MW00633278

The Emergence of Brand-Name Capitalism in Late Colonial India

Critical Perspectives in South Asian History

Critical Perspectives in South Asian History publishes innovative scholarship on South Asian pasts that will be widely accessible to a broad scholarly audience. Titles in the series interrogate existing themes and periodizations as well as open up new areas of inquiry by welcoming a range of disciplinary and theoretical perspectives within a historical argument. The series focuses on three broad scholarly developments: a growing engagement with the public life of South Asian history, a conceptual shift from South Asia being the "object" of study to becoming the generator or driving force behind new and distinctive research, and a concerted effort to study hitherto obscured regions, peoples, methods, and sources that point to a reframing of the current boundaries in South Asian history. This series invites new works that creatively engage with public debates about the past, draws attention to the distinctiveness of different South Asian contexts, integrates South Asia within global histories and draws upon South Asian material. Welcoming South Asian histories from the ancient world to the modern day, this series looks to bring scholarship on South Asia from different parts of the world in closer conversation and showcase the range and variety of new research in the field.

Published:
Forms of the Left in Postcolonial South Asia, Sanjukta Sunderason and Lotte Hoek (eds)
Political Imaginaries in Twentieth-Century India, Mrinalini Sinha and Manu Goswami (eds)
Workplace Relations in Colonial Bengal, Anna Sailer

Forthcoming:
The YMCA in Late Colonial India, Harald Fischer-Tine
Towards a People's History of Pakistan, Asad Ali and Kamran Asdar Ali (eds)

The Emergence of Brand-Name Capitalism in Late Colonial India

*Advertising and the Making
of Modern Conjugality*

Douglas E. Haynes

BLOOMSBURY ACADEMIC
LONDON • NEW YORK • OXFORD • NEW DELHI • SYDNEY

BLOOMSBURY ACADEMIC
Bloomsbury Publishing Plc
50 Bedford Square, London, WC1B 3DP, UK
1385 Broadway, New York, NY 10018, USA
29 Earlsfort Terrace, Dublin 2, Ireland

BLOOMSBURY, BLOOMSBURY ACADEMIC and the Diana logo are trademarks of
Bloomsbury Publishing Plc

First published in Great Britain 2023

A catalogue record for this book is available from the British Library.

Library of Congress Cataloging-in-Publication Data

Names: Haynes, Douglas E., author.
Title: The emergence of brand-name capitalism in late colonial India : advertising and
the making of modern conjugality / Douglas E. Haynes.
Description: 1 Edition. | New York, NY : Bloomsbury Academic, 2022. | Series: Critical
perspectives in south asian history | Includes bibliographical references and index.
Identifiers: LCCN 2022007248 (print) | LCCN 2022007249 (ebook) | ISBN 9781350278042
(hardback) | ISBN 9781350278073 (paperback) | ISBN 9781350278059 (pdf) | ISBN
9781350278066 (epub)
Subjects: LCSH: Advertising—Brand name products—India. | Consumer behavior—India. | Middle
class—India.
Classification: LCC HF6161.B4 H39 2022 (print) | LCC HF6161.B4 (ebook) | DDC 659.1—dc23/
eng/20220214
LC record available at https://lccn.loc.gov/2022007248
LC ebook record available at https://lccn.loc.gov/2022007249

ISBN: HB: 978-1-3502-7804-2
        ePDF: 978-1-3502-7805-9
        eBook: 978-1-3502-7806-6

Series: Critical Perspectives in South Asian History

Typeset by RefineCatch Limited, Bungay, Suffolk
Printed and bound in Great Britain

To find out more about our authors and books visit www.bloomsbury.com
and sign up for our newsletters.

This work is dedicated to Virchand Dharamsey, Makrand Mehta, and the late Dwijendra Tripathi, three scholars whose lifelong devotion to historical scholarship provides a model for all historians

Contents

Illustrations

Preface and Acknowledgments

This project began as a study of middle-class consumption patterns that would treat advertising simply as one useful kind of evidence. But newspaper advertisements served as a source of endless fascination, even amusement at times, and they had at the time of my initial forays almost never been a subject of serious analysis. In the interwar period, advertisements became one of the most significant forms of public discourse, and they may have been more firmly integrated into the everyday life of literate Indians than most of the sources we regularly use in our research. But historians have considered them tangential to their studies, passing them by as they go through the newspaper's pages or at best, drawing upon one or two to illustrate some argument about some other theme. Appreciating the logic and strategies that informed interwar advertisement increasingly became a central preoccupation. Eventually I decided to make advertising the main focus of my work and not just a vehicle to some other end.

Thanking students for their input is often a part of any list of acknowledgments. In this case, such thanks are no mere formality. Dartmouth College's Undergraduate Research program and the James O. Freedman Presidential Fellowship program, both administered by Margaret Funnell, have funded a series of superb undergraduates to help me with my work; these students have scoured through Indian, African and British newspapers provided through the Dartmouth Interlibrary loan office (which also deserves my thanks). Without their help, the approach I have taken to this project would not have been possible. I owe a special debt to two students who worked for me, Jeremy Schneider and Amita Kulkarni. Both of them wrote highly original papers or theses on advertisements that have informed this work, and have kindly permitted me to draw upon these papers in some parts of the book. Their research and their analysis is critical to this book; they are in effect second authors of parts of Chapter 1 and Chapter 5. I thank them for the permission they have given to draw upon these studies in this book. Other students who worked with me in my research, and who often offered valuable observations on the advertisements they dug up, included Joseph Balaban, Alice Crow, Kush Desai, Anmol Ghavri, Grace Hart, Elizabeth Janowski, Andrew Joseph, Hannah Kuhar, Sarah Kuologeorge, Ellen McDevitt, Samuel Neff, Max Pumilia, Rachel Rosenberg, Aditya Shah, Ananth Shankar, J. B. Thornhill, and Isaac Weber. In the classroom, my students have engaged with advertisements enthusiastically, often offering comments that have further deepened my thinking. Uma Mullapuddi wrote a paper based on research in London that has led me to recognize how profoundly eugenics influenced the mindset of middle-class Indians during the interwar period.

In India, I have also been helped immensely by several research assistants. These include Monalisa Dand, the late K. Hemlata, Suchita Patel, Chandni Shiyal, and Sarita Kadam. Shrikant Botre provided long periods of research support with Marathi materials and their translations. He soon became a close colleague and friend, and his influence on this book is profound.

The research in India for this book was supported by a grant from the American Institute of Indian Studies (AIIS) funded by the National Endowment for Humanities (NEH). I later received a fellowship directly from the National Endowment for Humanities for writing up the book manuscript. I am grateful to both AIIS and the NEH for their support. I greatly appreciate access to research materials provided by numerous archives and libraries, including the British Library, the Maharashtra State Archives in Mumbai, the Nehru Museum and Library, the Unilever Archives in Port Sunlight (UK), the History of Advertising Trust (HAT) in Norwich (UK), the J. Walter Thompson Company Archives at the Hartman Center for Sales, Marketing and Advertising History at Duke University, the Godrej Archives in Mumbai, the Tata Central Archives in Pune, the J.N. Petit Library in Mumbai, the Gujarat Samachar newspaper archives in Ahmedabad, the Asiatic Society Archives in Mumbai, and many other libraries. At these archives, several archivists or people who oversaw these libraries provided special help: Vrunda Pathare (Godrej), Rajendraprasad Narla (Tata), Eve Read (HAT), Shri Modi (Petit Library), Ruth Loughery (Unilever), and Nirmam Shah (Gujarat Samachar).

I owe special thanks to several colleagues with whom I have worked most closely. Most of them have been close associates almost from the project's inception. Arvind Rajagopal has been very generous in sharing his work and in offering advice even as his work overlapped with, and sometimes disagreed with, my own. Abigail McGowan has been a source of advice and collegial insights throughout this project. I have interacted with her extensively throughout the second half of my career; our intellectual interests somehow have often seemed to move along similar and complementary paths. Rachel Berger has pointed me to a large number of references that inform Chapter 6 and has given me considerable advice on its arguments. Tirthankar Roy and Prashant Kidambi have provided input throughout the research and writing of this study, and have read much of what I have written. Projit Bihari Mukharji and Charu Gupta read the whole manuscript and offered many valuable comments. In India, I could not have done without the special help of Vikram Doctor, Makrand Mehta, Anita Sarkar, and Virchand Dharamsey; Virchand has consistently been available to answer my questions, small and large, and to help refining Gujarati translations. I wish to dedicate this book to him, Makrandbhai, and the late Dwijendra Tripathi, all of whose careers of dedication to historical research has been an inspiration.

I have benefited greatly from many other friends and colleagues who have provided advice on sources, reactions to conference papers, and insights on how to interpret specific images. They have offered a variety of comments and advice, so I can not single out their contributions without going on too long. In the United States, I must mention valued advice from Indrani Chatterjee, Frank Conlon, Sandria Freitag, Veronika Fuechtner, Durba Ghose, Aparna Kapadia, Shekhar Krishnan, Prakash Kumar, Mark Liechty, Maya Malhotra, Alexandra Manchester, Lisa Mitchell, Shailaja Paik, Ishita Pande, Srirupa Prasad, Sumathi Ramaswamy, Nikhil Rao, Mrinalini Sinha, Howard Spodek, Ramya Sreenivasan, Robert Travers, and Anand Yang. Colleagues at Dartmouth during the last ten years who made valuable comments include Dwai Banerjee, Robert

Bonner, Bed Giri, Margaret Darrow, Kirk Endicott, Steve Ericson, Nisha Komattan, Richard Kremer, Ed Miler, Naaborko Sackeyfio, Holly Shaffer, and Leo Spitzer. Peter Quella of Boston University provided useful insights into, and translations of, South African advertisements, and he passed along comments from his colleague Zoli Mali. Michael Sacca helped tremendously in making the advertising images in this book presentable. Gail Patten has been extensively involved in preparing the manuscript for the press and in finalizing image permissions. Peter Sutoris helped with the proof-reading.

In Europe, I must thank the many scholars and others who have commented on my work. These include Ravi Ahuja, Bhaswati Bhattacharya, Markus Daeschsel, Henrike Donner, Ajay Gandhi, Mobeen Hussain, Sebastian Schwecke, and Stefan Tetzlaff along with many others. In India, a large number of people provided a variety of help, including insights into the advertising field, intellectual reactions to conference presentations, advice on sources, logistical support and collegiality. These include Iftikhar Ahmed, Neeladri Bhattacharya, Kaushik Bhaumik, Prithwiraj Biswas, Gerson D'Cunha, Marriam Dossal, Arvind Ganachari, Chhaya Goswami, Tapti Guha-Thakurta, Raj Kumar Hans, Neeraj Hatekar, Jyotindra and Jutta Jain (who also granted permission for the wonderful cover image), Arun Kale, Shailesh Kapadia, Shri Kshirsagar, Shekhar Krishnan, Manjiri Kamat, Rhishikesh Lakhote, Shirin Mehta, Naren Panjwani, Sujata Patel, Shri Rajadhyaksha, Aparna Rayaprol, Nisha Rupani, Bomi Umrigar, Ratan Sohoni, Shruti Tambe, Aroon Tikekar, Ravi Vasudevan, the late Haruka Yanagisawa and Shri Yangde. The Hiremath family and the Diwan family are friends whose support and companionship I must also acknowledge alongside my academic colleagues. Many others have made contributions that I cannot acknowledge individually here.

I wish to thank the journal *South Asia* and its editor Kama Maclean for allowing me to draw upon an earlier version of an article published there, "Selling Masculinity: Advertisements for Sex Tonics and the Making of Modern Conjugality in Western India, 1900–1945," vol. 35, no. 4 (Dec. 2012), 787–831. Taylor and Francis gave permission for me to use in chapter 7 a slightly revised version of my essay "Making the Ideal Home? Advertising of Electrical Appliances and the Education of the Middle-Class Consumer in Bombay, 1925–40," in *Globalizing Everyday Consumption in India: History and Ethnography*, edited by Bhaswati Bhattacharya and Henrike Donner (Delhi: Routledge Press, 2021). Hindustan Unilever and the Brihamumbai Electric Supply and Transport (BEST) have kindly provided permission for nearly half the images I have used in the text of this book. I thank them, and express my appreciation to Abigal McGowan, who originally pointed me to a picture of the BEST showroom printed here, to Yatin Pimpale and Vijay Karkera of BEST, to Rama Bijapurkar, and to Sudhir Sitapati and Viji Malkani of Unilever. I also wish to thank the many other companies and individuals who have consented or expressed no objection to my inclusion of advertisements of brands with which they were associated. In some instances, despite my best efforts, it was not possible to ascertain the current rightsholders, if any, of certain images, but I express my appreciation for the use of these images as well.

This book began when my son Tom and my daughter Rebecca were adolescents or children. They had to put up with my trips to India for research and many long hours in the office but provided much joy and entertainment between times of work. My wife, Nien Lin Xie, has been a source of support and companionship from well before the beginning of this book to its completion. She made many sacrifices to make this final stage possible, but the book also made possible great experiences together and with Rebecca in London and India. My greatest moment of satisfaction and pride in this project occurred when she remarked after attending one presentation on my research in London (I suspect comparing this study implicitly to my earlier work), "You know, this stuff is actually interesting."

Abbreviations

AA	*Advertising Abroad*
AW	*Advertiser's Weekly*
BC	*Bombay Chronicle*
BEST	Bombay Electric Supply and Tramways Company, Limited
BL	British Library
EA	*Export Advertiser*
EPW	*Economic and Political Weekly*
GA	Godrej Archives
GM	General Motors
GS	*Gujarat Samachar*
HATA	History of Advertising Trust Archives
IWI	*Illustrated Weekly of India*
JWT	J. Walter Thompson
JWTA	J. Walter Thompson Archives
KS	*Kanara Saraswat*
Levers	For various iterations of the Company, including Lever Brothers, Unilever, Lever Brothers (India)
MS	*Mumbai Samachar*
TCA	Tata Central Archives
TI	*Times of India*
UA	Unilever Archives

Introduction

> To the exporter the world must become a variegated chart of human wants. He must visualize peoples in their natural environment, limited by the special hardships which nature has imposed or enjoying the peculiar benefits of economic endowment. He must reconstruct their lives for a moment and endeavor to penetrate those barriers of ignorance or want which prevent them from fulfilling certain innate desires. He must look at their potentialities rather than their actualities and see whether in that vision he may glimpse a demand for the product which he has to sell them.
>
> Then dismissing this vision, he must turn to the conditions as they exist and plan to arouse those desires in his potential customers which will transform them into actual customers. Having determined that their purchasing power will enable them to buy his product, he must first create a demand on the part of his consumers. *This he may only do through the medium of advertising* (italics mine).[1]

When the American marketing expert F. R. Eldridge penned these words in 1930, the selling strategies of the world's largest manufacturing corporations were undergoing a transformation. Once content to confine themselves mainly to domestic markets, the makers of consumer goods ranging from soap, medicines, and clothing to food and drink products and small-scale technologies (flashlights, cameras, radios, electric fans, etc.) increasingly sought out buyers in eastern Europe, Latin America, Asia, and Africa. No longer accepting the poverty present in many of these regions as grounds for abstaining from aggressive sales efforts, they especially targeted an emerging category of "middle class" customers in these places. They insisted that the project required, as Eldridge's statement suggests, the collection of knowledge about the character of distant markets. Most critically, they believed that advertising their products widely would be necessary to their success. Partly in response to their efforts, consumers in many different areas of the world shifted their purchasing behaviors to include standardized, packaged *brand-name* commodities, and reoriented their bodily practices and daily habits to incorporate use of these products.

As international firms headquartered in North America and Europe sought to generate wider markets, they increasingly turned to trained advertising specialists to develop publicity campaigns. The men and women who deployed their skills in response styled themselves as "professionals"; they sought to deploy "scientific" techniques in creating ads, including the formulation of catchy "copy," the use of "commercial art," and a reliance on the latest technologies for producing high-quality printed images. Through the deployment of widely reproducible images in print form, advertisers sought to fashion cultural meanings that they hoped would inspire millions of people to buy mass-produced commodities. But though they applied universal advertising principles and sought to cultivate homogeneous consumption practices throughout the world—and thus were agents of an early twentieth-century form of "globalization"—they also insisted on the importance of adjusting their campaigns to local values and circumstances. Representatives of the U.S. advertising firm J. Walter Thompson in Bombay affirmed this approach when they wrote in 1936: "the sales record of clients is evidence of the ability of our staff to apply the advanced advertising skill of America, *adapting and modifying it as conditions and customs demand*" (italics mine).[2] Advertising specialists believed that to create committed consumers who would buy their products by brand on a consistent basis, they had to invest these commodities in powerful sets of cultural meanings that went beyond merely setting out the practical functions these items performed and that were rooted in the cultures of specific places. In Marxian terms, it was not sufficient to reproduce the fetishes surrounding given commodities in their original markets; these fetishes had to be refashioned and recreated in the new cultural environments the commodities now entered.

This book reflects an examination of professional advertising in one region of the world where this effort was particularly extensive, the Bombay Presidency in western India, focusing primarily on the interwar period. It explores how advertisers sought to advance *brand-name capitalism* among an emerging Indian middle class by promoting commodities manufactured by multinational companies during the 1920s, 1930s, and early 1940s, the period when advertising as a profession was first introduced in India. Though it discusses the application of principles and technologies first created in the United States and Europe, it focuses on approaches that advertising specialists used specifically to reach buyers in South Asia. As they sought to develop customers deeper and deeper in the Indian middle class, I argue, advertisers for many different commodities came to *converge* in their approach around principles of a *modern conjugality* then acquiring significant emotive salience within this class. This was not a universal pattern, and ads targeting expatriates and wealthy Indians typically did not reflect this tendency, but conjugality did become a common theme in campaigns designed to cultivate the regular customership of ordinary urban Indians who were educated and who worked in salaried jobs. Brand-name capitalism, in other words, gained a foothold in India through its association with emerging discourses concerning the modern family. At the same time, the book highlights the limitations of this effort, both its inability to develop markets in the countryside or among the urban poor and its failure to secure middle-class customership completely.[3] The book closes during the 1940s, as the role of foreign manufactures in the Indian economy contracted severely due to the effects of World War II and then as a result of policies of an independent Indian government that championed the principle of import substitution.

In exploring these developments, this study relies heavily upon a unique methodology for a business history: the textual and visual analysis of advertisements. While I draw upon the records of advertising agencies and other business firms and use an array of other archival materials, my primary approach here has been to analyze ads printed in newspapers from the cities of Bombay, Ahmedabad, and Poona. A close examination of these images in juxtaposition with one another, I stress here, illuminates the *cultural strategies* of multinational firms in India and the role of a variety of actors, both "local" and "global," in shaping advertisement.

While the book is conceived of as a history of capitalism, it thus suggests a significant rethinking of other central themes in the history of the Indian subcontinent since it demonstrates that branded commodities gained a purchase in Indian society by linking themselves with powerful cultural developments. Most obviously, it addresses the emerging historiography on consumption in South Asia and its role in the making of the Indian middle class.[4] This study departs from what became an implicit assumption in the history of the middle class: that its formation as a class can be accounted for with little reference to its material practices.[5] It stresses that consumption was a key ground on which the construction of the middle class as "modern" took place, and that advertising was an essential aspect of this process. At the book's core is an argument about the deployment of the principle of modern conjugality in advertisement and consumer culture. South Asianists have explored the formulation of "family imaginaries" in the context of intellectual, political, cultural, and legal histories[6]—but they have not examined previously how advertisers' efforts to develop markets for consumer products drew upon and reinforced this discourse, in effect adding a new dimension to it: that the objectives of the modern family could best be advanced or defended by the consumption of brand-name commodities. In short, this book depicts how brand-name capitalism became linked to other key themes of Indian cultural history, largely through the vehicle of professional advertising.

The book is also an addition to the visual history of India.[7] It is based upon the consideration of many thousands of images in western Indian newspapers. Like other works published in recent years, it challenges the dominance of written materials in historical analysis and pays attention to the special role of visuality in constructing modernity. That is, its interest is in images that are "products of the age of mechanical reproduction," that are "manufactured, circulated and consumed with new technologies of production and circulation that enable infinite reproducibility in ever more efficacious ways."[8] In extending visual studies to commercial publicity, the book highlights the most widely disseminated and visible form of visual culture in early twentieth-century India: the advertisement. Discussion of visual representations does not simply *illustrate* arguments based upon archival material; it demonstates instead, as Sumathi Ramaswamy has argued, that the "visual is constitutive of the social and political realities in which we live."[9]

Finally, as it addresses this range of issues, the book places more recent processes of "globalization" in South Asia into historical perspective. The expansion of consumption on the subcontinent during the last two to three decades is self-evident; an Indian middle class, one typically said to number several hundreds of millions of people, is now using a great variety of branded commodities in response to the "liberalization" of the economy and India's exposure to both global and national brands. The development of consumer culture has been stimulated in great part by Indian advertising agencies, who have played a critical role in adapting universalising discourses of consumerism to the subcontinent. But contemporary examinations of India's consumption culture by anthropologists and others lack significant historical depth, creating the perception that the post-1991 liberalization phase of India's economy is a unique moment that can be understood without an exploration of the past.[10] Developments in the interwar period, this book will demonstrate, suggest a much longer history of involvement by an international advertising profession in shaping attitudes toward commodities in India. The late colonial period was a time when many of the products that Indians assume have their origins on the subcontinent, such as Lux and Lifebuoy soaps and Horlicks and Ovaltine (both food beverages), were introduced by foreign companies. But as this book will also demonstrate, the path to contemporary consumption practice has hardly been one of a smooth, unfettered evolution. Instead, advertisers have constantly adjusted their techniques and appeals as they have struggled to attain and sustain Indian customership.

Historiography of advertising

This work seeks to establish for advertising a much more central place in the study of modern South Asian history. In contrast to works on North America and Europe, advertising has been a peripheral subject in the historiography of the subcontinent, in part because historians have long discounted the importance of consumption in a society characterized by widespread poverty.[11] Advertising has often fallen through the cracks even in work on subjects where it might have been expected to appear. Studies of capitalism on the subcontinent during the colonial period, for instance, have focused more on the export of agricultural commodities, production- and labor-related concerns in industry, the role of business communities, and the rise of individual entrepreneurs to prominence, than on the processes of marketing consumer goods.[12] Historical examinations of the Indian middle class have concentrated on the impact of English education and government employment, social reform movements, the development of Indian nationalism, and more recently, changing gender roles, rather than on the history of consumption practices, which elsewhere in the world have generally been seen as defining features of a middle class. Historians who use twentieth-century newspapers have regularly stumbled across fascinating ads in their research, and some have chosen an ad or two to illustrate some argument or other. But advertising *per se* hardly seemed relevant to the core concerns of South Asian historiography.

In the last decade, the landscape of historical work has changed, causing some scholars of South Asia to take up discussion of advertising in their work.[13] Much of this research has not regarded advertising as its main subject matter so much as a vehicle for appreciating other subjects: medical history,[14] visual history,[15] and the history of the middle class.[16] Advertisement, it has been clearly shown, intersects with these histories in major ways. Perhaps the scholar who has addressed the history of advertising most directly is Arvind Rajagopal, a media studies specialist who has examined the advertising profession both before and after independence. My own work shares, and is influenced by, many of the concerns present in Rajagopal's work: its recognition of the importance of markets in unbranded commodities, its delineation of a "vernacular" realm of advertisement distinguished from a formal, professional domain,[17] its emphasis on the pedagogical character of much advertising, and its recognition of the limitations of advertising efforts in reaching rural communities and the urban poor. But it departs significantly from Rajagopal's view of professional advertising in colonial India as an insular profession, generating its appeals primarily in accordance with imported (Western) cultural codes. On one hand, Rajagopal has suggested, advertising agencies participated in an "Anglophone" or modern domain associated with English-language papers in which the market was mostly the colonial elite and affluent city dwellers. On the other hand, at the same time, he argues, they sought to reproduce "the modernizing rhetoric of their Western counterparts"; their ads "did not stray far from the copybook of Western agencies, and assumed that Indian culture was little more than a veneer on the *homo economicus* already familiar to them."[18] Viewing advertising of the interwar period as enclavist, elitist, and Anglophone does not sufficiently acknowledge the profession's aggressive efforts to establish a foothold among a large lower middle class in India that was neither affluent nor thoroughly Westernized, and it misses important ways in which advertisers sought to accumulate cultural knowledge and lodge their appeals in forms they believed would be powerfully emotive to their consumers. While advertising campaigns fashioned pedagogical projects designed to persuade buyers that the use of branded commodites was critical to modernity, they modified their commercial messages significantly in an attempt to invoke specifically *Indian* middle-class notions of modernity focused on the conjugal family. This book shows how slogans intended to be used globally were substantially altered, or even abandoned, in the attempt to secure Indian consumers; it demonstrates how advertising art came to include visual cues designed to convey a sense of familiarity and persuasive power to Indian viewers; and it explores how the character of verbal "copy" was often "translated"[19] in terms expected to resonate locally. Advertising campaigns were often forged through processes of trial and error and experimentation as the designers of these campaigns tried to understand what worked and what did not in South Asia and as they received inputs from South Asian actors. Stressing the alien origins of the advertising industry may cause us to overlook the rigorous efforts made on the ground to market multinational commodities to an audience in India.

This book similarly departs from the work on global advertising that assumes the profession was largely a project to extend a hegemonic, uniform consumer culture from Europe and North America to Asia, Africa, and Latin America. Certainly it recognizes that advertising professionals were motivated in part by a desire to disseminate a civilizing mission they associated with the consumption of branded products[20] and that they propagated conceptions rooted in a capitalist universalism, such as those related to beauty and domesticity.[21] But it also draws inspiration from studies that have stressed how advertisers adapted their campaigns to principles gaining traction among local middle classes in particular regional contexts. For instance, Relli Schecter has argued in work about advertising in Egypt that: "the creation of exchange/sign values for commodities produced by multi-national companies entailed their 'localization'—the use of indigenous systems of meaning to facilitate their familiarization and their integration into local consumption."[22] Sherman Cochran, discussing the role of Chinese marketing efforts in the medical field, suggests that advertising entrepreneurs "poached" modern discourses of Western medicine, economic nationalism, and women's status then gaining cultural salience among Chinese reformers and "commodified them to promote his [their] products."[23] Julio Moreno's discussion of business strategies introduced by American firms in Mexico during the 1930s and 1940s highlights the effort of Sears, Roebuck and Company to depict itself as a champion of Mexico's industrial development and as a contributor to the upward mobility of the Mexican middle class. Moreno argues for a "middle ground" of cultural interaction between foreign advertising agencies and a variety of Mexican actors (rather than offer a perspective that sees advertising as an entirely alien intervention).[24]

This book draws most explicitly on Timothy Burke's *Lifebuoy Men, Lux Women*, a study of commodification in Zimbabwe from the 1930s through the 1950s.[25] Burke argues that advertisers evoked "prior meanings" to develop a base for their products, a concept he draws from the advertising theorist Judith Williamson.[26] As I understand his work, Burke delineates two different sorts of "prior meaning" in his analysis. First, he discusses the broad cultural perceptions that advertisers held about African values, notions influenced by strong European racial preconceptions and stereotypes. Second, he emphasizes how advertisers sought to draw upon the priorities and anxieties associated with the modernizing projects of educated Africans, particularly emerging notions of hygiene, masculinity, and domesticity. "Prior meaning," as I use the term here, is thus not an equivalent for "traditional culture." Middle-class values, I will show, were "in motion"; global brand-name capitalism insinuated itself in different societies by associating itself with changing value systems taking shape in the societies it entered. In India, advertisers came to ground their appeals in a language of a modernity then acquiring a hold among middle-class families as commonsense. Advertising in particular worked to elevate principles of a modern conjugality then under construction to a more dominant place in middle-class culture, and to link conjugality to specific consuming practices.

My examination of advertisement in effect analyzes India's place in three different kinds of global processes: the rise of new sorts of multinational firms focused on the provision of consumer goods; the dissemination on a world-wide scale of new principles and techniques associated with professional advertising; and the formulation of certain notions of modernity, especially those pertaining to conjugality and domesticity. It insists that such processes never reflected a simple, smooth transmission of principles from the "metropole" to the "periphery" or of "westernization." As the anthropologist Anna Tsing has argued, universalizing discourses "never fulfill their promise of universality"; they must become "engaged" in contexts far different from those in which they originated. In these contexts, universals become transfigured through *friction*, "the awkward, unequal, unstable and creative qualities of interactions across difference."[27] The character of global capitalism, conventions of professional advertising and notions of modern conjugality, I argue here, all became transformed as advertisers sought to create commercial appeals for brand-name commodities in western India's print media.

The concept of friction seems particularly apt in analyzing commercial appeals. As advertising professionals sought to advance the sales of the companies among a broad Indian middle class, they modified the cultural meanings associated with their products. In many cases, they rejected or adjusted imported approaches that they came to regard as being out of sync with the priorities of their consumers, they considered merchant complaints and advice from subordinates about marketing themes that did not seem to yield positive results, and they tried to counteract (or appropriate) sales pitches advanced by their Indian competitors. The book repeatedly demonstrates how international companies relying on advertising professionals tried to introduce advertising strategies, emotive appeals, visual conventions and slogans they had used outside India, sometimes in rather wholesale fashion, but then came to abandon, modify, and refashion these campaigns in ways they believed would have greater resonance for middle-class consumers. The core chapters of this study, Chapters 3 to 7, highlight the processses of trial and experimentation undertaken by advertising specialists as they encountered friction associated with their initial marketing strategies.

Methodological considerations

This study uses diverse sources to construct the cultural strategies of multinational businesses in India. First, it relies upon traditional forms of archival research, particularly the records of business firms such as the Godrej and Tata Archives in India, the Unilever Archives in Port Sunlight in the United Kingdom, the J. Walter Thompson Archives at Duke University in the United States, and the History of Advertising Trust in the United Kingdom. The first chapter of this book, on the advent of professional advertising globally and in India, especially draws upon archival sources. Such material, however, rarely provides explicit discussion of the processes of debate, negotiation, and strategizing involved in forging advertisement campaigns. We certainly have no historical records that could provide information comparable to William Mazzarella's fascinating ethnographic research on the formulation of contemporary advertising strategies in India.[28] The role of actors other than top executives, such as the translators and artists within advertising firms, is particularly murky.

As a result, I have turned extensively to an examination of what advertisements themselves suggest about such practices.[29] Drawing upon newspapers and magazines in a variety of archives, I developed a collection of many thousands of advertisements, which I use to detect general patterns deployed in advertising strategy and changes over time. In the pages that follow, I often engage in close readings of individual ads. Advertisement, I suggest, was a kind of rhetoric intended to persuade readers to buy the featured product and to accept the larger value system upon which ads were predicated. In an approach analogous to that I used in an earlier study on political rhetoric in western India,[30] I have sought to discuss the subject–audience relationship reflected in the ads. Such analysis requires considering how advertisers perceived the values and concerns of consumer segments they were targeting, most notably European expatriates and the Indian middle class. The book explores broader cultural discourses circulating among these groups, touching upon such matters as the family, domestic responsibilities and gender roles, household budgets, attitudes toward consumption, conceptions of the body and health, and even sexuality. My treatment moves back and forth between advertisements and these discourses as it seeks to understand the universe of "prior meanings" present in advertising messages.

An examination of the visual character of ads as well as their verbal aspects is crucial to my analysis; the imagery of advertisements was a central mechanism by which multinational businesses rendered global campaigns meaningful to local consumers. Professional advertising allocated a special importance to "commercial art." Advertising agencies typically included art departments, headed by specialists trained in conventions of commercial art who considered visual composition of advertisements closely. Often small visual cues were critical to an ad's purpose. For Indian middle-class consumers, a watch, a hair-style or a way of wearing a sari could signal modernity; a man wearing pajamas conveyed masculine lethargy and weakness; a bed in the background connoted frustrated sexuality; an armchair evoked comfort and economic security. Advertising artists often elicited ocular connections to prior visual forms present in other ads or in other media, such as the cinema or the theater, with which the viewer would be familiar and would know how to "read."[31] As Sumathi Ramaswamy has argued, no image "has a singular autonomous identity"; images are generated in a "plural sensory environment." "The concept of inter-ocularity/visuality is particularly useful in tracking how incoming ... practices ally with or disrupt more established ones, trigger prior associations, catalyze submerged memories, render the unfamiliar recognizable, and frequently reconfigure the recognizable."[32] I stress that advertising was eclectic in the visual connections it elicited, so I do not wish to insist on a systematic pattern of association between commercial art and any one genre of Indian visual culture so much as to point out relationships in the case of specific images.

Examined individually, advertisements can sometimes leave some uncertainty about whether similar sales pitches might have been used in other social or geographic contexts. At conference presentations of my work I have often been asked whether the images I have been discussing in my talk might reflect common themes of advertising throughout the world rather than cultural strategies designed for the Indian market. I contend here it is often possible to demonstrate clearly how advertisers adapted their ads specifically to an Indian middle-class audience by making *juxtapositions* and comparisons between different kinds of ads.

First, one can contrast the ways companies sought to market their goods to European expatriates in India and to middle-class Indians. Even as professional advertisers increasingly targeted the middle class during the 1930s, they still sought to perpetuate the customership of expatriates, who often possessed significant purchasing power, as well as wealthy Indians and Eurasians whom advertisers believed would emulate the Europeans.[33] Many global firms doing business in India made a conscious effort to develop appeals to expatriates that differed from those they made to middle-class consumers, for instance, by designing different ads for the *Times of India* and for vernacular newspapers or the nationalist paper *Bombay Chronicle*. Comparing such ads often brings into stark relief the cultural strategies that advertising professionals were considering in addressing these two audiences. Secondly and similarly, comparisons between advertisements for the same product in India and in other parts of the world elucidate the development of approaches designed for particular local contexts. As advertising professionals became increasingly involved overseas during the interwar period, they reshaped their campaigns to their new locations, addressing their perceptions of local priorities, sometimes dropping themes that assumed importance in the metropole. Third, I examine how campaigns from different multinational companies coalesced around similar motifs and images. Often international firms showed little compunction about replicating visual tropes and verbal appeals their rivals had devised earlier; when they did so, they in effect confirmed that they found these expressive modes valuable.

A fourth kind of juxtaposition explored in this book is that between ads associated with local Indian firms and those formulated by agencies advertising products of multinational corporations. "Vernacular" ads relied less on standardized forms of commercial art and the use of catchy phrases in their "copy"; often they provided a lengthy explanatory text. Drawing out contrasts between ads formulated by firms operating in Indian bazaars and ads generated by advertising agencies often sheds significant light on the objectives of the latter's campaigns. But in other instances, I suggest the cultural strategies of global businesses were forged in a kind of dialogue with advertisements devised by vernacular firms. As large corporations sought to develop consumer demand for their commodities and usurp local producers from their place in the market, they sometimes "poached" (to poach Cochran's term myself) from the cultural themes, the understandings of consumer anxieties, and the visual conventions reflected in vernacular advertising. The presence of such borrowing also suggests the involvement of Indian intermediaries in the construction of ads devised by professional agencies; these intermediaries may have possessed a stronger awareness of vernacular ads than did trained advertising specialists.

The most important kind of "juxtaposition" that I employ in this book, however, is to compare ads developed for the same products at different moments. Both whole categories of firms and the individual manufacturers of particular brand-name commodities reconfigured their appeals over time. Advertising professionals, I argue, were engaged in a process of experimentation. They tried some approaches in hopes of success, then dropped these strategies in order to take up new campaigns according to their sense of what might work better. In many cases, I show how global firms early in the interwar period simply imported advertising appeals they had been using in North America and Europe; by the 1930s, as professional advertisers became more important in formulating ads, they adopted new approaches specifically geared to Indian markets. These adjustments could be visual as well as verbal; existing artistic conventions from the metropole could be discarded and new ones taken up as advertisers adjusted their marketing efforts (the shift from using depictions of Hollywood actresses to relying on images of Bombay actresses in beauty soap advertisements may be the most straightforward example). Juxtaposing earlier ads with later ones elucidates the ways that multinational firms adjusted their visual and verbal strategies.

The stress I place on juxtaposition—that is, on highlighting comparisons between advertisements in different cultural and temporal contexts and in elucidating interocular and intertextual connections and contrasts between them—reinforces the importance of using a large and diverse collection of newspaper advertisements. I have collected ads in three languages—English, Gujarati and Marathi—that were most relevant to businesses seeking customers in western India. Multinational firms during the interwar period invested most heavily in English-language appeals, and often specialists designing their ads composed the copy in English before translation, though they increasingly placed ads in vernacular papers by the 1930s. I usually choose here English-language ads for my illustrations when these are sufficient to highlight my points at given moments but the inclusion of Gujarati and Marathi advertisements often brings out additional issues (about translation, transformation, and audience, for instance) that are critical to the central arguments of this study. While I trace in this book campaigns for many commodities, my overall use of these types of juxtaposition demonstrates that, during the late 1930s, advertising directed to the Indian middle class for a great variety of products tended to converge around themes related to conjugality. Advertisers at this key moment came to evoke regular concerns related to the modern family and the responsibilities it imposed on both husbands and wives then acquiring salience during the early twentieth century.

Organization of the book

This book consists of an introduction, seven chapters essentially divided into two parts, and a conclusion. The first part provides the critical background to the study. In Chapter 1 I discuss the rise of global consumer businesses and the development of global advertising agencies. The chapter briefly outlines the emergence of a local "vernacular" capitalism in India before examining the rise of the modern advertising profession, first on a worldwide basis and then specifically in western India. The chapter highlights the ways in which international consumer businesses came to rely on advertisers steeped in European and North American traditions of professional advertising during the interwar period. It then outlines the methods that these professionals developed for gathering knowledge about local societies and for adapting advertising messages in India to their understandings.

Chapter 2 then discusses the two major categories of consumers that advertisers sought to address in western India—that of "Europeans" on the one hand and that of the Indian middle class on the other—emphasizing that both of these categories were not stable sociological groups but were themselves involved in projects of self-fashioning. Consumer practices, I argue in contrast to the emphasis in much of the literature on the Indian middle class, were essential to these projects of self-construction. The chapter highlights the cultural priorities of modernity, specifically the ideals of modern conjugality, emerging in the middle-class audience that became relevant to advertising campaigns before World War II. That is, it outlines the universe of "prior meanings" explored in subsequent chapters.

The second part of the book—the study's core analysis—proceeds to discuss the evolution of advertising campaigns for a series of different products; I do not seek to be exhaustive in my coverage, but have chosen commodities that reflect some of the most prominent campaigns at the time, that provide some idea of the range of approaches used by global businesses, and that illustrate the processes of convergence in advertising appeals that were taking place. Each of these five chapters examines both the rhetorical and the visual message of advertisements. Chapter 3 studies the construction of conjugal masculinity by taking up the highly visible and extensive advertising for male "tonics." The chapter begins with the concept of male "weakness" in a variety of discourses, including colonial characterizations of the educated Indian man, nationalist counter-discourses centered on the rejuvenation of Indian masculinity, and medical discourses about male health. The chapter then discusses tonic advertisement by vernacular capitalists, which often portrayed particular products as critical to overcoming sexual weakness caused by seminal loss, a weakness that was seen as producing a series of other mental and physical incapacities. The chapter goes on to analyze the evolution of campaigns for tonics produced by multinational firms, showing how these campaigns came to pirate the notion of male sexual weakness from vernacular advertisement but increasingly welded these notions to conceptions of modern conjugality, fashioning forms of masculinity directly relevant to the family. Finally, the chapter turns to explore ads for Horlicks, a hot drink explicitly sold for its "tonic" qualities. The chapter demonstrates how Horlicks ads fused concerns about restoring middle-class masculine weakness on the one hand with emerging conceptions of male responsibilities within the family and anxieties about male employment on the other. Throughout the chapter, I illustrate the workings of "friction" by highlighting the abandonment of global campaign themes and slogans drawn from North America and Europe for ones specifically developed to appeal to the Indian middle class.

Chapter 4 turns to the increased importance of ads directed to women. The ground for female-oriented advertisements was prepared by three developments: the identification of the category of "woman" as the central target of social reform efforts from the late nineteenth century onwards, the emergence of new notions of the "female constitution" in indigenous and Western medicine, and the recognition by marketing experts that wives played critical roles in managing family budgets and determining household expenditures. The chapter then proceeds to examine ads for three types of commodities: (1) a South African medical product called Feluna; (2) the European hot drink Ovaltine; and (3) Levers' beauty soaps, Lux and Pears. Ads for the first two products came to stress middle-class anxieties about female abilities to perform domestic responsibilities necessary to sustain their families. The campaigns for Lux and Pears did break explicitly with a family-centered approach, in part because the main point of these campaigns was to convince consumers that women specifically needed their own soap to enhance their feminine qualities. Levers for a short time drew upon the concept of the "modern girl" so prevalent in global advertising, but it ultimately modified and tamed this concept, muting its challenge to the ideology of conjugality and motherhood. With every product explored in the chapter, the trope of the modern girl used outside India for the same products was to some extent repudiated for themes more compatible with the principles of conjugal domesticity.

In Chapter 5 I examine other kinds of soap advertisement, focusing primarily on Unilever/Levers' products, particularly Sunlight soap for washing clothes and Lifebuoy body soap. As I show, the soap market in India became a highly competitive one during the early 1930s, as many new entrants, both domestic and foreign, sought to secure middle-class customership. Levers continuously tried to develop a rationale that would motivate consumers to buy its soaps rather than others, and on a repeated basis. For Lifebuoy, the company adopted but then abandoned a campaign built around its international slogan of "B.O." (Body Odour), eventually settling instead on the theme of family health—"the Lifebuoy habit"—that it accepted as more resonant in Indian families that increasingly regarded maintaining the health of children as their foremost social responsibility The chapter then discusses changes in the nature of campaigns for Sunlight soap, which came to center on the housewife's responsibilities for the hygiene and physical appearance of family members in a world members of the middle class perceived as filled with considerable health risks.

The subject of Chapter 6 is the marketing of various cooking mediums. As in Chapter 5, the discussion in this chapter links the process of commoditization to what Pradip Kumar Bose has called "the medicalization" of the family. The chapter discusses a series of efforts, culminating in the campaign run by Lever Brothers for its product Dalda to usurp ghee and other indigenous cooking substances in the home by claiming the superiority of its brand in advancing family health. Here again, advertising converged around themes central to the emerging conception of conjugality. Still, at the end of the colonial period, brand-name cooking mediums had made only a partial inroad into middle-class consumption patterns due to reservations about the healthiness and tastiness of these products.

In Chapter 7 I turn to the advertising of electrical household technologies, a kind of product that has rarely been mentioned in discussions of pre-independence consumer culture. The chapter particularly examines the role of the Bombay Electric Supply and Tramways, Ltd. (BEST), which ran an extensive campaign to persuade Indian buyers both to use electricity and to purchase particular appliances, such as fans, refrigerators, vacuum cleaners, and electric water heaters. Much of BEST's advertising reflected an effort to stimulate middle-class families to do more than simply light their homes with a single bulb or two, an effort that was somewhat muted by the continued importance of the expatriate market and the limited potentialities of middle-class demand. The company often stuck to more global themes, including pedagogical efforts to persuade families to embrace electricity as neccesary to the achievement of a more universal (i.e. less localized) modernity. The evocation of family health and security was certainly present in some ads, but there was little convergence around these principles, evidence that the workings of friction were more muted when expatriates remained the main consumer base. The advertising of electrical products achieved only a very modest success before World War II. The last two chapters thus mark the limits of consumer culture, demonstrating the ineffectiveness of campaigns that could not establish their direct relevance to the reproduction of the family.

Finally, the book closes with a conclusion drawing together its different arguments with a brief exploration of post-1945 developments, when the field of professional advertising expanded considerably despite the ostensibly closed nature of the Indian economy. The chapter thus seeks to link the study of advertising, the emergence of brand-name capitalism and middle-class consumption during the interwar period to themes more typically associated with India's post-1991 globalization.

1

Brand-Name Capitalism and Professional Advertising in India[1]

The emergence of a consumer-oriented, *brand-name* capitalism in India during the interwar years was associated with a reorientation of the subcontinent's place in the global economy. Before 1914, much of India's world trade involved the export of raw materials such as cotton; most of this business was controlled by European agency houses headquartered in Calcutta and Bombay. There was also a vast import business in Lancashire textiles. After World War I, the relative importance of the international commerce in agricultural goods decreased, and the place of British cloth imports was challenged by Indian mills. The post-war context, however, was characterized by the aggressive entry of multinational manufacturers of consumer goods into the Indian economy; these firms sought to develop markets for their commodities, which included medical products, tobacco, soap, hot drinks like tea and cocoa, and everyday technologies like lightbulbs, bicycles, cameras, radios, batteries, and sewing machines.[2] Business experts in the United States now envisioned India as a "$600,000,000 market," with potential buyers well beyond the small set of colonial expatriates.[3] If international companies were to capture Indian markets, these experts reasoned, consumers on the subcontinent—particularly those identified as members of an emerging middle class—would have to be persuaded to buy their products.

At the onset of the interwar period, relatively few commodities consumed by Indians were branded. City-dwellers with middlish incomes usually obtained their goods in urban bazaars, and brand was only occasionally a significant consideration relative to price and qualities they could observe directly or were touted to them by hawkers and small shopkeepers.[4] Trademark legislation was limited and enforcement uneven; cheap imitations of branded goods proliferated in the market and rarely could be ousted by resort to the courts. In order to capture Indian markets, multinational manufacturers had to convince consumers of the superiority of their products and to discipline them into the habit of buying items that bore the official trademarks of global corporations.[5] This principle was championed in general messages carried by Indian newspapers, which sometimes claimed that branded goods were superior simply because they were advertised. One such ad ran: "The public has no better friend—no more trustworthy servant—than Modern Advertising.... Advertising is the manufacturer's expression of confidence in the goods he sells. It is a guarantee of Purity, Freshness, Efficiency."[6]

Even more ambitiously, the introduction of brand-name capitalism sometimes involved persuading buyers to abandon existing bodily practices and induce them to adopt new, "modern" habits: taking baths with soap rather than soda ash, soap nuts or sand; relying on laundry soap for washing clothes in the home rather than sending them to a *dhobi* (washerman); using a toothbrush and toothpaste rather than coal or neem twigs; drinking tea, cocoa or coffee on a daily basis; shaving every morning; and wearing ready-made clothes rather than draped clothing or clothing stitched by a tailor.[7] Newspaper advertisements stressed the links between the use of advertised commodities and modernity, sometimes castigating those who would not adopt branded items as hopelessly backwards.[8]

Professional advertising was seen by its advocates as critical to accomplishing these transformations in everyday practice. The expanding role of advertising experts no doubt grew out of their special role in championing a global consumer culture and their mastery over professional techniques believed to possess extraordinary persuasive power everywhere in the world. But, perhaps less noticeably, it rested upon a claim to understand local cultures and generate *cultural strategies* suited to the regions they sought to influence. Advertising men and women asserted to their multinational clients that they held a deep understanding of the subcontinent and its peoples that executives of distant manufacturing firms would never manage to develop on their own. This chapter explores how they created such commercial knowledge through market investigations and through contact with Indian actors.

The emergence of brand-name capitalism in western India

Commercial markets on the subcontinent long predated the twentieth-century expansion of brand-name capitalism. An earlier historiography viewed pre-colonial South Asia as possessing a simple pre-capitalist, non-commercialized society based upon self-sufficient villages with most of its manufactures destined for the courts of pre-colonial kingdoms or for export. This perspective has now been completely superceded; historians have demonstrated that Indian peasants were long involved in producing cash crops, that the subcontinent possessed substantial industrial activity, and that a dynamic set of mercantile actors engaged in trade along the coasts, into the interior, and overseas.[9] Historical literature has done much less to document pre-1850 consumption practices, but there is some evidence of significant consumer markets. Hew Bowen, for instance, has shown the existence of demand among Indian elites for some European manufactured goods—including glass, metal-ware and hard-ware, woolens and furniture—even before the 1820s.[10] Anand Yang's major study of nineteenth-century markets in Bihar documents the movement of consummables through a landscape of market networks that connected cities, small towns and religious fairs with the countryside.[11]

At present, our understanding of how commodity producers established demand for their products in distant locales before the twentieth century is limited. The picture we possess seems to emphasize the crucial role of "trading carriers,"[12] who typically purchased supplies at places of production, and then transported them to consuming regions by bullock carts, where they were sold in larger towns and religious fairs to more localized traders for sale in smaller bazaars and periodic markets.[13] Products were rarely sold by brand; cloth marketed at the Maheji fair in Maharashtra during the mid-nineteenth century, for instance, was known by its place of production rather than by its manufacturer's name.[14] In the absence of print-based advertising, merchants on the spot were critical figures, not only in the circulation of goods but also in the construction of the meanings by which consumers came to understand different commodities.[15] Tom-tom beaters and town criers, who are sometimes seen as representing pre-print forms of advertising, were typically hired by local shopkeepers rather than those who made these goods. Producers generally lacked the independent capacity to generate markets for their items, an often unrecognized step in the development of industrial capitalism. As a result, while business history can tell us a great deal about specific merchants and bankers in pre-colonial India, the documented past of individual manufacturers remains almost a blank slate.

During the early nineteenth century, British businesses began to flood the subcontinent with machine-made yarn and cloth. Though this trade became massive, relatively little research has been done about the marketing processes for Lancashire textiles. How did cloth reach the actual wearer in the Indian countryside? What network of traders transported foreign-made goods from the ports to interior markets? How did consumers transmit their preferences, and how did manufacturers learn about, and seek to influence, Indian buying patterns? Jyotindra Jain has richly documented the role of trade labels displaying mythological, imperial, and Orientalist themes in Indo-British textile commercial exchange during the nineteenth century.[16] But these labels seemingly were more meaningful in conveying the producer's name to importers and wholesalers than they were in influencing actual cloth users.

The emergence of brand-name capitalism during the late nineteenth century strongly depended upon the growth of cheap print media: newspapers, pamphlets, tracts, catalogues, and almanacs.[17] With access to print, communities of literate consumers living in towns spread over the South Asian landscape could be imagined and shaped through advertising.[18] Producing firms could now try to create cultural meanings that traveled with products, and thereby seek to usurp the role of intermediary traders and small shopkeepers in fashioning commodity images at their point of sale. Brand-name capitalism thus depended upon the production of mass-produced paper, the development of print technology, and forms of transportation that carried publications over long distances.

While this book focuses on the dissemination of brand names by international firms, thousands of small Indian businesses also participated in this process. A kind of *vernacular capitalism* utilizing advertisements in local newspapers and other publications emerged as small entrepreneurs took up production of cosmetics, medicines, tonics and aphrodisiacs, hair oil, soap, matches, handloom saris, and incense. Some of these firms' activities would be invisible to us if not for the survival of their printed advertisements. Many of these ads relied entirely on written text. When visual images were included, members of the business families often designed the images, drawing eclectically from various indigenous aesthetic traditions rather than from standardized commercial art. Using advertisements as evidence, Prithwiraj Biswas has reconstructed the history of a Bengali entrepreneur, Hemendramohan Bose, who began his career in the late nineteenth century as a hair oil manufacturer but who moved into making perfumes, bicycles, musical recordings, stationery, and fruit syrup.[19] Many analogous figures in the Bombay Presidency emerged after 1900.[20] It is tempting to view such businesses as reflecting an earlier stage of capitalism that ultimately gave way to larger corporations. But they were as much a twentieth-century phenomenon as their global counterparts, they often competed fiercely and effectively for markets with larger companies, they relied equally on print media, and they also targeted the urban middle class. They were in short co-participants in the making of brand-name capitalism, which was thus not simply a force issuing from Europe and America.

Appeals for patent medicines were the most common form of advertising by vernacular firms before 1920. As Jeremy Schneider has argued, "the allure of an expanding market, the requirement of only small capital outlays and the proliferation of medical manuals spurred the entrance of many entrepreneurs into the manufacture and marketing of indigenous medical products."[21] Medical advertisements were critical to the incomes of many small newspapers until their claims were regulated in the Drugs and Magic Remedies (Objectionable Advertisements) Act of 1954.[22] At the end of World War I, firms like the Punjabi manufacturer Amritdhara were among the most prominent advertisers in Bombay newspapers (see Figure 1.1).[23] In Maharashtra, one

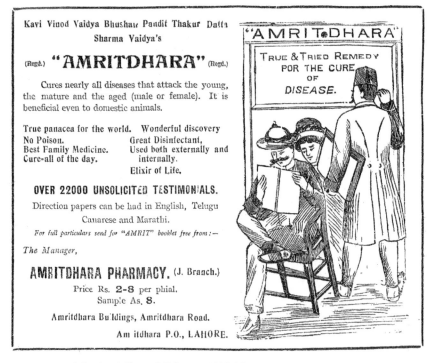

Figure 1.1 Ad for Amritdhara, *BC*, June 1, 1918, 13.

notable firm was the Ayurvedic business Dhootapapeshwar, founded around 1870 by the Puranik family, originally Brahman priests from Papeshwar in Ratnagiri district who located their workshop in Panvel in the Konkan. The firm continued to use as its trademark an image of the family shrine. It began advertising to *vaidyas* (Ayurvedic practitioners) in the late-nineteenth-century press. By the twentieth century it was publicizing its products directly in Gujarati and Marathi newspapers, and it started a monthly magazine, *Arogya Mandir*, to provide information about the principles of Ayurvedic science to vaidyas and storekeepers stocking medicines. By 1938, Dhootapapeshwar had developed a substantial industrial establishment, with 225 employees and an output of Rs. 3 to 4 lakhs.[24] During the interwar period, a printing press was set up in the workshop compound to print product labels and advertisements for placement in the popular media and *Arogya Mandir*.

Yet the role of advertising in disseminating brand names remained relatively limited before World War I. Large quantities of unbranded goods still circulated in Indian bazaars. Much press advertising was submitted by retail stores, which sometimes publicized consignments of goods for quick sales.[25] Many such ads possessed no artwork and no real "copy," only (sometimes lengthy) descriptions of the goods being sold and their qualities. Newspaper technology did not yet allow local producers to draw up and print sophisticated visual imagery.[26] International firms generally submitted ads that they had created in their home countries, often featuring images of white Europeans or North Americans (see Figure 5.1 for an example), as they possessed no local staff to design advertising. They rarely submitted their publicity to vernacular newspapers, lacking confidence in the accuracy of the papers' circulation figures and regarding the papers' readers as too poor to buy their products.

Around the beginning of the twentieth century, placement services began to play a part in submitting newpaper ads. B. Dattaram, sometimes regarded as India's first advertising agency after its founding in 1905, may have performed such a role in Bombay, though it apparently was hired mostly by Bombay retail stores, not international businesses.[27] In the 1920s, several foreign firms ran placement services in India, insisting that their special knowledge of the country made it possible for them to place ads most strategically.[28] The New York business of Eric Pusinelli, for instance, periodically sent its representatives to India to assess the merits of various papers for advertisement placement, and submitted ads to perhaps two dozen Indian newspapers, including the *Bombay Chronicle*, the *Times of India*, and *Mumbai Samachar*.[29] It also managed outdoor advertising on Bombay and Calcutta trams, public kiosks, and billboards, having secured a contract with the Publicity Society of India, "the largest outdoor advertising concessionaires in the East." It claimed: "Here is the Means of Reaching India's Millions," meaning the many Indians who did not read newspapers.[30]

Placement services contributed little to advertisements' form; the exporting companies in Europe or North America usually developed their own ads, then sent them to India where they would be published with only the addition of their local sales agent's name; the newspapers' staff carried out any translation required. Only rarely were new visual images designed; ads printed in Gujarati and Marathi usually continued to feature the original European figures present in the English-language originals. L. A. Stronach, a Bombay advertising professional during the mid-1920s, would later critique this approach: "the main press advertisements which came from Britain or America, and were placed direct with newspapers, to my mind were quite useless at product-selling, because they were prepared by and for the European mentality, and there were only a half million Europeans, including service personnel, in the whole of India."[31] Placement services increasingly proved unsatisfactory to many businesses as they sought to exert a more direct influence on Indian customers. Increasingly, they turned to professional advertising agencies.

The globalization of professional advertising

By the 1920s, advertising had emerged as a significant force in the domestic economies of countries in North America and western Europe. Top ad agencies like J. Walter Thompson and N. W. Ayer held hundreds of contracts and earned millions of dollars by designing and placing advertisements.[32] These agencies worked not for specific newspapers but for individual manufacturer-clients, choosing the media that they believed would yield the best sales at the lowest costs.[33] According to Richard Ohmann, there were two main factors responsible for the formation of the American advertising industry. First, the development of large-scale, "continuous-flow" factory production meant that manufacturers needed to create wider and more stable markets to absorb their products. Invoking the work of Alfred Chandler, Ohmann suggests that capitalists sought to "integrate forward" by adding a significant marketing dimension to assure they would have buyers for what they made. Second, advertising offered manufacturers a mode of connecting their commodities to new cultural norms of domesticity and gender emerging among the American middle class.[34] American advertisements in other words evoked "prior meanings" associated with changing cultural values in the United States.

Robert P. Hymers and Leonard Sharpe would write in 1939 that advertising had grown "from an undeveloped, ill-equipped, and often erratic advocacy to a well-defined profession of immense potentialities, well in the vanguard of that complex organization we are pleased to call 'modern civilization.'"[35] The assertion that ad men and women constituted a *profession* with its own forms of expertise became central to legitimating their commercial roles. The skills associated with this identity were rarely acquired in universities but were mastered through extensive apprenticeships within advertising firms. The field's leaders delineated the profession's key expectations in journal articles and books.[36] Advertising, they also insisted, was a "science" providing a reliable guide for future practice.[37]

Five major dimensions appear to have been critical in advertising's claims to possess a scientific and professional character. First, practitioners emphasized that their work was based on *market research*,[38] not on guesswork and hunches but on data collected through rigorous investigations conducted by the agencies. Second, they stressed the profession's strong grounding in the academic discipline of psychology. According to Walter Dil Scott: "Scientific advertising follows the laws of psychology. The successful advertiser, either personally or through his advertising department, *must* carefully study psychology. He *must* be a student of human nature, and he *must* know the laws of human nature."[39] Third, they highlighted the ability of the field's specialists to generate *copy*, the punchy rhetorical forms believed to carry persuasive power. Copy replaced earlier forms of appeal that simply offered descriptions of goods or that, alternatively, touted sensational claims to their efficacy. Advertising specialists viewed copy as a mode of communication unique to their profession; good copy caught the attention of readers, appealed to their logic or emotions, and persuaded them to purchase the product on a habitual basis. Fourth, advertising relied on *commercial art*, the modes of visual expression that complemented the verbal text. According to professional advertisers, "good illustrations add immensely to the power of the written word . . . the apt picture literally draws the eye to the copy and forces the attention of the prospect on to the product advertised."[40] Or, as one JWT executive put it more cynically, advertising art "leads the reader to the poison and makes him drink it."[41] Finally, professional advertisers claimed a mastery of technical processes involved in print advertising, such as engraving, the making of process blocks, the use of half tone screens, the deployment of metal stereoplates and electrotypes, and the methods of lithography and collotype printing.[42] Some agencies even began to make films for their client-firms.

Before the 1920s, many consumer-oriented manufacturers were selling products in Asia, Africa, and Latin America, sometimes through their own distribution networks,[43] but most would have considered it unreasonably expensive to employ advertising professionals abroad. To many manufacturers, countries outside the West, with their peculiar market systems, print media whose readership claims were often unreliable, and cultures that appeared exotic and commercially unfriendly, were unpromising locales for promoting brand recognition and high-volume sales. During the late 1920s, however, advertising went global. In some instances, entrepreneurs with an eye for opportunity opened individual ad agencies in new locales with commercial possibilities. In others, global advertising agencies established branches spread around the world.

J. Walter Thompson played a particularly prominent role in globalizing the advertising profession, largely as a result of its relationship with General Motors. In 1927, GM signed a contract with JWT to publicize its automobiles as it moved manufacturing capacity overseas. After landing this account, JWT opened thirty-four offices, including ones in Egypt, South Africa, India, Australia, and South America. JWT's international operations were initially dependent on its relationship with the car manufacturer; some branches simply folded when the GM contract ended around 1932.[44] In other cases, the establishment of an office in a new location attracted other corporations, often from the ranks of JWT's American clients, to sign agreements with the agency to conduct advertising there. Branches that successfully diversified their client base survived. JWT quickly became the world's most significant international agency (see Figure 1.2). N. W. Ayer, the biggest American agency during the 1920s, also opened international branches, prompted in part by a contract with Ford.[45]

The field of global advertising expanded as more manufacturers became convinced that a substantial body of consumers existed almost everywhere, even in very poor countries, who could be persuaded to buy their products. During the Great Depression, when domestic markets contracted severely, even meager profit opportunities abroad could stimulate firms to place a new emphasis on exports. In the United States, the

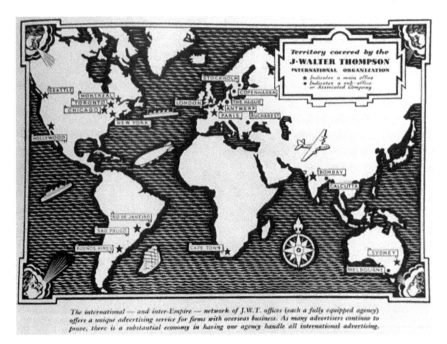

Figure 1.2 "Territory covered by the J. Walter Thompson International Organization," *Advertiser's Weekly*, September 30, 1937, 481.

Commerce Department encouraged such thinking by printing pamphlets that offered advice on how to carry out marketing efforts in distant locales.[46] The American trade journal *Advertising Abroad* and the British journal *Advertiser's Weekly* repeatedly ran articles stressing the potentialities of markets that once seemed daunting.

Advertising agencies overseas offered international manufacturers many of the same professional skills abroad they provided at home, but they also promised to serve as cultural mediators.[47] Specifically they claimed to possess an understanding of cultural and economic conditions in foreign locations and an ability to generate appeals that would accord with local "customs" and "circumstances." Advertising professionals became leading participants in forging a shifting global perspective on the cultures of Asia, Africa, and Latin America that might be called *commercial ethnology*, since (1) it was a body of professional expertise about (2) peoples conceived of as cultural others in ethnographic-sociological research, and it was (3) centered around assessing those peoples' potential to become buyers of brand-name goods.[48] It undoubtedly reflected the incorporation of ideas drawn from professional anthropology into the discourse of business expertise. During the interwar period, commercial ethnology acquired wider dissemination with the increased global role of multinational firms.

Commercial ethnology departed strongly from older colonial views that regarded humanity as being divided into peoples with fixed racial capacities and characteristics;

instead, it insisted that humans everywhere possessed similar potentialities and material proclivities. Clement H. Watson wrote in the JWT *News Bulletin* in 1928 that commercial export "sweeps aside national boundaries and regards markets as people—not as places."[49] In his view, Asians, Latin Americans, and Africans, whatever their race or nationality, possessed the capacity to become full-fledged customers if approached properly:

> Basically, most products are wholly international. A safety razor will shave the chin of a Frenchman, or of an Australian, or of a Hindu rajah, just as efficiently as it will of an American banker. A toilet soap doesn't care whether the complexion it cleanses is white or black, brown or yellow. A fountain pen will write Greek or French or Swedish as easily as it will English ....
>
> [P]eople are fundamentally alike the world over. Except for a few fanatics, all peoples seek protection, seek betterment of living conditions, seek added comfort, seek greater enjoyment of life.
>
> It has also been shown conclusively that by appealing to those fundamental traits of human nature, people in any stage of civilization can be taught to use products which serve their needs or fill their wants. This sometimes requires great patience, but it can be done—as many a successful exporter has proved.
>
> ... It is that adaptability of the human race to new ideas and new methods which makes the future of American exporting so bright.[50]

According to Watson, processes of social, economic, and cultural change were taking place across the world that could make many societies into major markets for Western goods. Interestingly he used the word "modernization" for these processes, well before that term entered the standard lexicon of anthropology and American foreign policy: "even the Far East is undergoing a rapid modernization that will soon bring the densely populated territories of China and Japan, Java and India, prominently into American export plans. Already in the journals published in these far-off countries one sees advertised many of the same products found on the shelves of our own local stores."[51]

While commercial ethnology rejected the notion that unchanging racial qualities characterized the world's peoples, it insisted on the principle of *cultural* difference. It stressed that people in non-European lands held beliefs, stuck to cultural *traditions*, followed social *customs* and *habits*, possessed different standards of living, and participated in distinctive market systems that businesses needed to understand. Cultural difference was at times portrayed in hierarchical terms; advertising discourse sometimes depicted people less familiar with branded products and the bodily practices associated with them as possessing lower levels of "civilization." But more importantly for commercial purposes, it portrayed culture as constituting a set of constraints that global businesses would have to recognize and adapt to as they developed selling strategies. Professional advertisers argued that the leaders of international firms, headquartered far away in commercial metropoles, could not hope to comprehend these differences or devise strategies to address them on their own.[52] The ability to spur sales on a brand-name basis required men and women on the spot, figures steeped in the profession's key principles but who also had acquired familiarity with the values and material practices of local consumers.

The advertising agency's supposed expertise in addressing cultural difference became critical to its claims to indispensability. While trying in 1931 to persuade the British consumer products company Scott and Bowne to open an advertising account in India, executives of JWT's Bombay branch asserted that their agency was able to offer the firm a special understanding of regional conditions, an awareness of the media needed to reach potential buyers, knowledge of marketing methods suited to India, and the ability to conduct local research needed to enhance the company's selling efforts. They argued that imported advertising was unsuitable and that Scott and Bowne's sales staff in India could not be expected to possess the knowledge necessary to generate effective ads itself.[53] An article in JWT's newsletter in 1929 similarly stressed: "What will attract the Britisher, the American and the German will not attract the average South African. He is, in matters of likes and dislikes, 'a thing apart,' but cultivate him in the right manner, approach him from the right angle, and you make him your friend—in his home and commercial life."[54] Writing about Asia, Roger Falk, director of Keymer's office in Calcutta, invoked starkly Orientalist logic in making a similar point: "Western sales dogma will never apply long to the paradox of the eastern peoples who, despite their ancient civilizations, represent the quintessence of human instability . . . who think of spiritual rather than material things, and whose standard of living is so different from that of the west."[55]

In overseas locales, commercial ethnology in effect displaced psychology as the key "science" informing understanding of the consumer. Advertising professionals working in Asia, Africa, and Latin America viewed foreign purchasers as motivated not so much by universal pyschological principles as by "customs," "habits," and "superstitions" (though also by "modernization"). Understanding these values required research. According to a JWT newsletter, the agency's effort throughout the world "was backed by the research experience and knowledge of the agency which is outstanding in this type of work, and [the agency] is conducting surveys of a type never before attempted in the countries which it covers."[56] Market investigations, carried out in every location where the firm had a branch,[57] analyzed demographic and economic factors like income, gender, the degree of urbanization, education and literacy; studied the nature of local marketing networks, and conducted assesments of local media for advertising placement. In countries where markets were relatively small, of course, few businesses could afford expensive investigations with large samples. Some surveys consisted of little more than the personal observations of an executive as he traveled; even relatively rigorous reports could include sweeping Orientalist generalizations that emphasized propensities of entire religious or regional groups without statistical foundation.

In the 1920s, the degree to which understandings of cultural difference should inform advertisements divided advertising professionals.[58] Some businessmen insisted that the manufacturing country's reputation for quality should be the key selling point to highlight.[59] The executive J. Francis Dement commented in *Advertising Abroad* that: "American merchandise abroad has won the respect of the foreign markets because of its manifest advantages. If that were not true, our manufacturers would be copying the styles and designs of our competitors. Therefore why not carry this individuality, which has proven successful in disposing of our products, to our advertising, thus completing the cycle?"[60] General Motor's initial appeals during the late 1920s were "pattern advertising," produced in America and often replicated abroad with only minor adjustments.[61] But many other actors were convinced that it was critical to impart a local character to copy. José Fajardo of the U.S.A. Corporation wrote: "The prime requisite of the advertising copywriter is to know and understand the people he is addressing." In his view: "Advertising copy, to be effective, must approach its prospect like a casual acquaintance who meets you unexpectedly, speaks in the familiar drawl of your section, and promises good news of the home town and your old friends. It must gain your sympathy in the short moment that you read it. Any hitch or strange accent can spoil that momentary feeling of sympathy and snatch away any chance for your message."[62] By the 1930s, the view that copy had to be adapted to particular cultures was winning out. JWT particularly championed its record of generating "copy written on the spot," proclaiming that in its offices "copy is written locally by experienced native writers: newspapermen, fashion writers, professors and economists—people thoroughly familiar with local preferences and prejudices."[63]

Specialists in overseas advertising argued that artwork also needed to reflect accommodation to local visual culture. Thomas Jarvis wrote: "Nothing will contribute more to the success of a foreign advertising campaign than the art work and typography. The selling appeal of the average export advertising campaign could be materially increased by the use of a higher type of illustration and arrangement."[64] He insisted that art should be carefully prepared, after "exhaustive research into manners, customs, dress, etc. of the readers; caste marks, facial characteristics, and variation in dress denoting rank and station." Commercial artists, he emphasized, needed to be conscious of "taboos" associated with certain colors or animals, drawing upon a word of special valence in anthropological research at the time.[65] A JWT article on South Africa similarly emphasized that both art and verbal appeals should be customized to fit specific circumstances: "Art work should have a local background, and 'copy' a local colour. It is a well-known fact that different fish in different waters are attracted by different baits. Anglers know this. Why, then, when angling for South African bites, use a uniform, world-wide bait?"[66]

The emergence of professional advertising in India

Almost from the beginning, India figured prominently in the globalization of the advertising professsion. JWT's establishment of an office in Bombay in 1929 followed the American agency's expansion to the European continent by only a few years.[67] By this time, India had begun to assume a place in the commercial imagination of European and American manufacturers in ways once reserved for the China market. Articles in business journals repeatedly pointed to India's population of more than three hundred million. While most of these people had limited income, these articles suggested, many millions might be reached if the right adaptations were made.[68] One U.S. government report reasoned that if only 1 percent of the subcontinent's population were potential buyers, manufacturers would have more Indian customers than in all of

Cuba. It continued: "it is obvious to market observers that more than 1 percent of the people in India are potential buyers of some products made by American firms who value highly their business in Cuba."[69] Other specialists emphasized that "modernization" was stimulating growth in the ranks of those who might respond to press advertisements. Roger Falk wrote in 1935 that the development of nationalism, the rise of education, and the spread of new ideas and movements "must inevitably bring in their wake the whole array of advertising material—better newspapers, the cinema, modern residential and commercial areas in which outdoor publicity finds its place, and the rest of the vast battlefield over which the sales conflict can be fought."[70]

The advertising profession took three major institutional forms on the subcontinent. First, some companies chose to develop relationships with local marketing "agents," who typically took responsibility for distributing and marketing the firm's products. A prominent example of this approach was Ovaltine, which conducted a massive worldwide advertising drive directed toward women.[71] In India, Ovaltine hired as its agent the firm of James Wright, headquartered in Calcutta and with offices in Bombay, Madras and Rangoon.[72] The firm clearly possessed a significant trained staff to generate copy, develop artwork, translate ad texts and place advertisements. James Wright ran a massive campaign for Ovaltine in India, publishing ads in both English and vernacular papers and generating outdoor advertising for public buses and trams, billboards and kiosks.

Second, the biggest firms in India developed their own in-house staff of advertising professionals, as was the case with the Imperial Tobacco Company[73] and Unilever. Unilever, the manufacturer of soaps, other toiletries, and cooking mediums, may have been the most substantial consumer-products business in the world at the time. In the later 1920s, its most prominent product, Sunlight soap, enjoyed a dominant place in the Indian market.[74] Some company executives were initially ambivalent about advertising to literate Indians, who, they reasoned, would likely buy Sunlight in any case. One wrote in 1928: "I have not, in 10 years in the East, met one advertiser who attributed the successful introduction of a new line or a sensational increase in sales to Press advertising."[75] The primary focus of advertising, these reports stressed, should be to "educate" paid laborers and small shopkeepers, some of whom did yet not use soap. Some company leaders lamented at the time that Unilever, in contrast to some other large companies, lacked an understanding of the subcontinent necessary to mount an effective campaign: "our contact with the real India is therefore non-existent and no European employed by us has any really deep knowledge of Indian life and customs or even of the individual peculiarities of the consumers of our goods at any specific point."[76]

The growing competitiveness of the Indian soap market after 1930 eliminated such hesitations; advertising became a major feature of Unilever's business. During the 1930s, executives of Lever Brothers, which had become incorporated as an Indian company, concluded that local resistance to ads designed in Britain was growing, and that it was critical to formulate appeals customized to a middle-class Indian audience. As sentiment within Levers for more extensive and culturally salient advertisements grew, it developed a significant staff in India to carry out its campaigns. Around 1932, John Rist was put in charge of the firm's Indian advertising. By 1936, he was so swamped with his responsibilities that his superiors recommended the establishment of "a real advertising organization."[77] In 1937, Levers sent the marketing expert Thompson Walker to conduct a market investigation of Indian soap use; Walker insisted that he be assisted by an Indian. Prakash Tandon, who later would become Chairman of Hindustan Lever, was hired in response. By 1939 advertising in India was handed over to a Levers' in-house advertising organization, Lintas.[78] At the time of its founding, Lintas in India already possessed art directors, account executives, media relations officers, and other features of a full-fledged agency, and it was handling submissions to 450 newspapers in thirteen different languages all over the country.[79] Levers was then spending 925,000 Rupees annually on advertising in India, four times what the advertising agency JWT spent on all of its clients in its Bombay office put together.[80]

The third mode of involvement by professional advertisers was the advertising agency. The first two international agencies in India to do more than just ad placement opened during the early 1920s.[81] Each brought in trained ad men steeped in British advertising methods, commercial artists, and printing experts with the ability to produce high-quality blocks. One of these companies, Alliance Advertising in Bombay, initially attracted significant customership among local merchants and manufacturers. Newspaper publishers, however, were unwilling to make the improvements in paper quality and printing techniques necessary to sustain the ads' quality in print, and resented the agents' usurpation of their traditional roles in preparing advertisements. Offered rate concessions by newspapers to return to typeset ads, many local businessmen ended their relationships with the advertising agencies, which then collapsed.[82] Purchasing Alliance Advertising's furniture after its closure, L. A. Stronach, an employee of the agency, founded his own firm in Bombay around 1925.[83] Stronach's would prove to be longlasting, surviving until its founder's retirement after World War II. Stronach worked hard at convincing newspaper publishers and product manufacturers that the use of modern print technology was in their mutual interest, informing the publishers that "if better advertising were created, greater sales of the advertised products would result," and asking manufacturers that "if they were convinced that advertisements I prepared for them were what they required, they should give me their full backing against the objections raised by the publishers."[84] Initially designing illustrations himself, Stronach prepared the process blocks and sent off the mounted stereos for processing. Stronach's won the ad business of General Motors in 1926. By the mid-1930s, it had also established an office in London, presumably to attract clients for its overseas operations, as well as three offices in South Africa, one in Egypt and one in Calcutta.[85]

The establishment of a JWT branch in Bombay in 1929—its office was initially in the Taj hotel[86]—marked the true arrival of the international advertising agency in India. The initial impetus behind this branch was JWT's effort to promote General Motors' sales.[87] Apparently, GM's Bombay representatives, who already possessed an arrangement with Stronach, were not informed of the company's global contract, and there were some awkward moments when Frank Gerard, the first local director of JWT, brought the contract's obligations to their attention (see Figure 1.3 for a GM ad probably designed by JWT).[88] With its place established on sound financial footing, JWT's Bombay branch was positioned well to add new accounts, especially from the

Figure 1.3 Ad for General Motors India Limited, *BC*, December 4, 1931, 3.

agency's established clients elsewhere in the world. In 1931 the firm's accounts included Kodak, Goodrich Tyres, Horlicks Malted Milk, and Pond's Face Creams. JWT also signed the Indian manufacturer, Tata Oil Mills Company (TOMCO), which made 501 laundry soap, Hamam body soap, and Cocogem cooking oil, as discussed later in this book.[89] In 1939, the agency had thirty-two accounts, having added such international firms as Elizabeth Arden, Binny and Co., Firestone Tyre (which had displaced Goodrich), Johnson and Johnson, Kellogg and Co., Philips Electrical, Standard Oil, and Smith Corona as well as Indian firms like Godrej and Boyce, Indian Hotels Co. (owners of the Taj), and Wagle Process Studio Press. JWT's biggest contract was Horlicks, for whom it ran a campaign in both English and vernacular papers. The branch's semi-annual income was more than Rs. 135,000, not a huge business but enough to sustain an office with a few Europeans and several dozen Indians.[90] The Bombay branch held on after termination of the global GM contract, continuing to make a modest profit.

The original branch manager in Bombay, Gerard, was a naturalized U.S. citizen with a background in banking, real estate, and newspaper publishing. He had worked earlier in India for an American office equipment business, and had received training in JWT's New York office. His assistant was Peter Fielden, a young man with a background in fine arts who became a trainee in JWT's art department and then worked in its London, Berlin, and Alexandria (Egypt) branches before coming to India around 1930.[91] The Bombay office also hired an English art director and an English artist, both of whom had been living in India.[92] In 1931, Gerard was replaced, apparently after revealing to his superiors his experimentations with the occult informed by theosophy.[93] Fielden, not yet thirty years old at the time, took his place, and would remain the branch head until 1966, well after Indians had filled all the executive ranks below him. He believed in India's potential as a market for branded goods, opining in 1938 that: "I have always been convinced that there is for us in India a very big future. India is year by year becoming a larger consumer of proprietary products and the history of our growth over the past nine years is evidence of our opportunities."[94] He appears to have been motivated in his activities by the idea that he—and JWT—would participate in India's modernization, writing his successor when he left the job: "I have lived in India since 1930, and many times I have been near despair with frustration and dissatisfaction. But *every time I have an* opportunity to work in the States or in Europe or elsewhere I have decided to stay with our very progressive business and the excitement of being part of history in the making."[95]

As the Indian nationalist movement increasingly questioned the dominance of foreign businesses in India, JWT decided in 1937 that ownership of the branch, its business and assets become incorporated in India under the Indian Companies' Act. The new entity was called J. Walter Thompson Company Eastern (Limited), and its top employees in India, including Fielden, were allocated ownership shares.[96]

From the beginning, the JWT office in Bombay was much more than an ad placement service. To its clients, the firm championed its experience in conducting market investigations, planning marketing campaigns, collecting data about the media, constructing copy and artwork, and handling engraving, type, and print block activities. It even claimed competence in making commercial films and in designing outdoor advertising. The branch set a minimum of 6,000 Rupees for any account that went beyond placement of already prepared advertising.[97] In 1935 JWT opened a second branch in Calcutta to strengthen ties with clients headquartered there; this office executed the planning of advertising campaigns, the design of copy and layouts, and the preparation of financial estimates. The Bombay office, which had added a process studio, still carried out all the mechanical tasks of preparing ads and artwork for both branches, along with billing and collections.[98]

Several other ad agencies were established in western India during the 1930s. Among these were at least two significant Indian firms in Bombay, Sista's Advertising and Publicity Services (later Adarts) and Studio Ravi Batra Private Ltd.[99] These agencies attracted little business from foreign manufacturers but did win Indian clients. Agencies opened in Ahmedabad as well.[100] During World War II, further Indian agencies were established. By 1945, when the Marathi newspaper *Sakal* identified the names of agencies placing every advertisement published during part of the year, most ads were placed by Indian firms.[101] By the end of World War II, the advertising profession was thoroughly established in western India.

Advertising agencies and the construction of cultural knowledge

Advertising specialists in India promised their clients the kinds of expertise their counterparts offered elsewhere in the world. But in making their claims to professional indispensability, they pointed to their possession of special cultural understanding. Stronach would phrase this point with clarity in an ad published in an advertising journal: "Only the co-operation of copy-writers and artists familiar with the methods of approach which appeal to the miscellaneous peoples [at its locations in South Africa, Egypt, and India] . . . can ensure presentation in terms suitable to the prospective buyer, correct in local detail and calculated in matter and form to attract their attention . . . to sell effectively in these markets requires specialized knowledge of the mentality, habits, prejudices and spending capacity of the people being addressed."[102]

Advertising professionals formed their understandings of India through various processes. First, they built a familiarity with the country through their experience of being stationed there.[103] Ad executives were often not the types to shut themselves off socially in exclusive European clubs. At JWT, Gerard may have interacted with local theosophical circles before his dismissal, and Fielden had an extensive record of participating in Bombay civic organizations during his career. In persuading clients to use his firm, Stronach especially pointed to the knowledge of India's landscape that he built up on a year-long, 7,500 km trip after leaving Alliance Advertising. Anvar Alikhan has suggested that "the wealth of the market information he collected [on this trip] would constitute the first market research study ever done in the country."[104] As Jennifer Scanlon notes in her work on Latin America, advertising executives abroad often developed strong identifications with the places where they lived and sometimes defended local cultural practices in their communications with home offices.[105] Their reputations as individuals a bit on the way to "going native" was sometimes part of the persona they cultivated.

Other aspects of the advertisers' special knowledge stemmed from their work activities. One part of every agency's functions was assessment of newpaper readerships, a tricky task in India where publishers were believed to inflate circulation figures. Each agency branch included employees who gauged circulations of India's newspapers and the socio-economic backgrounds of their readers.[106] Experts regularly debated in advertising journals the virtues of advertising in English-language publications relative to vernacular newspapers. While specialists during the 1920s sometimes argued that only English-language newspapers should be used due to the low circulation of most Indian-language papers,[107] they increasingly came to agree during the 1930s that it was necessary to place ads in vernacular publications, which reached deep into the lower middle class. While most experts insisted that the claims made by newspapers were exaggerated, it seems likely that sometimes the figures underestimated readership since the papers were often shared. Table 1.1 offers an illustration of the circulation figures of the biggest Indian papers published in the Bombay Presidency offered by one media researcher.[108]

Formal but mostly modest market investigations also contributed to the advertisers' understandings of India. From its very beginnings, JWT in Bombay was involved in conducting surveys with varying degrees of sophistication. While it acknowledged to clients that the extent of demand did not justify the expense of the kinds of studies with large sample sizes sometimes conducted in Europe and America, it stressed that the office was regularly involved in collecting information relevant to marketing efforts.[109] In 1935, the company reported, JWT's Bombay office had done significant statistical studies on "imports, exports, distribution of wealth, division of the population

Table 1.1 Circulation of major western Indian newspapers*

Bombay
Population—1,175,914—Industrial and Shipping Center

	Language	Class of readers	Est. circ. card rates	Scale
Morning dailies				
Bombay Samachar	English	Europeans and Indians	35,242	6s. 0d. per inch
Bombay Chronicle	English	Indians—nationalists	26,400	Rs. 1/12/0 per inch
Times of India (ex-Sunday)	Gujerati	Indians—chiefly merchants	22,000	Rs. 1/0/0 per inch
Jam-e-Jamshed	Gujerati	Parsee class	6,000	Rs. 0/14/0 per inch
Evening dailies				
Evening News (ex-Sunday)	English	Europeans, Indians, and Eurasians	8,000	2s. 8d. per inch
Indian Daily Mail	English	Europeans and Indians	5,000	Rs. 2/0/0 per inch
Hindustan and Prajamitra	Gujerati	Indians—largely provincial circulation	11,400	1s. 6d. per inch
Sanj Vartaman (ex-Sunday)	Gujerati	Indians—merchant class	8,000	Rs. 1/8/0 per inch
Weekly issues				
Times Illustrated Weekly (Sunday)	English	Europeans and Indians	34,256	9s. 6d. per inch
		National circulation		
Prajamitra (Sunday)	Gujerati	Indians—merchant class	10,700	1s. 9d. per inch
Kaiser-I-Hind (Sunday)	Gujerati and English	Parsee class	8,500	Rs 0/12/0 per inch

* Information on the *Times of India* and *Bombay Samachar* were almost certainly reversed by mistake at the time.

by race, language, etc., and motor vehicle registrations"; an examination of the relevance of Indian symbols in advertising; an exploration of the national market for fertilizers; a survey of swimming suit shops; a study of toothpaste use; a treatment of the selling situation of antiseptics; analyses of the markets for cameras, beer, and cigarettes; a large-scale consumer survey of the cloth market; and "several market studies by annual or semi-annual tours of the country."[110] In 1938, the company conducted an ambitious study promoting coffee consumption that involved setting up shops to acquaint customers with higher qualities of coffee.[111]

Only a handful of these surveys survive, but these documents clearly illustrate the contours of commercial ethnology. The most substantial was a 1931 JWT investigation probably written by Gerard in response to questions raised by Messrs. Lehn and Fink, an international cosmetics firm.[112] Assuming that most potential consumers in India lived in the largest cities, the investigation confined its most intensive examination to Bombay. It began conventionally by stressing the country's diversity, and emphasized that community divisions had important impacts on consumption patterns; most "orthodox Hindus," it observed, would avoid commodities using animal products, making it essential to mark soap and foods as containing no animal fat. The report then shifted into analysis of buying power. It stressed the limited spending capabilities of most Indians, devoting the majority of its attention to those with sufficient incomes to purchase consumer items, whom it divided into four categories: "Europeans, Anglo-Indians, Westernized Indians (all religions) and Educated Indians (all religions)." On the next page, it categorized the population differently, grouping Indians into eight classes—the well-to-do, landed proprietors, the professional class, the middle classes, small farmers and urban workers, cultivators, the unemployable, and dependents—providing estimates of monthly income at each level. The report also furnished an analysis of literacy in English and vernacular languages before considering the material habits associated with these categories. Included among the subjects discussed were travel, servants' roles in purchasing household goods, the participation of women in shopping, the effects of the climate, and the extent of health concerns among consumers. It gave significant attention to the level of women's interest in cosmetics (creams, lipsticks, and powder), the use of disinfectants in the home and in hospitals, and the utilization of feminine hygiene products and birth control, undoubtedly reflecting Lehn and Fink's special preoccupations.

The report also devoted a significant amount of space to discussing Indian markets. It estimated that India possessed millions of shops, classifying them in five categories including large European stores on one end, bazaar shops with inventories from Rs. 1,000 to Rs. 5,000 in the middle, and simple hawkers who purchased their stocks on a daily basis on the other end. It contrasted pricing behavior in these different kinds of shops, covering the role of haggling over prices between customer and shopkeepers in the bazaar. Price rather than brand, the authors insisted, was the Indian consumer's main concern:

> Price is 90% of the consideration. If the price of the product gives the dealer a
> chance to undersell his neighbour, he will push it. He will stock particular brands
> if he feels sure he will be called upon for them. He will undertake no special

promotion of any kind, unless ... there is a special profit in it for him. Indians care little for goodwill, as they know their customers will go elsewhere to save half an anna [i.e. a very small amount of money].[113]

Perhaps not surprisingly given JWT's interests, the report emphasized that any product had to be well advertised by an agency that could understand the market and promote sales.[114]

In 1938, JWT conducted another survey yielding some results that contradicted assumptions of its earlier study. To some extent, this survey constituted the ruminations of its anonymous author (Fielden?) on some statistics rather than a study reflecting deep research. It mainly classified Indians into strata based upon buying power. City-dwellers fell into an A and B class, with incomes over 400 Rupees a month, who composed 11 percent of the urban population; a C and D class with incomes between Rs. 50 and 400 a month, who made up the next 31 percent; and an E category with incomes below Rs. 50 who formed the remaining 58 percent. Western manufacturers, the report suggested, could hope to win customers in the A, B, C and some of the D categories; members of the E class were too poor to afford branded products. The report suggested that press advertising, however, typically only reached 13 percent of urban families, whereas up to 42 percent of the urban population, many illiterate, possessed the purchasing power to be buyers. It also pointed out that at least half of India's literate population lived in the countryside or in small towns,[115] and that many rural people who read newspapers could not be reached by existing distribution networks. Based upon these assessments, the report recommended more oral and pictorial advertising, traveling vans that would provide publicity and carry supplies to rural areas, and the possible use of film.[116] Despite these findings, much of the firm's activities remained focused on the press, which influenced people mostly living in cities.

Before 1937, Levers was less committed to formal market investigations. Annual reports mention a few surveys conducted by the company, including one on Eau du Cologne apparently carried out in the mid-1930s.[117] To a great extent, information about markets was conveyed to the head office in Bombay by the company's selling organization, which linked the bazaar, wholesale marketers, and foreign salesmen.[118] In 1938, however, the large-scale investigation of Thompson Walker on attitudes about soap ushered in a new era of commitment to market studies. The investigation hired a small team of young women to interview housewives in their homes in eight South Asian cities. In Bombay, the investigation was particularly rigorous. There, a thousand households were selected with the sample divided by community and class and located on a city map; and a questionnaire was drawn up to discuss habits of washing clothes and cleaning the body.[119] Unfortunately, the final reports do not seem to have been preserved.[120]

A final point to stress about the construction of advertising knowledge and practice was the contribution of Indian intermediaries. The advertising business on the subcontinent was never an exercise carried out by European agency leaders alone. The foreign professionals relied on Indian subordinates to perform a wide variety of functions; these individuals had input into the development of knowledge about

Indian society and the formulation of advertisements. In effect, the role of these actors was analogous to that of Indian pandits whose part in formulating nineteenth-century Orientalism is now well recognized.[121] Their impact was often invisible in the historical records. Here, however, I seek to highlight the evidence that does exist.

The interwar advertising agency—like nearly all multinational companies in India—was an institution stratified by race. The top positions in Stronach's, JWT, and the advertising section of Levers were all occupied by men and women from America or Europe.[122] When executives were given home leave—usually six months for every two-and-a-half-years in India—or when high-level officers needed to be replaced permanently—the agency gave little consideration to promoting Indians in their place.[123] The racial exclusiveness of executive ranks was an outcome of outright racism and the ethos of "professionalism," which assumed that only persons trained in the agency's home offices could acquire an understanding of the scientific advertising methods upheld by the firm. When Prakash Tandon became the first Indian at the executive level in the Bombay office of Lever Brothers in 1937–8, he lacked such training, but he possessed the next best thing: an English university degree.[124] Though educated as an accountant, he was hired in the advertising section, then about to embark on Thompson's marketing survey. During the war years, JWT sent one Indian student for training to America: Ajit Haksar, later head of Imperial Tobacco Company of India.[125] When wartime conditions made it impossible to hire a European for a new office in Delhi, the company sent an employee named Talyarkhan, previously an assistant account representative in Bombay. Talyarkhan believed he was being groomed to assume higher positions and would be sent to the New York office for training, but when it came to an expected promotion in 1948, he was passed over in favor of Europeans. In bitterness he resigned, writing:

> There is, however, a taxable limit to anyone's patience and I consider that instead of progressing with the changed times, the policy you are adopting in the question of recruitment is still reminiscent of days when Englishmen were 'koi hai walas' and the Indians ... well, they were just not good enough for executive positions. ... Are you really convinced that there is a dearth of talent within our organization here and in the country as a whole? Do you still maintain that you cannot find suitable Indians and were therefore forced to drafting two Europeans?[126]

Though Europeans dominated the executive ranks of advertising organizations, other levels were filled by Indians. The staff in an early JWT office consisted of four Europeans and fourteen "natives," "carefully selected for the positions they occupy." These included two copywriters, a mechanical production manager and assistant, an assistant artist, a media-research manager, a media-checking and block dispatch man, as well as accounting staff. The two "native copymen," reported the company in 1931, "are exceptional—one of them is the best man one of our clients was able to find during a number of years experience before our arrival in India—the other is the most capable native of all our staff, as is shown by nearly two years work with him." Mentioning the copywriters' crucial role in developing ads, the report concluded that "the combination of experience represented [in terms of background in professional advertising and familiarity with local culture] obviously permits us to adapt any copy methods which made J. Walter Thompson internationally successful to the local Indian requirements."[127] This balance of European presence and Indian participation roughly sustained itself over time. In 1942, there were nine Europeans (four English men, three English women, one German Jew and one European Armenian), fifty-five Indians, and seven Goans (Indian residents of the Portuguese colony) in JWT's Bombay office.[128]

The lower ranks of the art staff in advertising departments were predominantly Indian. Before the late 1930s, perhaps hundreds of Indians with strong artistic talents but without formal training in advertising participated in fields like printing, film-making, and advertising in western India, though the art directors in agencies were consistently European.[129] Most of these individuals are unknown to us now. We do know that V. N. Adarkar, later Professor of Commercial Art in the Sir J.J. School of Art, worked for Stronach's as a commercial artist for some time. With the establishment of a commercial art program in the J.J. School of Art around 1937, Bombay students gained access to a formal curriculum providing training in the art and technology of advertising, and some of these students made their way into advertising agencies.[130] In 1940, S. D. Khadilkar, drawn from the first batch of graduates of the commercial art program, was hired by Maeve Wood, then art director at JWT Bombay, after a grueling tryout of three days. Khadilkar later reported the presence of an art staff in the firm of about a dozen individuals at the time—only two were Europeans—and noted there were many Indian artists in the larger advertising field elsewhere in the city.[131] Soon after India attained independence in 1947, some Indian artists were positioned sufficiently well to quickly become art directors in their organizations. As we will see through much of this book, the images drawn in many advertisements often included very subtle elements that only persons with intimate knowledge of middle-class society would have been able to depict: for instance, a widow, an Indian "modern girl," a modest housewife, an educated office worker, a sexually dysfunctional male, a comfortable middle-class household, and so on.

Translation was another area where Indian employees had a role. At this stage, none of the agencies in India generated copy originally in Indian vernacular languages. Advertisements thus required translation before submission to the vernacular press. Since the European staff rarely knew local languages sufficiently well, the agencies hired Indians who knew English to do the job, sometimes on a contract basis. Supervising the translators' work posed a challenge. In one case, a man was hired to translate copy that began "When it is forty in the shade," which was meant to suggest the heat-relieving qualities of Horlicks (forty referred to Celsius temperatures), but his translated text in Tamil read: "When there are 40 people under the banyan tree." To counteract such problems, JWT checked translations by asking a second person in the office to convert the translated copy back into English. This policy undoubtedly encouraged the production of literal rather than idiomatic renderings.[132] But on other occasions, as we shall see, advertisements reveal the efforts of local figures struggling to transform copy into terms that would resonate with Indian newspaper readers. Again, it is not possible to identify most individuals who served as translators during this period. An exception is R. K. Swamy, who was hired by JWT in 1940 while still a teenager to replace an employee on leave, because he knew Gujarati as well as Tamil. Swamy would become a major figure in JWT after Independence, and would later form his own advertising agency.[133]

Copywriters, artists, and translators were only some of the Indian actors who shaped the character of advertisements through their everyday roles. Assistants on market investigations, such as the women who carried out Levers' soap survey, were important intermediaries between the company and middle-class housewives. Indian shopkeepers provided information on what did and did not work with their customers and they sometimes counseled salesmen to expand the dimensions of advertising efforts. The salesmen in turn played a critical role in providing the larger organization with knowledge about how to address advertising problems.[134] In his autobiography, Prakash Tandon recounts participating significantly in discussing Levers' marketing campaigns with his European bosses.[135] In short, the cultural strategies devised by advertising firms were not simply ones dreamed up by foreigners pushing a global set of values; they were socially constructed in the interaction between the professionals and Indian cultural brokers, many of whom were themselves drawn from the middle class.

Commercial ethnology and advertising practice

Advertising practice in India was strongly informed by the cultural knowledge developed by the professionals. Every advertising expert generated a list of cultural dos and don'ts to impart as advice to prospective clients seeking to do business on the subcontinent. Espousing a twentieth-century Orientalism, E. F. Pinner wrote in *Advertising Abroad* that "when getting ready to enter the Indian trade, however, it must be remembered that there are many religious and racial sentiments to be observed. Going contrary to the established customs, convictions and prejudices usually brings poor results, if any." He specifically warned against using inappropriate animals as commercial symbols and stressed the value of deploying specific colors for specific religious and regional groups before concluding: "Superstitions they are, naturally, but so ingrained in the fibre of the people generally through age-long observance and belief, that it is quite futile to attempt to go counter to them."[136] Others pointed to dangers of failing to consider caste sentiments; one observer wrote "an artist preparing a picture [probably in America] for a safety razor to be advertised in India drew a picture of a person of low caste sitting on the curbstone of a street shaving himself with this particular safety razor. A study of conditions prevailing in India with regard to the persons using safety razors would have avoided such an incongruity [that is, high-status buyers were likely to be put off by ads featuring individuals marked visually as 'low-caste']."[137] In a book he authored in 1939, Stronach pointed out possible mishaps that might result from ill-informed efforts. He mentioned one ad for carpets run in America picturing a Muslim nobleman sitting in a Delhi court with "lords and ladies on carpets of a wondrous texture, playing chess." When the same ad was placed in an Indian newspaper, he indicated, local readers responded with four impressions:

1) Muslim ladies never sit openly with men. Therefore, these women were not 'ladies'.
2) Their dresses were all wrong. No Indian woman, be she respectable or not, ever appears scantily dressed.
3) The game as depicted is a Western innovation. The old-time game was 'pachesi', which is a form of chess.
4) No one would have noticed the carpets.[138]

Advertising professionals stressed the importance of coordinating the visual appearance of ads with the copy, insisting, for instance, that illustrations of people should correspond with the community associated with their characters' names.[139] A JWT officer in Bombay wrote in 1936:

[A] campaign demands different artwork for different races. That is, an advertisement loses all reality in India if you show a Mahomedan and the text is in Singalese [sic]. This would not be necessary in a general advertisement but in cartoons, where the individuals are speaking, it would not be meaningful if the artwork were identical for all. These people always think of themselves as different races. The newspapers will never say that *a man* was knocked down; it is always a Burmese, or a Parsi, etc. etc.[140]

Advertising professionals sometimes advocated adjusting campaigns to regional audiences. A guardbook from the early 1940s for Sanatogen (a tonic) and Kolynos (a toothpaste) provides the visuals for ads targeted for later translation into regional Indian languages; these ads included illustrations geared to different readerships. Each Sanatogen ad featured a happy couple from different parts of India who were expressing satisfaction with their "marital" lives [i.e., sex lives] and each couple wears regionally distinctive clothing (see Figure 1.4 for three examples from the guardbook). It is interesting to note what did not change as well; all the images were marked as fair-skinned, middle class, and high status. Clearly the ads must have been drawn by artists with well-established notions about regional sartorial practices and the importance of signaling social distinctions. Artwork in Urdu newspapers clearly marked male and female figures as Muslims, primarily through the delineation of clothing.[141] In all of the Marathi, Gujarati, and English newspapers I examined, by contrast, no Muslims were included, an indication that regional advertisers had largely erased them in their conceptualization of the middle class. Images were generally marked in their clothing and ornaments as Hindu and high-caste, though some figures were clearly drawn to depict Parsis in Gujarati papers. This pattern existed despite the fact that educated Muslims in western India did enter middle-class occupations and the ranks of the consumers of branded items.

Offering their advice as cultural experts, advertising specialists regularly concluded that the print media by themselves were insufficient for publicizing brands in India, especially outside the middle class. Literacy levels were too low and Indians too visually oriented, they sometimes reasoned, for press campaigns to reach large sections of the population.[142] Some insisted on the value of "outdoor advertising," such as posters on

Figure 1.4 Three Sanatogen ads designed for different regional languages ("Urdu," "Hindi," and "Bengali," respectively), HATA, O+M Small Guard Books (Sanatogen-Therapeutic), OM (S) 12.

kiosks, tramways and buses, billboards and enamel signs. Such displays, they argued, needed to be visually striking. One specialist wrote that "[a] very important advantage of outdoor advertising is that it is possible to use bright colors in displays. As the Oriental is unusually receptive to color, he will soon identify a product by the color combinations of its display advertisements even though he may never know its name."[143]

The advertising professionals who devised these visual strategies claimed a familiarity with Indian bazaars and the commercial conditions prevailing there. Large retail stores, it was frequently observed, were rare in India, and catered only to Europeans or wealthy Indians. Elsewhere it was impossible to rely on window displays and other forms of publicity familiar to the manufacturers at home. In an internal memo, a Levers' executive indicated: "There are countless 'booths' in bazaars all over the land in which goods are stacked on shelves or on counters at small windowless fronts, and the opportunities to use showcards is limited. The pack itself . . . is the main display unit, and in designing new packs more attention should be given to the design and colour scheme of the actual pack, so that it will stand out."[144] Other accounts noted the value of displays on shop walls: "They [such displays] are raucously bright in colour, and visible from ten yards or more. They sell because they are the proper adaptation for India. The pictorial presentation means is extremely necessary in the case of these showcards. A name means nothing, but a picture tells a story."[145] In the bazaar, specialists regularly advised, there was need for messages engraved in enamel plates that could withstand monsoon conditions, again emphasizing the importance of bright colors.[146]

By the late 1920s and early 1930s, some advertising agencies in western India began to observe the popularity of film, noting that it might become a valuable advertising medium.[147] JWT championed its capacity to make films as early as 1931 and Gerard pointed out to a prospective client: "India, more than most countries, requires special treatment as compared with standard marketing procedure in westernized countries. The methods which are incidental in England and the United States are, in India, often of fundamental importance. Thus, we have made ourselves competent in India to handle motion picture and talkie production complete." He also mentioned some forms of outdoor advertising including "road demonstrations, caravan and sampling activities."[148] JWT persuaded GM around 1931 to fund an advertising film based upon an adventure story, and contracted out the work to a local studio. No other movies were made for years, but JWT's officers continued to believe in film's commercial potential if they could convince clients to invest in it.[149] Around the same time, an Indian company, seemingly in Bombay, became involved in making commercial films in "Hindustani."[150] In the early 1940s, JWT made a series of 1,000-foot films for Goodrich tires, TOMCO soaps, BSA cycles, Brooke Bond tea, Brand's Essence of Chicken, Horlicks, and Binny's textiles. Fielden would later write that: "Very shortly after I came to India in 1930 I became convinced that potentially the most powerful medium to influence people in this country is the movies, and never since that time have I had cause to change my mind."[151]

The script for one of these films, accompanied by some publicity photo stills (for instance, Figure 1.5), has been preserved.[152] Apparently made in 1941 by JWT's Bombay office, the film was entitled "Sacha Dost" (translated as "a friend in need") and advertised "Brand's Essence of Chicken," an extract of chicken product sold as a health food. The filmscript was first written in English but it was apparently translated into South Asian languages for actual production. Lasting a bit more than eleven minutes, the film featured a female character, Reba, who is in love with the character Shankar, but is being forced to marry Rai Bahadur, a wealthy old man who promises to cover her family's debts. Reba could pay off the debts if only she were able to give a public dance performance, but she has been weakened by a recent fever. A doctor advises Shankar that Reba could regain her health if she takes Brand's Essence of Chicken. Shankar in turn informs her that "after any illness and particularly after fever it is essential for recovering strength; there is no better and more easily digestible food known." Reba consumes the product, recovers, and goes on to perform successfully. The film apparently was punctuated by Reba's dance performances. In the final scene, Reba and Shankar depart the dance hall in a car, laughing happily, as Rai Bahadur shouts "Reba! Reba!" in frustration. With its reliance on familiar narrative devices from popular film, its heavy deployment of music and dance, and its use of costumes and scenery characteristic of Hindi film, the movie was clearly prepared by film-makers steeped in the conventions of Bombay cinema.

Levers, too, came to consider film as a significant method of advertising its products, particularly in rural areas. In 1928, one executive entertained the use of a traveling cinema on a motor-lorry to show films publicizing the company's products. Levers had

Figure 1.5 Still from JWT Film, "Sacha Dost," HATA, 50/1/17/ 3/1, Brand's Essence of Chicken, India/Ceylon, 1941.

consulted someone in British American Tobacco, which had already made an advertising film (the B.A.T. film had proven expensive and the complexities of making arrangements with local authorities and traveling over poor roads had made rural showings difficult). Levers planned to have its films made in Calcutta by a local cinema company and was considering showing them as part of a program arranged by British railway companies on cinema cars that stopped in rural areas.[153] In the mid-1930s, however, film was not mentioned as part of Levers' advertising expenses, evidence that it had not been adopted as a regular part of the company's campaigns. This changed in the early 1940s, when the company began to make films for some of its products, such as Dalda cooking medium, showing them extensively in a cinema van that traveled around the countryside.[154]

Such techniques suggest that advertising professionals believed the subcontinent to be a visually oriented society that would respond more strongly to the image than to the printed word. Unfortunately, as with the commercial films made by JWT and other companies, most elements of this visual culture have not survived. One major exception to this pattern, however, is commercial calendars, which have sometimes been preserved in excellent condition. These calendars, typically reproducing paintings by the late-nineteenth-century/early twentieth-century figure Ravi Varma or the twentieth-century artist M. V. Dhurandhar, featured mythological images, as in the cover image for this book, a 1934 calendar for Sunlight Soap, which depicts the god Vishnu riding the bird-like creature Garuda, a familiar Hindu motif. A number of multinational companies, such as Lever Brothers, Burma Shell, Imperial Chemical Industries, and Woodward's Gripe Water, printed calendars annually for Indian distributors and other merchants.[155] The images in calendars sometimes were worshipped by shopkeepers who received them.[156] As a 1926 report from Lever Brothers indicated, calendar distribution to dealers was not expensive and was quite valuable in fostering the traders' "interest and good will."[157] It is not clear, however, whether they were used directly in appealing to consumers; such images were rarely present in newspaper advertising. There is also little evidence that advertising agencies like Stronach's or JWT gave them much emphasis; seemingly, they were used primarily by manufacturers to create brand awareness.

While the advertising industry used a variety of media to publicize its clients' products, the largest item in advertising budgets remained the allocation for press advertising. In their newspaper ads, advertising professionals targeted two main strata of literate consumers: a small European community, living in Bombay or dependent on Bombay for its supplies; and a larger but poorer Indian middle class concentrated in western India's urban areas. To a great extent, ads directed toward literate consumers in the press were framed less around conceptions of cultural Otherness and they lacked the conspicuous colors and other striking visuals of ads associated with bazaar publicity. They reflected a different kind of cultural fine-tuning, an effort to address what the advertisers viewed as the priorities of a *modern* and *Indian* middle class, a class they conceived as becoming increasingly committed to principles of modernity. In particular, they gave heavy emphasis to preoccupations associated with the reproduction of the conjugal family.

Conclusion

European and American manufacturers with global ambitions thus increasingly turned during the interwar period to a special set of new actors—advertising professionals— to project their brands into farflung areas of the world where their influence had previously been limited. Advertising specialists offered to their client-firms different techniques for publicizing commodities generated through experience in the metropole, techniques that they now started to apply in Latin America, Africa, and Asia. But this chapter complicates any view of the advertising in India simply as an instrument of a Western economic system imposing alien values on Indian consumers. First, multinational companies were not the only forms of business seeking to establish brand names in India; "vernacular" firms also participated in this project. Second, advertising professionals couched much of their claim to indispensabilty to multinational firms on the grounds of their access to special knowledge about the subcontinent and their ability to generate cultural strategies needed to win Indian customers. To go global, in other words, the multinationals increasingly relied on experts who asserted the ability to appreciate the local (meaning here both all-Indian and regional) values. Third, advertising agencies generated their understandings of India and shaped their advertising campaigns through interactions with Indian actors, many of whom were drawn from the very classes whose consumption behavior they sought to influence. They developed specialized campaigns to cultivate customers in an environment they saw as characterized by cultural difference but with the potential to be absorbed into global material practices. As we shall see, this increasingly involved deploying the discourse of modern conjugality in printed advertisement.

2

Consumers: European Expatriates and the Indian Middle Class

Before the 1920s, most multinational businesses conceived of the Indian market as too small to deserve special attention. With some exceptions, global manufacturers of brand-name commodities often assumed that Indians were too poor or too difficult to reach, that reliable demand for branded products was confined largely to the small set of expatriates, and that expatriates possessed the same motivations as Europeans everywhere. Advertisements both reflected and perpetuated these convictions, usually relying on images and wording formulated in the home offices. Indians who purchased goods produced by international firms were often thought to be motivated by a desire to emulate the foreign ruling class; as a result global companies rarely developed advertising specifically targeting non-European consumers.

During the interwar period, however, global firms began to recognize new possibilities in India, expressing enthusiasm about reaching beyond enclaves of Europeans and highly anglicized or wealthy Indian elites. As E. F. Pinner wrote in *The Export Advertiser* in 1931: "It is the native trade that represents the big opportunity in India—the European population being very small compared with the total population."[1] Reaching this audience, he stressed, would require addressing distinctive concerns. "What appeals to the Indian in his advertisement?," lectured a newspaper man to the Rotary Club of Madras in 1938, "Pictures of soignee European women and delicious roast beef? I doubt it. I feel that [the] so-called educating of the public to the appreciation of European advertisements is really of very little use."[2] Particularly as advertisers began to recognize the force of Indian nationalism, the notion that emulation would motivate Indians to buy global commodities lost favor in the advertising industry.

By the 1930s, professional advertisers, relying on understandings grounded in commercial ethnology, came to emphasize that the Indian environment required a more targeted approach. Most significantly, they increasingly distinguished between expatriates and the Indian educated classes. Harold Elterich wrote in the *Export Advertiser* in 1931 that India offered two different markets for multinational companies, a set of Europeans constituting about 225,000 people—"to which can be added approximately 130,000 Eurasians"—and an Indian middle class.[3] Roger Falk of Keymer's Calcutta office reasoned that separate approaches were needed for these audiences: "Selling to the European is not difficult, but the upper-class Indian, with his growing interest in politics, his appetite for knowledge, and his ready adoption of the

English language, becomes more and more the object of our attention."[4] A Levers' document suggested a more nuanced approach, arguing that "all our advertising activity might usefully be divided into two sections, each of which has two classes. The sections are: 1) Appeal to the European Community [and] 2) Appeal to the Indian Community. The classes of each are: 1) Reminder and Prestige Advertising [and] 2) Educative Advertising." Some Indians, the report acknowledged, could still be influenced by prestige advertising oriented to Europeans, but educative advertising needed to be directed specifically to Indians.[5]

Members of the advertising profession reasoned, moreover, that the "native" market was itself divided, chiefly between literate Indians who could be won over by press appeals and a more heterogeneous category of non-literate and rural people, who were either too hard to reach or had to be attracted by other methods. While they concentrated their efforts on the former, they often toyed with dreams of a time when parts of the larger population might be persuaded to make significant numbers of small expenditures. In reality, none of these groupings—the Europeans, the Indian middle class and non-literate consumers—was homogeneous or stable. But they served as critical categories informing the logic of professional advertising during the interwar period.

Part 1: The Europeans

Despite dismissive comments they sometimes made about the size of the European population in India, representatives of global firms still regarded expatriates as a significant part of their market during the interwar period. While small in numbers, Europeans often possessed spending power far beyond most middle-class Indians; many of them, moreover, were accustomed to buying branded products at "home" and regarded continued access to these products as essential to sustaining their physical well-being and their social standing in the tropics.

According to the 1931 *Census of India*, "Europeans and Allied Races" in the Bombay Presidency constituted 22,913 persons in 1931, 15,652 males and 7,261 females.[6] In 1921, Bombay city itself possessed 14,726 Europeans, a little more than 1 percent of the city's population; by 1931, the total numbers had fallen to 8,400, largely due to the elimination of the Colaba military station.[7]

The category of "European" in the census was a constructed one that elided differences of nationality, language and class.[8] Roughly two-thirds of those so enumerated in Bombay city in 1921 were British, but the term also denoted Germans, Austrians, Russians, Swedes, the Swiss and Americans.[9] The category also included some poor persons, even vagrants, though these were not part of the imagined market addressed by global business.[10] Anglo-Indians, mostly the offspring of mixed-race relationships, sometimes listed themselves in the census as Europeans, and this self-identification certainly influenced their buying patterns. The category of "Europeans and Allied Races" together with Anglo-Indians in the Presidency was enumerated as 40,710 individuals in 1931 with more than 40 percent of them living in Bombay.[11] Bombay city's commercial significance for Europeans stretched into the mofussil.

Expatriates throughout the Presidency read English-language papers published in Bombay, visited the city to make key purchases, and sent mail orders to urban stores.

The European population in Bombay city itself was also unstable. Some people enumerated as Europeans, such as the crews and passengers on ships in the harbor area, were pure transients.[12] There were also seasonal movements. During the winter months, Europeans from different parts of India converged on Bombay as they prepared to take the boat trip to England for home leave or permanent departure; these individuals had usually left by the hot season. During the summer and monsoon, many Europeans resident in the city migrated to the hills to escape the heat, leaving an increasingly male society behind. At these times, some of the city's younger European men, who lived in "chummeries" (bachelors' quarters) or elaborate tent complexes during the rest of the year, moved into vacated flats or homes as renters or house-sitters.[13] Employees of British businesses typically signed five-year contracts but would return home after two-and-a half-years of service for six months' rest and recuperation, a practice believed essential to their physical and mental health. Many young men failed to last out these contracts, returning home after succumbing to illnesses and heat exhaustion.[14] Stanley Reed, editor of the *Times of India* during this period, later referred to European society as possessing a "bird-of-passage" atmosphere.[15] The European population was largely a set of sojourners, and European society an unstable formation that needed continuously to reproduce itself by cultural practices that outlived the presence of specific individuals or families.

Because of its mobile character, the European population in Bombay shared many of the general demographic characteristics of the larger city, which was, after all, a city of migrants. The Europeans were preponderantly male. In 1921, there were only 480 females per 1000 European males, slightly more than the ratio among Muslims (452) but slightly less than the ratio among Hindus (531).[16] They were highly concentrated in the working ages. Only about 10 percent of British residents were under the age of ten; European families who lived in Bombay often sent their children to boarding school. Only about 6 percent of Europeans were over the age of fifty; most apparently chose to return to the metropole by late middle age.[17] Advertisement geared to expatriates rarely acknowledged that a large portion of the European consumers would have been single males living outside families.

Literature on the Indian city has frequently emphasized the contrasts between native "black towns" supposedly characterized by houses and shops crowded together in unsanitary conditions and European "white" towns, often associated with army cantonments and with very, orderly, wide streets bordered by trees.[18] More recent scholarship questions this distinction for many cities.[19] Certainly by the early twentieth century there was no exclusively European section of Bombay; Europeans typically lived intermingled with the Indian upper classes and with others who possessed no homes. The highest concentrations of Europeans were in the cantonment area of Colaba, where a significant set of troops had been stationed until the 1920s. In Malabar Hill and Cumballa Hill, some Europeans had resided in large bungalows owned by Indians at the beginning of the century.[20] During the plague of 1896 to 1910, the house-owners often reoccupied these buildings to escape neighborhoods they regarded as unhealthy, and the European population was forced to spread itself more widely over south Bombay. The reliance of expatriates on a land market controlled by Indian property holders meant that they were in no position to dictate the urban population's spatial distribution.

Increasingly, most Europeans moved into flats in apartment buildings,[21] which they often found far from adequate to meet their needs. Housewife-columnists in the *Times of India* typically lamented the lack of closets and storage space, inadequate lighting, exposed wiring, poor water pressure and electric geysers that supplied hot water at a trickling rate.[22] While the expatriates often lived privileged lives, they frequently regarded their own living situation as one of discomfort.

The political position of Europeans in western India was also slipping during this period. Changes in municipal and provincial government associated with the Montagu-Chelmsford Reforms of 1919 and the Government of India Act of 1935 increased Indian representation and limited European influence. During the 1937 elections, in which Congress won control over the Provincial Assembly and eventually formed a ruling ministry, Europeans in the Bombay Presidency were reduced to the position of a small minority guaranteed only seven seats in the assembly. Developments like Khursed Nariman's exposure of European financial arrangements in the Backbay Reclamation Scandal of the 1920s, the Civil Disobedience movement of 1930–1, and the enactment of prohibition by the Congress Ministry in the Bombay Presidency after 1937 created a sense of embattlement among many expatriates.

In the private sector, foreign business firms with branches in Bombay typically reserved their top managerial positions for men hired in the European or American metropole. Prakash Tandon would later report that there were less than a dozen Indians working in management levels throughout the city at the time.[23] Employment policies clearly sustained a view of Europeans as "qualified" managers and Indians only as useful subordinates. But the changing industrial economy no doubt offered expanding opportunities to Indian businessmen. Indians, for instance, assumed positions of ownership in the city's textile industry, which was gradually freeing itself from its dependence on European managerial and technical expertise. Indian entrepreneurs built up powerful economic empires in other spheres. The Tata family, which entered the fields of steel manufacture, hotel management, hydro-electric power, consumer products, and even airline travel is the best-known example.[24] Elite business families often obtained high levels of schooling for their sons and daughters, sometimes in Europe itself, undercutting education abroad as an exclusively European marker of status.

As their place of pre-eminence became beleaguered, Europeans struggled to preserve their prestige and their sense of community. A. T. Robinson, who worked for two British companies during the 1920s, would later recall: "you were always rather concerned to be a sahib [respected white man], with the exception here and there perhaps a bloke didn't mind so much, but normally you felt that you definitely had a position to keep up."[25] Europeans worked hard to reinforce a social fabric that would sustain the appearance of privilege, one that sometimes admitted a few wealthy Indians willing to conform to the conventions of expatriate life. Critical to this process was an intense internal sociality, which continuously recreated extensive face-to-face relations among the Europeans even as individuals and families moved into and out of the city.

The central institutions of this society were the social clubs, which often continued to be based on racial exclusivity. But Europeans in Bombay organized patterns of interaction that extended well beyond the clubs, ones that during the winter months involved the exchange of visits to each other's homes for dinners, attendance at the cinema, theater and concerts, and outings to local hotels to listen to jazz, to view cabaret performances, or to dance. A key feature of evening-time sociality distinguishing it from Indian middle-class interactions was the mixing of unrelated men and women, and the search for potential romantic partners and courtship on such occasions. Sporting activity—tennis, yachting, hunting, golf and cricket—also served to provide a kind of social cement perpetuating a sense of European community.

The demands of expatriate society could be taxing. Wilfred Russell wrote in his diary that Europeans, "rarely think further ahead than the next party and do their best . . . to get asked if they have not. One gets in this attitude of mind very easily."[26] An Indian critic, D. Karaka, wrote: "The strong orthodox element which is in power plays a great part in moulding the young [European] man's character, and his mind is very soon full of all the prejudices, the taboos, the empty ceremonial which the British rule in India has stood for all these years. The threat of social isolation is so severe that even the toughest soon fall in line and . . . think as others have done and thought before him."[27]

Middle-class Indians were typically excluded from this society or kept on its fringes. Even "progressive" Europeans, including Russell, reported that they had Indian friends or encountered Indians at work, but never invited Indians to their homes and rarely if ever visited Indian residences.[28] Prakash Tandon wrote that his firm excluded him from conferences in which the remaining managers (all Europeans) were invited or in meals or drinks at the Taj hotel, where they would adjourn after the work day was over.[29] Expatriates living in the mofussil often participated vicariously in Bombay society, by reading reports printed in the *Times of India* and other English-language periodicals. On some social occasions—jazz at the Taj, parties at the homes of European officials and golf or bridge at integrated social clubs like the Willingdon club—mixing took place across racial boundaries, but the Indians present on such occasions usually were drawn from the upper classes.

European society and consumption

The maintenance of European consumption values was also critical to sustaining expatriate society and its boundaries. Elite Europeans could not hope to transplant life at home onto the subcontinent due to their minority status, shortages in housing, hardships of the Indian climate, the transient character of their society, and the demographic peculiarities of a sojourner population. But they could adopt selected material aspects of an imagined homeland that sustained distinctive identities and provided a sense of comfort in an alien environment. They brought with them from Europe extensive experience with buying mass-produced goods by brand. By the late 1920s, many Europeans expected their homes, even when these were only flats, to include a telephone, imported furniture, electric appliances such as refrigerators and hot-water geysers, a Western-style toilet and bath, and European interior decorations. For the top members of the bureaucracy and private businesses, a motor car became a necessity. The *Times of India* ran repeated articles on home design, the latest fashions in Paris and Hollywood, and recipes for European dishes needed to sustain the expatriate lifestyle.[30] The observance of European holidays such as Christmas and New Year's Eve, along with the food and music of home, was critical to this society's reproduction.

Advertising specialists recognized the importance of consumption to expatriate culture. JWT's 1931 report indicated that Europeans "have incomes rather larger than they would receive at home and are forced to live on a fairly extensive scale" and noted that "the [their] life corresponds to that lived by the upper class in England."[31] Besides expenditure on club memberships and entertainment, the report mentioned the importance of spending on clothes, beauty products and cosmetics, toiletries, and canned goods. Europeans purchased some of these commodities in "European and Indian stores though they occasionally go bargain hunting in the bazaars"[32] while European women in the mofussil did much of their shopping from city stores by mail.[33] Anglo-Indians, the report suggested, tended to follow sojourner Europeans in their tastes, though they often had less disposable income.[34]

Professional advertisers clearly drew upon their knowledge of expatriate social preoccupations, derived in part from their own membership in this society, to devise cultural strategies that would encourage the expatriates' consumption of their products. During the late 1920s and the 1930s, they increasingly found imported ads inadequate for this purpose and designed advertisements oriented to special priorities of expatriate life. Ads targeting Europeans living in India were placed primarily in British-owned publications, most notably the *Times of India* and the *Illustrated Weekly of India*.

Visually, ads designed for the expatriate community were marked by two sets of indicators. First, the human figures were drawn to suggest Europeaness—women typically were illustrated with fair skin (that is, the color of the newspaper page), short, often light-colored hair (depicted by a few wavy lines in otherwise blank spaces),[35] and dresses and skirts that came to mid-calf. Evening gowns, sports clothes, or even undergarments (in the case of ads for lingerie or for hot water geysers) could also be featured. Other indicators of a European home, such as household furniture or even a dog, might be included. But markers also frequently came to be used to signal the Indian context: servants, minarets in an urban market place, Indian men with turbans in the background, European men with *sola topis* (headwear often worn by expatriates in the tropics), Indian vegetation, or just a hot sun. These markers clearly distinguished many ads of the 1930s from those of the early 1920s, when imported ads reflecting European contexts were the norm.

Four themes were particularly prominent in these ads. First, they frequently sought to evoke a sense of luxury and prestige. In many cases, they specifically suggested to the expatriates the possibility that they might experience the comforts of an imagined homeland. An advertisement for Black and White cigarettes, for instance, suggests a club scene. A male audience in formal attire is being served dinner and drinks by uniformed servants of the establishment. One of the servants offers cigarettes to a European in the foreground while the others smoke and carry on conversations, all

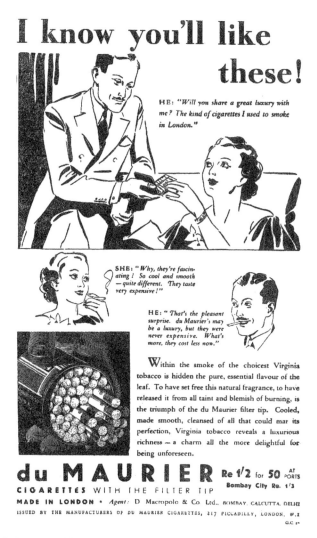

Figure 2.1 "I know you'll like these!" du Maurier Cigarettes, *TI*, February 15, 1937, 9.

conveying the relaxed nature of the occasion. The ads' text runs: "At all Important Functions, Where Only the Best is Good Enough—**BLACK and WHITE** cigarettes reign supreme."[36] In another cigarette ad, likely intended to suggest the context of courtship, a European man in a suit offers a European woman a Du Maurier cigarette made in London. "I KNOW YOU WILL LIKE THESE," he comments in the ad's central caption. The dialogue continues: "Will you share a great luxury with me? The kind of cigarettes I used to smoke in London"[37] (Figure 2.1). Both ads suggest the eliteness of the product advertised and a sense of separation from Indian society. Images of Indian women smoking were never present in any ad directed to Indians.

Figure 2.2 "Enjoy yourself without anxiety," Southall's Sanitary Towels, *Illustrated Weekly of India*, July 4, 1937, page unnumbered.

Second, advertisements regularly reflected the importance of extra-familial, often inter-gender sociality, among expatriates.[38] Ads directed toward Europeans—in contrast to those geared to middle class Indians—emphasized participation in social life at dinner parties, dances, and shows. An ad for "Long John Scotch Whisky," which pictures an Indian servant with a tray of whisky and glasses in the foreground and a group of European men in the background, makes an explicit case for "sociability," stressing the importance of interaction with community fellows after the "heat and burden of the day have passed."[39] Some ads built upon anxieties about being excluded from expatriate social life. For instance, Figure 2.2, an ad for sanitary towels featuring a couple dancing, evokes concerns about physical ailments—here a woman's period—that could prohibit participation in parties and limit the possibilities for romance.

Ads oriented to Europeans produced by the Bombay Telephone Company, which specially targeted expatriates, echoed the theme of endangered sociality. One ad ran: "She wasn't invited *because she was not on the* TELEPHONE" and stresses the lost social opportunities one could miss because of not possessing a phone. The image pictures a woman sitting at home alone juxtaposed with another image of her friends dancing at a party (see also Figure 7.1).[40]

A third repeated theme was the vexatious behavior of servants. Servants were featured regularly in ads geared to Europeans, in contrast to ads oriented toward middle-class Indians, where they were often invisible. In some cases, a servant in the visual frame functioned simply as a marker of India or a symbol of an exclusive social context like a club. But in others, servants were central to the advertisement's main message. Some ads emphasized the need to re-establish the full authority of the European sahib and memsahib over the expatriate household. Ads for electric irons and laundry soap, for example, often stressed the product's value in overcoming the damage a *dhobi* (washerman) could do to one's clothing,[41] while appeals for food products often emphasized the importance of supervising the household cook. An ad for an electric tea-pot suggested the product's key virtue was to circumvent dependence on the servant; "Why wait til the 'boy' arrives," it pleads.[42] An ad from Smith and Poulson food products makes the issue of the expatriate housewife's authority explicit (Figure 2.3), posing the question "Memsahibs! who's BOSS in your kitchen? you or your cook?,"[43] and exhorting readers: "Get rid of any inferiority complex as far as your kitchen is concerned. Rule it with a rod of iron and Brown & Polson's Cookery Book . . . ."

Advertisements similarly evoked the need to govern the household's market interactions. Most Europeans relied on servants, especially their cooks, to buy fruits and vegetables, meats, cooking oil and other essential home items in the local bazaar. Consumption decisions, in other words, were exercised jointly by the sahib, the memsahib, and the family's servants. In some cases, advertisements sought to prompt the Europeans to reassert full control of decision-making over household purchases. The ad shown in Figure 2.4 for Philips Lamps, entitled "The Boy's Misstep," focuses on a European woman educating an uninformed servant (who has bought the wrong kind of lightbulb in the market), about the importance of purchasing such items by brand. The ad's central message of course was actually directed to the European who might not recognize the superior virtues of Philips Lamps and the need to provide servants with specific instructions on the brand to buy before they set off for the market.

Finally, many ads appealed to European worries about the Indian environment. Fears that the European might constitutionally be susceptible to dangers from the tropical climate remained a preoccupation long after medical science had called such theories into doubt, and anxieties about the consumption of unhealthy foods were a major theme. As Chapter 6 will demonstrate, ads for cooking mediums regularly invoked concerns about using adulterated ghee found in the bazaar, and ads for tonics and food products were often sold for their supposed properties in bolstering the body's ability to withstand the draining effects of the heat and sicknesses like malaria and cholera. In one ad, Ovaltine was depicted as building resistance to the monsoon, a "depressing period of sickness, low spirits and vitality, which strains the limits of human endurance."[44] A 1939 advertisement for Horlicks pictures a woman in danger of having to return home and leave her busband behind due to the likely effects of the upcoming hot weather; taking Horlicks, however, allows her to recover (Figure 2.5).

Thus, in drawing upon themes of significant salience to expatriates—the promotion of the comforts of the homeland, the importance of extra-familial, inter-gender

memsahibs!

who's
BOSS
in your
kitchen?

you or your cook?

Never let yourself say—"Oh, my
dear, these Cooks are impossible !
I told him   " Get rid of any
inferiority complex as far as your
kitchen is concerned. Rule it with
a rod of iron and Brown & Polson's
Cookery Book. Realize that the
latter solves *all* food problems at
a glance. It tells you how Brown &
Polson Patent Cornflour and|or
Raisley Custard, even in the hands
of only a "fairly good" cook, can
perform culinary miracles.........

better still there's

BROWN
& POLSON

write to-day for free copy
of Brown and Polson's
"Cookery Book of Indian
Recipes" to:
CORN PRODUCTS CO.
(India), LTD.
Currimbhoy House,
Waudby Road, Bombay.

PATENT ★ RAISLEY
CORNFLOUR   CUSTARD

Figure 2.3 "Memsahibs! who's BOSS in your kitchen? you or your cook?" Brown &
Polson, *TI*, December 20, 1939, 13.

Figure 2.4 "The BOY'S MISSTEP," Philips Lamps, *TI*, April 8, 1933, 22. Produced here with acknowledgment of Philips, India, Limited.

Figure 2.5 "Young Couple Almost Separated," Horlicks, *TI*, June 8, 1939, 15. Produced with permission of Hindustan Unilever Limited.

sociality, the need to maintain control over servants, and the travails of the Indian environment—professional advertisers developed a set of appeals specifically geared to European readers of Indian newspapers (as distinguished from Europeans in Europe) even as a concern with gaining Indian customers grew. In effect this set of ads explicitly elicited the anxieties of an elite that faced losing the position of power and prestige it had long enjoyed.

Part 2: The Middle Class

While the expatriate market remained important, advertising professionals increasingly turned their attention after the mid-1920s to Indian consumers, especially those they identified as urban, as falling below the traditional aristocracy and the newly rich in status but above the poor, as employed in salaried occupations requiring literate skills, and as possessing incomes sufficient to buy brand-name goods. Professional advertisers did not employ any consistent language to identify these figures, but sometimes deployed the term "middle class"—which was coming increasingly into use during this period in the larger society.

The category of a "middle class" is, no doubt, a somewhat slippery one. As Mark Liechty has indicated in work on contemporary Nepal, "the more closely one looks at a class group, the more its boundaries dissolve and its supposed distinguishing features blur into a haze of contrasting and conflicting detail."[45] Historians of South Asia have defined the middle class in different ways, and some have even advocated rejecting the term altogether. Scholars like B. B. Misra argued that the middle class should be defined by sociological characteristics, chiefly income and occupation, and that the concept is self-evident: "most of us, without the aid of a specialist, understand what we mean when we use the term."[46] He included commercial, landed, professional and educated groups in his treatment. Nikhil Rao uses the term "lower middle class" in his discussion of South Indians in Bombay, referring mainly to the educated clerks who worked for salaries in government and in private business and excluding many of those Misra had included.[47] C. J. Fuller and Haripriya Narasimhan also give primacy to occupational categories in discussing the Tamil Brahmins who moved into salaried positions in the colonial bureaucracy during the early twentieth century (and more recently into fields like information technology), but also argue that such *economic* classes developed into *social* classes as they became increasingly closed in origins and formed shared lifestyles, beliefs, and values.[48]

By contrast, Sanjay Joshi adopts a constructivist approach, arguing that an Indian middle class, which came into being during the late nineteenth century, should be seen as a set of actors involved in self-fashioning a sense of group identity as agents of modernity rather than one that mechanically reflected occupational characteristics. He particularly stresses the stances that middle-class residents of Lucknow took up in the public sphere on cultural issues ranging from religion and gender to politics and nationalism. Joshi argues at the same time that the importance of these commitments to modernity was "fractured" by attachments to hierarchy, patriarchy and religious intolerance.[49] Ironically, he does not show that the subjects of his study regularly invoked the category of the middle class in reference to themselves.

My own work follows the term as it was coming into use during the early twentieth century—it was rarely employed in practice before this time in western India—which emphasized sociological and material dimensions. Around this time the language of class came to be used as a central mode of discussing the urban social environment in India. The idea of a "working class" was perhaps the most obvious sign of this development, but the term "middle class" also started to be regularly invoked.[50] In using this concept, the new urban sociology denoted a set of people who possessed education and salaried employment, and excluded middle-income commercial actors who did not hold salaried jobs or possess the same literate skills. The upper end of this category included professionals in such fields as law, medicine, engineering, university teaching and journalism, who often exercised considerable independence in their work. A much larger section, however, was composed of office clerks, whose jobs involved, according to S. N. Bhonsle: "writing, keeping accounts, operating typewriters or accountancy machines strictly in conformity with the instructions given by their superiors or the routine prescribed by them, copying, indexing, sorting, tabulating, filing and checking the information required by them, and in general keeping ready the raw material required by them in the conduct of business as far as correspondence is concerned."[51] As Sumit Sarkar has discussed in the context of late nineteenth-century Bengal, the predicament of the lower middle-class office employee was to submit to the discipline of the time clock and bureaucratic rules, often in psychically unrewarding work that received poor remuneration.[52] We lack similar studies on the Bombay Presidency to help us understand what middle-class men thought of their work environments, but sociological studies during this period depicted the middle class as including families who were struggling to make ends meet in an environment characterized by considerable unemployment and low salaries.[53] L. G. Khare entitled his writings on the subject the "depressed middle classes." Many other surveys focused on the problems of unemployment and the limited capacity for spending among the "middle class." As the term was deployed in interwar Bombay, it included a much wider range of families than the subjects of Joshi's study of late-nineteenth century Lucknow, who mostly occupied a higher status.

Though its origins may have largely been in academic discourse, the term middle class was taken up regularly in the public sphere. When newspaper articles discussed the "middle class," they typically referred to material circumstances of the middle class and the need for the state to address its difficulties. Issues like housing and rents, unemployment, educational costs, health care and the cost of living were the most common themes.[54] Letters to the editors of western Indian newspapers also used the concept, evidence that the term quickly became incorporated into everyday language and in self-identification.[55] Often the chief concern in these letters was the need of middle-class families to avoid falling into the material conditions faced by the poor and working class.[56] A public protest of clerks in 1921, which invoked the concept in pressing their concerns to the government, similarly emphasized that members of the middle class needed to uphold standards of dress and housing that would distinguish them from the poor.[57]

The emergence of the middle class in this sociological sense was to a great extent a product of the structure of British rule. As Bhavani Raman argues, the colonial order spawned a "document raj" that required a sizeable corps of Indian administrators and clerks with knowledge of English; these actors were concentrated in the administrative headquarters of district towns and provincial capitals.[58] The new professions—the law, medicine, engineering and journalism—usually required even higher levels of education. By the twentieth century international businesses and some Indian firms also employed a substantial set of clerks who could produce and process the vast documentation necessary to balance the company books, provide reports to superiors and home offices, and meet the expectations of the colonial legal system when disputes occurred and tax payments were required.[59]

In order to attain such salaried positions, young men needed to attend, and succeed in, English-language schools established in urban places throughout western India, and colleges and universities, which were concentrated in the biggest Presidency cities. By the 1930s, filling a position as a humble office clerk usually required at least a bachelor's degree.[60] In order to become marriageable to such men, middle-class girls were also expected to pursue education through secondary school and often college.

English schools and universities in the biggest cities typically enrolled students belonging to a variety of high-status groups, who mixed together in their educational lives, creating the possibilities for the formation of shared political and social outlooks.

It is quite difficult to estimate the size of such a "middle class," especially because the term was not used in the censuses of the time. The 1931 census counted 30,834 males and 1,452 females employed in public administration in Bombay city and 17,530 males and 2,467 females working in the "professions and liberal arts" but the numbers in the former category probably included some persons who were not literate or employed in office work, including ordinary policemen, street sweepers, and office cleaners in the former category and indigenous medical practitioners, "magicians," and "conjurers" in the latter. The same census additionally listed 50,017 males and 2,411 females in the category of "cashiers, accountants, book-keepers, clerks and other employees in unspecified offices and warehouses and shops," but then noted that "were it possible to classify this kind of employment more satisfactorily, much of this employment would be relegated to many different orders."[61] For the Bombay Presidency as a whole, the number of employees and working dependents in the category of public administration was 146,566, in the professions and liberal arts 152,607, and in the category of cashiers, accountants, book-keepers, clerks and other employees in unspecified offices 24,336.[62] JWT's 1931 report estimated the "professional classes (teachers, lawyers, clerks, and better-class shopkeepers)" in all of India as 2,000,000 people and the "middle class (small-shopkeepers, clerks, manual workers)" as 4,500,000 people, not including dependents.[63] The middle class of the Bombay Presidency—as the advertising profession viewed this potential block of consumers—might be estimated as several hundred thousand people, perhaps ten to fifteen times larger than the European/ Anglo-Indian population (but with less buying power on average), though we need to keep in mind that the boundaries of this category were somewhat fuzzy.

The social backgrounds of the middle class were highly diverse. Outside Bombay city, high-caste men—often Brahmans in Marathi- and Kannada-speaking districts, and Brahmans and Vaniyas in Gujarati areas—tended to occupy positions requiring literate skills. In Bombay itself, employment opportunities were more wide-ranging as were the communities available to fill them. Educated young men flowed into Bombay from different parts of the subcontinent: the Maharastrian countryside surrounding the city, Gujarat in the north of the Presidency, Goa in Portuguese-controlled territory and the Madras and Bengal Presidencies. Some Muslims acquired the education and employment necessary to be recognized as middle-class in status. The middle class in Bombay, like the working class, was largely a set of migrants. Bhonsle's 1938 report indicated that less that 10 percent of its sample of clerks in the city had been longterm residents of the city; the rest had origins outside of Bombay, and many retained strong ties with rural districts. Somewhat more than half of these people, he argued, originated from the three districts of the Konkan region.[64] Information on local occupations suggests considerable specialization by ethnic group. Brahmans and Kayasthas dominated government employment. Saraswat Brahmans were prominent in the municipal administration; high-caste Gujaratis filled positions as clerks in many local businesses; Pathare Prabhus were found in the banks and insurance companies; and South Indians occupied positions as accountants and as employees in the offices of commercial firms and railway administration.[65] Parsis played a major role in many British businesses.

Whatever their social origins, many members of the middle class were facing quite precarious employment prospects during the 1920s and 1930s. Immediately after World War I, jobs requiring education in western India expanded considerably, attracting large numbers of youth to migrate to the cities and to seek schooling. This situation changed dramatically during the 1920s and the 1930s. During the Great Depression, the colonial government instituted a severe retrenchment in staff and a reduction of salaries. There was a 10 percent salary reduction across ranks in 1932 and another cut of 5 percent in 1933. Banks, insurance companies, and other private firms followed suit; and salaries as low as 30 Rupees a month were present among younger employees. Unemployment was rife, especially for recent graduates; those with only secondary education often no longer could obtain appointments in clerical fields. This situation also created severe anxieties among those with employment about their job security and sometimes a strong sense of grievance that they were working in positions below the level of their educational accomplishment.[66] Awareness of these preoccupations strongly influenced the character of interwar advertisements.

Conjugality and the construction of the middle class

To what extent can it be said that the middle class was not just a category of economic actors exposed to similar sorts of work environments but also constituted a social class coming to share a certain social outlook? The answer to this question is complex. Certainly, the middle class of western India was heterogeneous in its identifications. In Bombay city alone, it would have included Gujarati Brahmans and Vaniyas, Maharashtrian Brahmans (with some non-Brahmans), Parsis, Goans, South Indians, Bengalis, and some Muslims from different parts of India. Many of these groups were involved in shaping their own distinctive senses of social identity. Frank Conlon, for instance, has discussed the sharpening of self-identification among Kanara Saraswat Brahmans in the context of twentieth-century urban life while Nikhil Rao has shown how the category of "South Indian" was created among Brahman migrants from Tamil-speaking areas during the same time.[67] Different middle-class groupings often inhabited distinct neighborhoods in Bombay; Maharashtrians predominated in Shivaji Park and Thakurdwar (with Brahmans and non-Brahmans often living in their own areas), Gujaratis in south Bombay and Bhandra, South Indians in Matunga, and Bengalis and Parsis in Dadar and Parel.[68]

On the other hand, many families who were identified as falling into the category of the middle class were coming to develop shared commitments to principles of science and rationality, societal progress, and political liberalism, partly as a result of their common educational experiences. Still "modern" notions of religiosity were often inflected by group identities. Members of the Gujarati upper castes, for instance, would not have worshipped regularly in the temples South Indians had built in Matunga, while Parsis and Muslims of course observed religious practices quite distinct from those of all Hindus. By the 1920s, most but not all middle-class persons would have developed strong identifications as Indian nationalists. But even nationalism could be a source of differentiation. There was considerable tension, for instance, between Gujarati and Maharashtrian nationalists. Gujaratis in the interwar period often were committed followers of Gandhi, while upper-caste Maharashtrians tended to associate with the nationalist approach of Lokamanya Tilak, the early twentieth-century regional leader who had championed the celebration of the seventeenth-century Maratha warrior-king Shivaji, whom Gandhi once labeled as a "misguided patriot."[69] By the 1930s and 1940s, the Rashtriya Swayamsevak Sangh and the Hindu Mahasabha, two Hindu right-wing organizations, acquired a strong foothold among middle-class Maharashtrian Brahmans. Members of the small non-Brahman middle class were beginning to develop strong critiques of Brahman dominance. Parsis were often depicted as being divided politically between staunch nationalists and those with pro-British inclinations; and some Muslims were starting to become attracted to the Muslim League, which increasingly became opposed to the Congress during the later 1930s. Both Prashant Kidambi and Nikhil Rao have highlighted moments when the clerks of Bombay came together in collective protest to advocate shared economic interests.[70] While the middle class was "in the making" in cultural as well as economic senses, this process had not gone so far as to raise class consciousness to a position of priority over the other identities its members had formed.

One significant social commitment that increasingly cut across the bounds of different groupings was an attachment to the principle of modern conjugality. In using the term conjugality here, I do not intend to refer primarily to the actual form of midde-class social organization. Instead I stress the importance of conjugality as an ideology or discourse that was gaining sway during this period, one that insisted that the conjugal family—the husband, wife and their biological offspring—should be the primary foundation of modern society.[71] Intrinsic to this conception were several critical tenets; that the central and sole legitimate basis of the family was the heterosexual relationship between the husband and wife (one confirmed by marriage); that the male head of household should be responsible through his salary for maintaining the family economically; that the wife's major role should be the raising of children, looking after the home and guarding family status; and that the central priorities of the family were to sustain the reproduction of its social and economic position from one generation to the next by maintaining the health of its members, ensuring the education of children and arranging favorable marriages for them. Conjugality was associated with a host of other themes central to middle-class modernity—the notion of marriage as a partnership based upon sexual and intellectual companionship, new concepts of masculinity and femininity, domesticity, the medicalization of the family and the stress on family hygiene, and the field of eugenics. The place of conjugality in middle-class value systems was not uncontested, but it was becoming a particularly salient and emotive principle among the groups that thought of themselves as middle class. The discourse of modern conjugality was set out in a wide variety of forms that proliferated at the time, including pamphlets providing moral instruction, women's journals, literature, film and art. And it certainly was coming to inform the construction of affect and intimacy within the middle class.

Commitments to modern conjugality grew out of the social and material preoccupations of the middle class. As Bhonsle brilliantly noted, marriage was central to the self-reproduction and status of middle-class families:

[A]s an institution marriage holds a very secure position in the lower middle class owing to its biological and economical advantages to this class. Tenets of respectability demand sexual integrity which can be secured only by a rigidly guarded matrimony. A position in the middle class demands educational equipment and economic well-being which presuppose sexual association with responsibility for the issue in the parents—a fit ground for the institution of marriage to prosper. With his limited economic resources, the clerk can substitute no other institution in place of marriage which can satisfy his biological, economic and aesthetic needs so well.[72]

As young men migrated to cities for education, they frequently left their extended kinfolk behind; often after marriage they would bring their new wives from the countryside to form conjugal units. Older conceptions of marriage often fit awkwardly with their new social and economic priorities. For instance, because of their need to complete their schooling and to obtain well-paying jobs, middle-class youth increasingly delayed their marriages much later than the previous generation had done.[73] Increases in middle-class marriage ages clearly began well before legislation prohibiting early marriages was passed.[74] The value of extended families declined as couples concentrated their resources on meeting their subsistence requirements and school expenses. Joint families were the exception rather than the rule in the lower sections of the middle class; in Bhonsle's survey of clerks, only 9 percent of his sample lived in joint families.[75] In Bombay at least another factor militating against large families was the rise in housing costs; most middle-class families in Bombay could not afford more than two small rooms in a chawl or modest apartment building. The attraction of delayed marriages, of discourses promoting sexual self-control, and of birth-control—all of which produced smaller family sizes—grew side by side among the middle class during this period.[76]

The priorities of jobs and education led to an enhanced emphasis on the conjugal unit. Unlike landlords and some peasant families, whose reproduction from generation to generation often depended on land ownership, or mercantile families who possessed business assets that could be similarly transmitted over time, the middle-class household rarely possessed fixed capital sufficient to guarantee the perpetuation of a family's social position. It instead depended upon obtaining salaried work anew in each generation. For families in western India with long histories of urban living, with access to education and traditions of providing service to royal courts, achieving such a goal might not have taken major adjustments. But many others had loosened their dependence on landed property only recently, after their migration to cities.[77] The Saraswats of Bombay—who possessed a strong rural legacy—became almost wholly reliant on clerical employment in the first two decades of the twentieth century. By 1938, one Saraswat would write: "Jobs are the goal of our lives . . . the Saraswat . . . looks down upon anything that does not savour of services."[78]

The propects for obtaining salaried positions were becoming increasingly uncertain after 1925. For many young men, long periods of unemployment could precede one's hiring, a process that could be, as one Saraswat noted, "soul-killing."[79] Parents of young women were often equally preoccupied with finding sons-in-law whose employment prospects could sustain their familial status. Such searches could be quite stressful, noted the *Kanara Saraswat*, "except in the very rare case where a pretty maid whose face is her future succeeds in bagging one [a husband with good prospects] herself."[80] In many instances the parents might not only have to spend extensively on a dowry and wedding expenses, but also become actively involved in seeking jobs for the new husband.[81]

To retain or advance its social position, as the writing of Pierre Bourdieu illuminates, the middle-class family needed to ensure that offspring could acquire the critical "cultural capital" required, most importantly the command over English or written vernaculars and other specialist knowledge (engineering, medicine, accounting, etc.) that made males employable and females marriageable.[82] The education of children thus was a central preoccupation of the middle class. One Saraswat author observed in a 1950 article entitled "Middle Class Habits of Mind," that middle-class parents were "determined that the children at least should make good. They go through incredible hardships to give their boys a good education."[83] Familial circumstances, another wrote, could be "strained to a breaking point in the process of providing funds for the education of the children."[84] L. G. Khare, writing about one lower middle-class family in 1917, reported that it represented a type of people who "spend remarkably much more on the education of their children than their limited exchequer can really permit. There is a sincere desire to offer the children the best educational advantages possible, with the ultimate hope that not only will the family place higher in the material scale when the young male wage earner of the coming generation has secured a better job, but also that the passage from the lower middle class life to higher middle society will be definitely established."[85] New entrants into the middle-class job world with modest resources were sometimes poised precariously on the brink of poverty and loss of reputation if their offspring lacked educational success, an event that probably occurred more frequently than has been recognized.

The strengthening of the conjugal principle among families from diverse community backgrounds, of course, was not simply a product of material concerns, but reflected a growing attachment to "modern" norms of appropriate family structure, norms advanced in schools, advice books for housewives and couples, literary works and the emerging genre of film. There is a wide range of research elsewhere in India that addresses the ways in which notions of conjugality and domesticity became central to modern identities. Dipesh Chakrabarty has suggested that the reformulation of family ideals in Bengal was strongly associated with nationalism, as educated men sought to create a sense of disciplined domesticity, one based upon notions of orderliness in the home and affection between husband and wife.[86] Pradip Kumar Bose similarly has stressed the importance of a new discourse surrounding the nuclear family that was focused on raising and disciplining children and on shielding its members from the disruptive influences of elders and in-laws.[87] These notions of conjugality were not simply foreign imports.[88] In her work on late-nineteenth-century women in Bengal, Judith Walsh has posited the notion of "global domesticity," arguing that domestic ideas and relationships were hybrid products reflecting the interaction of transnational discourses and "language, beliefs, ideas, and values of preexisting indigenous family relationships and domestic arrangements."[89]

Later chapters will examine conceptions of masculinity and femininity, sexual health, nutrition, and physical appearance associated with the middle-class family. Here I point to a feature of the new conjugality that is often overlooked but constitutes a regular theme in this study: the special onus it placed on parents for the family's physical health. As Bose has indicated, modern families came to possess a highly medicalized character; maintaining the subsistence and health of children was its most central purpose.[90] Health, he contends, "became one of the family's most-demanding objectives. The obligations that were imposed include those of a physical kind, like care, contact, hygiene, cleanliness, attentive proximity, breast-feeding of children, clean clothing, physical exercise and so on, which specified and finalized the corporal relations between parents and their children."[91] Hygienic education proved to be one of the most critical forms of lesson for the middle-class mother to impart.[92]

The medicalization of the family must in part be understood in the context of the ubiquitous eugenic discussions of the time, which squarely placed responsibility for a supposed decline in the physical state of the Indian nation on the practices of the traditional social order, particularly those related to marriage. A major debate over these issues was precipitated by Katherine Mayo's *Mother India*, which argued that the "inertia, helplessness, lack of initiative and originality, lack of staying power and of sustained loyalties, sterility of enthusiasm, weakness of life vigour itself" were due to oppressive societal practices such as childhood marriage and prohibitions against widow remarriage, excessive male sexuality, and inadequate health care.[93] Similar arguments were made in the debate over the Sarda Act of 1929, which raised the legal age of marriage. Eugenic theories suggested that early marriage, dowry, and other forms of traditional gender relations might be responsible for unhappiness, the physical weakness of women, and the production of children incapable of contributing to the nation's welfare.[94] "Child marriage," N. S. Phadke insisted, "leads to physical deterioration. It not only undermines the muscular strength of the people, but imperceptibly deprives them of all pluck and daring, all mental and moral stamina."[95] While Phadke's main remedy for this problem—love marriage—was endorsed only by a small minority, the modern family, headed by fathers who provided companionship and affection to their wives and material support to their children, was widely regarded as preventing physical and mental enervation and poor health into the next generation.[96] Such writings highlighted a host of dangers that threatened the family, including rapid social change, the sedentary character of urban life, and the propensity toward individualism (supposedly reflected in behaviors like masturbation).[97] Articles addressed to middle class men and women stressed the importance of exercise and improved food habits to combat these threats.[98] The highest priority was placed on observing household practices that would ensure the production of hardy, energetic children and thus promote the revitalization of the larger society.

In short, a diverse array of writings and other forms of public expression set out conjugal norms, often in terms that raised anxieties about the ability of middle-class households to meet them. This is not to suggest that the conjugal "familial imaginary"— to use Sreenivas' valuable concept[99]—was adopted without contestation. As Indrani

Chatterjee has argued, conceptions of the family and household in the Indian past have been multiple, layered, and fluid.[100]

Considerable diversity persisted in the character of intimate relations during early twentieth-century South Asia, and even among the urban middle class other powerful forms of affect existed alongside, often in competition with, conjugality. The joint family, where obligations to brothers, fathers, uncles, and senior women constituted the primary social bond, in many cases exerted a powerful appeal, even when urban flat-living rendered it difficult to realize in practice.[101] Celebration of male sociality sometimes flourished among young single migrants in chawls, tenements or small flats until they could afford to marry or to bring their families from rural areas.[102] Ascetic ideals were advanced by various religious communities on the one hand and by nationally prominent figures like Gandhi on the other. As Kaushik Bhaumik has argued, a culture of the young, associated with the value of individual freedom and with leisure activity such as cinema-going and tea-drinking, thrived in Bombay, championing the companionship of single men against the pull of conjugal relationships.[103] As we shall see in Chapter 4, the ideal of the independent modern girl, freed from familial obligations, competed with the notion of the domestic housewife. Small numbers of women entered salaried employment while female-headed households emerged in some cases, particularly when husbands died or proved incapable of exercising masculine responsibilities. And of course, multiple alternative imaginaries flourished outside the middle class. No one paradigm had fully won out by the interwar period, and some educated city-dwellers no doubt felt some ambivalence about the new conjugality.[104] Advertising, as we shall see, often served to advance the hegemony of the heterosexual couple against these other conceptions of social organization.

The middle-class family and consumption

The emerging middle class was characterized by a set of attitudes and dispositions toward consumption that in part flowed from its adherence to conjugal principles. Surprisingly, it is a rather novel assertion to say that the Indian middle class during this period was defined by its material practices. Scholars working on Europe and North America, or for that matter on contemporary South Asia,[105] whether informed by Marx, Weber, or Bourdieu, would find the contention that consumption is central to middle-class identity unremarkable. Historians of India, on the other hand, have typically paid little attention to material life in the construction of the middle class before independence. Following Prashant Kidambi, I argue here that the very ambivalence of its attitudes toward consumption should be seen as a defining characteristic of the colonial middle class.[106]

On the one hand, there were certainly factors promoting new kinds of consumption among middle-class households. The receipt of a monthly salary provided new opportunities for spending, absent among wage earners who obtained their payments in smaller amounts, as social reformers sometimes warned.[107] For established householders, the maintenance of family respectability required certain critical expenditures, as J. K. Mehta indicated in a talk to the Bombay Clerks Conference in

1920: "All of these [clerks] belong to a certain status in society and have certain appearances to keep up. They have to provide decent clothing for their wives and children and a decent education to the latter. Not only this, but they have to live in decent quarters and have faithfully to keep up certain social engagements."[108] Similarly Bhonsle wrote of the city's clerks in 1938: "They have to maintain a certain standard of dress and personal appearance...Their greatest endeavor is to maintain a respectability which would approach that of the middle class but for the economic inferiority in which they stand."[109] One 1936 account in the *Kanara Saraswat*, contrasting contemporary spending practices with those that had existed fifty years earlier, described the life of contemporary Saraswats as one of "extravagance and luxury":

> In food, dress and habits, as well as thought, word and deed, we differ from our great grandfathers to such an extent that if ever they chose to pay us a visit, they would have great difficulty in persuading themselves that we really were their descendants. It is instructive to compare a list of articles found in the eighties of the last century with a corresponding one for the present decade... What a difference![110]

As Kaushik Bhaumik has argued, a middle-class youth culture emerged during the early twentieth century that encouraged relaxed attitudes toward spending on leisure purposes.[111] The *Kanara Saraswat* noted that Saraswat young men attending colleges or starting new jobs participated in smoking cigarettes, drinking tea in local hotels, and attending cinema-houses, all activities that involved significant cash expenditures.[112] One community leader blamed "lack of parental control" and a "deplorable absence of a moral and religious background" for such practices, writing: "In Bombay, you find temptation at every corner—inviting cinemas which has the most insidious influence on character and a very perceptible one on eye-sight, and countless opportunities for dissipation of every kind, including gambling which begins innocently with cards, 'competitions' and lotteries, masquerades as business in cotton and shares, and ends ignominiously at the races."[113]

But any inclinations toward spending were strongly tempered by countervailing tendencies. Most critically, the purchasing power of most middle-class families placed severe constraints on expenditures. Perhaps 40 percent of these families lived at living standards only minimally above those earned by the upper end of the working class.[114] They spent most of their income on food and housing. Sample family budgets from the early 1920s reported that while working class families used about 28 percent of their income on items other than food, fuel, bedding and house-rent, middle-class families devoted only slightly more, on average about 35 percent, to such items. Middle-class households with incomes less than 125 Rupees a month, about two-fifths of the survey sample, devoted only 29 percent of family expenditures outside these four categories.[115] The cost of living space was one reason that such families were unable to free up greater resources for commodity purchases.[116] "The rising needs of a growing family," Bhonsle wrote, "generally outstrip the income. The demands for food, clothing, education and sundries rise day by day and the family has to devise all sorts of expedients to suppress expenses within the limits of income."[117]

Faced with limited resources, middle-class households often gave preference in their spending to items that perpetuated the reproduction of the family—and its middle-class character—into the next generation. Education of children, as we have seen, was a significant expense largely absent among workers. Spending on life insurance, which sought to guarantee that the nuclear family would survive if the male head died, had a high priority. Some income-earners devoted a significant part of earnings to remittances for dependents who remained in native places.

There were also strong cultural principles inhibiting consumption. Some Hindu and Jain traditions discouraged displays of wealth. Gujarati Vaniyas, for instance, had historically maintained spartan households, with little furniture or decoration.[118] Such attitudes, moreover, were often strongly reinforced by arguments made by reformers who warned that material indulgence would harm the progress of their communities and the nation. A host of publications, many written as songs or verse, admonished or ridiculed those who habituated tea shops or who tried to follow the latest fashions.[119] Writers in the *Kanara Saraswat* repeatedly urged community members to practice frugality for reasons of financial and physical health.[120] In one series of articles, H. Shankar Rau warned that Saraswats should watch their expenditures in a host of areas: leisure activities and the use of tea and coffee both inside and outside the home, the eating of rich and spicy foods, and the wearing of expensive clothing.[121] He argued for a "middle way . . . marked by moderation, ennobled by purity, adorned by simplicity and hallowed by faith."[122]

Nationalist leaders particularly expressed reservations about many visible forms of consumption. By the 1920s, virtually all nationalists were calling for the observation of *swadeshi* (the purchase of Indian-made goods). Writing in *Young India*, Gandhi commented, "There is not in the cities at least that real change of taste that the people will not touch foreign cloth whether it comes from England, Japan, France, or elsewhere. Though the intellect admits the desirability of abjuring from foreign cloth, the heart yearns after the fineries which come only from foreign countries. Love of self predominates over love of the country or rather love of the semi-starved millions."[123] Gandhi's statement clearly acknowledged his own inability to prevent urban people from engaging in conspicuous expenditures, but it also illustrates the pressures members of the middle class were under to conform to nationalist prerogatives. Often families had to steer a narrow pathway between using their resources to distinguish themselves from lower social strata and adhering to nationalist codes stressing restraint and uniformity.[124]

An emphasis on financial restraint and modesty in consumption was directed particularly toward women. As Partha Chatterjee has argued, nationalist discourse often drew a line between the acceptance of western models in the "material" and political world, which was to be controlled by men, and the "spiritual" world, which was in theory embodied by women.[125] "Women," Abigail McGowan has noted, "were expected to compensate for the Westernization of male, public life by adhering to Indian cultural traditions, food habits and religious observances."[126] Open breaches of "tradition" by women, particularly the public emulation of Western females in consumption practices, were often regarded as behavior responsible for social breakdown. Periodical literature repeatedly denounced women who sought to imitate foreign styles or to engage in the ostentatious use of material things.[127]

Finally, consumption patterns among middle-class households were strongly influenced by the form of their engagement with the market. Unlike Europeans and upper-class Indians, very few middle-class individuals purchased their supplies in department stores or big merchant shops. Instead, they did most of their shopping in urban bazaars, where goods made by vernacular firms proliferated and brand-name goods might be scarce or available only at fixed prices unaffected by the give and take of bazaar negotiations. In many cases, they made their choices of what to buy based not upon the manufacturer's reputation but upon price and qualities stressed by local shopkeepers and hawkers. Sometimes they even looked upon branded goods with suspicion, regarding the claims to higher quality made in advertisements as spurious or insufficient to justify their costs. In still others, the consumption of branded goods required them to make radical and potentially disruptive changes in their bodily practices or in the division of labor within the household.

The character of textile advertising exemplified these circumstances. Clothing was the largest item in middle-class spending outside of food and housing. But clothing was also a key symbolic battleground in the nationalist struggle; Congress organizers of the 1930s not only advocated the boycott of foreign cloth, but they also often urged upon the middle class a reliance upon simple and modest homespun textiles.[128] Textile manufacturers, both foreign and Indian, who openly encouraged expenditures on clothing beyond basic necessities, could run afoul of the Gandhians. Moreover, the adoption of clothing standards associated with specific social groups served to sustain the groups' sense of social distinction. Women's saris, often customized to cultural preferences associated with specific regions or communities, were one such item.[129]

With little possibility of developing mass demand that cut across community and regional boundaries, both cloth importers and Indian textile mills typically refrained from newspaper advertising. Most clothing ads designed by advertising agencies for English-language papers were geared to the European population. The ads directed to Indian consumers were usually more modest, reflecting limited investments by manufacturers, often designed without the involvement of advertising professionals.[130] After 1935, there were some exceptions to this pattern, for instance Arvind Mills of Ahmedabad in women's clothing and Buckingham and Carnatic Mills in men's wear.

In short then, middle-class city-dwellers were affected by contradictory pressures. In this environment, where suspicions of branded goods were rife, global firms tended to steer clear of sales pitches stressing the pleasures to be derived from their products.[131] Success in winning consumers often meant *selectively* overcoming middle-class hesitations about spending in general, especially on products made by foreign firms. Increasingly, advertising specialists regularly tried to overcome these hesitations by attempting to link expenditures to preoccupations of the conjugal family, as suggested by the advertisement for insurance shown as Figure 2.6, and as much of this book's narrative and visual material will confirm. The picture of a husband and wife with their two children on a picnic freed from anxieties reflected an ideal that had wide appeal. In some cases, they sought to accomplish this by providing a kind of scientific instruction to consumers insisting the use of branded commodities was critical to the family's self-reproduction; in others they adopted the posture of an intimate contact whose affective relationship with the family allows them to share special knowledge about the

Figure 2.6 *"Let'*UNITED INDIA' *take care of your wife and family,"* United India Life Insurance, *BC*, April 12, 1938, 3.

product's value to family well-being. Through such positioning they served to create strong psychic connections between the domestic realm and perceptions of specific commodities and the use of branded commodities in general.

Part 3: The Rural Population and the Urban Poor

While advertising professionals devoted most of their efforts to designing ads for expatriates and the middle class, commercial knowledge identified a third significant category for assessing market prospects: non-literate Indians, who composed about 93 percent of the population in the 1920s. Advertising professionals stressed that the material circumstances of people in this broad category were typically characterized by poverty. According to JWT's 1931 report: "only an extremely small proportion of the people of India, Burma and Ceylon can be considered in terms of possible purchasers of western manufactured products. The masses are pitifully poor, ignorant and slaves to custom and tradition. Their wants are confined to shelter, a piece of cloth and a handful of rice."[132] The report went on to conclude that "since the total number of persons with sufficient income to buy more than the bare necessities of life is very small," the cultural practices of most Indians need not be considered deeply. A Levers' executive writing in 1934 similarly commented on "the incredible poorness . . . of the Indian consumer," noting the average annual income in the country was between four and five pounds, and with most Indians concerned not with cost in rupees or annas but in pies.[133]

Still, some advertising professionals believed that market potential existed beyond the literate population. After pointing out that many of India's poor survived on "tuppence" a day, Roger Falk reasoned in *Advertiser's Weekly* that "to divert the attention of three or four million people . . . to an anna article produces a pleasant turnover and it is this sort of trade which is hardly touched at present."[134] He gave the example of aspirin sold at two pills per anna as a product that might attract extensive customership if village-to-village propaganda could be devised. While the 1931 JWT report mentioned in Chapter 1 dismissed all but urban literates as possible consumers, its 1938 report indicated that the majority of literate people actually lived in the countryside and some illiterate urbanites earned sufficient incomes to buy branded commodities, suggesting a potential for creating broader demand for such goods.[135] And the same Levers' executive who lamented India's poorness suggested that even the poor might be reached if prices were sufficiently low; "therefore small scale units are definitely necessary for this market and small tablets of soap weighing from 1½ oz. to 2½ oz. are getting more and more popular everywhere, especially in Burma. To educate the consumer to use our proprietary lines we must enable him to buy small quantities at a time, at a price which is within his purchasing power."[136]

By the later 1930s, some advertising specialists were convinced that significant untapped demand existed for branded commodities, and recommended innovative methods for reaching illiterate consumers. The main obstacle was the cost of such campaigns. Given the expense of making films to publicize their products or of purchasing vans and hiring staff to carry advertising into agrarian areas with dispersed populations, few multinational firms were ready to seek out rural, non-literate consumers. JWT officers, finding no client willing to commit the resources needed for such attempts, concluded that the agency itself would have to fund them if they were to get off the ground.[137] Advertising in newspapers by contrast did not require a sizeable investment to get started and could be incrementally increased as customership expanded.

Professional advertisers did, however, target specific non-literate groups whose occupations might motivate them to buy branded commodities. In 1928, for instance, Unilever suggested a plan to reach *dhobis* [washermen], who typically were independent operators, cleaning clothes for clients for a regular fee. Estimating that only 2 percent of Bombay's dhobis used Sunlight soap, with most of the others relying on soda ash and other non-branded cleaning agents, one executive recommended that free samples of Sunlight be given to ten dhobis each in different towns for a six-month period and that the company issue certificates to the dhobis who used Sunlight. The official reasoned that this scheme would prompt other dhobis to inundate the company for certificate requests, and thus convert most of them into purchasers; it might also have a demonstration effect for potential household customers (who were using Sunlight mainly as a body soap).[138] This scheme, however, seems not to have been put into practice. In 1936, JWT recommended a targeted campaign for Mobil Oil among the thousands of operators of small motor buses who, for a fee, carried a few passengers at a time between villages in the province's interior. The agency also produced a campaign "told entirely in pictures" for Mobil Oil geared to urban taxi drivers, who were described as "another illiterate group." This campaign consisted of distributing a strip folder of Mobil Oil images among the drivers and at petrol pumps.[139] Marketing experts for Singer Sewing Machines similarly sought to reach tailors through specialized advertising efforts.[140]

There were some commodities whose market was potentially great enough to warrant general campaigns that would reach into the countryside. The most notable of these commodities were cigarettes, body soap and perhaps tea.[141] A 1927 Unilever report, noting the large number of Indians who did not use soap, concluded that there were vast market possibilities in "educating" non-users with sufficient income to buy higher-quality soaps, arguing that Sunlight was well positioned to capture this demand, but it would have to overcome local producers who sold at cheaper prices.[142] By the mid 1930s, Levers had formulated a significant campaign in rural areas using advertising lorries. Each lorry toured the countryside in its region with a team of four people—a driver, a menial worker, a clerk and a salesman.[143] In arriving at a new location, the team would put up posters and distribute leaflets for Levers' products, and open a demonstration, with the salesman expounding on the value of different products and showing attendees how they were used. (For instance, the salesman might clean pots with Vim, Levers' product for cleaning in the kitchen.) Sales would be made beside the vehicle. About 300 units of soap were sold on the typical village visit at 1 Anna per unit. The products sold were obtained from local village shops, and the lorry crew would then resupply shopkeepers with new stock in anticipation of future demand. In 1936, the company reported that "lorries in fact form such an important factor in our Educative advertising and give such useful assistance to our Prestige and Reminder advertising that our advertising policy for some time must be centered round lorry work and must in fact be to add to the number of lorries as soon as we reasonably can."[144] The cost of this system per lorry was about 600 pounds per year plus 400 pounds of advertising material, a burden that companies with more limited rural sales prospects could not afford.[145]

After almost a decade of using this system, urban markets still constituted the bulk of the company's soap sales. When Levers raised its prices during the early war years due to increased raw material costs, peasants seemingly reverted to cheaper soaps and non-commercial cleaning substances. One company advisor warned that allocating too much of the advertising budget to lorries would inhibit the ability to intensify the appeal in cities, where competing soap companies were making inroads through newspaper campaigns. The advisor indicated that urban areas still provided the greatest marketing scope, and "spending in rural areas will only give results in the distant future."[146] The lorry system established direct contact with consumers but it was occasional contact, confined mostly to the days when the lorry's route could visit a particular village. Marketing experts, however, were concluding that for items requiring regular purchases (later termed "fast-moving consumer goods"), it was critical to hit the consumer with repeated appeals. Even in Levers' case, the commitment to target the non-literate population became tempered by a belief that it was members of the middle class who could be subjected to recurrent messages in the newspapers on an economical basis.

Conclusion

Thus, even though advertising professionals often imagined a day when they might reach India's many millions, they concentrated their efforts on two main target audiences that in India numbered in the hundreds of thousands: the tiny set of European expatriates and a significantly larger category of middle-class families that individually possesed restricted resources and had a limited exposure to brand-name goods. Advertising beyond these audiences often necessitated major resource commitments without the clear promise of significant returns, and it potentially meant keeping profit margin at near-negligible levels. It also required access to forms of knowledge that advertising agencies did not possess. Consequently advertising agencies developed more focused campaigns that they believed would have special resonance for literate consumers in the cities. As we shall see, they appealed to the middle class not primarily on the basis of the pleasures commodities might bring to the individual but around the ways these products might relieve anxieties about the conjugal family's capacity to sustain itself. And there were only limited efforts to advertise in major areas of the typical family budget, for instance, food and clothing. This chapter thus suggests the limitations of brand-name capitalism and the tenuous nature of any attempt to postulate a linear picture between early twentieth-century consumption practices and the mass marketing practices of the present moment.

3

Tonics and the Marketing of Conjugal Masculinity

At one point in Wilfred David's long-forgotten (and easily forgettable) novel *Monsoon,* a book set in early 1930s Bombay, a rather villainous British businessman named Alan Markham writes an advertisement for his new product "Yuvo" (youth) to be inserted in local newspapers. Employing techniques gleaned from an advertising specialist in his firm, Markham designs an ad stressing the rejuvenating properties of Yuvo and its value in enhancing virility. By using the product, Markham's ad claims, "all Nervous and Mental complaints rapidly disappear and Vigour and Vitality are reconsolidated to the actual pitch of youth. Yuvo is the source of a Veritable Vital Fluid, which floods the body with buoyant dynamic energy." The ad included a fake testimonial from a "P.R." in Indrapore. Markham also planned to add a "suitable illustration or a pseudo-scientific diagram." David goes on to comment sarcastically:

> In the case of Yuvo, however, there was no want-generating process required! Want had not to be created from non-existence, or stimulated from latency into active being. Want was there, a crying want, universal, insistent. Yuvo had merely to make itself known in order to direct that want towards itself. It was true that Yuvo was merely an aphrodisiac. All the more reason it should be advertised, extensively advertised. For through constant suggestion it was bound to be what it aimed to be—a rejuvenating force![1]

Apparently David was so struck by advertising in Bombay that he would give it a central place in his novel and his account is evidence of the profession's growing visibility. But the most striking feature of this passage is David's command over the language of advertisements for one specific kind of product, the male tonic. His use of such terms as "nerves," "vitiated manhood," "vigour," "vitality," "youth" and "vital fluid," and his inclusion of a scientific diagram, reflected a mastery of an idiom deployed widely at the time. Though the novel's suggestion that local consumers responded to such ads automatically was exaggerated, the account effectively captured a major set of "prior meanings" on which tonic advertisers in India regularly drew.

As David's reference suggests, tonic advertisements were ubiquitous in western India during the 1920s and 1930s. There was perhaps no other product advertised so broadly and regularly, and even ads for such unrelated commodities as sugar, chocolate, cigarettes, malted milk drinks, and alcohol sometimes claimed to possess tonic qualities. Many vernacular tonic manufacturers began running ads in local newspapers during the late nineteenth century; by the 1920s, multinational companies crowded the Indian market with tonic products. A substantial demand for tonics must have existed if they could be marketed so widely. Seemingly, if there was one item that would make middle-class Indian males loosen their purse strings, it was the tonic.

As the manufacturers of multinational tonic products sought to gain middle-class consumers, they drew upon a logic of male "weakness" and "degeneration" grounded in colonial discourses about Indian masculinity, one strongly reflected in the vocabulary of local tonic advertisements. During the early 1930s, advertising specialists, like *Monsoon's* Markham, increasingly poached upon the sales pitches of vernacular firms, hoping to capture a large market share from their competitors in the bazaar. They increasingly touted their products' ability to overcome sexual incapacity and other forms of "weakness" and they drew upon prevailing visual conventions of vernacular advertisement. But at the same time, they reshaped the concept of colonial weakness, linking it to notions about male responsibility for ensuring the reproduction of the modern conjugal family, economically, socially, and sexually.

Tonics

According to *Webster's Third New International Dictionary of the English Language,* a tonic is "something that invigorates, restores, refreshes or stimulates."[2] In early twentieth-century India, tonics could be tablets, liquids (including wines), laxatives, or even foods. Many tonics claimed to possess "secret formulae" whose powers had yet to be understood properly by the medical profession.[3] In the colonial context, the tonic also carried with it the sense of a rebuilding potential; through its invigorating power, it could overcome shortcomings of the male body, not just provide a temporary sense of pleasure or relief.

The frequency of tonic ads in India suggests two points. First, there was money to be made in tonics. According to the *Report of the Drugs Enquiry Committee, 1930–31*, a "craze" for medicinal products (including tonics) had developed in India.[4] The financial commitment that tonic sellers made to advertising could not have been sustained without a significant base of customers willing to spend money on these commodities.

Second, the market in tonics was highly competitive. Beginning tonic manufacture required little capital, and new tonic brands appeared and then disappeared frequently. With little significant regulation of drugs, no producer needed to establish evidence of a medicine's effectiveness or the standardization of its ingredients. Some horrified observers noted that the market was "flooded" with such medicines, and consumers had little way of assessing them.[5] In this commercial environment, advertising was crucial to winning over customers.

Medical notices in general, and tonic ads specifically, were critical to alerting readers to possibilities for self-diagnosis and self-treatment. By buying advertised medical commodities, consumers could hope to address health problems without intervention from medical specialists, thus sparing themselves the awkwardness of revealing embarrassing details about themselves and paying doctors' fees. Writing about the advertisement of Ayurvedic products (including tonics) during this period, Jeremy

Schneider has argued: "no longer was the trained and the experienced *vaidya* [Ayurvedic practitioner] seen as the anchor and irreplaceable element necessary to achieve health and strength, rather the drug itself assumed overarching importance."[6] The commodity advertised, Schneider suggests, displaced the regimen of bodily practices—diet, exercise, the use of medicines, the deployment of charms and the practice of sexual restraint—that indigenous practitioners might prescribe.[7] Advertisements similarly offered the possibility of bypassing professional doctors trained in Western biomedicine in British India's universities.[8]

Advertising proved particularly valuable for promoting products that claimed to correct male sexual dysfunction, since this was a subject surrounded by shame that men were reluctant to talk about with their partners, doctors or friends; ads sometimes referred to sex as a *gupt* (secret) subject. Both indigenous practitioners and bio-medical doctors might have well-established relationships with a patient's family or friends and could leak damaging information into his social circle. Testifying to the Drugs Enquiry Commission around 1930, V. K. Parulkar, a Bombay doctor, specifically tied the role of medical advertisements to fears about revealing personal habits such as masturbation believed to be the source of dysfunction:

> Specifically, these advertisements make great effect on men who have got weak nerves as a result of self-abuse [i.e, masturbation]. They are ashamed to tell their secret to doctors and expect doctors to find out the cause. In some cases therefore doctors are not able to find out the cause, in the absence of the clear history of which patients should give to medical men. Such patients therefore come to the conclusion that it is wise for them to try such remedies. Impotency in such cases is very common. Such men spend tremendous sums of money for getting virile again.[9]

Parulkar's comments highlighted a motif running through tonic advertisement: the preoccupation with the "weakness" and "degeneration" of Indian male bodies. The concept of weakness was polysemic, one that suggested different meanings in different contexts. Tonic ads drew upon, and extended, four sets of interlocking discourses about "weakness" prevalent at the time.

First, the ads grounded themselves in a colonial stereotype of the effeminacy of the high-caste, educated male. As numerous scholars have pointed out, the British rulers often thought of themselves in hyper-masculine terms while portraying high-caste groups such as the Bengali *bhadralok*, Maharashtrian Brahmans and Gujarati Vanias as "weak," "feminine" peoples.[10] In colonial discourse, the educated Hindu was imagined to be "degenerate in mind and body," "lacking in enterprise," and physically weak.[11] Such stereotypes questioned the ability of middle-class males to participate in military service, sports and other forms of activity that demanded bodily exertion, as well as the capacity to provide moral and political leadership. Weakness in turn was linked psychically to a concept of similar political weight and malleability, that of "degeneration," a supposed condition of the Indian male attributed to diverse personal and cultural practices ranging from masturbation to child marriage and a reliance on the pen rather than the sword as a means of livelihood.[12]

Nationalist discourse frequently reflected the internalization of these conceptions even as it sought to counter them. In a wide range of writings, nationalists frequently accepted the Indian male's current weakness, though they typically disputed the notion that weakness stemmed from racial characteristics; in some cases, they suggested, it was modernity, urban life, or the sedentary character of modern professions that produced bodily degeneration.[13] A number of historians have pointed to the centrality of physical culture—gymnastics, wrestling and paramilitary displays—in nationalist expression; such activities were intended to counter the current state of Indian masculinity.[14] Publications steeped in what Luzia Savary has suggested might be considered a "vernacular eugenics" stressed the potential danger of weak male bodies to the reproduction of a fit, energetic nation.[15] Gandhi's writings, too, reflected a concern that Indians needed to overcome physical and mental frailty and thereby establish their masculinity. On one occasion Gandhi remarked: "I have traveled all over the country and one of the most deplorable things I have noted is the rickety bodies of young men."[16]

Second, as Parulkar's comments mentioned, advertisements drew upon popular theories of tropical medicine that saw "weakness" of the nerves—"neurasthenia"—as the source of illness and bodily breakdowns. This discourse attributed weak nerves to a variety of causes that drained male bodies: the hot climate, overwork, the strains of urban life, and problematic moral behaviors, particularly masturbation. Such ideas were located outside the germ theory of disease causation yet at the same time they still carried the aura of Western science.[17]

Third, such notions intersected with bodily conceptions drawn from various indigenous medical sciences. Such conceptions were hardly products of a timeless Indian culture, but were themselves being reframed at the time in the context of colonial discourse, the nationalist search for a usable past, and modern conceptions of conjugality. For instance, Guy Attewell has discussed the importance of a concept of weakness thought to be caused by cultural dislocation and sexual immoderation in the reconceptualization of *unani tibb*, a flexible school of medical practice that typically traced its origins to Indo-Islamic traditions.[18] Mark Singleton has highlighted the importance of anxieties about weakness and bodily degeneration to the modern *asana* (postural) practice commonly known as yoga.[19] Projit Mukharji has delineated the centrality of concepts of weakness and debility to *daktari* medicine, a diverse field followed by numerous Indian practitioners who claimed to be following "western" medicine but whose practices and theories were formulated in an Indian context.[20] Notions of weakness and degeneration informed modern Ayurveda as well. All these ideas were inflected by the pervasiveness of eugenic logic at the time.

Finally, notions of weakness were rooted in understandings about what might be called the "sexual health" of men. That is, they drew upon well-established (and well-explored) Indian theories suggesting that semen wastage depleted male energy and strength and that its conservation was a means of generating vitality that could be deployed in the wider world.[21] These theories were reinforced by the influence of somewhat similar western notions.[22] Gandhi viewed *brahmacharya* (celibacy) as a means of developing the strength he needed to engage in his demanding forms of non-violent resistance.[23] As Bhikhu Parekh has indicated, Gandhi believed that semen was the body's sole source of energy, that "all power comes from the preservation and sublimation of the vitality that is responsible for the creation of life [i.e, semen]," and that sexual acts involving the loss of semen "impeded the generation of psychic and spiritual energy."[24]

During this period, a general theory prevailed that sexual excess—in one's youth or in the present—produced male debilitation. According to this theory, masturbation, wet dreams, the visiting of prostitutes, and homosexual sex wasted semen, which could lead the body to become run down and cause sexual incapacity.[25] Anxieties about sexual weakness may have flourished particularly among middle-class urban male migrants for whom a period of adolescence between childhood and adulthood emerged with the rising age of marriage, and who worried about their capacity for biological reproduction.[26] Though these views are often attributed to Hindu religious notions, they also found resonance among Muslims and particularly among Bombay's Parsis, who by the 1940s were beginning to express concern about their dwindling population and the supposed physical weakness of their community, developments attributed to a lack of interest in sex among Parsi males.[27]

These four sets of ideas about male weakness often intersected in both colonial and counter-colonial discussions. As Pande has demonstrated, moral excesses associated with masturbation, wet dreams and early marriage were often viewed as a cause of the physical weakness of the high-caste urban male.[28] The general condition of the nerves was regarded as a source of sexual dysfunction; conversely impotence was seen as producing problems of psychic and physical health. Racial discourses suggested that Indians might be especially prone to nervous conditions and sexual excess. The emphasis on moral failings and bad habits—the consumption of alcohol, the use of drugs and sexual indulgence—as sources of weakness also resonated widely at the time.[29]

Whatever its perceived source, middle-class discourses portrayed weakness as a tendency that could promote not only physical deterioration but also a more general debility pervading all realms of life, including the family. The modern conjugal imaginary prompted reconceptualization of male roles, elevating the husband to a position of new power but also foisting upon him an almost exclusive expectation to ensure the family's economic security. In the ideal, he should no longer rely on the joint family's collective resources, and he had obligations to insulate his wife from the meddlesome tendencies of extended kin. He was expected to propagate children, especially sons, who would carry on the family's status into the next generation. He also had a role in their upbringing, ensuring they got a proper education and participating in their intellectual cultivation and physical development. In short, men were to play a special part in the biological, economic, and social reproduction of the nuclear family.

Indian fiction in a variety of regional contexts repeatedly centered around the inability of husbands to protect their wives from powerful forces issuing from the extra-familial world. Even more common were writings that focused on men unable to resist parental interference or to overcome difficult family circumstances so that they could unite with their beloveds in marriage, including such famous novels as Saratchandra Chattopadhyay's *Devdas* (1917)—a Bengali work read widely in translation in western India—and Govardhanram Tripathi's *Saraswatichandra*, the leading piece in the canon of Gujarati literature (1993 [1887–1901]).[30] Much of the tragedy in the main character's situation in each case rested in his ultimate failure to take the actions needed to fulfill the roles of male householder, husband, and father. As Prashant Kidambi has argued for Bombay, preoccupations about the ability to sustain the family materially also became central to the middle class. Those with salaried jobs worried that their families might fall from the ranks of respectable people. Kidambi's discussion of Saraswat periodicals illustrates the heavy emphasis placed on the husband's responsibility for sustaining the family's social position; these writings usually omitted any potential role for extended kin. In effect the journals called for a disciplined, respectable kind of husbandhood that rejected frills to maintain the stability of the conjugal unit.[31] In short, notions of weakness and the ways men could fail the family by failing to satisfy masculine expectations were pervasive in middle-class western India, as they were in much of the rest of the subcontinent.

Vernacular tonic advertisements

By 1918, indigenous tonic producers had long been drawing upon this universe of prior meanings, using "weakness," and particularly sexual weakness, as a critical selling point. Notices for sexual products took up a large portion of advertising space in vernacular newspapers. Indeed, until the 1930s, many small Indian-language papers had considerable difficulty in attracting other kinds of ads and were compelled to rely on sellers of medicines, especially tonics, for a significant portion of their revenues.[32] Much as recent advertisements for erectile dysfunction treatments in the United States made possible the mention of sexual subjects that could not have been broached in the mainstream media earlier, the commercial interests involved in selling tonics opened up spaces for discussing sexual matters otherwise off limits in public discourse. Religious reformers and government officials alike frowned upon the publication of these notices.[33] In 1931, the Drugs Enquiry Committee recommended a legal ban on advertising medicines that promised greater virility, but these recommendations were not implemented until 1954.[34] The big English-language papers, which attracted a wider range of ads due to their large readerships with greater buying power, could afford to turn down sexually explicit advertisements. But they too ran appeals for sex tonics using more discrete language.

The advertisements for vernacular tonics were typically designed by their manufacturers rather than by advertising specialists. They usually reflected a limited investment in marketing. In many cases, their content consisted mostly of words; there was often little visual material, and any images were probably drawn by members of the family firm or employees in newspaper offices.[35] Some ads consisted of little more than a couple of lines indicating the availability of a tonic and the problems it was designed to address. But other ads could have quite lengthy texts, and thus provide considerable insight into prevailing notions of male sexual health.[36]

Often these ads evoked a logic stemming from Ayurvedic or Unani traditions, while others were steeped in bio-medical theories; most commonly, they evoked bodily conceptions where the boundaries of the two systems became blurred, where extensive "vernacularization" of western medicine had occurred and indigenous medicine claimed a "scientific" character.[37] No doubt, they drew upon a larger didactic literature about sex then in circulation,[38] and clearly took recourse to a set of notions about sexuality and health shared widely across different urban classes, not just "subalterns."

The idea of male "weakness" (in Gujarati *nabalai* or *kamjori*) was central in such ads. In advertisements for sexual products, the term usually served as a euphemism for impotence, which was typically conceived less as an issue of erectile dysfunction than of seminal thickness, perhaps hinting at reproductive potential rather than the ability to carry out sexual intercourse. But the concept of weakness in these ads also possessed at least two other layers of meaning: a lack of physical strength and vitality in the male body and public cowardice or ineffectiveness.[39] The ads' special power may have stemmed from their suggestion that addressing sexual health problems would correct other bodily, mental and political shortcomings.

Bazaar advertisements typically stressed the debilitating (and sometimes shameful) effects of sexual outlets other than heterosexual intercourse, especially masturbation, wet dreams, and spermatorrhea. Most commonly, they suggested that 'bad habits' in one's youth undermined a man's sexual capacity or seminal thickness as an adult, but promised that the appropriate potions and lotions could repair the damage caused by semen wastage so that a man could perform strongly in sexual intercourse. At the same time, the ads sometimes engaged the sexual fantasies of their customers. They encouraged men to indulge their imaginations in harems, relationships with courtesans, and the like. Males who had wasted semen in the past and had become weak could now hope—by using proper medical substances—to participate in forms of sexuality previously available only to the strongest, most potent, men. In other words, the discourse of advertisements embodied what Alter has called the "paradox of virility," that is, the co-existence of conceptions placing high emphasis on sexual self-restraint and those evoking the value of robust performance.[40]

Advertisements for medicines to correct sexual dysfunction indicated that they would cure other bodily problems, while ads for general medicines often included impotence or semen thinness in a longer list of symptoms they addressed. The ads suggested that a man's bodily fluids were important not just to his sexual life, but to his physical well-being, his mental capacity, even his moral character. The multiple meanings of key words in these advertisements added to this layering effect: *nabalai* or *kamjori* could mean impotence, weakness or ineffectiveness; *virya* could mean sperm, strength or courage; *shakti* could mean sexual capacity or strength, power, will-power or energy; "youthfulness" indicated not only age but ability to engage regularly in sexual intercourse; and the various words for manliness (for instance *purushatva*) could suggest sexual virility, a more general masculine vigor, and an ethic of proper male social conduct. The powerful resonance of these ads thus rested in their evocation of a double or triple register that related sexual performance to the general health of the male body and to the fulfillment of masculine political and social obligations.[41]

One campaign that reflected significant visual as well as verbal elements was a particularly fascinating set of bazaar advertisements for a group of products called Jadibuti Manliness Set from Ambala in the Punjab. These ads ran over several years in the *Mumbai Samachar*.[42] The image in one of these ads (Figure 3.1) highlights a holy man administering the product to a youth who is being choked by the snake of

Figure 3.1 "The True and Faithful Service to the Motherland," Jadibuti Mardai [Manliness] Set, *MS*, January 6, 1928, 4.

impotence. Written in English on the snake are the various causes of the young man's affliction: "masterbation (sic.)," "spermatorrhea," "premature ejaculation" and "nocturnal emission." To the left and above him are the phrases "no health, no happiness," "shyful disgrace," "anxiety," "no enjoyment," "dead life," and "dishonour of family"—all supposed consequences of impotence. Three angel-like figures with mustaches, one carrying a sign that reads "guaranteed extirpation of impotency," fly overhead. These figures were seemingly derived from Parsi theater.[43] The Gujarati text surrounding this image was entitled "the true and faithful service to the motherland," and the ad was signed, "Servant of the Nation, S. H. Hussain." In the text, Hussain related his life story. He confessed—taking the anxious male reader into his confidence—to have engaged in bad habits during his childhood so that he was not fit for marriage when he was twenty-five. He was ashamed of his non-performance, and after failing to find a remedy from local medical practitioners, he left home in despair. During his travels, he met a Mahatma (sage) in Kashmir who took pity on him, and who gave him herbs to treat his problem. Within five days the weakness in his penis was gone and his youth had returned; his semen had become thick. He later set out to perform the same "service for the motherland" that the holy man had performed for him by making these products available in commercial form. Hussain here implicitly invoked a eugenic logic that connected physical capacities diminished through masturbation to the nation's weakness.[44] By helping India's men to overcome sexual shortcomings that plagued them individually, he seemed to claim, he was making possible a more general revitalization of the country.

Slightly later ads for *Jadibuti* from 1934 (Figure 3.2), by contrast, stressed the value of the product to the enhancement of male reproductive capacity. Announcing that the

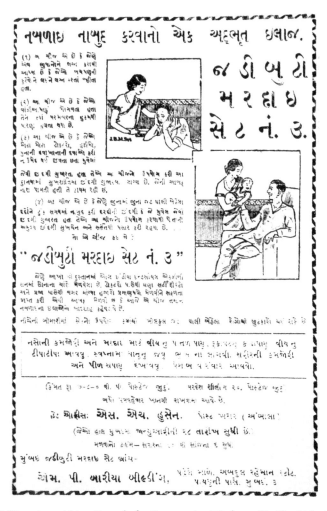

Figure 3.2 "One Astonishing Remedy for Overcoming Weakness," Jadibuti Mardai Set No. 3, *MS*, January 17, 1934, 5.

products were an "astonishing remedy for destroying weakness," these ads suggested that the medicines would be found valuable by young males about to marry after a childhood of bad habits, who were sterile, who had serious pains in their body, and who had failed to find any solutions from other doctors. *Jadibuti*, one of them claimed, promised that the product would address weak nerves, thin sperm, obstructions in semen, wet dreams, bodily weaknesses, jaundice and frequent urination. The ad thus invoked a medical logic in which a variety of body functions interacted together rather than one stressing symptom-specific remedey.

Particularly important to the ad's resonance was the evocation of shame, a message conveyed primarily through visual means. In the top image, a woman stands over a stressed husband, expressing compassion for his plight. The wife's position seemingly heightened the sense of abjectness and humiliation in the situation of the dysfunctional man and the urgency of addressing his problem. In the lower image—after the man has used *Jadibuti*—the couple have a child, and the man rests easily in an armchair, an emblem of the fulfilled, comfortable householder.[45] Clearly the ad addressed anxieties about reproduction.

The limited presence of women in pre-1930 ads is otherwise striking. When they appear, as in the appeal for *Jadibuti*, it is as figures meant to evoke male shame, with little sense of sensuality or marital companionship. The theme of women's sexuality was absent. Not only were males the audience of such advertisements, but the ads focused largely on restoring the man's capacity for enhancing his own pleasure, his reproductive power, and his contributions to society and family, with little reference to female participation in the sexual activity involved.

Global firms and tonic advertisements

Global firms had been advertising tonics in Indian newspapers well before the advent of professional advertising. These appeals were often generated in Europe, and placed in local newspapers by a distribution service. Many ads from this period carried a message oriented toward Europeans that the sellers may sometimes have hoped would also influence middle-class purchasers. Often, the only element changed from a European original was the name of the Indian bottler that had been added.[46]

A few ads for imported tonics during the 1920s, however, provide evidence of having been produced in South Asia. For instance, Figure 3.3 specifically addresses expatriate concerns with the debilitating effects of the heat.[47] It pictures a vigorous European man in a suit, but also wearing the *sola topi*, the characteristic headwear of the expatriate to guard against the sun. The product is described as addressing problems of the nerves and fevers, both health issues strongly associated in expatriate culture with the tropics. There was no allusion to sexual themes.

An ad for Burgoyne's Easton's syrup from 1926, by contrast, is addressed to the "manhood of India."[48] The ad specifically proclaims the product's tonic properties and suggests the syrup is intended for those who are "weak"; it promises the male user the ability to participate in a wide range of sports, which can only be played by those with

Figure 3.3 "For Good Health in Hot Climates—take Sanatogen" Sanatogen, *BC*, December 31, 1925, 10.

"the physical strength and the steady nerve which such physical exercise commands." The advertisement appears to be addressing concerns its designers expected to be shared by both expatriates and Indian males; indeed the ad features the image of a European. Again, the subject of sex was not mentioned. But in its stress on weakness, the appeal here was one that would be shared by many ads for commodities produced in India.

During the 1930s, however, the investment and strategizing put into global tonic ads clearly increased, and the effort to develop a customized message to a middle-class, male, and Indian audience became more conscious. With the rise of the advertising agency, both the copy and the visual elements in these corporate tonic ads were usually developed in India. Advertisers of global tonics also began to place more ads in Gujarati and Marathi papers, clearly seeking to win customers from deeper within urban society. Evidence in the ads suggests that multinational firms sought to usurp the place of vernacular tonics in consumers' spending patterns; there was a concerted effort to pirate the language of their bazaar competitors (as suggested by Markham's actions in *Monsoon*) while fusing this vocabulary to notions of conjugality and modernity.

As professional advertisers became involved, attention to the visual appearance of tonic ads increased. Business firms had begun to recognize the importance of eye-catching drawings. The allocation of space to verbal messages was often reduced and a variety of attractive type-faces were deployed. In their artwork, the ads' designers usually chose to signal their target audience through the clear delineation of the characters depicted. Hair color, clothing, and other such signs increasingly served as markers of the middle-class male identity of the figures; European bodies, however, were still sometimes used to depict strength and vigor.

Some advertisers of corporate tonics asserted a "scientific" basis for the healing power of their products. "Nature alone," an ad for a product named Vitophenes asserted (in language that seems to be directed against Ayurvedic medicine), "cannot guarantee health and happiness all through life. Nature needs the support of Science, the help that Vitophenes give. Whatever your age, Vitophenes will banish Headaches, Depression, Debility, 'Nerves,' Sleeplessness, and Poor Health."[49] Such ads frequently included medical diagrams of the body and mentioned the professional endorsement of physicians. Appeals for Sanatogen, a "tonic food," carried pictures of doctors attending a patient, and stressed that "25,000 physicians all over the world" recommended the product.[50] The notion that tonics repaired the nervous system, "cleansed the blood," "stimulated the liver," and "corrected blood pressure" were present in a wide range of advertisements. The use of numbers and names that carried the aura of serious chemistry—Leciferrin, Vitophenes, Magnolax, Phosperine, etc.—furthered the sense that these products were scientifically sound. The ads' designers clearly relied upon a biomedical language that they felt would appeal to the sensibilities of members of the middle class as modern persons with a world view steeped in western science.

The most dominant and insistent theme in the advertisements, however, became that of "weakness," a concept that could suggest physical debility, mental disintegration and sexual incapacity. Corporate ads now increasingly evoked the same middle-class bodily anxieties so widely stressed in vernacular advertising. One advertisement for Okasa, a widely publicized German tonic, mentioned that nerves became weak from "old age, malnutrition, tropical climate, over-work and excessive habits," and could produce "symptoms of constant ill-health in one form or another, nervousness, debility, lack of energy, sleeplessness, fatigue and premature old age." Okasa, the ad insisted, would "keep your NERVES strong and GLANDS fully Active." With a few weeks of use, "Brain, nerves, Eye-sight, Digestive Organs, Kidneys, are all made active and normal. Sleeplessness, Neurasthemia, Depression, Debility are completely removed."[51] An ad for Waterbury's

Compound juxtaposed comments from a man before and after taking the product. In the "before" statement, the man indicated that his "vitality [was] low, strength and vigour fading daily. [I was] totally discouraged about health. Knew I was getting weaker, and nothing seemed to help...." Waterbury's Compound, he states, "made a new man of me in fifteen days ... I did not know any tonic could help so much in such a short time."[52]

Tonics promised to revitalize the body's physical capabilities. Images of people (often Europeans) engaged in sports—boxing, cricket and tennis—were prominent as were those of body builders. Vikelp tablets, for instance, employed a photograph of a muscular Caucasian man and a curvaceous Caucasian woman wearing bathing suits. "THIN, AILING, NERVOUS BREAKDOWN ...!" the ad proclaimed before going on to say "How Minerals and Natural Food Iodine Build Worn-out, Ageing, Weak, Sickly People into Strong Redblooded, Virile, Men and Women."[53] The use of idealized, muscled and toned European bodies was likely intended to heighten the feelings of insecurity that might prompt middle-class men to buy the tablets.[54] Such ads sought to induce the feeling that "not measuring up" in athletic activity was a source of inadequacy and emasculation.

Medical ads increasingly depicted weakness as a condition that threatened to undermine the conjugal family. An ad for Harkers' Nervetone pictured a small boy talking to an angry father who is shaking his cane at a weeping mother. The caption ran *"Kiddie advises mummy and dad not to grumble over domestic troubles. Both are weak."* "Unruly Mummy and irritable Daddy," it went on "Its Weakness [weakness is] the cause of nervous prostration.... My school master takes Harkers Nervetone, because, he is the same like you [sic]. Why not try both and save the home."[55] An ad promoting Phosferine pictured a father in a turban, a mother in a sari, and a baby. The text ran: "The happy father, wise in his generation, protects the health of their [his family members'] constitutions against infection. He safeguards health and happiness too, when he replenishes lost energy in himself and his wife with a regular dose of Phosferine."[56] Here the unmentioned danger seems to be the disastrous effect on family well-being if the chief earner were to lose his physical capacities. In another Phosferine ad, the main character laments, among other things, his own lack of a son, implying that virility and the perpetuation of a "healthy, happy family" into the next generation was at stake.[57] In all these appeals to "family values" the family unit imagined was a nuclear one, usually with one man, one woman and a child (almost always male).

Most notably, corporate advertisements came to emphasize the theme of sexual weakness so prevalent in vernacular advertising. Most of the ads steered away from theories of "semen anxiety" (worries about depleting strength and energy through loss of semen in acts like masturbation) though they sometimes stressed the notion that exhausted nerves caused impotence.[58] But they did invoke a concept of weakness that functioned on a multiplicity of levels, including sexual capacity, the condition of the male body as a whole, and the ability to be effective in professional, political and family life. In these ads, corporate advertisers effectively drew upon a vernacularized scientific logic, one inflected significantly by understandings of the body associated with indigenous tonics. An English-language ad for Okasa illustrates this point (Figure 3.4).[59]

The most obvious feature of the ad was its bold claim to enhance "sex-vitality." Providing a medical diagram of the upper half of a male body, it stresses that Okasa

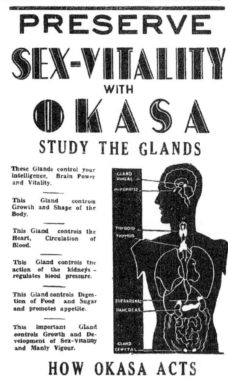

PRESERVE
SEX-VITALITY
WITH
OKASA
STUDY THE GLANDS

These Glands control your
Intelligence, Brain Power
and Vitality.

This Gland controls
Growth and Shape of the
Body.

This Gland controls the
Heart, Circulation of
Blood.

This Gland controls the
action of the kidneys –
regulates blood pressure.

This Gland controls Digestion of Food and Sugar
and promotes appetite.

This Important Gland
controls Growth and De-
velopment of Sex-Vitality
and Manly Vigour.

GLAND PINEAL
HYPOPHYSE
THYROID
THYMUS
SUPRARENAL
PANCREAS
GLAND GENITAL

HOW OKASA ACTS

Hidden inside the human body are some most mysterious cells
which control health, sex-vitality, vigour, physical and mental powers, strength of body and nerves. OKASA acts just on these cells
and definitely restores them to full activity making you a new man
with full vitality, strength and vigour of youth. By the use of OKASA
the cells, the nerves, the brain, the heart and all other vital organs of the body are strengthened. Your whole system is completely
rejuvenated. The results are beyond your expectations

BEWARE OF IMITATIONS!
DO NOT RUN ANY RISKS
ALWAYS USE OKASA
THE ORIGINAL GENUINE GLAND-TONIC
HIGHEST INTERNATIONAL AWARDS

For complete literature & fresh supply, write to:—
OKASA CO., BERLIN (India), LTD., 12, Rampart Row, Fort, Bombay.

Figure 3.4 "Preserve SEX-VITALITY with OKASA—Study the Glands," Okasa, *BC*,
January 11, 1938, 3.

addresses problems present in many "glands" from the brain to the thyroid, the
pancreas, and the genitals (described as an important gland controlling "Growth and
Development of Sex-Vitality and Manly Vigour"). The ad goes on to say:

Hidden inside the human body are some most mysterious cells which control
health, sex-vitality, vigour, physical and mental powers, strength of body and
nerves. OKASA acts just on these cells and definitely restores them to full activity

making you a new man with full vitality, strength and vigour of youth. By the use of OKASA the cells, the nerves, the brain, the heart and all other vital organs of the body are strengthened.

The ad relied on two themes present in vernacular ads: the connectedness of various bodily functions in a larger interacting system, specifically stressing the importance of sexual energy to a person's general health, and a concept of "manly vigour," both physical and mental. The ads also drew upon the increased interest in the endocrinal system and the effects of hormones, a theme derived from Western sexual science.[60] A Gujarati ad for Sanatogen evoked similar logics, claiming that the product addressed "weakness of the reproductive organs" while also suggesting that the product would deliver "vitality (*shakti*) and brilliant good health."[61] The ad moved between these issues in the text as well, referring to a general incapacity of the body and to impotence (*namardai*). The use of such polysemic words as "manliness" (*purushatan*), "brilliant manly power" (*tejasvi purushatva takat*), and "vitality" (*shakti*) in these ads alluded to concerns with virility, masculine physicality and honor. The intervention of Indian translators must have been essential to generating wording that skirted obscenity laws but left little doubt in the mind of adult readers about their references to sex.

The vocabulary of sexual shame was also part of the battery of rhetorical devices, drawn from vernacular advertising, used by advertisers. In another Gujarati Sanatogen ad (Figure 3.5), we see a man in a reclined pose, seemingly in a state of worry and presumably without the ability or inclination to get up. "How you can increase your manliness," the heading proclaims. The text became more explicit about what "manliness" entailed: "the man who is unable to enjoy worldly pleasures and carry out the *duties of a married man* is not only always anxious and sad, but also feels a lot of shame. He becomes frustrated, broken and bored of the world and jealous of the abilities and cleverness of others.... How can such a man regain strength and manliness?" (italics mine).[62] The advertisement drew upon the logic of shame present in vernacular ads, but it now linked sexual shortcomings to notions of male obligation in the conjugal household. Sanatogen was marketed quite differently in the *Times of India*, a newspaper where advertisers often sought to reach European expatriates. There the ads focused on enhancing the capacity to cope with the climate, improving the ability to recover from malaria and heat-induced tiredness, and facilitating participation in party life and other forms of extra-familial sociality.

Ads for Stearns tonic tablets directed to middle-class males similarly linked concerns about sexual incapacity, notions of shame, and the importance of fulfilling conjugal expectations. Figure 3.6 provides the *Bombay Chronicle* image of a debilitated male slumped in his chair, in this case one wearing pajamas and seemingly unable to move. His wife (marked by her sari and hair-style as both Parsi and modern) stands over him, emphasizing the context of shame in which he finds himself. Her own image does not seem to convey personal frustration, but concern with her husband's condition. An empty bed is visible in the background, the marker of unfulfilled sexuality in marriage. The ads reads: "Do You Feel like this? No Strength, No Energy, No Zest, No Manhood, No Joy." Regular adult readers of vernacular ads would have had no uncertainty about the implications of the words "strength," "energy", "manhood,"

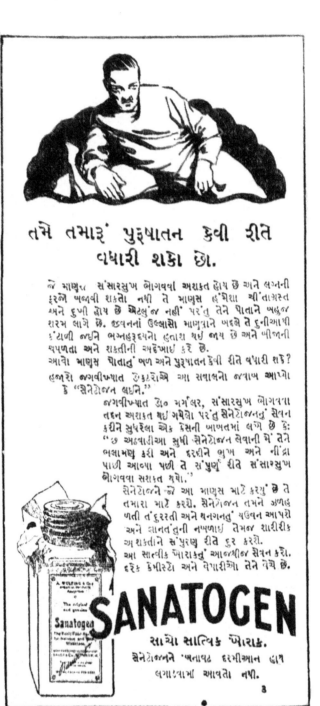

Figure 3.5 "How You Can Increase Your Manliness (Virility)," Sanatogen, *MS*, January 24, 1931, 12.

Do You Feel Like This?

NO Strength, No Energy, No Zest, No Manhood, No Joy? Sports, food, work, pleasure, amusements beckon you in vain. You can't be bothered.

We have all felt like that sometimes, but to feel like that always is dangerous. You want a thorough renovation. What is needed is a blood purifying tonic, digestive laxative and nerve builder. Take

STEARN'S DIGESTIVE and TONIC TABLETS

They will bring you back to life, vigour and enjoyment, increase your vitality, build up your nerves, strengthen your will and make you fresh, fit, forcible and fertile both in brain and body.

Obtainable of All Good Chemists and Stores.

Figure 3.6 "Do You Feel Like This?" Stearns, *BC*, August 20, 1934, 11.

and "fertile."[63] The size of the home (at least two rooms), the furniture, curtains and carpet all signal a somewhat prosperous middle-class context.

An ad for Stearns in the *Times of India* (Figure 3.7), by contrast, clearly addresses an expatriate audience, stressing the need to repair the debilitating effect of the Indian climate. The worn-out European male, being consoled by his dog (an image never present in ads targeting middle-class audiences), is unable to continue his work activity; he is "totally unfit for service in the tropics" and is being sent back home. The ad warns the European consumer not to let this happen to him. The ultimate disgrace, the ad seems to suggest, was to fail to meet one's obligations as a member of the ruling race;

Figure 3.7 "Health & Career RUINED!" Stearns, *TI*, October 20, 1934, 17.

the ad implied that embarrassing personal failures damaged the larger reputation of the European community. Stearns tonic pills, the ad contends, will help a man "ward off fever and other tropical illness."[64] In both advertisements, apparently, the artists and copywriters sought to highlight the most shameful shortcomings they could imagine. But they portrayed shame in culturally salient forms that they believed would be emotive to different target audiences.

Poaching from the approach of vernacular ads was also reflected in the visual conventions of ads directed to middle-class audiences. The figure of a wife standing over a worn-out, incapacitated husband became a common trope in corporate advertising by the late 1930s. Advertisements for different multinational tonics sometimes converged around this image. The Bayer's tonic ad depicted in Figure 3.8 clearly has a strong visual resemblance to the Stearns ad just discussed. The artists working for professional agencies, likely Indian subordinates, seemingly regarded this trope as a particularly powerful mode of conveying masculine sexual insecurity. The ads for Stearns and Bayer in effect both reflect the application of the conventions and techniques of commercial art and the use of modern printing technologies, but the inter-ocular relationship between these ads and the slightly earlier Jadibuti ad featured in Figure 3.2 is clear. The repeated borrowing of this visual motif from vernacular advertising reflected an appreciation of its power in depicting masculine abjection, weakness and lethargy, shame, and sexual inadequacy in a simple, straightforward image.[65]

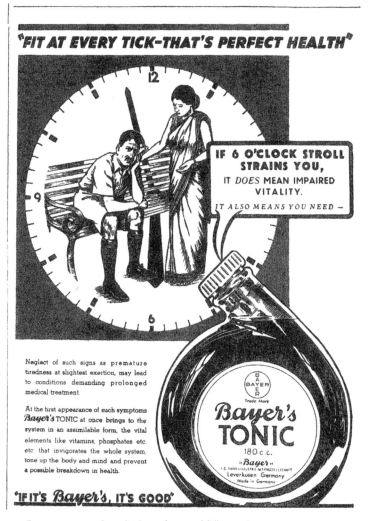

Figure 3.8 "Fit at Every Tick—That's Perfect Health," Bayer's, *TI*, May 9, 1939, 11.

Ads for multinational firms now also addressed the issue of reproduction. In one Gujarati Okasa notice, for instance, a happy European couple hold a new child, a product of having taken the "hormone compound." A caption indicates that the product is a miracle of science. The ad promises that Okasa would address *ashakti* (incapacity) and restore 'youthfulness' to those experiencing premature aging, both phrases present in bazaar advertisement that possessed sexual implications.[66]

Corporate tonic advertisements offered a somewhat different commercial paradigm than vernacular ads. Usually, corporate appeals were somewhat less direct (or more ambiguous) in their use of sexual terminology, more conscious of establishing a biomedical basis for their claims. These appeals left little room for the play of male fantasy; their language was mostly an austere one of anxiety with only limited suggestion of possible pleasures to be enjoyed in sexual activity. At the same time, the advertisements connected the notion of weakness explicitly to preoccupations associated with the modern conjugal relationship. And by invoking the familiar, multivalent notion of weakness, by using concepts with layered meanings that suggested both sexuality and other forms of bodily health, by indicating that sexual health and the health of other organs were interconnected by highlighting the shame of nonperformance, by using well-established visual tropes to convey this message, by promising to remove barriers to procreation, and finally by linking all of these themes to principles of modern conjugality, corporate tonic advertisers built upon an edifice of conceptions highly familiar to an Indian male audience.

Sex tonics and a "happy married life"

During the second half of the 1930s, a new kind of sex tonic ad emerged in western Indian newspapers, one that did not fit neatly into the categories of "vernacular" or "corporate" advertisement. These ads stressed the tonic's value in enhancing "marital happiness" and a "happy married life." The ads again targeted men, but stressed the male's ability to satisfy his wife sexually in the achievement of conjugal happiness. The "happy marriage" ads appear to have been almost exclusively placed in the vernacular press, perhaps because they targeted the middle class of western India (and not expatriates) but perhaps also because English-language papers refused to print them due to their explicit sexual meaning. In the *Mumbai Samachar* alone, at least five different medical products and the Chinese Medical Store in Bombay offered advertisements with this theme. Marital happiness ads thus reflected not the idiosyncratic approach of a single company but a larger paradigm different firms believed was worth emulating.

Marital happiness advertisements typically stressed the consequences of male sexual dysfunction for the sexual satisfaction of the middle-class housewife.[67] An ad for Jinsin (Ginseng?) Gold Tonic Pills (Figure 3.9) conveys a sense of despair by including the image of a dysfunctional husband with a rather sullen wife standing above him but with her back toward him. The image utilized the visual trope seen earlier in the ads for Jadibuti, Stearns and Bayer, adding to the sense of male shame a strong sentiment of female resentment (rather than pity and consolation).[68] The viewer,

Figure 3.9 "By Using Jinsin Gold Tonic Pills, Obtain the Sweet Contentment of Married Life," Jinsin (Ginseng) Gold Tonic Pills, *MS*, December 13, 1937, 11.

however, is not left on this negative note. In a second image in the same ad, we see a happy, younger looking and taller man after use of the pills embracing his beaming wife while she looks longingly up to his face, evidence of a renewed sexual life. Most married happiness advertisements suggested a special companionship would result from using the product. In ad after ad, husband and wife were pictured in poses of significant intimacy resulting from a mutually pleasurable sex life (for instance Figure 3.10).[69] Captions in such ads include "taste the true enjoyment of married life," "find enjoyment by doubling the passion/vigor of your marital happiness," "full success of conjugal sexual life," and "experience unprecedented pleasure in your married life." Each appeal asks the husband to imagine the value of his wife's "satisfaction" to his own happiness; in some cases, the ads may have also been intended to prompt wives to urge their husbands to take action to address sexual shortcomings.

Visually the happy marriage ads possess a distinctive character. Unlike most ads for vernacular firms, they reflect considerable investment in artwork; it seems likely that the businesses selling these tonics hired trained artists to draw these images. In many cases, the ads convey a cinematic feel, with the couple engaged in romantic settings and poses. The husband and wife touch in a way that conveys deep affection, for instance, with the man's arm around the woman and the woman's hand on his chest. A difference in height sometimes accentuates the husband's masculinity. In some instances, the intimacy went beyond what would be permissible in other newspaper material, as in one ad where the couple engage in an unmistakably passionate kiss.[70] The strong similarity between ads for different products is clear evidence of mutual influence, that is, of inter-ocularity.

Some ads stressing marital happiness brought up concerns about procreation. An appeal for Jinsin tonic pills, for instance, pictured a small boy stretching out his arms

Figure 3.10 "Enjoy Married Life by Doubling your Vigor," Mahabs Pills, *MS*, September 15, 1943, 6.

toward his delighted mother while his father, wearing a suit and seated in an armchair (again, the symbol of bourgeois householderhood), looks on contentedly. The caption refers to the scene as an ecstatic family, and points to the possible attainment of "real heaven in this world." The ad's lengthier main text indicates that the product overcomes the disappointments of married life (meaning both the absence of children and sexual problems) and gives new life by "eliminating every kind of shortcoming in manliness."[71] Most of the happy marriage ads, however, celebrated non-procreative sexuality.

An important feature of all these ads is the presence of overt markers of modernity, including the hair-styles of men and women, the clothes depicted (suits and ties are often worn by men, six-yard saris by women), and the furniture shown in the visual frame. In one ad, using a comic strip before-and-after sequence, one woman discusses with a friend her husband's sexual problems by telephone,[72] an instrument that would have been affordable only to the upper-most sections of the middle class; the phone symbolizes the highest forms of technological progress and of eliteness rather than simply being an instrument through which two women communicate. These markers indicated that the man's fulfillment of his wife was critical to the achievement of a truly modern marriage. Images of women in turn usually suggest a companionship based upon some intimacy and devotion, which might be signaled by flowers in the hair (which could indicate a desire to please the husband).

An important source of the meanings incorporated into the marital happiness advertisements were the discourses of scientific sexology and the birth control movement, which were beginning to reach members of the middle class through journals on sexual matters, marriage manuals, and lectures by experts.[73] The new writings asserted, among other points, the importance of understanding sexual function to sustaining the viability of the conjugal relationship. Consciousness of male and female sexual response, advocates of the new science argued, was critical to avoiding sexual incompatibility, which they viewed as the most important source of husband–wife friction. Knowledge of human biology and of "marriage hygiene," they posited, would lead couples to adopt practices in their sexual lives that would sustain conjugal intimacy and prevent unwanted conception. Marie Stopes' book *Married Love* (first published in 1918), which contained some discussion of birth control but focused primarily upon providing information about the physiology of sex in order to promote (to use the words of Sarah Hodges) "a happy and sexually fulfilling married life," was advertised in Indian newspapers and sold in urban bookstores, as were the works of other sexologists.[74] In her well-publicized debates with Gandhi in North India during 1936, the birth control advocate Margaret Sanger insisted on the importance of a concept of "sex love": "sex love is a relationship which makes for oneness, for completeness between the husband and wife, and contributes to a finer understanding and a greater spiritual harmony."[75] Indian advocates of sexual science like A. P. Pillay, R. D. Karve and N. S. Phadke, also published books and journals on sexual subjects, often emphasizing the importance of sexual knowledge to conjugal happiness.[76] The dissemination of sexological literature thus established a foundation of prior meanings for ads stressing the modern, scientific concept of a sexually compatible marital happiness.

Yet marital happiness ads did not simply replicate the logic of sexual science. Some of them, for instance, invoked the language of weakness as well as the reasoning of semen depletion and conservation (a notion dismissed by global sexual science). One ad for Mahabs pills pictures a modern middle-class couple underneath the caption of "taste the true enjoyment of married life."[77] But the ad's text begins by referring to the need to repair lost potency (*viryashakti*, literally semen-energy) resulting from a misuse of one's masculinity (likely a reference to masturbation). If the pills were used, the ad claimed, there would be "a magical effect on one's productive power." Then linking in familiar logic the health of semen to one's general physical health, the ad goes on to claim that "there will be a magical effect on your weak body and lifeless sexual organs acquire a new life" before stating that Mahabs pills would address problems ranging from poor memory power and nerve weakness to semen disorders. The ad concludes: "use it yourself and you will see that your married life improves within days." Another ad promised that Mahabs pills would permanently cure wet dreams, weak sperm, lack of manliness and impotence, and make one energetic and vibrant. "Your semen," the ad asserts, "will become thick like a stone and be unfailing."[78]

Thus many marital happiness ads reflected a hybrid conception of masculinity, one that welded together a new language drawn from global sexual science and modern conjugality with a well-established idiom of semen conservation and bodily strength present in vernacular tonic advertisements. The ads could at one and the same time draw upon worries about the accumulating effects of "bad habits" in one's youth, middle-class commitments to modernity, science and conjugality, and concepts grounded in powerful erotic/romantic fantasies.

Horlicks, male weakness and the office

The evolution of campaigns for Horlicks, a malted milk drink product made of barley and other grains, further illustrates the ways that corporate tonic advertisements creatively deployed the principle of male weakness to advance the new conjugality. Horlicks was founded by two British brothers, William and James Horlick, who set up a company for making this product in Wisconsin in the United States during the 1870s. A British factory was established near London in 1908; by 1918 Horlicks seems to have been primarily a British company. Transported easily in its powder form, it was used extensively by British troops during World War I and was sometimes brought to the subcontinent by Indian soldiers afterwards.[79] By the mid 1930s, it was one of the five most commonly advertised consumer goods in western Indian newspapers (the others being Okasa, Lifebuoy and Lux soaps, and Ovaltine, a competitor of Horlicks). In late 1938, Horlicks was the largest client of JWT, with an account of a bit more than 22,000 Rupees over a six-month period.[80] There was no inherent reason that Horlicks could not be marketed for its taste, but before 1945 it was advertised as a tonic drink with health benefits. A key objective of its advertisements worldwide was to convince buyers to make its consumption a daily regimen. In England or America, such persuasion might have involved substituting Horlicks for tea or coffee. In India, regular use of these other drinks was becoming established in urban India around the same time; creating a habit of consuming any kind of branded commercial beverage involved a transformation of everyday bodily practices.

Little archival information is available about Horlicks' ad campaigns in India during the 1920s. While the ads at the time were usually oriented toward expatriates, they were clearly designed on the subcontinent rather than imported readymade. The ads in both English and vernacular papers often stressed the importance of proper nourishment needed to withstand hot weather. Typical images were a European woman on an Oriental veranda with a Taj-like structure in the background or a European man wearing a *sola topi*. One ad relied on the image of a bearded Indian raja, a figure the advertisers sought to associate with power and wisdom.[81]

In 1929, JWT took over the account for Horlicks in India, and the effort put into formulating ads geared to Indian consumers clearly increased. Under JWT, Horlicks at first centered its campaign around two issues. First, there was a stress on the health of children, most often boys. As this theme was developed, the ads increasingly deployed a comic strip sequence, which allowed them to depict characters before and after taking Horlicks. One frequently run ad (Figure 3.11, here in a Gujarati version), for instance, depicts a boy who always comes in last in school games, and who is a major source of worry to his parents. By the last frame of the cartoon, the boy, after taking Horlicks, is pictured finishing first in a race. The campaign drew upon medical theories of enervation, which was depicted as a major cause of physical and academic non-achievement among children.

The second theme stressed was convalescence. Ads repeatedly portrayed Horlicks as a tonic food that would provide the nourishment needed to recover from lengthy illnesses. According to one JWT report, the two targets of children and the bed-ridden "were undoubtedly good specific markets since Indians really will spend money for their children and there are always a convalescent group who are immediate buyers."[82]

By 1937, JWT officers, perhaps prompted by the competition with Ovaltine, which was running a campaign in India urging women to provide the product to their husbands and children as a way of upholding family health (see Chapter 4), seemingly decided the Horlicks appeals were too narrow and turned to the middle-class man and anxieties connected to the office workplace. The new advertisements drew on prevailing notions about male weakness, but linked this theme to uncertainties about unemployment and professional advancement, a pervasive concern during the Depression.[83] At the same time, they evoked the ideology of the middle-class householder and his responsibilities in a medicalized conception of the conjugal family.

Horlicks advertisers quickly came to link the new approach to the slogan of "night starvation," an international theme inaugurated in Britain around 1931 but seemingly not applied in India before 1937. In Europe, the Night Starvation campaign had stressed the supposed value of taking Horlicks before bedtime to enable a good night's sleep so that the user would have energy to carry out daytime tasks. JWT, however, clearly found it difficult to translate this slogan into culturally meaningful terms in India, where starvation was not a metaphor but a reality. In English-language ads, the term night starvation was included but a translation into a local vernacular (in Roman letters) was then included, as the following images illustrate. The various translations (such as *savarni kamjori* in Gujarati) actually meant "morning weakness," thus alluding

Figure 3.11 "We were so worried about Chandrakant until . . .," Horlicks, *MS*, September 16, 1936, 7. Produced with permission of Hindustan Unilever Limited.

to the concept of male weakness, with its implication of sexual shortcomings. The value of the product in promoting sleep was mentioned only rarely.

Most night starvation ads, which were extensively run in papers across India, came to follow a common narrative in their cartoon sequences, one developed on the subcontinent. They featured a worn-out middle-class male figure failing at work, whose boss, sometimes a European, scolds him for poor performance. Often after advice from a third party, he seeks out a doctor, who diagnoses him as suffering from "night starvation" and urges him to take Horlicks daily. In the last frame, reinvigorated, he has achieved success and has won a promotion or has avoided being sacked. In one ad (Figure 3.12), for instance, a shipping clerk cannot keep up with his work due to his tiredness before he discovers Horlicks, which enables him to manage his job easily. Other ads featured railway officials, police inspectors, lawyers, government clerks, and film directors. There was even a hockey player from Jhansi. Men in these ads often wore spectacles, a sign of their midde-class status and of non-manual employment.

Figure 3.12 "Shipping Clerk's Failure Through NIGHT STARVATION," Horlicks, *BC*, August 6, 1939. 9. Produced with permission of Hindustan Unilever Limited.

In these ads, failures in the job world were sometimes explicitly linked with ideals of companionate marriage and the family. In "The Young Broker's Tragedy," the sequence begins with a young man talking with his beloved, professing his worry that her father will not let them marry because his earnings as a jute contractor are too low (Figure 3.13). In the second frame, the young man blames his shortcomings in business on his lack of vitality and energy. After consulting a doctor, he starts to take Horlicks every night. Soon after beginning this regimen, he wins a major contract from a jute firm. Three months later, we see the young couple prosperous and happily married.[84] The cartoon ends in a romantic setting, where the man, now invigorated by his daily consumption of Horlicks, professes his happiness at his successful marriage. His new wife praises him, saying "you are so clever and full of vitality." In using the term "vitality" (translated as *utsahi* or enthusiasm in Gujarati versions), the ad invoked a word used widely in vernacular tonic ads to suggest sexual capacity. The last frame of the ad, set in a romantic garden, seems to draw from cinematic motifs.

In some cases, the potential failure to keep a job or to achieve a promotion was tied to the possibility the male involved might be unable to meet familial obligations.

Figure 3.13 "Clever Young Broker's Tragedy Due to Night Starvation," Horlicks, *BC*, October 2, 1939, 9. Produced with permission of Hindustan Unilever Limited.

In Figure 3.14, a man laments that because of his own constant weakness, he is likely to be denied a promotion he needs to afford a good education for his son. After he begins taking Horlicks, the son's schooling is asssured.[85] The man in the ad is marked as middle-class and a Maharashtrian Brahman, through his clothes, spectacles, and the surname of Kelkar (another character is called Sen, an upper-caste Bengali name). In another Horlicks cartoon sequence, a father fails to perform expected roles in the home; because he is always tired and grumpy, the children avoid him rather than join him in play. The sequence ends with a rejuvenated father whose kids love to spend time with him.[86] In stressing a man's role in the recreational life of the family, the ad suggests an aspect of conjugal fatherhood that has yet to be explored by historians.

JWT placed these ads in English-language papers such as the *Bombay Chronicle* but also had them translated for publication in vernacular papers in western India (as well as elsewhere in South Asia). In such cases, the visual images were the same in Gujarati, Marathi, and English versions. A key difference is that the translations avoided mention of "night starvation" altogether, referring only to morning weakness. The advertising firm clearly monitored the rest of the translation carefully, making sure a close

Figure 3.14 "His child's future nearly ruined by NIGHT STARVATION," Horlicks *BC*, August 5, 1939, 16. Produced with permission of Hindustan Unilever Limited.

equivalence to the English-language original was maintained, but the naming of characters was often brought into conformity with regional usages. In the "Shipping Clerk's Failure Through Night Starvation" (Figure 3.12 in English and Figure 3.15 in Marathi), the key character in the strip has no name in English, is referred to as Raman in Gujarati and Ramrao in Marathi (most commonly, an upper-caste name). In other ads, names in the English version suggesting origins from different parts of India, such as Kelkar (Maharashtra) and Sen (Bengal), were replaced by Surendra and Rasik in Gujarati versions. Following common Gujarati usage, the ads used given names rather than family names. The English word "weakness" was translated in these ads as *kamjori*

Figure 3.15 "Shipping Clerk's Failure Through Night Starvation (Marathi version)," Horlicks, *Kesari*, January 13, 1938, 3. Produced with permission of Hindustan Unilever Limited.

and the word "vitality" was translated variously as *shakti* (energy) and *utsahi* (enthusiasm), all terms possessed double meanings (that is, non-sexual and sexual).

Advertising specialists with JWT placed in English papers like the *Times of India* clearly designed quite different kinds of Horlicks advertisements for expatriates.[87] The slogan of "night starvation" was featured in these ads while "morning weakness" was not mentioned, and the subjects of endangered masculinity and the insecurity of employment were absent. A common theme was the importance of functioning properly within expatriate social circles. One ad stressed the significance of a European woman's ability to entertain her husband's business clients at dinner parties (see Figure 3.16). Before taking Horlicks, she was too tired to do so, and her husband risked losing a client's business to competitors. After making Horlicks part of her daily regimen, she so charms the client that her husband's success is ensured![88] Another theme stressed in Horlicks ads for expatriates was the climate, as we have already seen in "Young Couple Almost Separated" (Figure 2.5).[89]

In short then, formulaic aspects of J. Walter Thompson's global campaign for Horlicks such as the comic strip format and the slogan of "night starvation" were adapted considerably in India after their introduction. Horlicks advertisers on the

Figure 3.16 "Wife Nearly Becomes a Burden through NIGHT STARVATION," Horlicks, *Times of India*, April 15, 1939, 17. Produced with permission of Hindustan Unilever Limited.

subcontinent clearly calculated that the theme of workplace anxiety would be one that would resonate widely among Indian middle-class men from different communities and in different regions. The ads built upon entrenched perceptions of the male, middle-class body as weak, enervated and lacking vitality, but stretched these perceptions from the realms of military activity, physical culture and politics into the office and the nuclear household. In the context of the Depression, advertising professionals sought to give their appeals a special emotive power by linking the crisis in the middle-class workplace with failure to live up to the expectations of husbandhood and fatherhood, manufacturing male identities suitable for productive office workers, committed consumers and responsible household heads.

Conclusion

The global manufacturers of tonics entered a commercial environment characterized by the proliferation of vernacular commodities claiming to invigorate the Indian male. During most of the 1920s, they typically did not differentiate in their advertising strategy between Europeans and the Indian middle class, using approaches that placed them at a serious disadvantage to their vernacular competitors; their general abstinence from the sexual potency business effectively meant relinquishing much of the local market to the products of the bazaar. But by the early 1930s, multinational producers, no longer satisfied with their position in the expatriate market, increasingly sought to move in on the territory occupied by local producers and to target the middle-class male. They stepped up their advertising efforts, increasingly inserting their publicity in a wide range of media, including both English-language and vernacular newspapers.

The advent of professional advertising gave tonic producers international techniques of formulating copy and advertisement design. But as the evolution of the verbal and visual form of advertisements suggests, they came to regard such imported methods as insufficient. Like the character of Markham in *Monsoon,* they began to appropriate the pervasive, polysemic language of masculine weakness and vitality that their bazaar competitors had long utilized; Indian subordinates, translators, and artists no doubt contributed significantly to this transformation. The new campaigns developed a two-track approach, using different logics for the middle class and for European expatriates, as the comparisons between different Stearns, Sanatogen and Horlicks ads clearly illustrate.

Professional advertisers especially introduced innovations into tonic ads by fusing the language of weakness to anxieties about the social reproduction of the middle-class family and survival in the middle-class workplace. Perpetuating the modern conjugal home and succeeding in the colonial job world, they implicitly and sometimes explicitly argued, required overcoming the educated middle-class male's "weakness." Advertisers drew upon a wide range of conceptions from a vast vernacular field, but transformed these conceptions through creative juxtapositions with notions rooted in the idea of the modern family, hoping to make Indian husbands and fathers into consumer-subjects ready to buy brand-name tonics.

4

Advertising and the Female Consumer: Feluna, Ovaltine, and Beauty Soaps[1]

Soon after he joined Lever Brothers in 1937, a young Prakash Tandon began his participation on the first major marketing survey in India based upon household research. This survey involved a small team of female interviewers asking middle-class housewives in several Indian cities about their soap preferences. A set of adventurous young women, including several Christians, defied social conventions and conducted the interviews, visiting households of people they did not know before. Previously Levers' executives had been convinced that in India men controlled family choices about consumption. Tandon concurred. But Tandon's supervisor on the project, Thompson Walker, who possessed considerable experience analyzing soap consumption worldwide, was convinced otherwise. Tandon argued with Walker: "I explained to him that our Indian housewife always deferred to her husband, for she had been brought up traditionally to look to him for decisions. I grew quite eloquent about the classical training of girls as future wives, the place of the husband as lord of the house, while she is its *devi*, *grihalaxmi*, the goddess of the home, demure, submissive and deferential to her master." Walker countered: "If from that you conclude that she is so submissive as to leave all decisions to the husband, you are mistaken. I bet she not only has much to say, but it is she only who decides most things in the home. What she wants, like women anywhere in the world, she gets, including her soap." He instructed the team of interviewers to press further after receiving the stock answer: "husband chooses." Tandon recounts the housewives' response in his autobiography: "The result was funny and demolished me. At the very first call Ada [one of the interviewers] made, the housewife as usual said 'husband chooses.' Ada began to probe as instructed. Suddenly a light dawned on the woman's face and she said quite simply, 'Oh I see what you mean. My husband chooses, but of course I tell him what to choose.'"[2]

Soon after the survey's completion, Levers began to develop advertising campaigns targeting housewives, an indication that the company quickly applied its discovery of female centrality in decision-making. In arriving at this new strategy, the firm was participating in a broader trend. Advertisers of many other products had already concluded, usually without formal market research, that it was critical to address women in their campaigns. The 1930s was a watershed in this respect, marking the dramatic advent of the female consumer in the multinationals' marketing efforts.

This chapter examines advertisements centering on women for three kinds of commodities: (1) Feluna, a South African medical product widely sold in India; (2) Ovaltine, a hot drink product; and (3) Lux and Pears soaps (both sold by Levers). Ads for these commodities focused around three different themes: female health, domesticity, and beauty. In each case, this chapter shows, campaigns initially formulated outside the subcontinent were seriously modified or sacrificed altogether in India. The cultural strategies used by multinational firms clearly reflected an effort to adapt to emerging discourses about Indian middle-class domesticity, a key dimension of conjugality.

The event of woman in twentieth-century western India

The focus on women in 1930s advertisements was not an inevitable outcome of sex difference. Instead the ground had been prepared for this development by decades of discursive attention in India to the category of "woman." Writing on the emergence of female-focused advertising in China, Tani Barlow has argued that what she calls the "historical catachresis *women*" was an historical novelty or "event" that "requires explaining the conditions under which its having been thought became possible."[3] Barlow traces this development to broader historical processes as the category of woman became crucial to the construction of Chinese modernity and as advertisers came to understand China in light of a "vernacular sociology" in which women played crucial parts. In Chinese advertising, she shows, woman assumed an iconic visual form, that of a "modern girl" with short hair surrounded by objects of advanced technology, Western books, and, of course, advertised commodities.[4]

In India, too, the imagination of modernity hinged on the women's question. The major reformist thinkers of western India, such as Justice Mahadev Ranade and his wife Ramabai Ranade, Pandita Ramabai, and Dhondo Keshav Karve, devoted considerable attention to what they regarded as the abject position of high-caste women, epitomized in low levels of female education, the early age of marriage, social seclusion, and prohibitions against widow remarriage.[5] Some reforming efforts were led by men, and were often preoccupied with what Indian women's "backward" condition suggested about the state of Indian civilization. As Meera Kosambi has shown, however, a set of Indian feminists also emerged, operating mainly as individuals in the late nineteenth century,[6] and as part of larger women's organizations in the twentieth.[7] Western India figured prominently in these developments. The All-India Women's Conference, the most important feminist organization of the time, was founded in Poona. A central focus of all these movements was the view that women's position in Indian society needed "reform" and such reform was critical to making the nation modern.

By the early twentieth century, these developments started to influence gender conceptions deeper in middle-class society. Among high-caste city-dwellers, for instance, the age of marriage began to rise steadily, seclusion disappeared as a social practice, and schooling for women became the norm.[8] For ordinary middle-class women, one of the most widespread consequences of reforming efforts was the formulation of new norms of domesticity based in the nuclear family. According to the dominant perspective, the middle-class housewife was to be educated, to be freed extensively from joint-family strictures, to be released from seclusion and to participate, modestly, in new forms of public life. At the same time, she was expected to refrain from embracing "western" social values, which nationalist discourse viewed as signs of moral decay, including forms of public sociality involving interaction with men outside the family or ostentatious consumer expenditures. Finally, she was to exercise significant new responsibilities in the household, serving her husband and taking care of her children.[9] Modern women were to possess considerable authority—independent of male elders, mothers-in-law and other senior women, and sometimes even their own husbands—in matters falling within the home.

Articles in the *Kanara Saraswat* stressed that the housewife was to be married but only after her schooling had been completed, to guard her reputation fastidiously, and to serve as an intellectual and emotional companion of her husband. An educated Saraswat woman, one author wrote, "would make a better housewife and would influence the life of the household and the people around her to a much greater extent than one who is not similarly qualified."[10] The article insisted, however, that she should not seek to compete with men in the job world, and criticized the tendency the author found present among Christians for women to work as typists, saleswomen and shop assistants.[11] According to another author, women would "lose their most precious possession—'womanliness'"[12] if they sought employment, though he allowed for the possibility that a few jobs would not interfere with the happiness of home life or male employment opportunities. Saraswat male and female commentators both reasoned that the duty of a woman was to manage the home, a realm often depicted as being of equal importance to the work world dominated by men.[13] "The Grahini [housewife]," a Saraswat woman argued, "will always be the dominating ideal of the Hindus. The conservation of the home—the haven of rest, the centre of happiness and usefulness, is a sacred necessity. Motherhood is a supreme privilege and is the most responsible institute in the world of human affairs."[14] Child care, especially looking after children's health, was a particularly critical task. Women also played a central role in building their offspring's moral qualities. Woman's duty, one author reasoned, "is … to mould the character of future citizens of the world in this miniature parliament [the family]. The atmosphere of the house should be such that boys and girls should be brought up with the idea that the home is a sacred place and in it the behavior of the parents should be exemplary."[15]

Articles in women's journals such as the Gujarati *Stri Bodh* and the Marathi journal *Stri Masik* often echoed these understandings. *Stri Masik*'s publication during the 1930s and 1940s, its high production values and its regular inclusion of well-designed ads, many submitted by multinational firms, was an indication of the expanding readership of women's journals and the recognition of women's market potential. It often advanced "progressive" stances, such as the value of women's education, the importance of men helping with domestic tasks in the home, and greater economic freedom for women. But it also published articles focusing on women's domestic duties and obligations. Poems in the magazine praising the housewife articulated ideals for all married women to follow. One such poem (converted here to prose form) ran:

> The true housewife is the one who makes her home happy with her intelligence. She is the one who makes everyone happy and satisfied in family life. It doesn't matter whether her husband is rich or poor. She is the one who is always satisfied and happy and faces every problem with determination and with a smile on her face. She is the one who teaches good habits and passes on culture to her children and makes them good human beings.[16]

The new ideology of domesticity gave wives a significant role in shaping the family's material practices. Abigail McGowan stresses two especially relevant aspects. First, middle-class housewives were to assume considerable control over household budgets, managing family expenses even though the husband supplied the necessary income. Articles in women's journals and other media provided extensive instruction to women about household budgeting.[17] Wives were expected to make sure that the expenditures needed to sustain health, education, and servants' wages were met without exceeding familial means. In practice the housewife's financial authority was circumscribed by continued cultural limitations on women's participation in shopping and by the power of husbands as income-earners. Second, as noted in Chapter 2, women were to exercise significant self-restraint in their acquisitions. Nationalist discourse discouraged women from using foreign goods, and frowned upon signs of display, luxury, and ostentation on their part.[18]

An increased appreciation of women's role in determining family consumption practices came to inform advertising campaigns. In Levers this conclusion may have arisen from its 1938 marketing survey. Other firms had recognized the role of women in household decision-making well before this time, and geared their campaigns accordingly.[19] Ads often steeped their sales appeals in the ideology of domesticity, emphasizing that a woman's role as manager of family finance and upholder of family health, as a person who shaped her children's character and their chances of achieving educational and professional success, required her to buy the advertised commodity. Evocation of the conjugal model conveyed the necessity (as opposed to the luxury) of adopting certain commodities.

Visually, advertising linked itself to these discourses, not only appealing to women as decision-makers in matters of consumption, but also drawing upon and reinforcing the pressing new ideals of reformed womanhood and domesticity. Advertising increasingly came to forge an image of the modern Indian housewife through a set of verbal and visual conventions that emerged through experimentation over time. The iconic *grahini* came to be represented as clad in a sari, sometimes pulled over her hair, to convey her personal modesty and her thoroughly Indian identity (sometimes reflected in regionally specific forms). If her head was uncovered, flowers might be tied in her hair, symbolizing the desire to bring happiness to her husband and family.[20] The sari depicted usually represented a modern style (typically six yards in length) made of cotton with a modest border, one befitting a woman who managed a household budget with frugality and prudent judgment. She wore a marriage mark on her forehead, limited makeup, lipstick and simple jewelry, perhaps some modest earrings and a couple of bangles. The light color of the newspaper page, rather than black or some shade of grey, was used to depict her skin color, clearly suggesting fairness and potentially distinguishing her from middle-class images of lower-class communities. Artists in western India were careful to mark her as Hindu or Parsi, clearly avoiding sartorial or facial features that might suggest Muslimness, thereby precluding the possibility of identifications across "communal" lines. In some ads, the husband and/or children (either a son or a son and a daughter) would be pictured in the visual frame as the beneficiaries of her efforts. Members of the joint family were typically absent, unless their inclusion might draw further attention to the conjugal relationship (a picture of a mother-in-law, for instance, might symbolize potential pressures for the housewife to overcome, as we shall see in Chapter 5).

While the housewife became the predominant female image in advertisements, a second, more radical trope was introduced in India: the model of the "modern girl." As the Modern Girl around the World Research Group has discovered, the concept was a global one, stretching from North America and Europe to South Africa, Japan, and China. Modern girls, they have shown, "wore sexy clothes and high heels; they applied lipstick and other cosmetics. Dressed in provocative attire and in hot pursuit of romantic love, Modern Girls appeared on the surface to disregard the prescribed roles of dutiful daughter, wife and mother."[21] Though the modern girl image was represented differently in different cultural contexts—a short flapper dress might indicate the modern girl in North America, a tight *qi pao* in China—they were typically signaled by short hair, the use of modern cosmetics and cigarette-smoking, and they were often connected to the possibilities of romance or even sex.

Indians were exposed extensively to the concept of the modern girl during the interwar period through advertisement, film, and observations of European expatriates. The Bombay cinema during the 1930s produced a host of films featuring women who challenged gender stereotypes, wore unconventional clothing, chose their own romantic partners and even engaged in athletic exertions for instance, in horseback chase scenes.[22] Certainly some vernacular advertisers experimented with the concept. For example, Figure 4.1, an ad for a uterine tonic named Stri-Mitra (a woman's friend) provides a hybrid image of a young woman with a modern hair-style (one that at first appears to be short hair but on closer examination is tied back) and lipstick, dressed in a modest six-yard sari, though she is also clearly marked as married through her *mangal sutra* (necklace) and *bindi* (forehead mark). In effect a kind of competition developed between two ideal types that were both derived from global models, of the modern girl on the one hand and the modern housewife on the other. The modern girl became the subject of some controversy. Some Indian leaders condemned the figure of the modern girl. Gandhi on one occasion wrote critically "I have a fear that the modern girl loves to play Juliet to half a dozen Romeos. She loves adventure . . . dresses not to protect herself but to attract attention. She improves upon nature by painting herself and looking extraordinary."[23] In the context of growing nationalism, which frowned upon "westernized" behavior and the desire to maintain the company of unrelated men, the modern girl concept gained only a somewhat temporary and limited traction in advertising culture.

Figure 4.1 "Stri-Mitra (A Woman's Friend)," *Stri Masik*, September 1933, A-2.

Cultural opposition to the modern girl concept profoundly influenced marketing campaigns of multinational companies. As we shall see, advertisements for Feluna and Ovaltine addressed to the middle class came to steer away from this model, though the same companies were heavily invested in it elsewhere in the world and among expatriates. When the trope of the modern girl was deployed, as sometimes happened in beauty product advertisement, it was usually done in a muted form that would not evoke the same sense of independence, sexuality, and romance reflected in representations from China and other world contexts. By contrast, the dominant advertising approaches of brand-name corporations often came to dovetail with the concept of the modern housewife, who was to embody principles of an enlightened conjugality in her concern with health, the raising of children along scientific lines, and the sound management of the household but whose activities outside the home and family were carefully circumscribed.

Feluna, "the female constitution," and conjugality

The development of medical commodities targeted to address women's health became highly conspicuous during the interwar period. As with ads for men's tonics, the emergence of medicines oriented toward women and their health issues was a response to the middle-class demand for "self-medication" through use of commercial products. Consulting a local specialist or biomedical doctor might involve revealing embarrassing information about a woman's physical state, such as irregularity of periods, infertility, and sexual infirmities. Use of commercial products could be discrete but also scientific and modern in appearance.

The logic used in advertisements for women's medicines was shaped by reforming discourses and the emerging conception of conjugality. Arguments about women's bodies, for instance, were critical in debates over the age of marriage. The main contention raised by advocates of increasing the legal age of marriage or consent during the 1920s was actually a eugenic one, that is, that childbirth to females who had not reached adulthood would result in weak, sickly babies and thus undercut the fitness of the next generation.[24] Embedded in this argument was a logic insisting that mothers needed to be hardy women who had reached maturity. Urban middle-class life, with its sedentary character, was also depicted as a threat to the health of women's bodies. A writer in the *Kanara Saraswat* noted that:

> Our women living in Bombay look more refined and may be more educated . . . But that is not all. Can they live long and bear the strain of a family life? Decidedly not. Most of our women fall easy prey to consumption and other diseases and consumption is spreading like wildfire, both among men and women and especially the latter. Women are more prone to this scourge on account of their sedentary lives, and they have to live their whole lives confined to their small rooms in a barrack-like place called a "chawl." It is dirty, noisy, ill-ventilated and evil-smelling. Our women depend mostly on servants for their housework . . . It is hard work that keeps up the health.[25]

New notions of domesticity may have specially influenced the social construction of menstruation. Menstruation had conventionally been viewed among the upper castes as a polluting activity, one to be experienced in the company of women away from the larger household. Reforming discourses questioned the norms of seclusion while principles of modern medicine challenged the notion that exposure to menstruation posed a danger to male health. There was no reason, the logic of modernity suggested, that menstruating women should not participate in public life. Practically, when families lived in chawls or small flats with one room for sleeping, women could not be easily insulated from male family members.

By the 1920s, local capitalists in western India had developed numerous medical commodities that promised to address women's health. Such companies ran ads extensively in vernacular newspapers. Three themes feature prominently in these ads. First, they depicted women's bodies as constitutionally exposed to pain and susceptible to a range of ailments; medical ads typically promised to address a whole range of conditions a female might experience. For instance, advertisements for "Sundarisathi" sold by Dave Chemical and Pharmaceutical Works in Bombay promised to address any kind of pain, including those related to irregular menstruation, urinary problems, hand and foot pain, general lassitude, hysteria, and uterine disorders. The ad printed testimonials from about a dozen individuals, claiming that both Western doctors and Ayurvedic *vaids* used the product.[26] Ads for a medicine offered by Gangabai Pranshankar, a pioneering female entrepreneur from Ahmedabad who also established a branch in Bombay, claimed to address a similar range of maladies, also offering testimonials.[27] A Gujarati ad for "Ambrosia" pictured a woman in agony with hands in her face, and asked the reader: "Why should you needlessly suffer pain?" before again running through a litany of ailments that the medicine claimed to address.[28] Menstrual difficulties were prominent in some of these ads. The Chinese Medical Store in Bombay, for instance, ran a Marathi ad for Chi King Ki, picturing a woman suffering alone within the household, with a text indicating that menstrual problems were one of the most important questions of female life (Figure 4.2). A prone female, enduring pain privately while others went on with their lives, was a common visual trope in such advertisements.

Vernacular ads for women's medicines sometimes offered to provide assistance with infertility and the rigors of childbirth. The above-mentioned Sundarisathi ad indicated that "if a woman has no offspring, she will certainly be able to bear children [after taking the product]"; testimonials followed from men whose wives gave birth after taking Sundarisathi.[29] Similarly, an ad placed in an Ahmedabad newspaper by Gangabai for a product named Garbharashak, promised to prevent premature births and weaknesses during pregnancy, assuring the mother that she could reach full term.[30]

Ads for multinational products came to draw upon the logic of these vernacular appeals, but often came to link this logic explicitly to concepts of domesticity and conjugality. By far the most widely advertised medical commodity for women during the late 1920s through the late 1930s was Feluna, which was manufactured and distributed by Graham Remedies, a South African company. The medicine, originally created in 1908, apparently included iron and may have been intended originally to address anaemia. But it was rarely marketed exclusively on this basis; it was sold everywhere as a general medicine for a wide range of ailments, though always for "females only." By the 1920s, Feluna was in effect a global commodity, sold extensively in Africa and India.

In South Africa and other settler colonies, Feluna's marketers had clearly devoted an extensive budget to advertising. During the 1920s and 1930s, many ads were apparently designed in South Africa before being sent to other colonies without modification; some ads in the *Cape Times* published in Cape Town and *The Rhodesian Herald*, for instance, were identical. Many of these English-language ads drew upon a concept of imperial domesticity, that is, a view of the European woman's role in the home as critical to the preservation of the family and the safeguarding of the imperial race.[31] Imperial domesticity not only provided European populations living abroad with a sense of comfort—the colonial housewife was responsible for the creation of "European" spaces in the home—but also served to separate and distinguish the settler from the "native," and furnished a social glue that obscured class differences among Europeans.[32]

Figure 4.2 "A highly important issue related to a woman's life," Chi King Ki, Chinese Medical Store, *Kirloskar*, July 1939, 1174.

Drawing upon these cultural priorities, Feluna advertisements emphasized the importance of carrying out household tasks, bearing healthy children, and performing as mothers. One ad in the *Cape Times*, for instance, stressed Feluna's value in ensuring successful motherhood. Entitled "May I See Your Baby?" the ad goes on to say: "Despite all the birth-control talk, married people, especially women, want children of their own. Do you doubt it?" The ad then claimed "there are many women in South Africa who have been lifted from the tragedy of thwarted Motherhood to a realization of their cherished goals by Feluna. This preparation, compounded for females, has probably corrected a weakness, stimulated certain glands, regulated functions or conditions which put them internally 'out of step' with Nature."[33]

Most Feluna ads addressed to Europeans in South Africa, however, featured single, "modern girls" outside familial roles, including engagement in athletic activity such as tennis, swimming, and golf. An ad from the *Cape Times*, for instance, pictures a female character watching others at tennis after playing a disappointing match, suggesting she could never live up to her potential as an athlete: "Real tennis is not a *pat-a-cake* game. It calls for speed and stamina. Weaklings can't stand the pace. If Feluna Iron had given the girl the extra strength *plus energy* springing from rich quality blood, . . . there would have been a *drive* behind her racquet that would have made her hard to beat" (italics in ad).[34] The figure of the sportswoman, an important manifestation of the modern girl, addressed the desires of a new generation of women motivated by notions of individual accomplishment outside the family context.

Other ads focused on modern girls seeking to participate in forms of white sociality—parties, dances, etc.—where young men would also be present, and evoked anxieties about the possibility of failing to execute this participation successfully. Typically the women in the ads possessed short hair or a "perm" and wore flapper dresses and hats that reflected modern, glamorous styles. In Figure 4.3, a white woman standing in front of a mirror in her slip—a form of undergarment reflecting a break with the tight corsets and bustles of earlier periods—laments that despite her eager preparations for a dance, she would not enjoy the occasion because of "an old sex enemy" (presumably, her period).

Feluna ads also began to be published in South African papers with a predominantly black readership. The *Bantu World*, for example, ran ads in several African languages, including Sesotho, Xhosa, and Zulu. But these advertisements carried a different focus, claiming to meet the cultural priorities of literate blacks; the newspaper mentioned in one notice that it had "a highly qualified staff of Native translators," as well as advisors willing to suggest "copy of particular appeal to the Native Mind," both free of charge.[35] Visually, the ads featured images intended to be meaningful to black South Africans, such as village scenes or a maternity room in a mission hospital. While all the ads concerned issues of women's health, they were often addressed to male household heads. Figure 4.4 includes a two-frame comic strip sequence, and is directed to South African husbands.

The first of the frames features an urban couple who have come to the woman's village because of her failure to bear children; the husband is returning her to her father in exchange for the dowry. The father instead advises the couple to take a course of Feluna to overcome childlessness. In the second frame, the couple have come back a year later with a baby. As the South Africa specialist Peter Quella noted in viewing this ad, it would have been somewhat unusual that a young man would discuss such a matter directly with his father-in-law rather than going through an intermediary; this feature may have been intended to indicate the actors' modernity. Clearly the ad brought up a concern common to both whites and blacks—that of reproduction—but did so by placing this concern in a setting potentially evocative for literate blacks. In another Sesotho ad, Feluna is advertised as treating a variety of female bodily problems brought on by the stresses of modern life. It pictures a heavyset woman surrounded by material objects that perhaps suggested prosperity, but also in a state of serious discomfort. The ad stresses that Feluna addresses a wide range of ailments of "pains, tragedies and debilities."[36] The artistic styles in *Bantu World* ads also contrast strongly with ads oriented to Europeans, as is self-evident from these examples.[37]

Figure 4.3 "I *did* want this to be one of my *good* nights," Feluna Pills, *Cape Times*, July 8, 1935, 6.

In the 1920s, Graham Remedies came to develop a significant campaign for Feluna in India. Feluna first found an audience among Indians living in Natal, who sometimes wrote their kinfolk in India about the pills' supposed benefits. The company later reported that before 1925 "we received an occasional enquiry and then a growing volume of orders from India" before the company had done any advertising on the subcontinent. Then "Indian wholesalers wrote asking for trade terms, saying they were having persistent enquiries for this line." In 1926, Graham Remedies made deals with

O Ne a Batla Hore a Khutlisetsoe Bohali Ba Hae.

Mosali eo oa batho o ne ale mahlomeng ha monna oa hae are o mo khutlisetsa ha habo ho ntatae. O ne a lebeletse ka mahlo a matso ho bona hore na li Feluna Pills ha li tlo mo thusa na.

Re ka bolela ka 'nete le ka bótsepehi bohle hore re na le makholo-kholo a mangolo a tsoang ho batsuali ba bolelang kamoo li Feluna Pills li ba entseng hore ba fumane bana ha ba ne ba se ba tetse ho ka fumana nguana. Feluna, tabeng tse joalo, e hlasimolotse setho se neng se fokola kapa se sa sebetse ka tsuanelo. Feluna e fihlile ea tsosolosa ea matlafatsa setho seo 'me mokhoa oa hlaho, ka thuso eo, oa etsa hore ho fumanehe nguana eo ba neng ba mo lakatsa ba mo lebeletse hakalo.

Hape li Feluna li lisa bophelo bohle ba mosali. Lipilisi tsena lia eketsa 'me li nchafatsa mali hore abe mafubeli hantle. Ke ka lebaka leo mosali ea sebelisang Feluna a bang le bophelo bo tletseng bo khothetseng, a bang le thabo 'me a ratehang. O ikutlua a phetse hantle me basali ba felang ba phetse hantle ho monate ho lula le bona.

Haeba lipontso tse latelang tsena li teng ho uena li supa hore u ka fumana thuso ka ho sebelisa li Feluna Pills:—

Ho fokolloa ke mali, Mokhathala, Ho fokola, Ho sokela, Lehatlelo le lesoeu, Mahlo a lerotho, Mokokotlo, Mahlaba ha u ile khueling, Ho pipitleloa, Ho bona linaleli mahlong, Molikoalikoane, Hlooho e opang, Ho nyeka pelo, Nyooko le likhathatso tsa mala.

Re hatisa lengolo leo re le amohetseng ho Ezekiel Nkosi, oa P.O. Karino, Transvaal, eleng le leng la a mangata a mona ofising ea rona.

"Ho felile lilemo tse tharo ke nyetse mosali oa ka pele re fumana nguana oa rona oa matsibolo. Ke ne ke hlomohile ke bile ke hopola ho mo khutlisetsa ho batsuali ba hae. Empa motsualle, e mong a re eletsa hore a sebelise li Feluna Pills, a etsa joalo. Ho makaleng ha ka ho hololo le thabong eaba o nka mpa kamorao ho likhueli tse 'ne 'me a ntsualla nguana e motle ea nonneng oa nguanana. Kapa eleng ho hlaha ha nguana kapa eleng lipilisi ke sitoa ho ka hlalosa feela haele bophelo ba hae bo bile botle haholo ha esale a qala ho sebelisa li Feluna. Kajeno re na le bana ba bararo; banana ba babeli le moshemane ale mong. Kaofela ha bona ba phetse hantle ba matla."

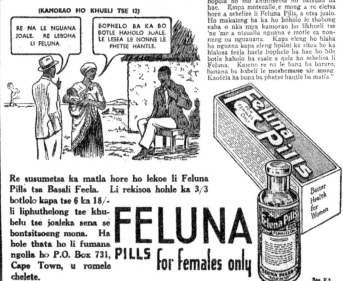

Re susumetsa ka matla hore ho lekoe li Feluna Pills tsa Basali Feela. Li rekisoa hohle ka 3/3 botlolo kapa tse 6 ka 18/- li liphuthelong tse khubelu tse joaleka sena se bontsitsoeng mona. Ha hole thata ho li fumana ngolla ho P.O. Box 731, Cape Town, u romele chelete.

FELUNA PILLS for females only

Better Health for Women

Sea. P.I.

Figure 4.4 "O Ne A Batla Hore A Khutlisetose Bohali Ba Hae," Feluna Pills, *Bantu World*, October 20, 1934, 13.

agents in Bombay, Calcutta, Rangoon, Karachi, Columbo, and Madras to sell Feluna, and arranged contracts with Indian newspapers to publish advertisements. In 1928, the commodity was distributed in western India by the firm of Patel and Dhondy of Bombay, who advertised it in both English-language and vernacular newspapers.[38]

At first, such ads were probably drawn up in South Africa and then exported to India for placement in English-language newspapers or for translation in vernacular papers. The company did not always differentiate in its advertising oriented to expatriates and those geared to middle-class consumers. A few ads in vernacular languages featured Indian figures; more commonly they simply retained European images used in English-language versions. For instance, an ad translated into Gujarati in the *Mumbai Samachar* in 1927 pictured European women in three different periods of life—youth, motherhood, and old age—touting the advantages of Feluna in each stage.[39]

Other Feluna ads published in English-language papers in India targeted unmarried expatriate women, evoking the importance of thriving socially within European mixed-gender parties, echoing the ads oriented toward South African whites.[40] Advertisements with this theme were never published in vernacular papers; one suspects that local commercial agents placing the ads pointed out that they would have been deemed irrelevant or even scandalous in Indian middle-class society, where families closely guarded the reputations of unmarried females. Otherwise advertisers' efforts to calibrate Feluna ads to the concerns of Indian buyers were limited.

By the early 1930s, however, Graham Remedies was formulating targeted campaigns that sharply distinguished expatriate and Indian consumers. Some ads in English-language papers continued to address the priorities of imperial domesticity or the concerns of "modern girls" with parties and sports. In some cases ads with these themes designed in South Africa were simply reproduced in India. One such ad, captioned "Admiration: Every Woman Craves It," also published in both locations, explicitly linked the beauty culture of the modern girl—mentioning "lipstick, face cream, powder, rouge," a "perm," "eyes," "nails," "teeth," "breath," "dress fashions"—to issues of female health.[41]

Feluna ads directed toward the middle class were no doubt developed in conversation with Indian actors, such as traders, translators, and artists.[42] These advertisements, seemingly poached from the logic used in the ads of vernacular firms, emphasizing for instance Feluna's special value in overcoming female ailments, including menstrual difficulties. They distinguished themselves from bazaar ads in their explicit efforts to evoke values of modern conjugality. The visual images stuck close to the iconic Indian housewife, picturing a woman marked as modern but whose primary obligations lay with her family and childcare.

The rhetorical contours of these advertisements have been discussed by Amita Kulkarni.[43] In the early 1930s, they often addressed the husband most directly, reflecting the assumption that the Indian male was the person who controlled family purse strings. They portrayed husbands as figures who also bore special obligations to guard their wives' health, but ones who needed schooling to understand the pain women endured regularly. "Your wife—is she suffering?" ran one ad, "It is your duty to give her Feluna made specially to combat weakness in women and to build up a sound healthy feminine constitution." Drawing upon eugenic reasoning, the ad linked conjugal concerns with India's well-being: "And to you as husband, we ask you of the enormous influence Feluna must wield, through the mother's improved inner-health and vitality, towards producing robust children instead of those delicate weaklings who go to swell the ranks of the unfit, or to increase the rate of infant mortality."[44] Captions in other ads indicate: "Husbands, guard the health of your wives," "Are Your wife and Child as Healthy as These?," and "Your Wife Cannot Enjoy Life if She is Anaemic."[45] One Gujarati ad opened with the caption: "Women don't tell men what they have to endure."[46] In the later 1930s, as understanding of women's familial roles in financial decision-making improved, Feluna ads targeted women more directly, but without sacrificing the conjugal ideals or conceptions of the body involved.

Kulkarni highlights two specific themes stressed in Feluna ads of the period: motherhood/reproduction and the character of the female constitution, both themes prevalent in eugenic literature. Feluna advertisements typically featured the health of women as mothers. Figure 4.5, for instance, is an ad run extensively in both English-language and vernacular versions. Entitled "Motherhood," it pictures a sturdy woman wearing a modern but simple sari, a couple of bangles and some earrings, with two children, one a baby and the other a small girl wearing a dress, a clear sign of the family's modernity and middle-class status but also its lack of ostentation.[47] The light skin and hair of the baby makes him appear almost European, a trope indicating good health. The English text of the ad alludes to the "strains of motherhood," referring to motherhood as the highest expression of a woman's life, and warns husbands:

> If your wife is one of those irritable, impatient mothers standing on the border-line
> of a health breakdown, or if her health has already broken as a result of the miseries
> of nerve weakness or physical debility or functional disorder, you should *insist* that
> she takes a course of Feluna . . . let her have the health to be a MOTHER in the real
> meaning of the word.[48]

Feluna's ads regularly portrayed women's bodies as possessing constitutions with special vulnerabilities and thus requiring a uniquely female medicine. A woman's life was depicted in these ads as one of pain, especially pain associated with childbirth and menstruation. Some ads listed a host of female complaints that only women had to bear, from "womanly distress" and "nerves" to anaemia and digestive problems. These appeals avoided images of Indian women preparing for parties or engaged in athletic activity, themes Feluna ads had mentioned in appeals directed to an expatriate audience; they mostly focused on the family context. One particularly interesting exception, however, provides especially telling evidence of the modification of Feluna ads in the Indian context. Figure 4.6 pictures an Indian woman carrying a tennis racket, who plays two or three sets of tennis a week and who is described as someone who always "looks healthy and happy." Mrs. Mehta regularly defeats Mrs. Vakil, a woman described as sickly and unconcerned about her health. While successful on the tennis court, Mrs. Mehta does not wear athletic garb but a simple sari with modest forms of jewelry. She possesses a modern but hardly revolutionary hair style. Her married status is emphasized; she wears a *bindi* on her forehead and a *mangalsutra* around her neck,

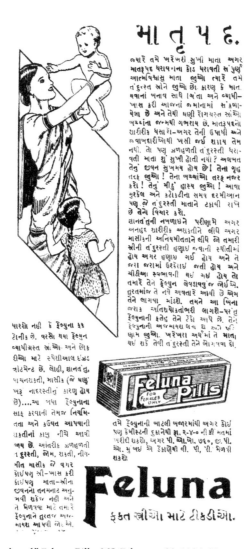

Figure 4.5 "Motherhood," Feluna Pills, *MS*, February 23, 1934, 11.

both signs of marriage. With her volume of athletic activity limited to two or three sets a week, Mrs. Mehta seems to possess no ambitions in her sport beyond defeating the hapless Mrs. Vakil. By interjecting in one sentence that she "runs her house very well," the ad openly tries to dispel fears that the modern woman might neglect her responsibilities in the home if she engages in sport. Here again, the ad addresses the husband, asking in its caption: "Is *your* wife as healthy as this?" In short, Mrs. Mehta has been divested, visually and verbally, of the dangerous attributes of autonomy embodied in the figure of the athletic sportswoman. The names given to Mrs. Mehta and Mrs. Vakil indicate an exclusively high-caste context.

Figure 4.6 "Is your wife as healthy as this?" Feluna Pills, *TI*, September 28, 1933, 11.

Thus, as they experimented with approaches designed to win middle-class customers in India, Feluna advertisers discarded recourse to the image of the modern girl, either as an attender of parties or as a competitive athlete, that they had used in cultivating South African expatriates. Instead they drew largely upon notions of domesticity and motherhood, themes that had certainly been present in South African advertisements, but ones that were significantly modified for an Indian audience. They often directed their ads to husbands, borrowed extensively from concepts of the female constitution present in ads placed by vernacular capitalists, and otherwise fine-tuned their ads verbally and visually to Indian conjugal conceptions and eugenic logic.

Ovaltine and the middle-class housewife

In many ways, advertisement for Ovaltine closely followed the pattern set by Feluna appeals. According to company histories, the Swiss manufacturers of Ovaltine, Wander AG, established manufacturing plants in Britain and the United States in the early twentieth century and began advertising the product extensively.[49] By World War I, Ovaltine was exported widely throughout the British Empire. After the war, Wander pursued an aggressive marketing policy oriented to consumers around the world. Jeremy Schneider, surveying the company's ads globally, found advertisements for Ovaltine published in newspapers in Britain, in English-language newspapers in Africa like the *Nigerian Daily Times* and the *Kenya Daily Mail*, and in English-language papers in India like *The Hindu* [Madras], the *Bombay Chronicle*, and the *Times of India*. My own research has confirmed that Ovaltine advertisements were published widely in Indian vernacular papers as well. In each context, the ads' designers came to include elements believed to have local appeal while eliminating themes they considered irrelevant in new contexts.

In Britain, Schneider has discovered, Ovaltine typically directed its campaigns to women. These ads ran on two main tracks. First, they drew upon ideas of domesticity, reflecting a conception of a "professional" housewife who managed her home on scientific principles. These advertisements featured homemakers who responsibly supervised household consumption, ensuring the health and vigor of their husbands and children. "Mother—how many in your family are fit?" asked one English-language ad before going on "Are You—your Husband—your Daughter—or your Son?" These questions were accompanied with a picture of a mother and smaller images of other family members. The ad confirmed the special scientific awareness expected of the modern housewife, stressing that "You know that the very foundation of health is correct nourishment." After mentioning the presence of "vitamins and other vital food elements required to ensure perfect fitness of body, brain and nerves," the ad insisted on the value of developing the "Ovaltine habit." It also linked these concerns with family well-being to the health of the nation, proclaiming that "Britain must be fitter."[50]

Other advertisements featured independent modern girls: explorers, athletes, and movie stars.[51] As Schneider points out, these campaigns centered upon depictions of heroic and active women, engaging female consumers who envisioned a significant life outside the home. Some ads highlighted women whose exploits had been publicized prominently in newspaper headlines, particularly aviators like Amy Mollison, Josephine Nadin, and a Mrs. Bruce. During this period, news stories about female pilots and explorers circulated widely.[52] Other ads focused on athletes, particularly tennis players. The emphasis in these cases was on the claimed capacity of Ovaltine to generate "tireless energy" and overcome the physical and mental strains that vigorous sports entailed. Still other ads featured glamorous British film stars, such as Adele Dixon, Aileen Marson, and Polly Ward. All these women were pictured with short hair, wearing unconventional clothing (whether aviators' garb, tennis clothing, or fashionable dresses), and usually with no men or children in the visual frame.

In India, Ovaltine ran a vast advertising campaign in a variety of media, including English-language newspapers, vernacular papers, street hoardings and bus signs. By the 1930s, Ovaltine's ads had clearly developed two distinctive approaches in India. The first was geared to expatriates and elite Indians thought to possess European consumer values; the second targeted the Indian middle class. Both types refrained from evoking the modern girl (whether as party girl, explorer, tennis player, or film star), instead stressing familial contexts.[53] Ads in English-language papers like the *Bombay Chronicle* and the *Times of India* overwhelmingly featured European characters, reflecting themes of imperial domesticity associated with expatriates throughout the Empire. A few of these may have been drawn up in England, only adding the name of the Indian agent, James Wright. In other cases the ads' designers in India added some small element to indicate the colonial context—a man wearing a *sola topi*, tropical vegetation, or a minaret in the background. The addition of these little local touches in a frame otherwise little different from a European home or social club may have suggested to the expatriate that Ovaltine could be a vital element in sustaining a sense of familiar domestic space in an alien environment. Figure 4.7, which features an English woman announcing breakfast is ready by ringing a gong, almost ostentatiously signals the Indian context by using the expatriate term "barra hazri" for breakfast: "Barra Hazri ready! The gong sounds its familiar message in flat and bungalow up and down the Country. And in countless thousands of happy health homes delicious 'Ovaltine' is served at the breakfast table, making the call of the gong doubly welcome."[54] Addressing the colonial housewife, the ad stresses Ovaltine's value in sustaining family health in India. Other ads emphasized Ovaltine's utility as a "hot weather drink" that helped the female consumer cope with the Indian climate, a familiar theme in ads targeting expatriates, as was discussed in Chapter 2. One advertisement pointed out, "Unless you take steps to conserve your energy and strength, you feel too listless to take part in games or other recreation—though everyone knows that regular exercise is particularly desirable at this time of the year."[55] Still others depicted the expatriate homemaker's special role in supervising servants[56] and in overseeing the cook's purchases in the bazaar.[57]

In vernacular papers, James Wright followed a different strategy, one likely influenced by the translators and artists involved in producing the ads or the Indian merchants who sold it. Many of its advertisements featured domestic contexts. In these ads, the European home was replaced by its Indian middle-class counterpart. Its furnishings included simple Western-style dining tables, chairs, curtains, and framed beds, items that would have been available only among the upper middle class. The family members' clothing sharply signaled their Indian identity. In ads published in western India, husbands, for instance, typically wore headwear associated with Parsis or high-caste Hindus. The modern housewife occupied center stage in the visual frame. In most cases, she wore a simple sari, apparently made of cotton and no gold thread, pulled over her head in a common sign of modesty. She was pictured with unostentatious jewelry, perhaps a couple of bangles around her wrist, and some earrings. In most cases, no servants were present. None of these ads highlight Indian women engaged in sports or other adventurous activities featured in European appeals.

The predominant theme in the ads published in vernacular papers was the role of the housewife in ensuring familial health. The ads offered a medicalized conception of the modern conjugal unit, one in which mothers and wives possessed special responsibilities for upholding family well-being. Joint families were entirely absent in these ads.[58] "A Healthy family," one ad proclaims in Gujarati, "is a happy family." The ad

BREAKFAST IS READY—
'OVALTINE'
CALLING

BARRA Hazri ready! The gong sounds its familiar message in flat and bungalow up and down the Country. And in countless thousands of happy healthy homes delicious "Ovaltine" is served at the breakfast table, making the call of the gong doubly welcome.

Throughout the changing seasons—hot, cold or wet—by far the best way to ensure the health of every member of your family is to make "Ovaltine" their daily beverage. Its delicious flavour appeals equally to young and old.

"Ovaltine" is a complete and perfect food, prepared from Nature's foods which are richest in nourishment. It provides all the nutritive elements essential to health. It contains proteins, mineral salts and calcium, organic phosphorus, carbohydrates and vitamins, all in correct ratio and form to maintain brain, body and nerves in vigorous health.

Make "Ovaltine" your family's daily beverage for health. But be sure you buy "Ovaltine" and not some imitation. Unlike imitations, "Ovaltine" does not contain any cheap ingredient, such as household sugar, which is only added to give bulk and to reduce manufacturing costs. Nor does it contain starch or a large percentage of cocoa. For quality and value, nothing can compare with "Ovaltine," which is 100 per cent. pure concentrated nourishment.

Remember that "Ovaltine" is packed in tins containing 4½, 9 and 18 ounces. Compare these weights with imitations. "Ovaltine" gives more in quantity—more in quality—therefore more in value.

Sold by all Chemists and Stores

Agent: James Wright, 65a Ripon Street, Calcutta; also at Bombay and Madras.

OE:298

Figure 4.7 "Breakfast is Ready—Ovaltine Calling," Ovaltine, *BC*, June 16, 1937, 4.

stressed the housewife's role in "providing every member of [her] family ... the necessary and pure nutrition."[59] Some Gujarati ads particularly praised the housewife's critical financial initiative in purchasing the product to advance the vitality (*shakti* or *jom*), vigor and strength of their families. Figure 4.8 again pictures a family with both a son and daughter, proclaiming that Ovaltine is for the value of the whole family.

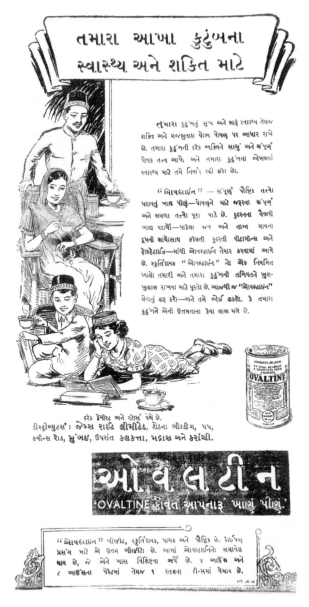

Figure 4.8 "For the Health and Energy of Your Entire Family," Ovaltine, *Prajabandhu*, January 15, 1939, 5.

Figure 4.9 similarly asks the housewife to buy Ovaltine for the health and energy (*jom*) of her family. While the caps in 4.8 suggest a Parsi family, the man's headwear in 4.9 indicates a Brahmin husband; both images would signal middle-classness to the reader. The clothing of females is modern but conservative, marking domesticity. The table (and the window in the second image) indicate both modernity and significant comfort; lower middle-class homes and working-class dwellings would not usually have such features. In many Ovaltine ads, the vocabulary of health associated with eugenic discourse and with male tonic advertisments was extended to the family as a

Figure 4.9 "Give Ovaltine to Your Family for Health and Energy," *Prajabandhu*, January 12, 1936, 15.

whole. Some ads, for instance, gave the wife a specific responsibility to prevent male weakness, and feature a female figure providing Ovaltine to an exhausted husband, though without the sexual overtones of tonic advertisements.

Ovaltine advertisements directed to expatriates and Indians did refer to the housewives' domestic duties, but the latter steeped themselves more frequently in a eugenic language suggesting the possibility that middle-class weakness might undermine the nation's advance. Implicitly, Ovaltine ads suggested, the Indian female had a special role in countering this potential within her own family. In ads directed to Indian middle-class women, party life, athletic participation and the effects of the draining tropical heat simply disappeared. In short, the ads came to feature prevailing themes in middle-class discourses of domesticity.

Lux, Pears and the construction of modern beauty

The proliferation of global commodities specifically designated to enhance female beauty was largely an interwar development. Before World War I, a number of businesses devoted to beauty products had emerged in England, France, and the United States. These companies marketed goods that included perfumes, creams, lipstick, makeup, and beauty soaps at costs within the reach of women in families with middlish incomes.[60] Increasingly they turned to advertising agencies in their efforts to fashion demand for these products. JWT, for instance, designed special campaigns featuring testimonials by actresses to sell Ponds facial and skin creams.[61] It was only during the 1920s, however, that these firms began making concerted attempts to market their goods outside North America and Europe.[62] Some of the companies—Ponds, Elizabeth Arden, Unilever, and Messrs. Lehn and Fink—developed major international campaigns oriented to women.[63] These campaigns soon stretched to India.

In the United States and Europe, advertisements typically formulated for these campaigns utilized images of women outside roles as wives and mothers. As the firms engaged in the beauty industry fine-tuned their appeals to Indian, middle-class audiences, however, they increasingly steered away from commodity images that would contradict the ideology of domesticity. An examination of the campaigns for Lux and Pears beauty soaps demonstrates how autonomous conceptions of beauty were contained and refashioned into ones more compatible with emerging ideals of the conjugal family.

Early-twentieth-century notions of beauty, as Holly Grout has brilliantly discussed in work on France, reflect contradictory social tendencies. On the one hand, modern conceptions of beauty perpetuated the notion that a woman's social worth is dependent upon the valuation of men and that women should adhere to certain conventions of appearance. Beauty icons—models, movie stars and others—enforced the idea that "women's bodies were made to be looked at, admired and desired."[64] As feminist scholars have argued, the idealization of the female body—and of particular body-types—associated with the commodification of such beauty products as cosmetics were intended to encourage perpetual dissatisfaction among women about their appearance.

On the other hand, at the same time, Grout points out, beauty culture provided a mode of disrupting and even transforming social conventions that restricted women. Beauty was an ideal that did not depend upon fulfilling rigid familial roles as daughter, sister, wife, or mother. The advocacy of new, "modern" standards of beauty often jibed with challenges to traditional gender practices, for instance in campaigns to undermine foot-binding in China, to stop teeth blackening in Japan, and to challenge the veil in various Islamic societies. Such campaigns achieved successes not simply as a result of debate in the print media and social movements, but also due to transgressive acts of women, including the flouting of norms concerning appearance. The adoption of new forms of beauty culture was often associated with the greater visibility of women in public life.[65] Denise Sutton has demonstrated how JWT (advertiser for Ponds) and cosmetics manufacturers appealed to forms of expression that promised women release from confining social expectations in a variety of global contexts.[66] The paradigm of the modern girl itself relied upon ideas of beauty suggesting oppositional social possibilities even if these notions were partly generated by the male gaze.

The ambivalence of modern concepts of beauty was certainly present in the context of middle-class western India. No doubt, in some cases, new beauty standards involved winning male recognition, as some advertisements certainly stressed. "Will he like me?," ran one ad for Oatine Snow printed in both vernacular and English-language newspapers during the 1930s, which featured a seemingly single woman concerned with winning male admiration.[67] Another Oatine ad stressed the importance of keeping oneself beautiful for the husband returning from his office. Picturing a middle-aged woman in a sari, it suggests: "THE LOVING WIFE desires to be ever beautiful in the eyes of her husband. THE WISE WIFE knows the way to the fulfillment of that desire. That is why she regards Oatine as indispensable."[68] To use Pierre Bourdieu's terminology, beauty represented a form of social capital in the marriage market;[69] families with daughters perceived as beautiful could arrange better matches and negotiate lower dowries; beauty, as one ad for Mysore Sandal Soap put it, was a "social necessity" with concrete but unspecified benefits to a woman and her family.[70] The development of beauty culture in twentieth-century India undoubtedly promoted new forms of anxiety about appearance for middle-class women.

At the same time, new ideas about beauty stressed social identities not explicitly connected to familial roles. These notions offered channels for self-expression among women when they had little role in the work world, when their opportunities for exercising an independent political voice were limited, and when their options for advanced education were circumscribed by the expectation they become housewives. Modern standards of beauty were made possible by transformations in women's places in public life, as norms stressing seclusion in the home or restricting the presence of females in public space—marketplaces, tramways and buses, sporting venues, and cinema houses—were undergoing challenges. Wearing blouse-pieces and six-yard saris rather than no blouse or a nine-yard sari became subjects of intense conflict between young women and social elders and between conjugal couples and community leaders. In some cases, women sometimes enthusiastically embraced beauty culture as a way of challenging norms they regarded as oppressive and outmoded, particularly those associated with the joint family and seclusion, even as they became enmeshed in new forms of subordinated relationships with their husbands. In short, the new beauty culture went hand in hand with challenges to traditional gender restrictions, challenges that then were often reformulated to be compatible with new conjugal norms.

The commoditization of beauty was a critical development of the 1920s and 1930s that has largely been ignored.[71] Beauty of course was hardly a new conception, but it was now articulated differently. Among the wealthy, beauty secrets had historically been carried over generations through chains of transmission between women. Often women utilized a great variety of non-commercial substances, some obtained from the natural environment, others brought to women's quarters by itinerant traders. Sharada Dwivedi and Shalini Devi Holkar's account *Almond Eyes, Lotus Feet: Indian Traditions in Beauty and Health*, richly documents the wide range of oils, pastes, and fragrances and the numerous body practices (bathing, massage, etc.) used by women in a princely *zenana* (women's quarters).[72] Based upon extensive research and the personal experience of Holkar (an American-born woman who married into a princely household), the book includes recipes for beauty products derived from familial traditions. The account locates the concern with beauty squarely in the sociality of women:

> Beauty care was part of this ultimate goal [sustaining the traditional family] and part of maintaining a delicate balance in life. Performing all those elaborate beauty rituals and using all our home remedies at least gave us the feeling that we had some defense against harsh climate, health problems and wagging tongues in the family—all of which could unbalance life badly. Of course, there was the question of vanity, too, but we never thought of beauty as a matter of fashion. We thought of it as a tradition, obligation, habit, health care, and yes, as good recreation. It was such a lot of fun! We women were always together for whatever it was—for massaging or bathing or washing our hair, and even for tending our children.[73]

Dwivedi and Holkar also describe the amazed encounter of some young women from this background with commercial cosmetics and their provocative packaging in visits to Bombay shops in the early twentieth century; these women previously had associated items like facial creams and lipstick with courtesans and prostitutes, not respectable women. "These women [featured on product labels] flaunted their freedom so openly," the narrators indicate. One member of the group bought some Western cosmetics but "No one ever used them; we were far too familiar with the natural things we'd always used."[74] The use of commercial beauty products thus involved daring behavior. Advertisements encouraged transgressions that initially appeared revolutionary at times. They offered women access to a beauty culture partly freed from the joint family, the *zenana*, and dependence on face-to-face interactions with pedlars (though likely still grounded in female sociality).

By the 1920s, many different products for enhancing beauty were already on the market. These included hair oils, perfumes, soap, and "snow" (that is, vanishing cream). Both vernacular producers and multinational firms manufactured these products. Foreign makes of snow included the products Afghan, Oatine and Hazeline, but there were also vernacular brands like Himani, which was produced by the Bengal Perfumery and Industrial Works, and Alembic, a Baroda company. Most ads for these products had as their main premise the importance of keeping the skin looking "young" and light-complexioned. One Himani soap ad from 1923 (Figure 4.10), for instance, featured an image of a female deity with the caption: "BEAUTY REIGNS SUPREME from the day of creation to this date. And beauty is created for beauty's sake—retained for so long as is possible. Try to Retain it to your Old Age by using HIMANI, the mysterious toilet snow."[75]

Makers of beauty products sometimes issued calendars with images of Indian goddesses. For instance, Vinolia (a soap brand within Unilever's larger company) developed calendars for their goods using paintings of the famous late-nineteenth/early-twentieth century artist Ravi Varma. In one case, Vinolia and the Indian brand Kerala Sandalwood Soap produced calendars using the same Ravi Varma image of the goddess Lakshmi, the first in 1926, the latter in 1940.[76] In 1936 the *Bombay Chronicle* published an ad for Oatine Snow entitled "A Gift from the Gods," featuring a woman discovering a jar of the product on a lotus, an auspicious religious symbol (Figure 4.11). The image seemingly alludes to the goddess Lakshmi, who in mythological accounts emerges from the churning of the ocean and who is often pictured sitting on lotus flowers.[77]

Mythological themes, however, were relatively rare in newspaper advertisements. During the late 1920s and early 1930s, ads issued by multinational companies more

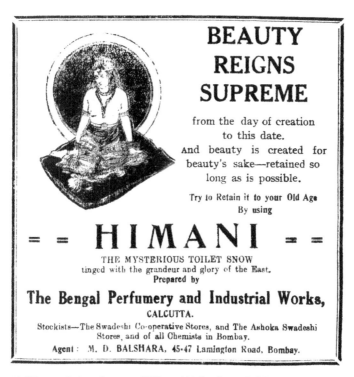

Figure 4.10 "Beauty Reigns Supreme," Himani Toilet Snow, *BC*, June 11, 1923, 11.

A Gift From The Gods

To Beauty Lovers

The OATINE preparations come as a precious gift for the growth and preservation of loveliness even into old age.

OATINE CREAM is modest in its requirements. It asks only the devotion of five minutes' gentle massage every evening before bedtime, and it offers you in return a lifetime of skin health, the warm glow and bloom of youth. A complexion smooth and free from blemish and the enjoyment given by the possession of beauty unsurpassed.

OATINE CREAM nightly and OATINE SNOW daily. These two are all you need for—Beauty.

THE OATINE CO.,   GRAHAMS BLDG., Parsee Bazar St., Fort, BOMBAY.

Figure 4.11 "A Gift from the Gods to Beauty Lovers," Oatine Face Cream, *BC*, March 2, 1936, 9.

commonly relied on drawings of European women; producers of beauty products persisted in this practice well after other types of business had moved to using Indian figures in appeals to the middle class. Pears ads, for instance, typically either featured short-haired, young European modern girls or elegant, expensively dressed European women conveying the values of luxury and superior quality. In other cases, partial nudity was suggested through images of European women at their baths with crucial body parts strategically covered.[78] A Palmolive ad in Marathi included a view of the back of a short-haired European woman in her bath, an image intended to convey sensuality.[79] The same ad included smaller images of the Dionne quintuplets, a set of Canadian infants used worldwide to suggest the product's health-promoting qualities, as well as a picture of palm trees, the source of the oils used in Palmolive (crucially signaling the soap's reliance on vegetable products rather than animal fats). During the later 1930s, even as the advertisers of some products like Ponds Cold Cream, a client of JWT, came to feel that it was imperative to mark the figures in ads as Indian, they sometimes used photographs of models who appeared to be Europeans dressed in saris, wearing bindis on their foreheads and Indian jewelry (see Figure 4.12).

Such campaigns in effect involved propagating notions of whiteness that female executives in JWT believed to have universal appeal.[80] The continued reliance on Europeans or light-skinned Indians in beauty ads stemmed largely from the perception among advertising specialists that Indians, too, associated fair skin with beauty and status. Advertisers began to pay close attention to the issue of skin color held by both Europeans and Indians; a 1931 JWT report, generated for the cosmetic firm Lehn and Fink, devoted significant attention to this issue.[81] An American advertising expert conveyed, in mocking terms, his view of local fascination for light skin:

> I once ran across the advertisement of one of these products [pharmaceuticals] in an Indian periodical. It pleaded with the Hindu who took his daily bath in a pool covered with green slime to spray his throat [with a spray produced by a multi-national company] before entering crowds. The advertisement intrigued me. I called on the distributors, a Parsi merchant in Bombay. Did he sell much of the product? Yes, it was going very well. I was non-plused. India is full of surprises, but I thought I knew my India better than that. "Ah yes, sahib. All the Eurasian girls buy it." "Eurasian girls," I gasped. The plot was thickening. "Oh yes. Three or four applications and the skin turns three shades whiter." [82]

In some cases, advertisements for multinational products appealed openly to preferences for lighter skin. A skin cream called Cremozon promised to make "Dark Skin Permanently Fair." It pictured two seemingly European women, one shaded much lighter than the other, suggesting the cream's use could transform a woman's skin tone. The ad provided a pseudoscientific explanation for this supposed capability: "CREMEZON is an oxonised cream, each jar liberating 200 cubic centimetres of fresh, active Oxygen. Ozone, the most active form of Oxygen, has proved a remarkable skin bleaching agent scientifically. Continuous application of CREMEZON to the skin therefore gradually but surely bleaches [the skin]."[83] Other ads more subtly claimed that their products promoted skin freshness, fostered a new luster in the skin, or created a bloom and vitality in the skin, all codes for fair skin tones. Even as advertising artists shifted to depicting Indian rather than European female figures, they used the blank, white page to indicate light skin color, suggesting Indianness through other visual markers, particularly saris. Such ads doubtless drew upon prevailing notions simultaneously influenced by colonial preoccupations with whiteness, with textual

Figure 4.12 "Pond's new Creams contain Skin-Vitamin," *IWI*, August 28, 1938, 36.

traditions in India favoring lighter skin, that have ancient antecedents, and with caste conceptions that demarcated status based upon skin color.[84] In a context where awareness of genetics was beginning to enter middle-class outlooks, fair skin served as a kind of biological asset ensuring the likely perpetuation of the family's perceived social position or checking the potential for degeneration that was associated with darker skin color.[85] Advertising certainly bolstered these concerns, in effect fostering color as an important marker of demarcation between middle-class and lower-class/caste bodies and bolstering the importance of lighter skin as a form of social capital for middle-class women to possess.[86] At the same time, ads promised that color was actually not a fixed physical trait but an attribute that could be manipulated through practices involving the use of brand-name commodities.

By the 1930s many Indian firms, too, were producing beauty products and advertising them. Their ads visualized female beauty in a variety of forms, featuring images ranging from modest Indian housewives to unconventional modern girls. TOMCO ran ads with a cinematic flavor of women in romantic settings with men wearing Western-style suits on moonlight nights; they pictured women dressed in saris but also wearing wristwatches signaling modernity.[87] Godrej utilized drawings of the Egyptian princess Cleopatra, who had been the subject of a 1934 Hollywood movie starring Claudette Colbert.[88] Such firms as Godrej, Ajanta (Figure 4.13), Mysore Sandal Soap, and Bosfa Tearose Soap even

Figure 4.13 "Beauty—A Nature's Gift But Men's Own Choice," Ajanta Soap, *BC*, February 11, 1935, 34.

ran ads featuring women at their baths to suggest sensuality; the conventions against nudity for Indian females, which would later characterize Indian advertisement, were as yet not so strong to inhibit their use in soap advertising.

Occasionally vernacular advertising was involved in appropriating visual tropes of beauty from multinational ads, just as global tonic sellers poached on themes stressed in vernacular male tonic ads. The main value of using such images was to differentiate beauty soaps strongly from ordinary soaps, to associate the product with status, youthfulness, comfort, and sensuality, and perhaps to provide husbands with a degree of titillation, so that families would loosen budgetary constraints to consider buying a soap exclusively for women, an item that might otherwise have seemed an unreasonable luxury.

Lux

During the later 1930s, however, Levers, the biggest multinational, guided its commodity messages away from the themes of the modern girl, sexuality, and nonconformity toward images that were less culturally transgressive. Unilever apparently introduced Lux toilet soap into the Indian market during the late 1920s.[89] Many of the early ads for Lux simply featured a bar of soap in its packaging. Lux began to be intensively marketed as a beauty soap in India around 1933. As the next chapter discusses, Levers did not fully differentiate its major soaps from each other until that time when Lifebuoy became clearly delineated as a health soap, Sunlight as a soap for washing clothes, and Lux as a beauty product. The growing sales of Palmolive and Pears demonstrated that there was a market for beauty soaps, and that it was important for Levers to demarcate the rationale behind each of its products, since middle-class households would otherwise economize by buying only one brand for the entire family.

In order to deepen consumer associations of Lux with beauty, Levers' advertisers introduced into India appeals featuring Hollywood stars, which it had been using elsewhere in the world before this.[90] By 1935, the firm was conducting a full-fledged campaign with this theme, relying on illustrations of such actresses as Joan Blondell, Ginger Rogers, Miriam Hopkins, and Carole Lombard in order to suggest the product's value in sustaining or improving one's complexion. The use of such images was prevalent both in English-language publications and in vernacular papers (see Figure 4.14 for one example).[91] This global strategy of utilizing testimonials from these stars fit with well-established patterns of testimonial use in Indian advertisement.

By the later 1930s, however, Levers' executives concluded that "The Film Star appeal is not pulling as much as formerly." A main reason, they argued, was that the ads featured only American and European stars, while Indian consumers were increasingly viewing Bombay films with Indian actresses. Such cultural friction prompted the brand's promoters to enter into discussion with some (unnamed) Indian female stars, who ultimately refused to allow the company to use their images.[92] Producers of other beauty soaps, however, soon overcame such hesitations and signed up important actresses from the Bombay cinema for endorsements. The first firm to do so in western India appears to have been Swastik, an Indian company headquarted in Bombay, which in early 1938 used an image of Sabita Devi, star of the social film "300 Days and After,"

Figure 4.14 "Ginger Rogers," ad for Lux Soap, *Prajabandhu*, May 8, 1938, 7. Produced with permission of Hindustan Unilever Limited.

to promote its Chandan brand. Devi is quoted in the ad as saying, "I use CHANDAN (Sandalwood) Soap to preserve my beauty." The ad proclaims that Swastik is the "soap that the stars recommend."[93] Oatine also ran ads in 1938 of Pramilla (Figure 4.15) testifying that she had been using the vanishing cream for years. The caption under her image argued, "The complexion of a film star needs the best possible treatment for cleansing, nourishing and revitalizing ... Oatine Cream satisfies every requirement of the standard."[94] By the end of the year, Colgate Palmolive was running ads for Palmolive that came to feature such major stars as Devika Rani, Sulochana, Padma Devi, and Khursheed.[95] Sulochana's short hair, makeup, and lipstick in Figure 4.16 clearly mark

Figure 4.15 "Pramilla Prefers 'Oatine,'" ad for Oatine Face Cream, *IWI*, October 23, 1938, 3.

her as a "modern girl" and the text explicitly reinforces this reading. Some of these ads began to use photographs more systematically, perhaps as a result of improvements in the technical processes of reproducing photographic images.[96] Photographs particularly proved valuable with soap and cosmetic ads because of their perceived authenticity in carrying information about skin appearance. Perhaps because of Palmolive's coup in signing up Sulochana and Devika Rani, two of the biggest stars of the time, Lux had to continue its reliance on Hollywood actresses,

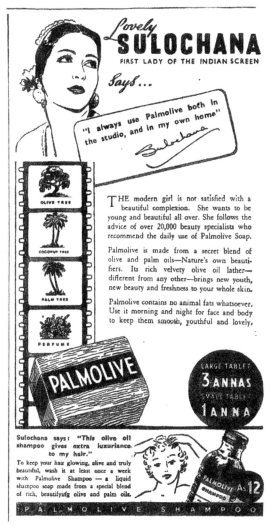

Figure 4.16 "Lovely Sulochana: First Lady of the Indian Screen," Palmolive Soap, *TI*, October 17, 1939, 3.

but added an emphasis on the appeal of the soap's perfume to Indian women.[97] A 1939 ad (Figure 4.17) also coincided with Levers' new recognition of women's role as the key decision-makers in consumption matters, as discussed at the beginning of this chapter. The ad's largest image was an Indian housewife experimenting with two soaps, one an ordinary soap and another Lux; she notes the superior qualities of the latter. But the ad still included a smaller picture of a Hollywood actress providing testimonials supporting the use of Lux, thus sustaining the cinema-star theme despite significant Indianization in the appearance of the ad.

Figure 4.17 "The Active Lather of Lux Toilet Soap Gives Greater Skin Beauty," Lux Soap, *Prajabandhu*, February 26, 1939, 9. Produced with permission of Hindustan Unilever Limited.

Palmolive's choice of Sulochana was particularly striking. She had been a star of the silent era, and by 1939 her career was winding down. As Priti Ramamurthy has argued, Sulochana epitomized the Indian "modern girl." She was "sexy and provocative; she was long-limbed (or made to look so) and sported bobbed hair, dark lipstick, mascara, and long, painted nails. At times she wore Western-style dresses, pants, hats and shoes . . . and at others she wore saris, Indian-style jewels and braids."[98] Her makeup and lipstick evoked the modern girl trope. In some movies, she played swashbuckling, athletic roles, riding up on horseback to save the day. Her light-skinned, almost

European appearance (she was actually a Baghdadi Jew or Eurasian) was common among the silent era film stars. Ramamurthy stresses the sartorial innovativeness of modern girl actresses in Indian films; they wore Western clothing or saris that gave a cosmopolitan impression: "The Indian Modern Girl was coded and coded herself as global and Indian modern through the hybrid fashioning of her body, her body language and her sartorial zest."[99] Devika Rani was also referred to in her Palmolive ad as a "modern girl" and a "glamour girl" and was depicted with short hair (or with hair tied back in a modern style), lipstick and modern earrings.[100] Ramamurthy argues, however, that Devika Rani's persona was informed by the advent of what she calls the *Bharat Nari*, or the Indian woman—"a good wife, now in the modern role of companion within the confines of a heterosexual, middle-class marriage"[101]—an ideal associated with the growing influence of nationalist norms stressing the values of respectability and Indianness.

By mid-1941, Palmolive soap's presence in the Indian market seems to have faded, perhaps because the war had limited its importation. By contrast, Levers, with its strong presence on the subcontinent in the form of office and factory, retained the ability to supply Indian demand. Palmolive seemingly left the field open for Lux to appropriate a campaign using Indian film actresses. In late 1941, Levers launched ads for the soap initially featuring Leela Chitnis; during the years that immediately followed, it signed contracts with a number of other actresses including Ratanbai, Shobana Samarth, and Mumtaz Shanti.

Chitnis no doubt possessed the potential to be a subversive figure akin to Sulochana. She had married another actor while just a teenager and had been divorced from him for several years by the time of her selection in 1941. She played romantic parts in many of her movies. But the image associated with her name in the ads was of a demure woman, light-skinned and wearing lipstick and eyebrow liner no doubt, but with a conservative hair-style marked by flowers and a marriage mark on her forehead. In Figure 4.18, Chitnis provides instructions to the consumer on how to use Lux before praising the effects of the soap for a woman's skin (using a quote box). The photographic image combined with the quotation added a strong sense of authenticity that was both visual and verbal; the viewer was supposed to imagine the words being spoken at the moment of her gaze. Lux ads featuring other actresses around the time used a similar combination of devices to achieve this effect. These stars, portrayed in a photographic image, noticeably used lipstick and other Western makeup, but wore their saris pulled over their long hair and comported the ubiquitous marriage mark on the forehead. The image of female film stars proved to be an enduring theme in Lux advertisement.[102] By the 1950s, images of actresses from some regional film industries were also used in vernacular advertisements in addition to those of Bombay stars.

In reaching this moment, Levers' advertisers clearly were drawing upon advertising tropes used by other soap manufacturers in India, who had in turn been influenced earlier by Lux's use of Hollywood stars. The actresses featured were not straightforward emblems of docile femininity; they were pictured alone, often in poses suggesting strength of character, and they wore Western makeup and lipstick, signs of a willingness to challenge traditional expectations. Their roles as romantic figures in the parts they

Figure 4.18 "Leela Chitnis provides the key to obtaining beauty," Lux Soap, *MS*, March 17, 1942, 4. Produced with permission of Hindustan Unilever Limited.

played, sometimes pursuing love unfulfilled or temporarily blocked by social norms, also implied an unconventional character. At the same time, they increasingly displayed key markers of respectability. While they did not always actively promote the ideal of modern conjugality, they did not represent an open challenge either, a potential that had existed with earlier figures like Sulochana.

Pears

Advertisements for Pears similarly came to reflect a negotiated effort between notions of female autonomy and modernity on the one hand and respectability and Indianness on the other. Pears was a British company that had developed a unique and somewhat expensive process for manufacturing soap in the late nineteenth century. It was acquired by Unilever in the early 1920s but it maintained a distinct manufacturing plant, soap quality, and product image. While Levers managed its distribution in India, Pears was often not mentioned in the company's reports. Clearly, however, the company maintained a strategy of sustaining Pears as a high-end soap with an ability to enhance female beauty, and it hired a set of talented artists in India to carry out this task.

Before the late 1930s, Pears ads often featured European figures who epitomized principles of glamor and modernity in their hair styles and their fashionable clothing (including furs), sustaining the commodity's associations with prestige and eliteness. But around 1938, Pears shifted to using distinctively Indian images. In 1939, the company carried ads with youthful Indian females in a remarkable, striking style of commercial art that reflected a special economy in its use of detail. Figure 4.19 pictures

Figure 4.19 "That's Pears Tonic Action!," Pears Soap, *BC*, May 25, 1939, 10. Produced with permission of Hindustan Unilever Limited.

a woman with a sari and the forehead mark signaling marriage, but also strongly suggests the modernity of its subject through the woman's makeup and lipstick, and especially through its striking artistic style. Other ads featured young, seemingly unmarried women.

During the early 1940s, however, Pears developed two other campaigns that distanced themselves from the straightforward modern girl. Both campaigns were extensive, and were run in both English-language and vernacular papers with the same visual images. The first emphasized the importance of the inter-generational transmission of knowledge from mother to daughter. There were at least four distinct ads in this series but in each the younger woman is represented with short hair and lipstick and no marriage mark and she wears her sari over her left shoulder in a modern style; the mother, by contrast, wears her sari draped over her head and her long hair parted in the middle. In each ad, the mother is shown imparting her knowledge of family beauty secrets, while the daughter listens in rapt attention. In Figure 4.20 three generations of women are represented, the eldest depicted through a painting of a deceased grandmother.

The mother's place in the ad highlights the principles of skin care that her mother had transmitted to her and that she now was expected to pass on to her own daughter. The ad in effect mutes the radical potential of the modern girl, represented by the daughter, suggesting the possibility of a modernity that does not involve a break with family authority. Both elements of the house décor and the dress of the two women also suggest wealth, marking the product as prestigious.

The second campaign relied upon a series of richly detailed images of women whose appearance delineates distinctly Indian but modern conceptions of beauty. Again, there were several different ads in this campaign, and they were placed extensively in vernacular papers. The figures in the ads were drawn with lipstick and makeup but with sari styles, hair-styles and jewelry signaling "tradition." Most strikingly, each woman wears a nose-ring, sometimes on the right (in South Indian style) and sometimes on the left, clearly differentiating the subject from a Westernized female.[103] The artistic technique may indicate the influence of the Shantiniketan school of "Indian" art" founded by Abindranath Tagore[104] and perhaps particularly the painting of Kanu Desai, who had been trained at Shantiniketan and who was influenced by Tagore and Nandalal Bose.[105] The Shantiniketan artists were strongly concerned with generating a form of national painting that would reflect Indian aesthetic themes, such as the art of Mughal miniatures and images of the village; female beauty was a major subject of work in this school. The facial appearance of the woman in Figure 4.21, an ad for Pears, suggests conventions of female beauty found in Desai's work though she wears lipstick and cosmetics. Her jewelry and sari seem to suggest an upper-class, almost aristocratic bearing. Such messages about identity were carried out largely through visual means. The ads' text is phrased in especially flowery terms, emphasizing the special effect of using Pears on the skin, and the tonic qualities of its lather. The ads thus indicated that it was possible to incorporate the product of a multinational company in constructing a very Indian conception of beauty.

Figure 4.20 "Retain the family beauty," Pears Soap, *GS*, August 3, 1945, 3. Produced with permission of Hindustan Unilever Limited.

By the early 1940s, the period of beauty advertising's experiment fully with the modern girl ideal and with overtly sexual appeals was largely over. The ads retreated from the use of nudity and most of the campaigns now centered on the effects of beauty products on the face rather than over the whole body. European and Hollywood

Figure 4.21 "The Best Method for Acquiring Beauty," Pears Soap, *MS*, May 15, 1942, 5. Produced with permission of Hindustan Unilever Limited.

models were increasingly rejected, though the emphasis on light skin was reinforced. Multinational firms were clearly adapting their advertising pitches to a climate of rising nationalism that was affecting a variety of cultural media, most strikingly the world of film culture and painting. Different companies developed different approaches for conveying these messages, but they all increasingly rejected the most highly sexualized images. The ads sought to establish that use of their products could be easily integrated into an ideal that was modern but did not depend upon Western conceptions. While most campaigns over beauty products still offered to women the possibilities of self-expression outside their relationships to men, they did so through approaches that did not challenge the ideals of the conjugal family.

Conclusion

During the interwar period, especially during the 1930s, multinational companies began to introduce a host of products into India that they had marketed to women elsewhere in the world. In India, they began to devise advertising campaigns directed specifically toward women; the notion that women were consumers making decisions about commodity purchases fully emerged in capitalist understandings of the subcontinent. But these companies did not simply transplant the marketing appeals used elsewhere. Instead they altered their campaigns in a series of adjustments to their understandings of what mattered to Indian consumers, particularly female members of the middle class. They certainly were influenced by global models of womanhood such as the modern girl and the modern housewife but these models were adapted significantly to the Indian context.

The interwar period was a critical moment when women's societal position became central to the very constitution of modernity in western India. For the middle class a host of unsettled questions pervaded circulating discourses about these roles. Did urban life and the loosening of traditional social bonds pose physical dangers to women's health and their ability to sustain the family? How might mothers in particular contribute to the family's well-being and social reproduction? How should women appear in public and how could women's appearance contribute to the family's social capital? How would women marshall family resources in the marketplace to ensure the priorities of the family were met? The model of the modern girl potentially offered a threat to the conjugal ideal, and a plethora of commentators expounded on the danger posed by her potential ascendance. Advertising did not initiate or invent these discussions but it did come to contribute to them, mostly siding in the end with a model of womanhood that bolstered conjugal roles. In the case of Feluna and Ovaltine, explicit appeal was made to notions of a new modern form of domesticity. In the example of beauty products, advertisers no doubt experimented with alternative models of femininity, including ones suggesting non-conformity, female sexuality, and female independence. But as they sought to develop wider consumership among the middle class, they tended to bring their campaigns into line with changing conceptions of female responsibilities, social respectabilty, and nationalism. Global firms largely eased away from the image of the modern girl as articulated outside India—whether as aviator, athlete, party girl and romantic partner, or Hollywood actress—embracing appeals that often bolstered emerging conceptions of the modern housewife. The potential that women's growing presence and visibility in the marketplace might become a ground for challenging patriarchal controls in India was thus defused and tamed in the culture of brand-name capitalism.

Lever Brothers, Soap Advertising,
and the Family

At the time Prakash Tandon first found employment in Bombay with Lever Brothers in 1937, the company was probably the largest consumer products business in India. Though educated as a chartered accountant, Tandon was put to work in the firm's expanding advertising section under John Rist. Tandon's experience in the company was at first awkward. Indian clerks in his office watched closely to see if he would be served tea like the other managers and they initially would not let him sign papers that needed a "European" signature (until then synonymous with a manager's signature). He was paid one third less than Europeans at the same level and he was excluded from social gatherings of the other executives. Tandon, however, soon carved out a career in the company, playing a critical role in conducting market research and assessing the circulation levels of different newspapers. He was promoted to covenanted manager within the year. He continued to move through the ranks, becoming a director in 1951 and later the first Indian chairman of Hindustan Lever Ltd.[1]

Tandon's rise within the firm is an aspect of what he called the "Indianization" of Unilever, a development that stretched far beyond just adding and promoting Indian personnel. During the 1920s and 1930s, Unilever went from being a British-based company without a significant physical establishment in India to a business with an extensive local administrative office, revamped marketing networks reaching into the countryside, recognition as a limited liability company as Lever Brothers (India), and a large manufacturing plant in Bombay.

Changes in the company's methods of advertising consumer products, including about a dozen kinds of toilet soaps, clothes-washing soaps, household-cleaning products, and a cooking medium, were also part of this process. During the 1930s, Levers expanded its advertising efforts, and adjusted its sales pitch to middle-class consumers, increasingly gearing its advertising to themes steeped in the new conjugality. A new set of advertising specialists rose within the firm and, after 1939, the company set up an advertising offshoot named Lintas, which became committed to developing appeals for Levers' products that would discourage local consumers from turning to cheaper Indian goods. In part due to the success of these early campaigns, many Indians today would no longer recognize such Levers' brands as Sunlight, Lifebuoy and Lux soaps, and Dalda vanaspati, as ever having had foreign origins.

This chapter examines the evolution of Levers' advertising campaigns between the 1920s and the early 1940s, focusing on the promotion of Sunlight clothes-washing soap and Lifebuoy body soap. Levers' campaigns became part of an effort by the multinational firm to domesticate its sales pitches as it responded to the growth of nationalist sentiment and intensely competitive markets. As it committed hugely enhanced resources to advertising, engaged in new forms of market research, and experimented with a series of advertising appeals, Levers arrived at campaigns for Lifebuoy and Sunlight that drew deeply on conceptions of the conjugal family as a medicalized entity.

Soap and the middle-class family

By 1918, using soap for cleaning the body was widely accepted in the Indian middle class, and soap advertising certainly reflected this fact. As Harminder Kaur has pointed out, Indians had long used different agents in bathing: soap nuts and soap berries, gram flour, abrasive soils, yogurt, and various kinds of vegetable oils.[2] Projit Mukharji has shown that early vernacular advertisements for "soap" often did not distinguish between cleansing oils, hair oil, and soap bars.[3] But over the course of the nineteenth century, as soap use in Europe became nearly universal, British observers began to critique Indians for not using soap (in the form of a bar). Colonial discourses portrayed soap as a civilizing agent and as a marker of racial difference. As Anne McClintock has argued, "Victorian cleaning rituals were peddled globally as the God-given sign of Britain's evolutionary superiority, and soap was invested with magical, fetish powers."[4] The various smells associated with Indian oils, by contrast, were characteristically portrayed as "disgusting" and "nauseating."[5] Under the impact of such critiques, men and women with significant levels of education came to see soap use as essential to their health and their modernity.

The enhanced reliance on soap was incorporated into changing conceptions of the middle-class household. As a result of what I have called the medicalization of the family, the conjugal unit became a site where hygienic practices were to be strictly enforced and supervised, usually by the housewife. Reliance on soap also became a critical marker of middle-class stature. Just as soap had once differentiated the European from the Indian, it came to delineate distinctions between the middle class and other actors in Indian society. Adoption of modern sanitary standards in effect became a new yardstick along which caste was reconstituted, even as traditional notions of purity and pollution based upon hereditary characteristics were challenged by reformers. Shantabai Kamble, an educated young Dalit woman who began school teaching in rural Maharashtra during the early 1940s, remembered that during her youth, "high-caste people like Marathas and Brahmans used these [commercial] soaps, and looked down upon people who did not use soap."[6] Her rural family had itself relied on salty white soil, which it found near a local river in her village, as a cleansing agent. She remembers adopting soap around the time she began her first job as a teacher, both because she could now afford it and because of its healthy associations. Soap consumption became tied to assertions by Dalits to higher status during the mid-twentieth century.[7]

But while soap use for personal hygiene had been widely adopted by middle-class families, the same would not have been true for clothes-washing. Quite often such families would send their clothes to a *dhobi* who performed this role for multiple households; families with higher incomes employed their own washermen. Dhobis typically cleaned clothes outside the family's direct supervision and generally used methods that did not require soap, such as rubbing wet clothes aggressively on rocks or beating them with a kind of bat. In Bombay, many dhobis carried out their profession at Dhobi Ghat, which was established by the municipal corporation in 1890 and provided standardized facilities for hundreds of washermen. In the early 1930s, Sunlight soap was still used primarily as a body soap; according to one estimate, only one quarter of its consumption in India was devoted to clothes washing.[8] The use of laundry soap for washing clothes became more extensive during the interwar period, as housewives increasingly assumed the dhobi's function. Advertising was critical to this transformation.

Soap advertising during the 1920s

Since soap manufacturers did not have to create a middle-class market for body soap in India, advertising efforts during this time were devoted to promoting particular brands. The soap market was dominated at its upper end by foreign producers, who possessed a reputation for superior quality; Indian soaps were typically cheaper but were generally regarded as inferior. During the period of intense nationalist activity between 1919 and 1922, many Indians shifted to *swadeshi* (Indian-made) soaps, but by 1923 this tendency had faded and preferences for foreign soaps re-emerged for those who could afford them.[9] Most multinationals selling soap had no permanent establishment in India, but imported their products through Indian or European agents who were responsible for their distribution and who probably made most ad placements. In many cases, the ads themselves were generated outside of India; often the only sign of any local adaptation was the printing of the agent's name on the text of the ad. Figure 5.1, an ad for Erasmic soap printed in the *Bombay Chronicle*, features such a transplanted image. The image in the ad, of a European woman in a bathrobe admiring herself in a small mirror, evokes a concept of beauty but not overt sexuality; the ad's wording specifically stresses the values of "purity" and "daintiness."[10] Ads for foreign soaps in vernacular newspapers were few and little adaptive effort to cultivate Indian customers was made. In some cases an English-language ad was placed in vernacular newspapers with no translation. In others, the ads touted the English character of the soap and pictured European women in ball gowns.[11] Association of soaps with Europeanness was clearly a key selling point associated with quality, hygiene, and prestige.

By the 1920s, a significant local soap industry had emerged, though its products usually occupied the lower end of the market spectrum. Soap making, in contrast to textile manufacture, was a process requiring only limited investment; the necessary raw materials were widely available, and local soap-makers acquired easy access to the requisite techniques, sometimes from publications designed to encourage swadeshi industry. Cheap labor and low transportation costs gave the vernacular producer clear price advantages, and many Indians became concerned about relying on soaps containing animal fat, a characteristic of many imported soaps. Indian entrants into the field of soap

Of that delicate & refined
purity which is essential
to the ideal toilet soap.

"ERASMIC"
The Dainty SOAP.

ERASMIC, 13a, New Bond St., LONDON.
perfumers.   15, Rue du Temple, PARIS   Agents:—D. CHOTHIA & Co   BOMBAY.

Figure 5.1 "Of that delicate and refined purity which is essential to the ideal toilet soap," Erasmic Soap, *BC*, June 11, 1918, 12.

manufacture were many; the majority found the creation of sufficiently high qualities to sustain consumer commitment difficult and their efforts were often short-lived.

A few Indian manufacturers, however, were substantial enough and survived long enough to develop sustained newpaper advertising campaigns. Some of their advertisements were very limited, providing little more than the name of the company, the cheapness of the price, and testimonials from reputable or powerful individuals who used the product. Often, only a text mentioning the soap and some of its characteristics was provided with no visual imagery. Some producers proclaimed the swadeshi character of their goods hoping such emphases would win out over claims to other qualities. In Figure 5.2, an ad for soaps for the Hindustan Soap and Candle Works, stated that its soaps were made in India but also mentions that the soaps were used by the Governor of Bombay and other "influential ladies and gentlemen." Ads also might stress the cheap price of the soap and its freedom from animal fat. Vernacular capitalists sometimes provided a lengthy didactic text in their ads, evidence of an effort to win over potential consumers with logic rather than visual appeal.

Perhaps the most interesting vernacular advertisements of this period in this region were those run by Godrej Oil and Soap Ltd., which would later emerge as one of India's

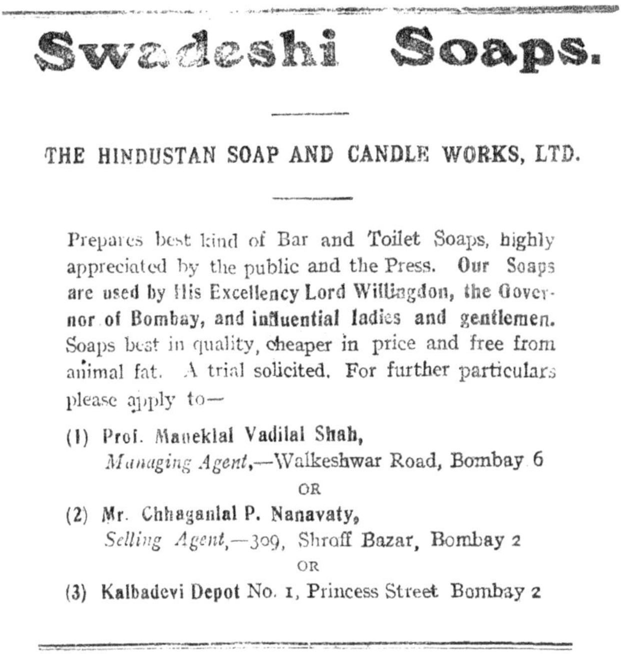

Swadeshi Soaps.

THE HINDUSTAN SOAP AND CANDLE WORKS, LTD.

Prepares best kind of Bar and Toilet Soaps, highly
appreciated by the public and the Press. Our Soaps
are used by His Excellency Lord Willingdon, the Governor of Bombay, and influential ladies and gentlemen.
Soaps best in quality, cheaper in price and free from
animal fat. A trial solicited. For further particulars
please apply to—

(1) Prof. Maneklal Vadilal Shah,
     Managing Agent,—Walkeshwar Road, Bombay 6
                    OR
(2) Mr. Chhaganlal P. Nanavaty,
     Selling Agent,—309, Shroff Bazar, Bombay 2
                    OR
(3) Kalbadevi Depot No. 1, Princess Street Bombay 2

Figure 5.2 "Swadeshi Soaps," The Hindustan Soap and Candle Works, *Bombay, BC,*
November 4, 1918, 3.

most substantial companies. The firm was founded by Ardeshir Godrej, a relentless
tinkerer highly motivated by the ideal of challenging foreign manufacturers. According
to company histories, he first became involved in an experiment to make surgical
instruments, but gave up this attempt when potential buyers insisted that they would
need to claim the products were made in Europe.[12] He turned to producing locks and
safes, and founded a very successful company, Godrej and Boyce Ltd., in 1897 to pursue
this purpose. Godrej began making soap around 1918, creating a soap bar made from
vegetable products that, in contrast to most indigenous soaps, produced a significant
lather and retained its shape even as it became wet.

In the 1920s, Godrej began to advertise extensively. Its ads directly challenged
imported products, admonishing readers to "Read and Learn" about the advantage of
Godrej soaps relative to foreign soaps (Figure 5.3). Imported soaps, these ads warned
sometimes in sensationalist form, were made of animal products and other kinds of
waste. A longer version of this advertisement, originally developed in a short Gujarati
pamphlet in 1918 and then printed in abbreviated form in local newspapers through
much of the 1920s, argued that many foreign soaps were made from parts rejected by
butchers, from diseased animals, including pigs that died of cholera and cows that died
from smallpox, and from human and animal excreta whose smells were disguised by
perfumes.[13] The ads clearly were intended to shock Indian consumers, particularly
Hindus and Jains with strong beliefs in the principle of non-harm to animals and the

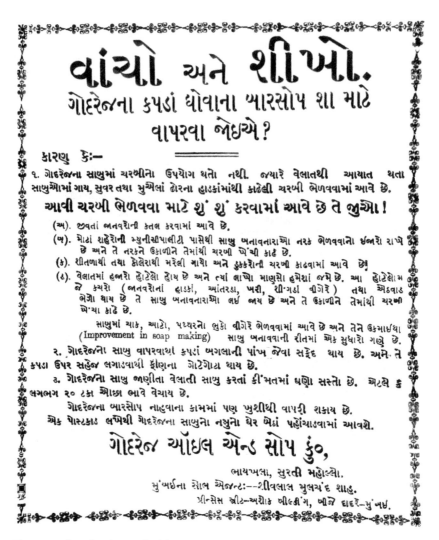

Figure 5.3 "Read and Learn," ad for Godrej Soaps, *MS*, September 4, 1926, 27.

polluting effects of human and animal waste; they also invoked Muslim conceptions of the unclean character of swine. The ads at first lacked any imagery and reflected little evidence of the role of professional advertisers in layout or design.

The challenge of Godrej and other competitors was at first insufficient to provoke Unilever into making major changes to its marketing operations, including advertising. Throughout the 1920s, Unilever had the largest sale of any soap manufacturer, foreign or domestic. At this time, the company was actually a conglomerate, selling the products of several significant British soap manufacturers during this period: Lever Brothers, J. Crosfield and Sons Ltd., and W. Gossage and Sons Ltd. By 1929 Levers, through another company it controlled, United Exporters Ltd., was handling the exporting business for all three.[14] Levers' own soaps acquired a special market position, expanding their sales by a factor of four between 1923 and 1929, and profits had risen accordingly.[15] This growth, however, had been achieved without offices in India that could supervise local distribution networks year-round. While the company had entertained setting up its own factory in India during the early 1920s, it retreated from that idea when the plan's costs began to appear prohibitive and when the local prestige of foreign soap revived after the end of the non-cooperation movement.[16] The firm instead sold its goods through a set of large European and Indian commission agents in India, who were paid based on sales and the risk they undertook. Traveling company representatives negotiated arrangements with these agents and Indian wholesalers on a regular basis. Indian shopkeepers were sometimes willing to sell Sunlight and other Levers' products at limited profits, in part because the prestige of these goods attracted purchasers to buy other items.[17] But because it lacked any permanent personnel on the subcontinent, Levers was unable to develop a strong appreciation of the Indian market.

In contrast to other multinational companies, Levers tended to place its ads directly in the papers rather than rely on its agents, who were not mentioned in the ads' texts. The company did not employ advertising professionals in India during the 1920s, perhaps because sales were expanding rapidly without this investment. The firm's ads were usually simple, often just featuring the packaging of Sunlight soap, the company's most important brand. Typically ads mentioned the commodity's popularity throughout the world, the purity of the soap's qualities, the freshness of the soap and its sweet scent. "If it is Sunlight," the ads insisted, "it must be pure." By 1928 Levers was submitting ads to vernacular papers and was developing some ads in India rather than simply placing its transplanted appeals. For instance, this image from a 1928 ad in the paper *Prajabandhu* published in Ahmedabad (Figure 5.4), picturing an Indian woman washing her son, clearly was generated for the Indian market. The ad contained a one-word caption in bold: *tandurasti* (health). The longer verbal text that followed stressed the product's value in promoting good health while stressing its worldwide reputation. A similar ad, picturing an Indian dhobi washing clothes, also stressed the same slogan, while emphasizing freshness, the product's sweet smell, and its purity.[18] In both ads, however, the observer is remote from the human figures pictured, whose facial features are not emphasized. The skin color of the people in both ads is black; this rendering would have been at odds with the self-perception of high-caste, middle-class families (who typically contrasted their own skin color with the supposedly dark skins of the poor and lower-caste). Thus, even though Levers' ads during the 1920s were forged in an Indian context, they do not appear to reflect a sophisticated attempt to incorporate "prior meanings" that would have carried weight among the middle class. This is not surprising of course for a firm with limited means of gathering significant knowledge about its potential consumers. Levers' advertising in India clearly involved limited financial investment. In short then, the age of professional advertising had not yet fully arrived by 1930 for soap manufacturers seeking a market in India.

Figure 5.4 "Tandurasti [Health]," ad for Sunlight Soap [Gujarati], *Prajabandhu*, February 5, 1928, 14.

The soap wars of the early 1930s

During the late 1920s and the 1930s, the competitive environment for Unilever and other multinational companies intensified. A host of new firms, both local and foreign, entered the market, often selling their products at prices well below what Levers and other high-end producers could manage. According to Lord Leverhulme and W. P. Scott in 1929: "We are now in the position that our own rather rapid success is beginning to react upon us. The increase in the sale and use of good quality soaps has encouraged local soap makers to increase their output and greatly to improve their quality while keeping their prices well below our own."[19] By 1934, there were perhaps 5,000 to 10,000 manufacturers, most quite small, producing soap in India.[20] New European importers, particularly from France, were also increasing their efforts. Japanese imports, too, began to appear, often selling at about 60 percent of the price of Unilever soaps.[21] The directors of Tata Oil Mills Company (TOMCO), which had entered the soap business, suggested "the competition from cheap soap made within the country has been so severe that organized soap manufacturers are receiving a setback" and claimed that the situation was "not only injurious for human use but is likely to retard the progress of the industry,"[22] phrasing that seemed to refer to the advance of brand-name capitalism. The company began to insist that the import of cheap, poor-quality foreign soaps should be legally prohibited.[23] Such firms also had to cope continuously with imitations. Makers of cheap soaps would sometimes concoct a trademark similar to those used by major producers, and then sell at low prices. As one Levers' officer wrote in 1939: "If 'imitation is the sincerest form of flattery,' there is no doubt that we are being flattered by our Indian competitors who produce soaps and cartons and wrappers startlingly like our own but yet sufficiently different to keep themselves out of the clutches of the law."[24] Imitations not only cut into sales but also endangered the reputation of the high-end companies when consumers found the products to be inferior.

These developments represented a serious threat to the manufacturers who had invested significant capital in more expensive technologies, and whose production costs prohibited radical rate reduction. Importers were also constrained by the wage rates they paid, which were several times higher than Indian levels. Advertising became a crucial means of trying to convince buyers to purchase brand-name products without drastically lowering prices.[25] In some cases, producers published ads explicitly warning the public against using imitation goods.[26]

The resurgence of swadeshi sentiment also threatened foreign manufacturers. The years between 1923 and 1928 had marked a lull in nationalist activity, permitting preferences for foreign soaps to re-emerge among people able to afford them. But in 1928, the appointment of the Simon Commission, which was considering a new round of constitutional reforms for India, sparked new protests, most notably because all the Commission's members were Europeans. In early 1930, the Congress under Gandhi inaugurated the Civil Disobedience Movement with the goal of obtaining independence. Indian producers began to emphasize their swadeshi credentials again in their ads. The tendency for multinational soaps to command prestige merely because of their foreignness collapsed. According to Leverhulme and Scott: "the preference for British goods in some places has given way to a direct antipathy to them." They went on to add, however, that "this need not worry us if our prices and our appeals are right—patriotism in India, as elsewhere and probably more than in many places, is still subservient to the pocket."[27] As the word "appeals" in this statement suggests, Levers was coming to regard advertising as critical to sustaining brand consciousness in the new environment.

The early 1930s was also marked by the growing visibility of middle-sized and large Indian firms that had mastered the technology of making higher-quality soaps. Some of these firms had existed for some time, while others had begun manufacturing soap only during the 1920s. Such firms made substantial investments in physical plants and all of them were deploying advertising extensively to build and sustain their products' reputation. Included in the ranks of these middle-sized companies were the Bombay Soap Factory, Margo, Mysore Sandal Soap, Bengal Chemical Company, Godrej and TOMCO. These brands directly competed with each other and with the foreign brands.[28]

Godrej's campaigns during this time continued to perpetuate themes it had been stressing during the 1920s. Its attacks on foreign soaps became even more insistent. The caption in the most dramatic of the company's ads ran "Soaps from dead Rats, Cats, Dogs, Cows, Etc. & from Human Excreta." The image in the picture features some very scruffy looking pigs wallowing in the mud (see Figure 5.5).

The text of the ad was equally sensational, even accusing foreigners of adulterating medicines with animal matter.[29] The ad guaranteed that Godrej products were free

Soaps from dead
Rats, Cats, Dogs, Cows, Etc.
& from Human Excreta

Says Frederick A. Talbot in his Book 'Millions from Waste':—
"All skins rags, bones, feathers and hair were collected. All waste arising in the slaughter of animals was carefully gathered. The carcases of animals which had succumbed to disease were also treated. A farmer was not even permitted to bury the corpse of a dog. The authorities were vested with the power to handle diseased animals to secure the fats for soap-making."

Many medicinal preparations are very ex-

pensive to make. Such preparations, when made for export to our poor country, are largely adulterated as is well-known to medical men in India. When foreigners, do not care whether we live or die after taking their medicines, does it not stand to reason that they would quite unscrupulously make such articles as soaps from greases recovered from such sources as dead rats; cats, dogs, cows and even from human excreta. In Europe fats recovered from human excreta are sold to soap-makers at half an anna per pound. Godrej pays from two to four annas for the same weight of pure Indian vegetable oils.

All Varieties of Godrej's Toilet Soaps
Are Guaranteed Free From Animal Fats

Godrej Soaps, Limited,
Delisle Road, Parel,   -   -   -   -   -   -   -   -   -   BOMBAY.

Figure 5.5 "Soap from dead Rats, Cats, Dogs, Cows, Etc.," Godrej Soaps, *BC*, August 29, 1934, 3.

from animal fats. The illustration used certainly suggests its designer was not trained in commercial art. But while the Godrej ads strongly attacked the use of foreign products, they sometimes still invoked the authority of the European. A number of ads cited European experts in critiquing the quality of Godrej's rivals in the soap market. Figure 5.6 pictures four scientists, three European and one Indian, sitting around a

Figure 5.6 "When Scientists Agree *you can be Sure that their findings are* TRUE," Godrej Soaps, *BC*, April 6, 1935, 3.

table taking notes on the discussion before them. Testimonials from each of the depicted figures were printed in the ad's text. The ad also included a short comment marked off from the ad by a textbox: "German and French tradesmen import Godrej's toilet soaps into their country." The ad certainly implied that European expert opinion was a more valuable form of evidence about quality than the views of Indian users.[30] Another ad insisted that "Europeans in India Largely use Godrej nos. I and II soaps." It went on to claim that "among thousands and thousands of our European customers in this country, residing in all towns from North to South and East to West, there are thousands who have enough discrimination to stick only to our Nos. 1 and Nos. 2 soaps."[31] Again, the drawings in Godrej ads did not observe the stylistic conventions of commercial art, suggesting the artists did not have formal training.

The company's soap sales expanded significantly throughout the decade. In 1937, the sales of its soaps had increased to more than 600,000 Rupees and it employed around 500 workers.[32] By this time, trained artists appear to have taken over publicity for Godrej. Images in the ads follow much more closely the styles of commercial art, sometimes featuring pictures of an Indian female consumer. Both the swadeshi appeal and the invocation of the authority of the European expert disappeared from the rhetorical framing of the product. The ads stressed instead the use of oils made from indigenous plants and trees like neem and sandalwood, and of perfumes based upon familiar scents. In other words, an explicitly political approach had been replaced by appeals based upon the use of ingredients widely accepted as healthy and pungent.[33]

For Levers, an even bigger source of competition than Godrej was the Tata Oil Mill Company. TOMCO was founded by the Tatas, a Parsi family that had already become wealthy through its investments in such ventures as textile mills and hydro-electric power.[34] Its entry into the consumer products field was almost unintentional. Initially the Tatas had established a mill around 1918 for crushing coconuts to make coconut oil for an overseas market, modeling their effort on a similar project in the Philippines a few years earlier.[35] But soon after the mill was up and running, the export market collapsed, and TOMCO had to search for alternative ways of using the mill. Increasingly, the company turned to manufacturing consumer products derived from vegetable oil. As we shall see in Chapter 6, the company initially focused its efforts during the 1920s on selling Cocogem, a cooking substance derived from crushed coconut. The demand for this product, however, never satisfied the company's directors, and by the early 1930s they had come to see soap as a commodity with greater prospects. TOMCO's two major products were Hamam, a toilet soap that was to become the most important Indian soap, and 501 clothes-washing soap, which challenged Sunlight. These soaps began to make rapid advances, despite the fiercely competitive environment. In 1932, the company reported that soap sales had doubled during the previous year, and TOMCO's plant would need expansion to meet demand. Levers executives viewed TOMCO, with an overall production of soap about 30 percent of Unilever sales, as their chief Indian competitor by 1937.[36]

As in the case of Godrej, TOMCO's directors saw advertising as crucial to success. Advertising served to sustain the soap's prestige and price, which they could not lower to the rates charged by the cheapest local manufacturers because of the major investment they had made in plant. Through much of the 1920s and early 1930s, they employed as their agent for distributing their goods Messrs. Foster and Co., the multinational seller of Glaxo, which made milk products for babies, this despite TOMCO's own claim to swadeshi credentials. When Foster withdrew from the account in 1933, TOMCO took full charge of its own distribution system, and hired JWT for advertising. For the second half of 1939, Thompson budgeted almost 6,000 Rupees business for TOMCO, making it one of the agency's top six accounts. Discussions were underway at the time for JWT to handle the account of all the companies in the Tata group for 30,000 Rupees a year.[37]

TOMCO's soap advertising underwent a transition during this period. Several TOMCO ads from around 1930 provided only a simple print message.[38] But in 1931 the company had decided to run more elaborate ads for 501 laundry soap. These ads pictured discussions among women who used the soap to wash clothes, and often carried a nationalist message, for instance by featuring a spinning wheel, a key symbol of Gandhi's campaign, and women washing *khaddar* (homespun) cloth. Figure 5.7 pictures one woman with a child and another hanging up clothes on a line. One says to the other "Have you tried using 501 soap for washing Khaddar? I find it makes clothes wonderfully fresh and clean."[39] The artwork bears evidence of investment in professional commercial art. The nationalist message was conveyed much more quietly than in Godrej ads, without the outright attack on foreign producers and their use of animal products. In some cases, testimonials from well-known Indian leaders were included.

By 1934, after the switch to JWT as its advertising agency, TOMCO's campaigns began to focus on the economical value of the product. Ads for Hamam (Figure 5.8) inaugurated a slogan that would last for many years, "The big bar at a small price," which they used in both Gujarati and English papers.[40] Perhaps because of a desire to emphasize the trademark, many of these ads typically pictured just the bar of Hamam, though some did introduce human figures. By contrast, 501 ads were focused on housewives, who were featured in visual form. An ad for 501 "Special" Soap suggested the user always got more value for the rupee because the weight of the large bar meant there was more soap in it. "Get your wife 501 'Special' for washing all the best clothes," urged the ad's text while emphasizing the cleaning power of the soap.[41] Advertisements for both products typically mentioned that they contained no animal fats, echoing Godrej's campaigns. By the early 1940s, 501 ads came to picture dhobis with wooden mallots for beating clothes and highlighted the damage such methods would have inflicted, an approach also used in Levers' ads for Sunlight. Both company's campaigns included instructions to the housewife for washing clothes.[42]

Any survey of the competitive environment for soap must also mention the role of Palmolive, a Canadian product, which was clearly trying to pry open the Indian market, as we saw in the previous chapter. Palmolive's campaign became increasingly ambitious during the early 1930s. In early 1934, it packaged its soap with Colgate toothpaste, providing one soap bar free with every tube purchased. Its ordinary bar sold at a price 15 percent less than Levers' comparable soaps.[43] Perhaps most significantly, Palmolive was conducting a campaign stressing its exclusive reliance on vegetable oils, specifically palm and olive oils, thus contrasting itself to the Unilever soaps. In short, it sought to rely on a reputation for quality while trumping Levers' products on cost and ingredients. Levers' executives expressed concern about the threat to the Indian market Palmolive represented.

Figure 5.7 *"Have you tried 501 Soap for washing Khaddar?,"* 501 Soap, *BC*, June 6, 1931, 3. Produced with permission of Hindustan Unilever Limited.

In sum, a host of factors created a much more challenging business climate for Levers than had existed in the 1920s. As modern notions of hygiene associated with soap took deeper root among the middle class, as the ranks of those considering themselves middle class increased, and as lower-status actors took up the use of soap as they asserted claims to upward mobility, soap consumption expanded. But there was no guarantee that Levers would sustain its share of this market, especially because its prices ranged above those offered by the other Indian and foreign soap manufacturers. This situation, moreover, arose in the context of the Great Depression, which reduced wages and created significant unemployment. The sales of Levers' soaps in India fell from 20,238 tons in 1928 to 12,045 tons in 1933 and net profits from 206,046 pounds

Figure 5.8 "Now: A Big Bar for a Low Price," ad for Hamam Soap, TOMCO, *MS*, February 19, 1934, 11. Produced with permission of Hindustan Unilever Limited.

to 61,309 pounds.[44] In this environment, the company developed new forms of advertising campaigns that were intended to neutralize the commercial appeals of their opponents. For the most part, these ads came to center around the hygienic mission of the conjugal family.

The Unilever response

During the early 1930s, Unilever fundamentally reconfigured its operations in India, creating a firm better able to respond to this competitive situation. The company brought the sales operations of its constituent companies under a single marketing organization.

A system of Unilever depots was created to distribute the firm's products all over India; only three local agents remained to do Unilever business as intermediaries in different regions. A new company, Lever Bros (India) Ltd., was soon incorporated in India in 1933, and it purchased the trademarks of the parent company's soap products. Though for a brief time the firm entertained handing over 60 percent control to Indian stockholders, it remained a multinational one with foreign ownership. A company that had only a limited physical presence on the subcontinent in 1929 developed a significant local administration to oversee the sales of Levers' soaps.[45] A substantial office of eight Europeans and seventeen Indians was established in India with headquarters in Bombay, and several dozen Indian salesmen sold the soaps in different parts of the subcontinent to about 3,500 wholesalers. Only the accounting office remained in London.[46]

The company also transferred the manufacturing of its most significant products to the subcontinent. A particularly important step in this process was the construction of a large factory in Bombay in 1934. The advantages of setting up production in India were many. First labor costs were cheaper. Second, Levers now became better able to deflect the nationalist argument that the importation of consumer goods was undercutting the country's industrial development; company officials reasoned that middle-class Indians would not be so ready to abstain from buying goods actually manufactured in India. Third, relocation provided a means of avoiding new tariffs established by the Government of India; the Japanese soap trade, in contrast, was devastated by the tariffs. Fourth, the close connections between the factory and sales operations made it easier for Levers to adapt the products and packaging to local tastes.[47]

The company also made a series of important adjustments in its marketing. It reduced its prices significantly for a while, driving some some local soap manufacturers out of business in the process.[48] It adjusted the color and appearance of its packs for Indian buyers, creating, for instance, a small cheap tablet of Sunlight that sold for one anna per carton and a cheap laundry soap called Empress Pale[49] to attract customers who would only spend small amounts on each purchase. Levers altered the ingredients of Lux and Lifebuoy soaps to produce colors believed to have local appeal and there was also extensive experimentation with soap perfumes.[50] Levers eliminated the use of animal fats in the manufacturing process, creating soaps that were made entirely of vegetable oils to meet local concerns about contact with animal products.

The company also stepped up its advertising efforts. Levers executives came to regard advertising as critical to perpetuating the prestige of their top-line products. Advertising expenditures were heavy compared to other companies. In 1934, for instance, the company spent Rs. 311,000 on advertising Sunlight, a figure that was more than 60 perccent of the total margin before advertising.[51] By 1939, Levers projected devoting Rs. 925,000 a year to advertising.[52] The amount spent on advertising increased from 5.7 percent of total turnover in 1935 to 9.7 percent in 1939.[53] Seemingly, these levels suggest, the company was willing to sacrifice some profit in the short term to build up a dominant position. It also increased the size of its staff in Bombay devoted to advertising, as discussed in Chapter 1. In 1939, the complexity of advertising had become so great that Levers set up Lintas, Bombay, to handle the creation of ads and their placement in newspapers.[54]

Levers now made a series of adjustments in its advertising appeals. In 1936 and 1937, one subtle innovation was the addition of the phrase "Made from pure Vegetable Oils Only" at the bottom of every ad; this was soon changed to "Made in India from pure Vegetable Oils by Indian Labour." Seemingly this language was a direct attempt to counter the extensive campaign run by Godrej over the previous fifteen years and the more recent efforts by Palmolive emphasizing the vegetable-derived character of its soaps. As one Levers' report indicated:

> "Consumer investigation seems to indicate that there is a definite antagonism to L.T.S [Lux Toilet Soap] on grounds of the Swadeshi and Vegetable Oil appeal of local competitors, and we therefore arranged for advertising to bear the words (without featuring it unduly) 'Made in India from Pure Vegetable Oils.'"[55]

Still, as late as 1936, many ads remained rooted in an assumption of an Indian consumer who regarded foreign products as more prestigious. European images were generally used. Sidney Van den Bergh, in charge of the Bombay office at the time, wrote that "Our Advertising department here still works very much on home lines and in my opinion too little attention is given to local circumstances." He indicated that Thompson Walker would soon be sent from London to "investigate local conditions" and to develop "advertising schemes which should appeal to the local consumer."[56]

The character of Walker's survey has already been discussed in Chapter 4. While the final reports were apparently not preserved, they clearly reflected a more extensive effort to accumulate knowledge about the priorities of the middle-class household and of decision-making processes in which housewives played critical roles.

The campaign for Lifebuoy soap

By the mid-1930s, Levers began to seek to establish a distinct personality for each of its major soaps. Vim was depicted as a product for cleaning around the house, Lifebuoy was to be a health soap, Lux a beauty soap, and Sunlight—which had been extensively used for the body before this—a soap for washing clothes. While ads for Lux were discussed in the previous chapter, I turn here to campaigns for Lifebuoy and Sunlight.

The decision to throw significant resources behind advertising Lifebuoy in India was made only during the mid-1930s. Before 1930, few Indians used Lifebuoy, which was quite different in character from other available soaps.[57] Its distinguishing characteristic was that it was made with carbolic acid, an organic compound with disinfectant, bacteria-killing qualities. It had developed a significant market in Europe by the 1920s and its advertising there initially featured health-related themes, such as the responsibility of mothers to care for their families. In 1930, Unilever in Europe had launched the famous "B.O." (Body Odour) campaign to market Lifebuoy; this campaign had attempted to promote a preoccupation among consumers with overcoming body smells. The slogan "B.O." was used extensively in ads there and in North America in the context of courtship and inter-gender, extra-familial sociality (Figure 5.9).

Figure 5.9 *"This might be your story too," Evening Telegraph* [UK], May 14, 1936, 1+. British Library Newspapers. https://link.gale.com/apps/doc/JF3237615118/BNCN?u=dar tmouth&sid=BNCN&xid=6e7e309d. Accessed October 18, 2020.

According to Julianne Sivulka, B.O ads typically suggested a series of social disasters resulting from body odor, including damaged friendships, lost businesses, and failed romances.[58] Both women and men hoping to attract members of the opposite sex were encouraged to bathe regularly with Lifebuoy to eliminate offensive "B.O."[59] When the soap was sold in India, these concerns were expected to carry over to expatriates, who at first constituted the vast majority of Lifebuoy's purchasers. As the most significant carbolic soap available on the subcontinent, the product may have had a special appeal for Europeans concerned about heat-induced sweat and other health issues they associated with India.[60]

By 1934, however, Levers' executives reported that Indians were beginning to use the soap. Sidney Van den Bergh reported: "I believe that in a country like India, a soap such as Lifebuoy, behind which we can put the health appeal, has a great future."[61] Levers reduced Lifebuoy's price and inaugurated its manufacture in the new Bombay factory, which made it imperative to develop broader markets for the soap. By 1937, Lifebuoy consumption was achieving "remarkable progress" backed by a campaign stressing its health benefits. One Levers' executive in India commented in his annual report that "the Health and Freshness appeal is a wonderful subject for an advertising story [in India]."[62] Levers devoted significant effort to producing these ads, which were published both in English-language and vernacular papers. At first, however, these ads showed only limited evidence of being adapted to Indian customers. They typically featured European adult male figures or European children taking baths after playing in the dirt, even in ads for vernacular papers (for example, Figure 5.10).[63] The B.O. theme, so prevalent in Europe, was initially absent. In 1938, however, Levers stepped up its advertising effort for Lifebuoy, launching an extensive appeal in fourteen different languages.[64] European figures largely disappeared from the ads, even those printed in the *Times of India*, reflecting a strategic decision to go after a middle-class audience. In 1940, Levers was spending 98,000 Rupees a year on advertising the soap; the proposed figure went up to 130,000 in 1941.[65]

Initially there were two different prongs to this campaign. The first of these emphasized the importance of preserving the health of children from the danger posed by germs. The ads pictured various creatures about to attack children, beginning with dangerous animals such as snakes and tigers, but then turning toward the depiction of fantastic imaginary monsters, as Figure 5.11 indicates. If the reader (imagined as a parent) were to encounter a creature like this threatening his or her child, the advertisement's logic stressed, he or she would certainly intervene. But germs were an invisible threat, and the modern consumer needed to learn that they posed an equal danger: "If germs looked like this you'd rush in to protect your child from them, but unfortunately, they don't—you can't see them at all. Doctors testify that germs are the cause of disease and illness—and you can't even see them! But they are there just the same and you can defeat them! They breed in ordinary dust and dirt and you can wash that away with Lifebuoy."[66] The ads addressed the middle-class consumer as a parent—gender unspecified—who was fully committed to the principle of scientific medicine but did not fully appreciate the danger germs posed to family health or recognize the body practices (i.e., regular washing with Lifebuoy) that could overcome this danger. The use of the fantastic monsters was intended almost to jolt families imagined to be lacking in knowledge of proper health habits into Lifebuoy consumption.

The second prong involved the introduction of the "B.O." concept to India. Clearly, much effort was made to adapt the theme to the imagined cultural priorities of the Indian audience. Notions of romance, courtship and marital relationships were avoided. Instead Levers centered the campaign around the uncertainties posed by the middle-class couple's entry into new, modern forms of public sociality. Typically, these ads pictured a crowd of

Figure 5.10 "All kinds of filth pose a danger to health," Lifebuoy Soap, *Jam-e-Jamshed*, March 18, 1936, 21. Produced with permission of Hindustan Unilever Limited.

men and women (always multi-gendered and composed of middle-class Indians from different communities) in public places, for instance in a bus, in a cricket match, or outside a cinema hall (for example, Figure 5.12).[67] The ads stressed the danger that body odor presented to public respectability in these novel contexts. To some extent the logic in these ads ran parallel to that used in the health danger campaign; the ads were predicated on the notion that B.O. (like germs) was something that one could not readily perceive, but nonetheless constituted a threat lurking in new forms of urban existence. "Many people have been failures in their public and private life because of Body Odour—for it's so easy to

Figure 5.11 "Save that Child," Lifebuoy Soap, *TI*, October 6, 1939, 10. Produced with permission of Hindustan Unilever Limited.

offend without knowing. We never notice Body Odour in ourselves! And though our friends notice it, particularly in crowded places, they rarely have the courage to tell us."[68] The person with a truly modern sensibility, this ad suggests, needed to recognize that body odor could prevent proper functioning in the new, unfamiliar society that was emerging. In effect, the advertisers sought to inculcate new standards of bodily practice that consumers should adopt in order to participate in public life. The places illustrated undoubtedly were critical urban spaces where middle-class Indians were increasingly tending to congregate.

There is, however, significant evidence that the B.O. campaign did not have the desired impact on the Indian middle class. Prakash Tandon, for instance, insisted to his

Figure 5.12 "It May be You! Protect yourself from B.O. (Body Odour)," Lifebuoy Soap, *TI*, October 5, 1939, 17. Produced with permission of Hindustan Unilever Limited.

boss that the B.O. theme had little resonance in India. Writing many decades later in *Punjabi Saga*, he would recall:

> Poor Rist [his boss] was to persevere dutifully and vainly at making 'B.O.' a household expression. We do not use initials in our languages, nor are we particularly worried about body odour. If you smell of sweat it is because sweat has a smell and not because you have not washed. Most people have a daily bath; from a bucket, at a well, at a pump in the street or in a river. When water dries, you smell again, and sweat soon smells. I tried mildly to suggest that the internationalness of

the campaign perhaps did not apply here. Rist listened politely, but probably considered this a part of the problem of training an Indian to appreciate modern ideas. If people sweat and smell and do not mind the smell, they can be made to mind, they could be taught to think of it as 'B.O.' and want to buy the only soap that would prevent it. Rist was totally uncynical, and to him this campaign, like all advertising, had a mission and was sacred in belief and concept.[69]

The fate of the "B.O." slogan in vernacular languages provides further evidence of difficulty in the campaign's translatability. "B.O." of course referred to no Indian word or phrase, so in vernacular ads, Levers included the English letters in the text followed by a full translation of the body odor concept (such as Sharirni Vas in Gujarati, Sharirache Vas in Marathi), as illustrated by Figure 5.13. This juxtaposition, however, was apparently so confusing to readers that, within months, Levers had dropped the mention of the English term B.O. in its ads and developed new abbreviations based on vernacular languages (as is indicated by the abbreviation "sha va" in quote marks followed by the full Gujarati wording in Figure 5.14, which depicts a cricket match). However in doing so, the purpose of creating a universal slogan that resonated among all consumers across India had been sacrificed. As Tandon himself suggested, the use of abbreviations for such purposes was not likely in any case to be meaningful to Indian audiences. By 1939, just a year or so after it was introduced and soon after the results of Thompson Walkers' market survey would have circulated among Levers' executives, the whole B.O. campaign was abandoned as was the emphasis on an extra-family, inter-gender, inter-community sociality.

By contrast, the campaign stressing the threat of germs to children lived on, though in somewhat less dramatic form. The monsters disappeared from the ads. The key theme now became "dirt danger" and the promotion of the "Lifebuoy habit" (see Figure 5.15 for example). The ads pictured individual children studying or engaging in play that would lead to encounters with dirt and germs. The pedagogical tone continued, with ads addressing parents on the risks of children exposing themselves to unsanitary conditions; the ads reminded the consumer of the "antiseptic" character of Lifebuoy. The figure implores: "Every wash with Lifebuoy gets rid of dangerous germs, guards against infection and illness ... there is a special health element in Lifebuoy."[70] In addition to the main image, a smaller drawing of a mother was often inserted, clearly indicating the specific family member the ad was targeting. "Teach her [the girl pictured in the ad] the Lifebuoy Habit," another ad warned the reader: "Of course you cannot keep her away from dirt—but you can let Lifebuoy protect her against its dangers. You see dirt breeds germs. Many illnesses can be caused by the germs in dirt. But antiseptic Lifebuoy soap—with its wonderful health-protecting lather—gets rid of the danger in dirt."[71] The figures in the ads were clearly marked as Indian, even in newspapers with large European readerships.

The ads were based upon an asssumption of a highly medicalized family, that is, of conjugal parents who were intensely preoccupied with the health of children, appreciated scientific theories of disease causation, and recognized the importance of soap to the continued reproduction of the modern family. By stressing the value of the Lifebuoy habit, advertisers sought to inculcate a long-term commitment to the project

Figure 5.13 "No one is safe. B.O. (Body Odour) might emerge from your natural sweat." Lifebuoy Soap, *Stri*, September 1937, A-1. Produced with permission of Hindustan Unilever Limited.

of securing the health of children through the sustained use of a specific brand-name product. Since middle class households typically purchased only one soap for all members of the family—unless a beauty soap was bought for women—there was no need to have a second approach providing motivation for adults if the parents could be convinced to buy soap on the basis of priorities related to their offspring. Thus the ad campaign was brought in line with hygienic discourses associated with the modern family, discourses I have suggested were linked with eugenic reasoning then gaining a considerable audience in India. To a great extent, a campaign based on the danger of

Figure 5.14 "Don't Run the Risk, If you are careless, you will develop Sha. Va. (Body Odour)," ad for Lifebuoy Soap, *Prajabandhu*, January 22, 1939, 5. Produced with permission of Hindustan Unilever Limited.

dirt and germs and the importance of the "Lifebuoy Habit" slogan in effect persisted for many decades afterwards.[72] If longevity can be viewed as evidence of how effective Levers' managers came to see the campaign, it is clear that the firm regarded the health-based approach as a success.

The example of Lifebuoy strongly suggests a set of cultural strategies had been reformulated through processes of experimentation, informed by responses to Walker's market survey and by interaction with Indian employees (such as Tandon himself and Indian translators), shopkeepers and possibly customers. The carbolic

Figure 5.15 "Dirt is Unhealthy," Lifebuoy Soap, *BC*, August 1, 1940, 5. Produced with permission of Hindustan Unilever Limited.

soap's sales pitch clearly altered, less in response to the changing themes of the company's global campaigns than to an evolution in Levers' understanding of the priorities of Indian, middle-class customers. The "B.O." slogan was ultimately abandoned in part because it proved untranslatable, and a campaign that was hyper-focused on children's health was adopted. While health had certainly also been a secondary theme in Lifebuoy ads in Europe, the campaign for the soap in India had been fine-tuned to focus intensely on the parents' (and often specifically the mother's) responsibility for the well-being of their children, a central concern of discourses oriented to the middle class during this period.

Sunlight soap

In contrast to Lifebuoy, Sunlight was a product that Unilever had long been selling to Indian consumers; it had clearly been the company's most important commodity in the 1920s and early 1930s. In 1938, its sales were still about five times the sales of Lifebuoy.[73] Sunlight faced direct competition from a variety of lower-cost Indian laundry soaps, whose manufacturers sometimes offered special discounts to wholesalers.[74] The company stepped up its advertising efforts significantly, with expenditures on advertising for Sunlight almost five times that of Lifebuoy.

Changes in Sunlight advertising paralleled changes in the campaign for Lifebuoy. Ads in the mid-1930s still featured, for example, expatriate women discussing the importance of convincing their dhobis to use Sunlight (Figure 5.16). The ads emphasized the importance of relying on Sunlight in order to ensure the longevity of clothing. By 1938, however, ads even in English-language papers generally used Indian figures, often highlighting middle-class housewives getting advice on the importance of washing clothes at home and of circumventing the dhobi's methods of rubbing and beating clothes.[75] The ads for Sunlight did not presume familiarity with the use of laundry soaps; instead they insisted upon the need to transform bodily practices involved in cleaning clothes. At the same time they warned against the use of cheaper soaps and mentioned Sunlight's manufacture in India and its exclusive use of vegetable oils.

Over the next several years, Levers repeatedly returned to such motifs, pitching its appeals directly to women, who were instructed in the value of using commercial laundry soap instead of cheap unbranded products or methods of cleaning clothes not requiring soap. They stressed to purchasers the importance of Sunlight to proper household management, the maintenance of family hygiene and appearance, and the handling of family finances (Figure 5.17).

There are two interesting points to make about such images. First, the ads counterpose the up-to-date methods the housewife could choose with the inefficient, costly, and outmoded methods of the dhobi. They implicitly urged the housewife to take over the dhobi's role or at least to supervise that role closely, thus in effect creating a new division of labor along gender lines and greater familial control over the process of clothes-washing. Sunlight advertisements often juxtaposed an image of the outdated washerman slamming clothes against some rocks with a picture of clothes shredded by such a process. Second, the ads' designers also felt compelled to provide step-by-step instructions on how to use Sunlight. The housewife is shown visually taking the clothes through a four-step process of soaking, soaping, working the soap into the clothes, and then rinsing, a process the ad claimed would save considerable wear and tear. Such visual instructions, which seem to reflect borrowing from some earlier 501 ads, strongly suggest the need to instruct the female consumer on how to use laundry soap, under the assumption she did not currently know how to do so.[76] In short, the ads provided schooling on how to become a modern housewife by fully taking charge over cleaning clothes.

In some ads during the early 1940s, the core message of the advertisement was conveyed through a picture of two women in conversation, the more experienced and

Her dhobi uses Sunlight Soap now
—and clothes last longer

"Here's another heap of dirty clothes. —I do wish washing didn't harm the clothes so much, and they never seem to be really *clean*."

"Take my advice and insist on your dhobi using Sunlight Soap. Sunlight's 'extra soapiness' gets out the dirt without the need for harmful beating and rubbing."

A MONTH LATER

"How smart your children look to-day. Did you take my advice about Sunlight Soap?"

"Yes. I'm so glad I did. The clothes all look so fresh and clean now. And Sunlight *must* clean them gently because they last much longer."

Sunlight Soap makes it possible to clean clothes without harming them. Whether clothes are washed by a dhobi or at home always be certain that Sunlight is used; its "extra soapiness" gets dirt out so easily, and leaves white things dazzlingly white, washable colours bright. Always keep Sunlight in the home; there are many uses for it, and it costs so little now.

SUNLIGHT SOAP

LEVER BROTHERS (INDIA) LIMITED

Figure 5.16 "Her dhobi uses Sunlight Soap now—*and clothes last longer*," Sunlight Soap, *TI*, December 11, 1935, 6. Produced with permission of Hindustan Unilever Limited.

competent in the shadows informing the less knowledgeable—who occupied the position of the reader—of the need to use Sunlight. In figure 5.18, a woman is pictured talking with a female friend. The caption reads: "My clothes always used to seem dull and grey [sic] after they were washed. Then a friend told me about Sunlight Soap. She said that *kutchha*[77] soaps are wasteful because they give very little cleansing lather and it's the lather from the soap that cleans clothes."[78] By attempting to create the illusion that instruction on the importance of washing soap was coming from someone in the

Figure 5.17 "The washerman has torn the cloths! Just imagine how much it would cost to buy new ones," Sunlight Soap, *Kesari*, March 27, 1945, 11. Produced with permission of Hindustan Unilever Limited.

female consumer's immediate social circle, the ads sought to close the cultural distance between the manufacturer and the household decision-maker.

In some ads run by Unilever during the early 1940s, a cartoon sequence was developed in which a woman learns how to wash clothes properly by using Sunlight soap. As with Lifebuoy ads, an original English-language version was translated into various vernaculars using the same images. Each ad featured a woman in a state of

Figure 5.18 "Sunlight Soap washes clothes cleaner than any soap I know," Sunlight Soap, *BC*, September 7, 1940, 13. Produced with permission of Hindustan Unilever Limited.

panic because she might develop the reputation for being unable to fulfill her wifely responsibilities. Often focusing on the face of the housewife, they promoted a sense of identification on the part of the female reader with her plight. A female friend—the figure was always a woman—provides the critical advice to meet the crisis. In one case it is the husband's sister who offers the crucial suggestions needed to relieve the housewife's burdens.[79]

In the final cartoon box, the housewife has learned of the value of Sunlight soap in washing clothes, and she overcomes the situation threatening to bring her social opprobrium. In Figure 5.19 a group of men—perhaps neighbors—are gossiping about the unclean state of clothes worn by the son Ramu (in Marathi ads, the character is named Rambhau) and his father.

The issue such ads sought to evoke is not just the need to improve the appearance of her husband and son, but what their state suggests about the domestic capabilities of the wife and the hygienic condition of the household. The modern housewife, the ad suggests, will readily recognize the critical importance of using the proper laundry soap to her reputation as someone who maintains her household well. Figure 5.20 features a circumstance that would have been familiar to most families with servants. In a cartoon sequence captioned "I Must Go to My Native Village," a crisis is precipitated

Figure 5.19 "How Miserable And Dirty Ramu And His Son Are Looking," Sunlight Soap, *BC*, December 4, 1941, 9. Produced with permission of Hindustan Unilever Limited.

Figure 5.20 "I must go to my Native Village," Sunlight Soap, *Kesari*, January 13, 1942, 2.

by the family servant departing suddenly for a visit to his native place. A female friend again comes to the rescue, advising the wife of the need to employ Sunlight soap now that she will have to do the work herself. Ultimately, the ad suggests, the family will be able to dispose of the need for a servant. The servant is clearly drawn to signal his membership in a lower-status caste, while both the women in the frame and the detailed furnishings in the room featured are markers of the middle-class character of the ad's main subjects.

Perhaps the most interesting examples of Sunlight advertising are ads that stress tensions between a wife and her in-laws in the joint family, a theme of much emphasis in literature and in domestic manuals at the time. These ads come from the early 1940s (I found no advertisements before 1940 even mentioning the joint family). In the first, the housewife confides to a friend that she can never please her mother-in-law. She is again advised of the proper method of washing clothes before the problem is resolved.[80] In the second image, an English ad from 1942, we see women engaged in conversation, in this case two mothers-in-law (Figure 5.21). One complains that her son must be "mad" because he has taken his wife out to a cinema-house when she should have been home doing the clothes washing. "What of me if my daughter-in-law does not stay at home and do the work?" The other mother-in-law replies: "My son often takes his wife with him. But she does not neglect the work. She knows modern ways that do work easily." The second housewife's secret, the ad reveals, is that she has taught the household servant how to use Sunlight soap, again suggesting that this is a method that does not involve the beating of clothes. "Behn,[81] I will bring her tomorrow to teach this easy Sunlight way to your servant." In both ads, the almost ubiquitous instructions for using Sunlight to wash clothes are present. The ad clearly stresses some of the most prominent themes in the discourse of conjugality: the tensions between housewife and mother-in-law and the value of release from the tyranny of in-laws, the primacy of the companionate relationship between husband and wife over other family ties, and the critical importance of the wife's household management skills.

The post-1939 Sunlight ads clearly reflected a rather intensive transformation of Levers' efforts to gather and deploy knowledge about consumers the company had accumulated during the previous few years. Whereas earlier ads used images of Europeans and themes evocative for expatriates, these ads were fashioned around popular middle-class discourses about the dynamics between husband and wife, wife and mother-in-law, and housewife and servant; they used idiomatic language, even in English-language versions ("kutchha," "behn," and "what of me"); they are based on common household situations; and they seek to replicate familiar modes of transmitting information within middle-class society, particularly the importance of conversation between women and gossip. Visually, Levers'/Lintas's artists had generated a novel set of techniques for depicting the Indian housewife and the different situations she faced in everyday life.

In effect Sunlight soap ads tried to link their appeal to powerful "prior meanings" about conjugality, discussions then at the core of emerging conceptions of modernity. Advertisements relied on global notions of domesticity, but did not merely replicate European motifs and tropes. Instead they steeped themselves in ideas and values, particularly those of the housewife's responsibility for family hygiene, that reflected

Figure 5.21 "My Son Must Be Mad," Sunlight Soap, *BC*, August 26, 1942, 3. Produced with permission of Hindustan Unilever Limited.

Levers' understanding of Indian middle-class priorities. In effect, they sought to instruct the housewife that the achievement of the modern conjugal ideal required the adoption of specific bodily practices set apart from behaviors marked as "traditional" and unscientific, ones that involved the extensive consumption of brand-name commodities. Visually, they used a variety of techniques to suggest the world of conversation among women and the identification of the female reader with the figures featured in the ads.

Conclusion

Within a short time period—from the late 1920s to the early 1940s—Levers underwent a major transformation from a company with a limited ground presence in India to one involved in an extensive effort to adapt to the changing political, cultural, and market environment of South Asia. The "domestication" or "Indianization" of Levers' operations was a creative response to the crisis posed to its business operations occasioned by dramatic increases in competition and changing attitudes toward foreign products. Levers set up a manufacturing plant in India, adjusted its products to the Indian market (particularly by replacing animal fats entirely with vegetable oils), and made an unprecedented investment in advertising. The company brought advertising specialists to the subcontinent who worked with local artists, copywriters, and translators to design ads. The character of the advertising message shifted through a series of campaigns that were repeatedly tried out, evaluated, and then reformulated. Levers in effect tried to counter many of Godrej's claims about foreign soaps, now stressing that its products were also "made in India with vegetable oils only." The B.O. campaign was abandoned, largely because it proved difficult to translate it into terms that would resonate among consumers of western India; Prakash Tandon's objections to the campaign are perhaps the most explicit evidence in this book of the friction that could be produced by the attempt to introduce universal appeals into a South Asian context. Another major shift followed Thompson Walker's market surveys around 1938 which highlighted the importance of female decision-making. Armed with extensive knowledge about the Indian household, Levers developed a series of campaigns for both Lifebuoy and Lux directed explicitly to the Indian housewife and her role in sustaining the hygienic mission and the respectability of the conjugal family. The campaigns of 1939 to 1943 also seem to have reflected a richer appreciation of idiomatic language as well as knowledge about the everyday character of Indian social interactions that likely came from Levers' subordinate employees and from traders dealing in the company's products. Most critically, the visual appearance of Levers' advertisement was transformed. No longer was a picture of a package of a Levers' soap and a few simple lines of text deemed sufficient; images of Europeans were no longer used. Now depictions of human figures specifically delineated as Indian, largely Hindu (or at least non-Muslim) and middle class, often engaged in familiar patterns of female sociality, were deemed to be essential to winning customers. When one considers this evidence alongside the Lux campaigns using film stars that were being formulated around the same time, it is clear that the company was involved much more consciously than before in efforts to formulate cultural stategies directed to the emerging Indian consumer.

6

The Invention of a Cooking Medium: Cocogem and Dalda[1]

If there were any segment of middle-class budgets that would seem to offer the possibility for stimulating a dramatic expansion of brand-name capitalism in India, it would be the domain of food. In India food constituted by far the most significant component of middle-class household expenditures.[2] And elsewhere in the world, agri-business and food processing have often played a critical part in the development of consumer capitalism. In the United States, for instance, commercial foods packaged and branded by large agricultural corporations came to constitute a critical part of the American economy by the mid-twentieth century. Their role has become so engrained in everyday life that it would be easy to assume that food everywhere possesses the same potential to contribute to the making of modern capitalism.

Such an assumption, however, simplifies the European and American experiences, and overlooks the uneven process of commodification in food markets. Undoubtedly, by 1950, most Americans had come to purchase their dietary needs in large-scale chain stores, and many foods they consumed were supplied by industrial-scale producers. But large-scale firms assumed this position of ascendancy only through a conflict-ridden process shaped by resistance from consumers and consumer activists and by extensive federal regulation.[3] Supermarket chains achieved their dominant place only after World War II, when many housewives had entered formal employment, reducing their time for shopping and food preparation. Advertisement stressing such themes as motherly love for the family, the need to please menfolk, the release of women from the drudgery of housework, and women's role in promoting familial health, proved critical in overcoming widespread hesitations about foods manufactured or distributed by large corporations.[4] Many items became dietary staples in late twentieth-century Europe and America only after decades of struggle. Margarine, for instance, was regarded in Britain as a marker of low status and poverty and as an inferior food in taste and quality through the 1950s;[5] its standing in European and American society became established only after concerted advertising efforts.

In India, food products manufactured by multinational corporations took up only a minor place in middle-class diets during the interwar period. In contrast to the marketers of tea, coffee, and other drinks like Horlicks and Ovaltine—whose efforts made serious inroads into middle-class consumption patterns during the interwar period—global firms involved in the food industry had relatively limited success in persuading Indians to buy and consume what they produced. Advertising devoted to food was limited compared to tonics, soaps, and other commodities that have been explored in this book, partly because businesses were so pessimistic about the possibility of creating mass markets for their products. Ads for Quaker Oats, Kelloggs' Corn Flakes, and Brands' Essence of Chicken did appear in English-language newspapers but such brands found a limited consumer base outside the ranks of expatriates and the most anglicized Indians. Figure 6.1 provides one attempt, showing

Figure 6.1 "How a young man recovered his strength," Brands' Essence of Chicken, *TI*, January 29, 1937, 13.

how an ad from Brands' Essence of Chicken drew upon the trope of male weakness, which was discussed extensively in Chapter 3. But such advertisements hardly made deep inroads into middle-class consumption patterns. The commercial production of foods in India no doubt increased during the early twentieth century, but the output was sold predominantly in unbranded form in urban bazaars and rural markets.[6] Most urban consumers of all classes continued to buy their foods in local shops or from hawkers on the street. The supermarket—or any institution resembling it— did not really exist in India, and processed foods constituted only a tiny portion of household diets. Seemingly the advance of brand-name capitalism stopped when it came to ingestible commodities.

This chapter discusses the advertising of a type of food product that producers did come to view as one with potential to generate significant demand: cooking mediums, that is, the oils and fats used in preparing foods in the household. It examines the efforts of two major companies to sell standardized, packaged cooking mediums in urban India: (1) TOMCO, the Indian edible oils and soap company that used international marketing and advertising firms to promote a cooking oil derived from crushed coconuts called Cocogem during the 1920s; and (2) Unilever and its subsidiary, Hindustan Holland Vanaspati Trading Company (hereafter HHVT),[7] which began to sell a new commercial cooking medium, *vanaspati* (hydrogenated vegetable oil) under the trade label Dalda during the later 1930s. Campaigns to promote Cocogem largely proved a deadend, despite significant efforts to market it as a safer alternative to unbranded forms of ghee and cooking oils. Dalda, by contrast, eventually carved out a place among many middle-class budgets through a campaign touting the product's value in promoting family health and masculine energy, in short by linking the product to central preoccupations of the middle class. Even so, Levers was not able to overcome significant consumer concerns about Dalda's healthiness or continued preferences for ghee (clarified butter). The story of both these commodities strongly illustrates the serious hesitations of middle-class families to subject their digestive systems to industrial capitalism.

Food, consumers and the bazaar

As anthropologists and other social scientists have long recognized, food plays a critical place in the construction of South Asian culture and society. Arjun Appadurai has pointed to the myriad of roles food exercises in everyday life:

Food in India is closely tied to the moral and social status of individuals and groups. Food taboos and prescriptions divide men from women, gods from humans, upper from lower castes, one sect from another. Eating together is a carefully constructed exercise in the reproduction of intimacy. Exclusion of a person from eating events is a symbolically intense social signal of rank, or distance, or enmity. Food is believed to cement the relationship between men and gods, as well as between men themselves. Food is never medically or morally neutral. Whatever the perception of the purely gustatory aspects of particular foods, the issue of their implications for the health, the purity and the moral and mental balance of the consumer are never far out of sight.[8]

But despite its centrality, efforts to explore the importance of food in the South Asian past have been limited. Only in the last decade or so have scholars begun to make concerted efforts to examine such topics as the dissemination of new foods and spices during the Columbian exchange, the role of food in the cultural construction of domesticity and the family, Gandhi's theories of diet, and the development of an identifiably "Indian" cuisine in national and global contexts.[9] And even this new literature has largely ignored the commercial history of food. But given the widespread adoption of branded forms of hot drink—Lipton and Brooke Bond tea, Ovaltine and Horlicks, and various lines of coffee—the weakness of global capitalism in transforming food consumption patterns in India needs to be understood rather than simply accepted as inevitable.[10]

The most straightforward explanation for the relatively limited adoption of mass-produced foods during the interwar period is that of taste. It would be a commonplace to say that food products being imported into India were often strange to palates accustomed to spices, regionally specific flavors, and the freshness of ingredients and preparation. Corporate manufacturers did not yet design their products specifically for Indian markets, as they would later do for masala-flavored noodles, packaged savory snacks, and boxed sweets. Canning and packaging, along with the processes necessary to prevent spoiling before they reached consumers, altered the flavor of foods in ways that were novel in early twentieth-century India. Not surprisingly, when most of the expatriate population left the subcontinent after 1947, the market for canned foods in India almost collapsed. Given the strong preference for fresh vegetables and produce in India, only the military and restaurants remained as significant sources of demand.[11]

Attitudes toward branded foods, moreover, must also be understood in light of Indian theories of alimentary health, even as these were undergoing transformation during the early twentieth century.[12] According to some Ayurvedic notions, food metabolism was powered by digestive fires that allowed the body to process food intake, eliminating wastes but also transforming foods into the energy necessary for carrying out the tasks of everyday life or for engaging in clear thought.[13] The ingestion of *satvic* foods, foods possessing the *guna* (quality) *satva*,[14] a word with multiple positive valences, was believed to sustain this process. According to a writer from the Kanara Saraswat community, in 1934, a satvic food was one that "augments vitality, energy, vigour, joy, and cheerfulness, delicious, bland, substantial and agreeable."[15] By contrast, food with a *rajas* quality, he suggested, was "bitter, sour, saline, over-hot, pungent, dry and burning, and produces pain, grief and sickness," while food with *tamas* qualities was "stale and flat, putrid and corrupt, leavings and also and unclean (sic.)"[16] These categories were strongly associated with purity and pollution. Shrikant Botre has pointed out that in Hindu texts, *Satva, raja* and *tama* are "caste-hierarchised and corporealized qualities (*gunas*) of the person's mind mapped on the Brahmin, non-Brahmin and the untouchable bodies."[17] Practitioners of indigenous medicine claimed that non-satvic foods failed to completely carry out the transformative processes involved in digestion, producing fermentation in the body, gas, listlessness, constipation, and cloudy mental capacity. Satvic foods were also seen as essential to seminal balance, which, as we have seen, was regarded as critical not only to sexual potency but also physical vigor and mental clarity.[18] High-caste Indians often watched their diets carefully, regarding foods consumed by Dalits, Muslims, and others as polluting or as endangering the proper functioning of the body. How different foods fit into these understandings was varied and subject to change. But commercially-prepared foods were especially suspect as containing ingredients that might harm digestion.[19]

Finally, it is apparent that consumers often held significant uncertainties about manufacturing processes themselves. Some were undoubtedly concerned about unsanitary conditions in factories. Others worried about *who* or what had touched the product as it was processed. As is well recognized in the literature, South Asians often have held beliefs that food, particularly uncooked food, carries pollution associated with those who have been in contact with it.[20] From the perspective of some high-caste Hindus, imported foods could have been contaminated by foreign industrial workers perceived as unclean, while food made in India might have been defiled by Dalits and Muslims. During the colonial period rumors abounded that foods processed in unknown factories might contain traces of meats and other unclean substances. In India food manufacturers had to constantly assure potential customers in their advertising that their products were made with the purest of ingredients in the most sanitary of processes.

Throughout the interwar period, middle-class consumers in western India exhibited a pronounced preference for fresh, unbranded items. While changes in the household economy in North America caused women to opt increasingly for processed and packaged foods requiring less time to buy and prepare, modern conceptions of domesticity in India may have actually intensified women's interactions with the hawkers and small shopkeepers who supplied their foods. Before the 1920s, social norms discouraging women's presence in public places meant shopping in middle-class families had often been left to men or household servants. During the interwar period, these norms slowly gave way to new attitudes increasingly placing the onus on women to look after household food purchases. Domestic manuals spelled out the enhanced responsibilities for women in the home; these included preparing healthy and tasty meals while observing household budgetary constraints, a balancing act that required significant skills in selecting foods and negotiating with shopkeepers.[21]

Such concerns certainly influenced household choices about cooking mediums. In simplistic terms, there were two main forms of cooking medium available to urban families in the early 1920s, unless they were willing to use animal fats. The cheaper of these was the category of vegetable oils—made from groundnuts, sesame seeds, castor, linseed and other oil seeds. Such oils sold in western Indian urban centers were often produced by small businesses in mofussil towns that ran forty to fifty oil presses and that shipped the processed oil off for sale through merchant-intermediaries.[22] By World War I a range of more mechanized methods emerged and oil-pressing was often carried out in factories (including some in Bombay), though these rarely sold their products on a brand-name basis.[23] The poorer classes in the cities and most rural areas relied heavily on vegetable oils.[24] Advertising for vegetable oil did not have a regular presence in Indian newspapers during this time.

A second major medium was ghee. Ghee was typically prepared through a labor-intensive process, either in households or by shopkeepers, that involved melting butter and then pouring off impurities. Ghee could be heated to higher temperatures than most vegetable oils before producing smoke, and was believed to make cooked foods tastier and healthier. It could also be spread onto cooked foods, such as breads, to produce a flavor appraised highly in local society.[25] It certainly possessed significant cultural backing. For instance, it was strongly associated with Brahmanical socio-religious rituals, such as offerings to deities in temple ceremonies. According to K. T. Achaya, the mere presence of ghee and milk in the cooking process "confers ritual purity on the dish."[26] Classical Hindu works—and the modern writers who cited them—sometimes referred to it as a life-enhancing substance. As one nationalist observer argued, the "best *satvic* food is milk and ghee," and a person with a diet that included these products, "can develop his powers of the brain to the utmost. It is mainly through a milk diet that man can attain worldly as well as spiritual powers."[27] While not all twentieth-century observers might have accepted ghee's qualities in enhancing spirituality, middle-class families often associated ghee with good taste, high status, and auspiciousness. Indigenous medical practitioners claimed that ghee had significant health values, including mitigating illnesses and fevers and purifying the blood.[28]

During the early twentieth century, however, the price of ghee rose significantly, pushing its regular use out of reach of many city-dwellers.[29] One consequence of such inflation was to compel urban households to rely more extensively on vegetable oils, often with deep dissatisfaction. Publications by Ayurvedic practitioners at the time lamented the fact that the middle class was being cut off from ghee's auspicious and health-inducing qualities.[30] Shopkeepers sometimes responded to the rising prices by adulterating ghee, typically mixing it with vegetable oils, such as cotton seed oil, groundnut oil and coconut oil, or even animal fats.[31] During the 1920s, whale oil and fish oil from Japan also became used extensively as adulterants, a fact that often could not be detected by consumers.[32] According to one account, thousands of cases were detected and prosecuted by authorities of the Bombay Municipality during the 1930s.[33] Adulteration became so common that one observer reported, perhaps with some exaggeration: "It is probably true to say that the only persons who have tasted pure 'ghi' are those who own milking-cattle, make their own butter and convert this butter into ghi."[34] Concerns about the purity of ghee found in the market—regarded as a culinary, ritual, and sanitary matter—became a regular refrain.[35] Ghee sold in Indian markets came under the watchful eyes of local municipalities and the colonial government,[36] but in practice any new rules regulating it were almost impossible to enforce. Observers sometimes held lower-class, lower-caste milkmen responsible for the unsanitary character of dairy products available in the cities, but more commonly blamed unscrupulous merchants.[37]

A new product available in the market after 1917 was hydrogenated vegetable oil, which came to be known as *vanaspati* (literally meaning "lord of the forest" but indicating it was derived from vegetables).[38] This was a commodity created by refining and hydrogenating various vegetable oils, processes that removed dirt and other impure elements, transformed the oils into a hardened fat, and eliminated the oils' characteristic colors and smells. In some cases, vitamins could be introduced.[39] Additives could make the appearance, texture and even taste of vanaspati approximate that of "real" ghee. The cost of vanaspati generally ran 35 to 50 percent less than pure ghee during the 1920s and 1930s. In writings of the time, the product was often referred to as "vegetable ghee."

Most South Asians today would probably find it surprising that vanaspati was first manufactured in early-twentieth century Europe. Exports of the product to the subcontinent began around the end of World War I and India became its main market. In the 1920s, one Dutch commercial firm, the Van den Berghs, was a particularly dominant producer; it merged with Lever Brothers to form Unilever in 1930.[40] But other manufacturers were involved as well. Figure 6.2 provides a 1928 ad for one such producer, Lily Brand from Ralli Brothers.

From the beginning, concerns about vanaspati's healthiness led to hesitations about its use. In the early 1920s, the government refused to endorse vanaspati over ghee for maritime crews, despite its cheapness.[41] Household adoption of vanaspati was limited. Even though vanaspati was a global commodity manufactured by multinational firms, it typically reached the consumer in unbranded form. Perhaps its main use during the 1920s and early 1930s was as an adulterating agent in the ghee market. Most

Figure 6.2 "Lily Brand," ad for Lily Brand Vegetable Product, *MS*, January 5, 1928, 12.

vanaspati produced by HHVT, for instance, was sold in 40 lb. tins, too large and expensive for household purchase, that merchants and others used to mix with ghee to create a product indistinguishable from pure ghee in color, smell, and taste but at a lower price or higher profit. As TOMCO indicated in its annual report of 1926: "every manufacturer of edible vegetable oils in this country is feeling the competition of German and Dutch goods, mostly in the shape of hardened oil, in our market... The imported hardened oil is mostly used for the purpose of adulteration with ghee and the production of various mixed products, wrongly described as ghee has increased, which in turn has brought down the price of natural ghee."[42] The amount of adulterant used in mixing could range from 5 percent of the total to 90 percent. In some cases, one observer noted: "the adulteration has gone on to such a limit that pure vegetable ghee is being sold under the name of butter-ghee."[43] At first vanaspati manufacturers refrained from trying to advertise their commodity directly to consumers, unsure whether any independent market could ever develop.[44] Adulteration with whale and fish oil died out during the 1930s after protective duties on these items were established and they were required to be marked as animal products. This development only enhanced the use of vanaspati.[45]

By 1930, Indian manufacturers became involved in producing vanaspati, taking advantage of protective tariffs on its import. Messrs. Indian Vegetable Products Limited established the first Indian factory for its manufacture but it was soon joined by several others, including Ganesh Flour Mills, HHVT, and TOMCO.[46] As tariffs on European production increased, imports were reduced to a trickle.[47] But the Indian commodity was still mainly used in adulteration, as an officer of the HHVT admitted in 1934: "although Vegetable Ghee is a sound and nourishing fat produced under much more hygienic conditions than the natural ghee to which it is a substitute, our industry has not yet quite lost its secret and backdoor character. Only a very small percentage of the trade is sold as Vegetable Ghee. It is either sold as Tawda, mixed product, or cheap ghee."[48] Two years later the same officer reported:

> the very great majority—perhaps 95% of all the actual consumers of our product— think they are buying real ghee and would be horrified to know that it was Vegetable Product they were really getting. The cow and the ghee produced from the cow's milk are holy, according to the Hindu religion, and therefore the prejudice against our Vegetable Product is much stronger than the prejudice that used to exist in Europe against Margarine and will be far more difficult to overcome.[49]

At the same time he predicted that the proposed laws' regulation of mixing would be unenforceable because the "big ghee Merchant is a wealthy man and the servant of the law enjoys a poor salary [i.e. he would be subject to bribery]."[50]

Cocogem

The development of advertising for mass-produced cooking mediums must be understood in the context of middle-class preferences for ghee and of the concerns consumers held about the healthiness and purity of commercial items. Advertisers sought to displace consumer reliance on ghee merchants, casting branded goods as more trustworthy in quality than ghee and other products found in the bazaar. But the advertising campaigns themselves reveal the great hurdles that the manufacturers had in overcoming aversions held by many consumers against industrially produced and branded commodities. Ultimately the most successful of these campaigns again stressed the modern conjugal family's preoccupation with the health of its members, particularly children.

During the 1920s and 1930s, many local merchants posted ads in the papers for pure ghee, hoping to take advantage of consumer anxieties about the genuineness of products actually present in the bazaar. A 1926 ad posted by M. Motilal Masalawala (Figure 6.3), a ghee merchant in Bombay, insisted on the necessity of pure ghee for the Diwali holidays, stressing his product had been tested for purity by the Chemical Analyzer.[51] The ad quoted Masalawala's rates and promised a reward of 5,001 Rupees to anyone who could prove that any of its ghee had been adulterated (an offer made to publicize that the chance of such a finding was remote). A 1929 ad for pure Barda ghee from Jamnagar, a product sold in large tins, specifically alerted readers to the presence of ghee adulterated with imported products elsewhere in the market and promised that its own ghee was pure, guaranteed by Jamnagar State.[52] Such ads were not part of sustained campaigns; they appeared intermittently and for short periods. In contrast to merchants dealing in ghee, the sellers of locally produced vegetable oil seemingly felt little occasion to tout the qualities of their product in advertisements.

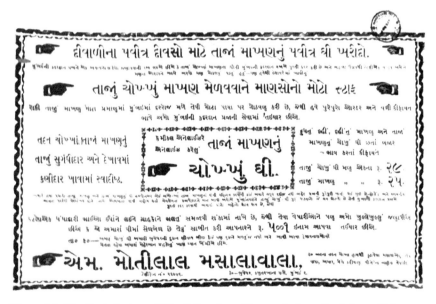

Figure 6.3 "For the holy days of Divali, Buy Pure Ghee made from Fresh Butter," M. Motilal Masalawala, *MS*, October 20, 1926, 5.

The first significant campaign for an industrially produced cooking medium was conducted for Cocogem, a coconut oil manufactured by TOMCO. Though TOMCO was an Indian company, it came to rely on international advertising firms in its marketing. TOMCO's entry into the domestic consumer market for cooking mediums was almost inadvertent. As mentioned in Chapter 5, TOMCO established a mill in Cochin for crushing coconut and groundnuts in order to sell oil and oilcake on the export market; the mill included the latest in modern equipment, and obviously involved considerable investment.[53] But after the export market for these products collapsed, the company in 1921 devised an alternative scheme, that of producing consumer commodities for the domestic market. Included in TOMCO's plans were substitutes for cooking butter, a deodorized salad oil made from groundnut and sesame seed, soap, and Cocogem, which was produced out of white Malabar copra. As the 1922–23 annual report of the company indicated, "there is a much larger margin of profit in these products than in the crushing of crude oil though it will take time to find a market for them."[54]

By 1924, TOMCO decided to focus its promotional efforts on Cocogem, which it found to be "the most suitable for everyday use and the most marketable of our products."[55] It established a sales organization to distribute the oil on a commercial basis, slowly overcoming merchant reluctance to sell the previously unknown commodity. The company made Cocogem available in a variety of sizes—1 lb., 2 lb., 6 lb., 9 lb., and 35 lb.—so that consumers with modest available cash could buy it. Almost from the very beginning, advertising was a major aspect of the sales effort. The 1923–24 Directors report indicated:

> With proper propaganda we hope to convince people that it is better to use a pure and economical ghee substitute like Cocogem than to allow themselves to be carried away by false sentiment in using the impure and, frequently, adulterated bazaar ghee. If we can succeed in doing this and our sales reach the maximum production of our Products Plant, which must take some time, our mills will begin to show a small profit and we can afford to await the improvement in the oil markets of the world which is bound to come sooner or later.[56]

TOMCO stockholders and board members increasingly urged an aggressive policy involving advertising. A participant in the stockholders' meeting of 1924 praised the commodity—indicating that he had almost totally switched from ghee use at home to Cocogem—but observed that general awareness of its attractive qualities was limited. He recommended to the directors that they publicize Cocogem in the vernacular newspapers of every district headquarters and also hire canvassers to conduct publicity. He also suggested providing free samples to Irani restaurants (in Bombay, presumably) in order to encourage them to use Cocogem in preparing their meals.[57] In 1926, the company developed an arrangement with Messrs. H. J. Foster and Company as an agent to sell Cocogem throughout Asia.[58] A major advertising campaign followed, one initially directed toward winning an Indian middle-class clientele. In 1933, after H. J. Foster asked to be relieved of its obligation to sell Tomco products (its leading figure had died), the advertising account was turned over to JWT.

Initial ads for Cocogem made multiple claims, including the tastiness of foods made with the oil, the purity of the product, and its cheapness. This 1926 ad in the *Bombay Chronicle* (Figure 6.4) stressed Cocogem's superior qualities relative to animal fat and vegetable oils. The ad clearly targeted middle-class consumers. The central image in the ad was that of an Indian housewife in a six yard sari, and it included silhouetted figures seated around a stove, with water pots and other vessels characteristic of a simple middle-class kitchen. The puris carried by the woman suggest a food largely inaccessible to the poor and working class, one often prepared with ghee. TOMCO also conducted advertising in vernacular newspapers. A Gujarati ad from *Mumbai Samachar*, for instance, stressed the cheapness and high quality of Cocogem, but also

Figure 6.4 "Better Cooking," Cocogem, *BC*, December 19, 1925, 14. Produced with permission of Hindustan Unilever Limited.

the fact that there was no risk of adulteration since it was sold in sealed tins.[59] Clearly the comparison suggested was to the ghee available in local bazaars, which was typically dispensed in measured quantities from open containers.

Acceptance of Cocogem, however, was hesitant. The new commodity not only had to overcome preferences for ghee and traditional oils, it also had to establish the incorporation of coconut oil in cooking, a practice largely confined to South Indians, whose preference for the product could be the subject of jokes elsewhere in India.[60] By the late 1920s, TOMCO's sellers had clearly recognized that gaining a foothold for Cocogem was going to be an uphill climb. Figure 6.5, a 1927 ad in the *Bombay Chronicle*, is entitled "Overcoming Prejudice" and specifically indicates that "Cocogem, too, [like other products once subject to suspicion] has suffered...from public misunderstanding,"[61]

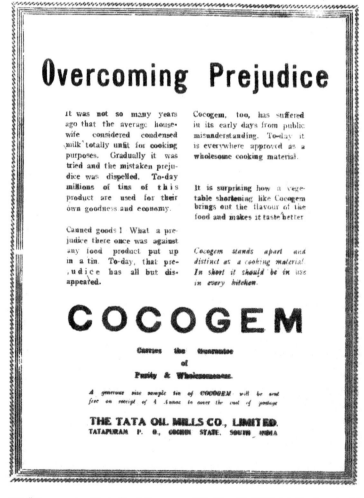

Figure 6.5 "Overcoming Prejudice," Cocogem, *BC,* May 21, 1927, 14. Produced with permission of Hindustan Unilever Limited.

at the same time expressing confidence that this perception would ultimately give way to widespread acceptance. The ad's references to a similar trajectory for condensed milk and canned goods in the past were ones that would have been understood most strongly by expatriates. For middle-class buyers, the widespread presence in the market of ghee adulterated with vanaspati continued to render Cocogem's price advantage over pure ghee irrelevant. Even European households sometimes continued to use ghee (perhaps due to their cooks' preferences) or animal lard.

By the early 1930s, TOMCO's ads increasingly inveighed against using bazaar ghee. One *Times of India* ad warned "You never know, with bazaar ghee. It may be (often is!) heavily adulterated or contaminated before it reaches you." The advertisement pictured a shop with swarming flies.[62] Highlighting the fact that Cocogem was packed in vacuum-sealed tins, the ad stressed that the consumer could count upon its quality. Another ad (Figure 6.6) pictures two European women conversing, one indicating: "You *never* know what you are getting in ghee, or what filth it has been exposed to." The other replies "No, but you can guess! No guess work about Cocogem. You *know* it's safe." The text in another ad reinforces this point: "Much ghee sold as pure is heavily adulterated with cheap, rank fats. And it's easy to imagine the contamination to which it is often exposed in the bazaar—yet too many people still leave this important matter to the cook."[63] Other ads targeted animal lard for criticism along with ghee.[64]

As these images make apparent, the campaign for Cocogem had shifted by this time to targeting the European housewife. More ads ran in the *Times of India*, the main newspaper read by the expatriate community, and they typically featured images of European women and testimonials from women with European names spread over the subcontinent. The discussion in advertisements of the items to be cooked also makes this clear: fishes, meats, "rissoles," scalloped peaches, and pastries. Ads for Cocogem in vernacular papers and English papers with nationalist reputations such as the *Bombay Chronicle* declined significantly. Seemingly, TOMCO had largely abandoned its pursuit of middle-class customers and apparently had not considered creating campaigns steeped in the values of conjugality as ads for tonics, women's medicines, soap, Horlicks and Ovaltine were starting to do by the 1930s.

One particularly fascinating feature of these ads was the constant warning to memsahibs that they not leave the purchase of cooking mediums to their cooks. Since cooks did much of the actual food shopping in expatriate households, their preferences had a significant effect on purchases. In Cocogem ads, European women were asked to take charge of their homes and not to trust their cooks to make such an important decision as the choice of cooking medium. As mentioned in Chapter 2, the need to exert control over servants' market activity was a regular theme in advertisement to expatriates. In one advertisment a housewife is illustrated instructing the cook how to prepare the family meal. "Don't leave it all to the cook!" the ad commands, "Show him how Cocogem will improve the food he prepares."[65] One particularly remarkable ad features a letter from one Goan cook (Luis da Silva) to another, replete with misspellings, cross-outs and grammatical errors. In the letter, da Silva praises his memsahib for providing him with Cocogem—which he suggests had improved the quality of his cooking immensely— and he urges Rodrigues to do the same (see Figure 6.7).[66]

Clearly TOMCO advertisers mounted a serious effort to market Cocogem in India during the interwar period. The company had made some small profits, but the results

BAZAAR GHEE

—a risk not worth taking!

P̲ure, vacuum-sealed
COCOGEM cooks better,
costs no more to use

E̲VERYONE knows that much ghee sold as pure is heavily adulterated with cheap, rank fats. And it's easy to imagine the contamination to which it is often exposed in the bazaar—yet too many people still leave this important matter to the cook.

Don't risk it—insist on pure, *sealed* Cocogem. Costing no more to use than so-called "pure" ghee, it is *always* safe, and it cooks (fries especially) infinitely better.

Why? Simply because ghee and other animal fats burn more than 100° below the temperature chefs regard as ideal—450° Fahrenheit. Food cooked at a low temperature

absorbs fat, becomes soggy and indigestible: food properly fried in really hot Cocogem is invariably crisp and delicious because it is *instantly* browned, the flavour sealed in, and all greasiness sealed out.

Cocogem is tasteless itself and does not absorb flavours—so it can be economically used again and again. And, being tasteless, it can be liberally used for shortening cakes and pastry without imparting any greasy flavour.

Use it also for pillaus, kedgerees, sauces, salad dressings, mayonnaise and many other dishes. It is rich in food-value and also contains bone-building Vitamin D.

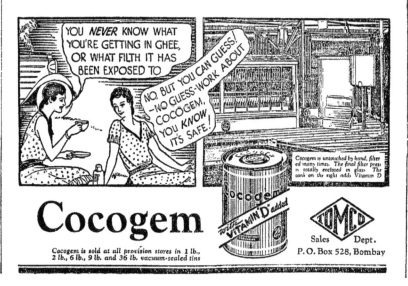

YOU *NEVER* KNOW WHAT YOU'RE GETTING IN GHEE, OR WHAT FILTH IT HAS BEEN EXPOSED TO

NO, BUT YOU CAN GUESS! —NO GUESS-WORK ABOUT COCOGEM, YOU *KNOW* IT'S SAFE!

Cocogem is untouched by hand, filtered many times. The final filter press is totally enclosed in glass. The tank on the right adds Vitamin D

Cocogem

Cocogem is sold at all provision stores in 1 lb., 2 lb., 6 lb., 9 lb. and 36 lb. vacuum-sealed tins

TOMCO
Sales Dept.
P. O. Box 528, Bombay

Figure 6.6 "Bazaar Ghee—A Risk Not Worth Taking," Cocogem, *TI,* May 31, 1933, 14. Produced with permission of Hindustan Unilever Limited.

Figure 6.7 "Dear Rodrigues," Cocogem, *TI*, February 5, 1933, 15. Produced with permission of Hindustan Unilever Limited.

of its campaign were disappointing. In 1934 less than 250 tons of Cocogem were sold nationally, less than 5 percent of the country's total production of vanaspati, an industry still in its infancy.[67] Despite the attractive packaging, the addition of vitamins to the product, and an ambitious advertising effort, the middle class had failed to show any real enthusiasm for the commodity. While Cocogem had seemed the most promising product made by TOMCO in the 1920s, the company increasingly turned its efforts to selling soaps in the 1930s, as discussed in Chapter 5. TOMCO also started up its own plant for making hydrogenated vegetable oil, and by 1934 was producing about three times as much (in weight terms) of this product as it was of Cocogem.[68] By the later 1930s, the number of advertisements for Cocogem had declined significantly. Resistance of middle-class families to industrially produced goods—what one TOMCO official called "the innate conservatism of the average Indian household"[69]— had in effect rendered the campaign a failure.

The campaign for Dalda

The most significant effort to promote a cooking medium before 1950 was Levers' campaign for Dalda, its brand of vanaspati. Dalda was a product launched by the Unilever subsidiary HVM.[70] The company was importing hydrogenated vegetable oil into India until it established a plant for manufacturing vanaspati in Bombay around 1931. The new factory made vanaspati from groundnuts and other plant substances. According to its records, HVM's product was regarded by shopkeepers as "superior" to its competitors (probably meaning that it resembled real ghee best). In 1936, the company produced 11,500 tons of hydrogenated oil, somewhat less than demand because of the limitations of productive capacity. Sales representatives of the company reportedly refrained from "pushing the sale of Vegetable Product in up-country villages and far off territories as they might have done if surplus capacity had been available in our plant."[71] Because the requirements of shopkeepers who mixed the product with ghee were consistently greater than what could be produced, there was no reason to advertise it independently.

By the mid-1930s, the HVM product had achieved considerable "goodwill," but seemingly much more among traders than among individual consumers. Undoubtedly most of the company's product was being sold for mixing, with the ultimate consumers being unaware of the manufacturer's name and often believing that they were buying pure ghee. Some ghee merchants even requested the company to package the product in 35 lb. tins with removable labels, which would make it possible to pass it off as real ghee. HVM refused, in part because it wished to sustain the brand's reputation and in part because such an action might provide a further temptation for government to regulate the industry.[72]

The fact that Levers' output was sold largely in adulterated form was clearly making company representatives uncomfortable. Discussions about regulating vanaspati and ghee adulteration were becoming widespread in government circles and in provincial council debates throughout the 1930s.[73] Vanaspati was repeatedly attacked for its foreign origins, the absence of vitamins and nutritive fats, its deceptive use in adulteration, and even the ritual dangers that adulteration posed in religious ceremony where ghee was a critical element.[74] Some Indian leaders emphasized the importance of encouraging the use of dairy products as part of projects to regenerate the nation and to protect the cow. Significant laws for grading and marking ghee were adopted by different provinces.[75] In Bombay, major legislation to quash adulteration was first adopted in 1925, and then was strengthened considerably in 1936. Ghee sellers and anti-vanaspati activists continued to lobby aggressively for the vegetable product to be banned altogether or to be forced to add a deep red color,[76] a practice that would have destroyed consumer interest in the product, which depended upon its resemblance to pure ghee.[77] Levers' executives reasoned that the development of a branded product that could be sold directly to consumers and possessed its own independent market might reduce the danger of government intervention. Under such pressures, one officer in Levers would write several years later, "Our whole business depended on our ability to develop quickly a trade for Vegetable Product in a household size of packing which would prove conclusively the existence of a worthwhile consumer demand."[78] The emergence of rival brands, such as Lion and Swastik Vanaspati, may have constituted another reason for

Figure 6.8 "A True Family Friend," Swastik Vanaspati, *GS*, August 30, 1945, 6.

pitching vanaspati directly for home use. Ads for these commodities often stressed the contribution of their products to the household, picturing happy families who used it at home. In Figure 6.8 the kitchen furnishings in the image and the kerosine stove in the left corner clearly suggest an upper-middle-class home, one that would have been at once familiar and an aspirational model for most of its intended audience.

By 1938, HHVT was marketing a new vanaspati product that resembled pure ghee in color and smell even more closely than its predecessors, and that would not be used for mixing.[79] Proposing to sell this product at a price a bit below that of pure ghee, the company proposed to call this product HVM Vanaspati, though it would be marketed under five more specific names, each sold by a different distributor. One of these brands was Dalda (the others were Lotus, Ganpati, Tiger, and Butterfly) and it was sold in 2, 5, and 10 lb. tins. The name Dalda itself was coined by adding an L (for Levers) to the name of the chief selling agents of the company's vanaspati, Hoosen Kasum Dada. Advertising these brands was essential to success, since consumers had to be convinced to buy a new and unfamiliar commodity in place of ghee or products purporting to be ghee. The company proposed 62,000 Rupees for advertising in the initial year. Such an amount would not likely be justified by the immediate sales, but the real issue was, as one executive put it, to develop "a proprietary trade in vegetable product as such," presumably reasoning that potential government regulations would end the vanaspati business altogether.[80] This 1938 ad (Figure 6.9) provided a picture of the different tins. The ad stressed the purity of the product, the fact it was made from vegetable oils, and that it " keeps your family strong and healthy and makes your meals more delicious." In effect, the principle of conjugality was now being introduced.

Soon the company apparently committed itself to promoting the Dalda brand alone, and it launched an extensive advertising campaign in English and vernacular newspapers. The ads were designed by Levers' new advertising company, Lintas, which was also promoting Levers' soaps. While sales were initially slow, they grew significantly by 1940, and the company decided to intensify its advertising, which rose to 265,000 Rupees in 1944.[81] Harvey Duncan of Lintas was made responsible for creating the campaign for the product. An initial 1939 ad announced Dalda as "India's new cooking food; *pure, wholesome*" and stressed the product "contains no animal fat" and is "untouched by hand," likely in an effort to address high-caste concerns about the possibility of exposure to substances (and persons) thought to be polluting in the manufacturing process. The ad posed the question;"Why use cheap oils or bazaar ghee when pure nourishing HVM Vanaspati can be bought so economically?," and mentioned that the product was available in packed tins rather than in open containers in the bazaar, echoing sales themes employed earlier by Cocogem. The ad stressed that the product could be used in many of the same ways as real ghee. It pictured a group of housewives who appear to be undergoing instruction on the virtues of the product. Dalda's use was thus clearly linked to the concept of domesticity from its inception as a commodity.

By 1940, Levers had clearly decided on the main lines that Dalda campaigns would take for the next decade. These advertisements, I contend, sought to counteract the serious doubts that existed in consumers' minds about Dalda: the questions about its nutritional value, uncertainties about incorporating mass-produced commodities into personal diet, and worries about replacing a dairy product believed to possess special

HVM VANASPATI

make delicious meals with wonderful

Packed in airtight tins to keep it pure and wholesome

USE H.V.M. VANASPATI FOR

Frying of every description. Place a lump of H. V. M. Vanaspati in the frying pan (in the usual way) and allow it to dissolve.

Flavouring rice. Melt the H. V. M. Vanaspati, and then pour over the rice, just as you usually do.

Spreading on hot chappatis. Spread H. V. M. Vanaspati on the chappatis and they will taste delicious.

H. V. M. Vanaspati also gives splendid results when used for making sweetmeats and for every other kind of cooking—it makes all your food far more delicious.

WHEN you first open a tin of H. V. M. Vanaspati, you'll be looking at a new product that has come to work wonders with your meals. It will seal all the juicy goodness inside fried food, add a welcome richness of flavour to a simple dish of rice, and make chappatis really tasty and appetising.

Think of this, too—H. V. M. Vanaspati is made from highly refined Indian vegetable oils. All impurities are removed, making H. V. M. Vanaspati one of the most valuable and health-giving foods obtainable. The Public Analyst of Bombay issued a Certificate stating that H. V. M. Vanaspati:

1. is absolutely pure,
2. contains no animal fat,
3. is manufactured under the latest and most hygienic conditions,
4. can be recommended with confidence as a pure, wholesome article of food.

H. V. M. Vanaspati is sold in 2 lbs., 5 lbs. and 10 lbs. tins, it keeps your family strong and healthy and makes your meals more delicious—so buy a tin of this marvellous H. V. M. Vanaspati TODAY!

Look for the name on the top of the tin!

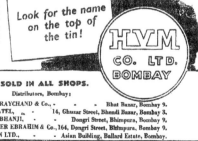

H.V.M. CO. LTD. BOMBAY

MADE IN INDIA FROM PURE INDIAN VEGE-TABLE OILS. UNTOUCHED BY HAND.

H.V.M. VANASPATI IS SOLD IN ALL SHOPS.

Distributors, Bombay:

DALDA BRAND	- BHAILAL RAYCHAND & Co., -	-	Bhat Bazar, Bombay 9.
LOTUS "	- A. M. R. PATEL, -	- 14, Ghuzar Street, Bhendi Bazar, Bombay 3.
BUTTERFLY ,,	- ALIBHOY BHANJI, -	- Dongri Street, Bhimpura, Bombay 9.
TIGER "	- ABOOBAKER EBRAHIM & Co., 164, Dongri Street, Bhimpura, Bombay 9.
GANPATI ,,	- H. PARSON LTD.,	- Asian Building, Ballard Estate, Bombay.

H.V.M. 1-348

THE HINDUSTAN VANASPATI MANUFACTURING CO., LTD., BOMBAY.

Figure 6.9 "Make delicious meals with wonderful HVM Vanaspati," HVM Vanaspati, *BC*, May 20, 1938, 11. Produced with permission of Hindustan Unilever Limited.

health qualities as well as religious significance. Dalda publicity addressed these concerns by connecting the commodity to medicalized conceptions of the modern conjugal unit focused intensively on the health of family members.[82]

In artistic form and often in theme, Dalda ads closely resembled the ads for Lifebuoy soap examined in Chapter 5. The visual similarity between the two types of ads was no coincidence; presumably the same artists at Lintas were responsible for drawing the images. One set of Dalda ads stressed the value of the product to male health. One such ad (Figure 6.10) provides an image of a smiling, energetic man with erect posture accompanied by the copy phrase: "Strength ... because he uses Dalda vanaspati."

Figure 6.10 "Strength ... because he uses Dalda Vanaspati," Dalda, *MS*, March 7, 1941, 4. Produced with permission of Hindustan Unilever Limited.

The text goes on: "he is one of thousands of men who have begun using Dalda and who, as result, obtains good, healthy food." The ad promises that there had been no adulteration of the product and it had been untouched by any human hand. The vocabulary of such ads—stressing the *shakti* (energy), *takat* (strength of fitness), and *utsahi* (enthusiasm)—were words that referred overtly to physical vitality, and that frequently carried connotations of sexual potency, and would have been familiar from campaigns for such products as tonics and Horlicks.[83]

Even more common in the emerging Dalda publicity was an overt emphasis placed on the health of children. In effect the campaign was brought in line with hygienic discourses associated with conjugality. These ads highlighted images of happy, healthy children often engaged in play, as in Lifebuoy ads. But whereas the Lifebuoy ads sometimes mentioned the inevitability of a child's contact with germs and dirt when the parents were absent, Dalda ads typically marked the presence of parents in the same visual frame, particularly fathers engaged in vigorous play with their children. In Figure 6.11, for instance, a father hoists his happy son over his head. A smaller image in the corner shows the mother engaged in cooking a meal over a kerosene stove, again an indication of a middle-class kitchen. This image strongly parallels the use of the mother's image in Lifebuoy ads, and was clearly an intentional strategic decision. The ad thus simultaneously evoked three critical images valuable to the imagining of the modern family: a healthy son, a father interacting with his children in leisure time activity, and a mother preparing food that would ensure familial well-being. The ad stressed the energy (*shakti*) that cooking with Dalda would provide, and mentioned that vitamins had been included. It also emphasized the product's purity, and the nutritious and healthy quality of foods prepared with Dalda. A visually identical ad was printed in English-language newspapers.

By the early 1940s, Lintas had added a second health-related element to its appeal to literate consumers: the *Dalda Cookbook*. The first such cookbook, generated by the Dalda Advisory Service, was published in 1942. Mrs. Z. P. Kukde was its compiler. According to later editions, it quickly sold out as did the second edition. Based upon the third edition that I was able to see, the cookbook was as much a domestic manual for the housewife as a compilation of recipes. It began with general instructions on how to prepare food, how to serve food, and how to keep a kitchen organized and clean. There were significant sections on food values, the meaning of a balanced diet, and examples of insufficient and unbalanced diets. One chapter emphasized the kitchen's importance as the health center of the family, and stressed the tasks a housewife must perform to make it a sanitary place: cleaning the floor, cleaning the shelves, and cleaning utensils. There were also sections on how to use Dalda in a variety of cooking methods. The cookbook's pedagogic message was self-evident: the company was adding this information to "provide an easy means for thousands of housewives to improve the well-being of families." Overall, the cookbook was designed to effect a transformation of household hygienic practices needed to ease the introduction of Dalda into everyday use.[84]

The cookbook also specifically advanced the healthiness of Dalda in ways that were likely intended to counter widespread doubts about the product. It stressed for instance the value of Dalda in improving digestibility, and addressed worries about the

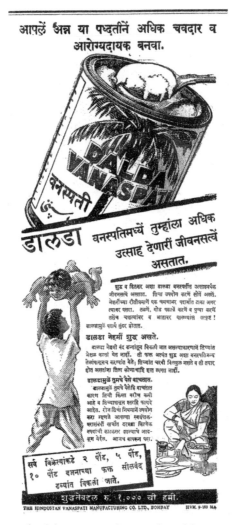

Figure 6.11 "Cook your food this way in order to make it delicious and healthy," Dalda, *Mumbai Samachar*, March 7, 1941, 4. Produced with permission of Hindustan Unilever Limited.

manufacturing process involved in making Dalda, stressing that the product was manufactured under "highly supervised circumstances" and then sealed securely in a tin. Finally it mentioned that Dalda was entirely made from vegetables, and should not affect "religious scruples." The cookbook warned about the dangers of some other cooking mediums, including impurities and rancidity.

Given the attention allocated to the sections on health and domestic routines in the cookbook, the actual provision of recipes appears to have been a subordinate consideration, even if these sections took up the majority of the volume's pages. The cookbook supplied in very brief and dry form recipes from different regions of India, and was divided up into parts on foods from the north, south, Bengal, and so on. The middle-class household that used such recipes would be transforming its dietary behaviors as well as its cooking and sanitary practices by experimenting with dishes from other regions. It was an initial foray into the creation of what Arjun Appadurai has termed a "national cuisine," and supplied housewives who were suddenly being called upon to demonstrate their cosmopolitan capabilities by acquiring techniques that required considerable versatility in the kitchen.[85] Along with the cookbook itself, Lintas submitted newspaper ads to vernacular as well as English-language papers that included individual recipes for specific regional dishes, often with pictures of the foods that would add to their appeal. The advertisements for these dishes championed the new and diverse expertise a housewife could acquire by using Dalda but did not forget to echo the larger campaign's stress on purity and health. Figure 6.12 is a Marathi ad from the women's magazine *Stri* that features an appetizing image of samosas prepared with Dalda alongside smaller images of healthy children at play and their happy parents. The caption at the top of the document read: "Food should be tasty and filling, but it should also increase enthusiasm [*utsahi*]." The woman in the frame is seen as commenting: "This happens only with Dalda; Look at our family!" A further line at the bottom reads: "Dalda is full of vitamins [*jeevansatava,* also translatable as life essence]—for enthusiasm."[86]

Lintas would soon develop significant forms of advertising to attract non-literate consumers. These forms included extensive demonstrations of Dalda in the streets of Bombay and other cities, where cooks prepared sweets, which were then consumed by those in attendance while demonstrators touted the virtues of the product. Mobile vans

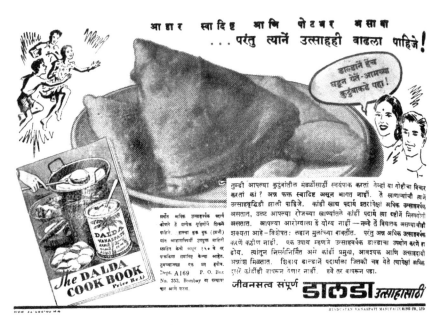

Figure 6.12 Dalda Cookbook ad featuring Samosas, *Stri*, March 1944, 2. Produced with permission of Hindustan Unilever Limited.

took such demonstrations into the countryside. Levers also made a film for Dalda, which apparently ran in rural areas, beginning in the early 1940s. This film was perhaps the second such commercial effort in western India, after JWT's GM ad. According to later accounts, it was projected onto a van that was given the shape of a Dalda tin. The film stressed the dilemma of a father who can not afford the expenses of using ghee for preparation of a wedding feast, and resolves this problem by adopting Dalda, providing great satisfaction to all present.[87] It clearly emphasized very different themes than the press campaign, which had been centered on the needs of the middle-class family. This emphasis may have stemmed from an assumption that in the villages, which typically used vegetable oils on an everyday basis, Dalda's best chance for entrée was by displacing ghee's centrality on special occasions.

As advertising for Dalda increased, the commodity significantly expanded its clientele. Between 1939 and 1943, for instance, Dalda production grew from 320 tons to 9,774 tons. Some of this expansion was no doubt due to demand from the military, which adopted Dalda in its kitchens. Dalda's rise was also caused by a shortage of dairy products at the time, brought about partly by the increased provision of beef in the army, which caused ghee prices to rise.[88] Increasingly, urban households regarded vanaspati as a viable option. One Levers report during the war indicated that "traditional prejudice" against vanaspati remained, but "much more headway has been made recently toward acceptance of straight [unmixed with ghee] Vegetable Product as a suitable item of diet."[89] Dalda itself gradually became synonymous with vanaspati in the public mind.[90] In 1943, the company was projecting rather dramatic increases in its production over the next ten years.

Still, the quantity of Dalda produced was only a bit more than one-third of HVM's manufacture of "vegetable product"; most of its vanaspati presumably continued to be used for mixing. Rising prices and profits moreover were encouraging a host of new competitors to take up hydrogenated oil; HVM's share of the market in vanaspati contracted significantly. While Dalda became the dominant form of vanaspati sold directly to householders, many consumers continued to buy unbranded cooking mediums in the bazaar. This pattern clearly reflected the strong persistence of preferences for ghee, which people often believed they were obtaining when they purchased the commodity in the market.

During the 1940s, Levers' problems with the perception of Dalda's healthiness persisted. Nationalists increasingly questioned the value of hydrogenated oil, insisting that true dairy products were superior both on the grounds of health and the economic welfare of farmers, whose incomes, it was argued, would be damaged by the development of the large-scale vanaspati industry.[91] Gandhi himself weighed in on the argument, authoring a widely read article in 1946 that critiqued vanaspati and praising real ghee.[92] The food minister of the central government made a statement in the Central Assembly that the substance should be banned altogether.[93] In 1947 an article by two Indian scientists reported that rats fed with vanaspati on a suboptimal diet (apparently designed to mirror the limited diets of India's poor) suffered serious growth and eyesight problems as well as serious vitamin deficiencies.[94] Levers countered by citing other studies, and by arguing it never intended Dalda to be used without other nutritive foods, but the damage apparently had been done, and the company struggled to counter the impression left by the study. Decades later this episode still lingered prominently in the memories of retired officers of Levers and Lintas.[95] Prakash Tandon would later write: "in all my years with vanaspati there were always problems."[96]

In general, societal preferences for real ghee remained strong. Many housewives even publicly denied their use of the hydrogenated vegetable oil when it was actually their primary cooking medium. Men reportedly smuggled Dalda into the home under cover of night to make sure their neighbors did not know the family could not always use ghee for its regular needs.[97] In the 1950s, Rajni Chaddha of Lever Market research offered the explanation in a brainstorming session of advertising experts that, as company executive Alyque Padamsee later wrote, housewives "were ashamed of Dalda because it symbolized their fall in status, that is, they were unable to afford ghee, and had to use a substitute product, and they transferred their resentment onto the ubiquitous Dalda."[98] In this climate of sustained suspicions coming from many different directions,[99] Lintas would later design a new campaign in the early 1960s that combined a health theme together with one stressing the emotional importance of motherly love. The English version of this was worded "mothers who care, use Dalda";[100] in Hindi the key phrase of copy was the more emotive Hindi equivalent, *Mamta ki Kasauti par Khara* (tested on the touchstone of a mother's love).[101] The campaign was carried out in a massive way—with new formulations first developed in various regional languages rather than translations and with the extensive use of film. Though it is impossible to know whether the advertising effort was responsible, demand for Dalda expanded dramatically after this point.[102] But such successes came after a long period of considerable struggle to establish positive associations with the product's brandname. The preoccupations of modern conjugality—particularly of parental responsibilities for the health of children—were invoked over and over again in this struggle to uphold Dalda's reputation.

Conclusion

In accounting for the relationship between food and capitalism in India, one might expect a simple narrative of a step-by-step process in which industrial producers seeking to create national markets triumph in some straightforward way over pre-capitalist actors, with advertisers playing a key role in molding the minds of consumers. The historical trajectories associated with Cocogem and Dalda, by contrast, suggest a more complicated picture. The companies responsible for both commodities intially began their manufacture not because they had imagined vast market possibilities by inducing Indians to use the products but because unforeseen circumstances had almost compelled them to take up sales directly to consumers. In the case of TOMCO, the evaporation of the international oil markets led the firm to shift to the manufacture and marketing of Cocogem, while in HVM's case, the danger of government regulation of vanaspati use prompted the company to try to create an independent market for Dalda among middle-class households. Through much of this period, corporate manufacturers of cooking mediums had to compete with actors in the bazaar and often did so rather unsuccessfully. Middle-class consumers in effect offered resistance to mass-produced commodities by maintaining prefences for ghee, which they typically purchased (sometimes unknowingly) in adulterated form. The relative cheapness of commercial cooking mediums was insufficient in itself to capture a significant customer basis. The friction created by these economic and social forces represented a challenge to professional advertisers, compelling them to reshape the character of their campaigns in order to address consumer anxieties, values, and priorities. Advertising was necessary to usurp, even partially, ghee's place of centrality in deeply-seated conceptions of purity and pollution, social hierarchy, and health. The publicists of Dalda tried to achieve this end to some extent by asserting the superior cleanliness of the manufacturing process used in making the product. Most significantly, however, the advertisements claimed that use of Dalda was critical in furthering the housewife's obligation to uphold the health and vitality of the middle-class family. Levers clearly made a concerted effort, achieving significant success, but the entrenched place of ghee in South Asian culinary logic was difficult to challenge until well after the colonial period.

The case of cooking mediums in India is a particularly instructive one because big corporations did eventually win over millions of consumers, in contrast to the case of fruits, vegetables and many other foods, where hawkers and small businessmen continue to play critical roles today. This was achieved, however, only through a very uneven, conflict-ridden and extended process.

Electrical Household Technologies:
Fracturing the Ideal Home

Perhaps the most central image that occupies our imaginings of middle-class consumerism, whether in North America, Europe or post-1991 India, is of a home filled with modern appliances and technological gadgets: electric lamps, refrigerators, vacuum cleaners, fans and air-conditioners, washers, radios, telephones, and of course, after World War II, the television set. Advertisement of these items has been seen as a key force driving the endless creation of new consumer wants and desires necessary to sustain modern industrial capitalism. In the history of modern India, however, household technologies have figured very little, at least until the advent of the TV-VCR age during the 1980s.

It is thus somewhat surprising to find that the print media extensively ran ads promoting new household technologies to residents of Bombay and other western Indian cities during the interwar period. Such products, mostly manufactured by multinational firms, made their way into Indian marketplaces, not long after the same goods became widely available to the middle-class public in Europe and America and before they were sold in Japan. Bombay itself had gained full access to a public electricity supply generated by hydro-electric projects by the end of World War I, when only 6 percent of British households had electric connections.[1] Other cities in western India soon followed with electricity produced by coal-burning plants. Local electric companies tried to broaden their customer base beyond the ranks of industrial producers, introducing electricity in urban neighborhoods where middle-class families lived. Newspapers in cities like Ahmedabad, Poona, and especially Bombay—in English, Marathi, and Gujarati—carried large numbers of ads for electric commodities. In Bombay, a particularly noteworthy aspect of the attempt to popularize such commodities were the campaigns of the Bombay Electric Supply and Tramways Company, Limited (BEST), which was a pioneer in advertising household technologies and regularly ran print ads to promote individual products as well as electricity consumption in general.[2]

Despite the widespread presence of such advertisements, middle-class families adopted the new technologies very selectively. Electric light undoubtedly became critical to the middle-class home. The effort to sell a wider range of appliances, however, met with significant obstacles, in part because their purchase placed serious strains on middle-class budgets, in part because their use potentially involved upsetting existing divisions of labor in middle-class households. The ubiquity of advertisement for electrical technology thus appears somewhat perplexing.

I stress here that advertisers of electrical appliances and telephones developed marketing strategies that implicitly acknowledged the hesitancy and skepticism of Indian consumers about the new kinds of technology even as they conducted extensive campaigns. First, they continued to seek European expatriate customers more strongly than they did Indian buyers. Second, electricity companies, especially BEST, tried to encourage middle-class households to make incremental purchases of the new household technologies, recognizing that mass consumption was unrealistic but hoping to stimulate marginal increases in expenditures on electricity, their main source of profit. But because of the perceived limitations of the potential markets for electrical goods, the kinds of pressures that prompted international manufacturers to abandon global appeals for ones targeting the middle-class consumers of western India more directly were largely absent. Advertisers of new household technologies juggled a variety of approaches in their advertising. On the one hand, they continued to espouse a universal modernity that seemed closely modeled after the appeals being made in Europe and North America at the time. In many of their messages to middle-class consumers, they gave voice to a "pedagogical project"[3] that involved berating householders for not embracing the full possibilities of modernity and not recognizing the increased opportunities for pleasure and leisure that the new technologies might make possible. On occasion, no doubt, they introduced notions of an alternative, Indian modernity focused on anxieties about reproduction of the conjugal family. But in contrast to the advertisement for other commodities discussed in this book, there was little tendency toward convergence around this theme; these two kinds of approaches existed alongside one another. The conception of the home offered in interwar ads thus appears to be a fractured one, marked by contradictory approaches that were never fully reconciled.

Electricity and the ideal home

The public advertisement of electrical goods emerged at a time when novel ideas about the home were taking shape in western Indian cities. Many of the men who worked as clerks and other low-ranking office jobs in Bombay, for instance, lived in "chawls," with or without their families. According to Bhonsle, a chawl was "a long barrack-like construction, two or three storeys high, partitioned into a row of rooms of uniform size. The depth of the room is 25′ feet by 30′ and they are partitioned into two by means of a brick, cement or wooden partition which may or may not reach the ceiling."[4] Most families were crowded into spaces with two rooms or less. Typically there were water closets on every floor and a water tap for every five families. In spite of municipal laws requiring a certain amount of open-air space in these buildings, chawls were usually dark and poorly ventilated. Trash was often strewn in the buildings' halls and common places. Living quarters were, for the most part, sparsely furnished and decorated.[5] Observers at the time regularly commented on what they viewed as the special dangers to personal physiques and health of living in such cramped, sedentary and unhealthy conditions.[6]

During the interwar period, the more mobile middle-class families increasingly sought out quarters that would distinguish their living spaces more strongly from the urban working class. In Bombay, where housing availability was tightly constrained, some families turned to the self-contained flat as a more desirable form of living space.[7] In other cities, as Abigail McGowan has suggested for Ahmedabad, they increasingly regarded modest, self-contained houses as their aspirational goals.[8]

These new forms of built space possessed standardized features that house-dwellers associated with modernity. Nikhil Rao has argued that a primary characteristic distinguishing the urban flat in suburban Bombay from the chawls was the presence of the toilet *within* the home; toilets required more elaborate systems of internal plumbing to facilitate the flow of water into the flat and waste waters out.[9] Rao argues that high-caste, middle-class migrants from South India to Bombay, with strong concerns about purity and pollution as well as self-conceptions as modern individuals, played critical roles in influencing the suburban flat's design in Bombay. The internal toilet, no doubt, became characteristic of flats elsewhere in the city as well as in self-contained houses in other urban centers.

A further feature that increasingly differentiated post-World War I middle-class flats and houses from working-class housing was a connection to the public electricity supply. After 1920 new housing increasingly included electric installations;[10] and older homes were gradually wired for electricity as well. In Bombay, electric lights became nearly universal in middle-class homes, replacing the use of kerosine lamps. Once connected to the electric supply, middle-class families apparently needed little persuasion to add a couple of fixtures with a single bulb each so that they would have light at night.[11] In some cases, male spaces in the home, where men read and boys studied, possessed electric lamps, while female-dominated areas like the kitchen continued to depend upon the light of a charcoal stove.[12] The use of electricity, however, often went no further than the adoption of electric light and perhaps an electric fan.

Local architects, journalists and other urban professionals, however, came to articulate a much more ambitious vision of the home in the interwar period. This consumerist vision included the types of building material to be employed, the positions of various rooms within the flat, the specifications of plumbing and the furniture to be bought, the cooking facilities to be included, and the electrical appliances to be utilized.[13] Often the attributes championed by advocates of ideal homes had little to do with the practical realities of urban life in India, including middle-class financial capacity and household labor practices.

Local newspapers increasingly ran articles on housing forms that their authors felt should be emulated. The image of the ideal home that the visionaries articulated was inextricably linked to an expectation that consumption patterns and household bodily practices might be transformed. Discussed in these articles were specific products such as electric stoves, water heaters, electric mirrors, hair dryers, washing machines, irons, and refrigerators. One article emphasized the importance of moving beyond electric lighting to adopt a new, modern mentality that would embrace electricity more broadly:

> Within the last few years, many revolutionary changes for the better have been made possible in our houses in India, and perhaps the most important has been

the gradual spread of electric power and light systems. These systems have given us liberty to take advantage of refrigerators, fans, electric cookers and other kitchen necessaries—and now we pampered dwellers in cities and other places where there is electricity can even heat our water by it.[14]

Another article went on in a similar vein, focusing on the ways such appliances would offer housewives relief from tiresome household labor.

Recent advances in the application of electric power would, if generally adopted, make a twentieth-century paradise. Here is a kind of short-hand existence where to press a button or turn a switch is to set moving each essential service of the home...

The application of electricity to ironing, washing, cooking, drying, heating and freezing makes an end of drudgery of a woman's work.[15]

In May 1936, the *Times* devoted several pages to the newly built Dhunraj Mahal, a state-of-the-art building complex of perhaps one hundred flats and offices located near the Gateway of India.[16] The articles praised the project's architects and builders for applying the most advanced methods of construction. Manufacturers of various features used in the structure—from concrete to floor tiles—ran advertisements stressing that their products reflected the highest standards available. Makers of new household technologies, too, employed the occasion to champion their manufactures. The sellers of His Master's Voice Refrigerators stressed that there was an H.M.V. Refrigerator in every flat in Dhunraj Mahal while Siemens advertisements highlighted that three hundred of its ceiling fans had been installed. Under the caption of "Carefree Cooking for all tenants of Dhunraj Mahal," the Bombay Gas Company proclaimed, "Modern housewives in modern flats do all their cooking on clean, quick, efficient BURMA gas cookers." Such ads implicitly urged homemakers everywhere to emulate the residents of Dhunraj Mahal (whom, I suspect, were predominantly expatriates).[17]

Perhaps the most significant effort to publicize the new models for the middle class was the Ideal Home Exhibition in Bombay in 1937.[18] Sponsored by the Indian Institute of Architects (IIA) and held in the Bombay Municipal Town Hall, the exhibition ran over two weeks and attracted as many as 100,000 visitors, both European and Indian. IIA members were seeking to establish their professional identities on sound footing; their promotion of futuristic housing conceptions was perhaps rooted more in a quest to establish their credentials as architects than in any realistic notion of ideas residents might adopt.[19] The whole exhibition was also planned with an eye to the pedagogic function it would play for the Bombay public, as the *Bombay Chronicle* stressed: "This Exhibition will show completely furnished and equipped rooms—designed to show how the best of the most modern equipment can give a genuine comfort which human beings are entitled to enjoy."[20] Visitors to the exhibition found themselves moving from bedrooms to living rooms to bathrooms, all reflecting the latest in furnishings and equipment.

Some of the rooms in the exhibit, including a billiard room, a cigar room, and a bar had no counterpart in Indian homes whatsoever; there was even "an ideal operating theater," probably included at the behest of local doctors or hospital administrators.

Little thought was given to housing for workers or even the lower middle class, a fact highlighted in the exhibition's keynote address by Prime Minister B. G. Kher of the newly elected Bombay provincial assembly, who chided attendees by reminding them of conditions present elsewhere in the city:

> We cannot afford to lose sight of the practical realities of life. The housing conditions of the majority of people inhabiting this city are far from satisfactory. The slums of Dharavi, the chawls of Parel, and many other parts are a standing reproach to the fair name of our beautiful city. And I cannot help feeling that it is the duty of every citizen to do all that lies in his power to do away with the slums, which I repeat are a disgrace to our fair city, and to provide decent housing conditions for the large number of people living there.[21]

The Ideal Home Exhibition was a *consumer* spectacle, in which attendees were asked to entertain a radical transformation in their material practices. The ideal home conception imagined by the exhibition's planners involved a transformation of the technologies of everyday life: the preparation and preservation of food, the treatment of clothes, bathing, and so forth. According to the *Times of India,* one of the exhibit's purposes was to provide visitors with an understanding of how technology might address some central questions about modern living: "How can the housewife be spared some of the totally unnecessary drudgery known as 'housework' and devote her time to the running of an ... every way pleasant and efficient home? What has modern industry, in numerous new and fascinating materials, to contribute to amenities of house and home?"[22] The exhibition included rooms with lighting provided by the Eastern Light Company, electric cookers and electric fittings supplied by BEST, and electric geysers for heating kitchen and bath water furnished by Johnson and Philips.[23] The exhibition was in effect a performance of an emerging brand-name capitalism, an occasion when multinational corporations displayed the virtues of mass-produced commodities and advertised them in print media.

Articles in the *Times* and other newspapers at the time of the exhibition specifically promoted electricity use. One writer touted the importance of good house lighting: "In these days of cheap electric power and frosted electric lamps, there is no reason why even the meanest city home should not be brilliantly illuminated yet how often does one find even adequate illumination in the wealthiest of Bombay homes?"[24] Another article, discussing the value of appliances and gadgets including toasters, irons, shavers, carpet cleaners, scalp brushes, and clocks, insisted that these commodities "do something useful more quickly and efficiently than was done before," before setting out a larger endorsement of electric motive power (and new modes of utilizing servant labor):

> This is indeed an electric age. I am probably prejudiced in my views but I find it almost impossible to conceive of existence without electricity. Almost nothing seems to have escaped the manufacturers' eagle eyes, but it might almost literally be said that we depend upon it for very nearly every form of heating and cooking, lighting and action.
> Boy, switch on the punkah! [fan].[25]

Newpaper columns about the exhibition were accompanied by ads from companies touting the value of their products in creating ideal homes. An ad run by the BEST showroom, for instance, made a general plug for the use of electricity, arguing:

ELECTRICITY IS THE ESSENTIAL SERVICE IN THE MODERN HOME
IT PROVIDES:

GOOD LIGHTING Correctly designed fittings
COOLNESS Fans and Air Conditioning
LUXURIOUS HOT WATER Geysers and Storage Tanks
SAFE FOOD Electric Refrigerators
HYGIENIC COOKING Electric Cookers
CONVENIENCE

A thousand Electrical Appliances which make life easier, healthier and better at a trifling cost."[26]

Collectively, therefore, the discourse of the exhibition's organizers, newspaper coverage of the event, and commercial advertisements reinforced one another, creating a consumerist fantasy that equated electricity on the one hand and modernity, material comfort, and sanitation on the other.

The realities of middle-class housing

Middle-class families in western India were thus exposed in public exhibitions and in some advertisements to new conceptions of the home animated by universalist ambitions rather than ones that reflected efforts to adapt those conceptions to the priorities and preoccupations of Bombay's middle class. The Ideal Home Exhibition, the publicity surrounding it, and the housing notions articulated by architectural professions and journalists were mostly pure spectacles, like a zoo populated by exotic animals or a science museum filled with fantastic, futuristic objects, rather than displays of practices local residents might realistically adopt. Existing evidence, including oral recollections of the period, suggests that the idea of a home filled with labor-saving devices gained limited traction. Middle-class families took up new household technologies on a piecemeal basis, adopting electric light and perhaps an electric fan. Relative to other electrical goods, these two types of commodity were cheap, and they allowed household members to carry on existing activities without upsetting household social relations. Virchand Dharamsey recalls in his youth (during the late 1940s) the presence of electric lights in his house, with kerosine lamps (*kandeel*) kept in reserve, but without fans until decades later. Cooking was done on a charcoal *saghadi* (stove). And there was only one family in his building with a phone or radio, which other residents dropped in occasionally to use. The electric washing machine, the most significant major appliance adopted in American homes, was completely absent in Indian contexts until many decades later.[27] Refrigerators were purchased or rented to a very limited extent, hot water heaters were adopted rarely, and telephones did not become fixtures in middle-class homes until the 1980s.[28]

The most obvious reason for the inapplicability of the ideal home concept to everyday household practices was the limited purchasing power of middle-class families. As mentioned in Chapter 2, many of these families lived only slightly above the standards of the more prosperous working-class families, and expenditures on items other than food, clothing, and house-rent were limited.[29] In reports issued by the Bombay Labour Office, the category of fuel and lighting—with fuel more important than electricity—constituted 5.5 percent of a typical family budget, that is, about eight rupees for a family earning 150 Rupees a month. In 1938 H. Shankar Rau, discussing recommended family budgets for Chitrapur Saraswat Brahmans earning 175 Rupees a month (somewhat above average), suggested three rupees a month as an appropriate allocation for electricity. He advised Saraswat families to take baths in cold or tepid water and to avoid using bright lights; Rau assumed the use of charcoal stoves for cooking.[30] Refrigerator *rentals* in Bombay during the 1930s cost 14 Rupees a month and telephone use 16 Rupees, that is, about one third of an average middle-class family's expenditure on *all* items other than food, housing, and clothing; monthly instalments toward the purchase of a refrigerator would have run somewhat higher.[31] These costs were obviously prohibitive.

The middle-class household in India also did not face the same internal transformations that were stimulating the adoption of capital-intensive methods of doing housework in North America and Europe. The use of household appliances in the United States and Britain during the 1920s and 1930s was not spurred so much by the lure of modern technology as by the declining availability of domestic labor, as working-class women entered factory employment, clerical positions, and jobs as shop assistants that yielded higher wages than work as servants in middle-class households.[32] These developments compelled housewives to take up the slack at home (since men rarely assumed these responsibilities). The adoption of electric technologies served in part to counter these new pressures so that housewives could continue meeting societal standards for home maintenance and childcare. But in western India no such a compulsion was present. The potential ranks of those willing to act as servants may have even expanded during the interwar period as more migrants entered the city while opportunities for women in industrial employment contracted.[33] Even lower-middle-class households often hired a servant to help at home, sometimes in collaboration with other families in their chawl, apartment building, or neighborhood.

Cultural norms surrounding women's work often strengthened middle-class reliance on household labor. As previously mentioned, domestic manuals alerted readers to the danger of Westernized women who indulged themselves in leisure activities and the consumption of luxury items at the expense of responsibilities within the home.[34] These texts set out a heightened array of female responsibilities; the idea of freeing women from the drudgery of housework certainly did not become a significant priority in middle-class ideology in India.[35] On the contrary, as commentary and some advertisements suggested openly, societal standards clearly frowned on housewives who escaped their obligations such as clothes-washing, cooking, and child care in order to attend cinema houses or engage in idle gossip; the idea that women might seek employment outside the home was entertained by only a tiny minority. Middle-class norms thus clearly militated against the use of scarce familial resources to displace household labor with machines.

The commercial rationale of advertising

Given middle-class qualms about embracing new forms of material consumption, why then did manufacturers and sellers of electrical goods invest such extensive efforts in advertising household technologies? In comparison to the archival material on Lever Brothers and JWT, there is limited information available about the people who designed newspaper advertising for electrical products or about the processes by which they generated knowledge about Indian consumers. We do, however, know something about the market for electric products at the time, and we can construct the logic of advertisement based upon an understanding of its peculiarities.

There were at least two factors encouraging significant advertising of electrical technologies despite the absence of mass consumer demand. First was the sustained importance of the demand of expatriates (and an Indian upper class that sometimes followed the expatriates' lead). While the Europeans were small in number relative to the Indian middle class and could never constitute a large market for small-cost items—a European, like an Indian, required only one toothbrush or bar of bathing soap at a time—they often individually possessed substantial disposable incomes and often held strong expectations of the comforts needed to compensate for the rigors of living in exile.[36] They could be expected to make some high-value purchases that lower-middle-class Indians could not hope to match. Even poorer Europeans and Anglo-Indians, with aspirations to upward mobility and with a concern to be included in the ranks of the ruling race, may have seen the acquisition of electrical appliances as a crucial marker of identity. Many of the ads run by BEST for electrical products were submitted to the *Times of India*, whose readership came disproportionately from expatriates.

Many advertisements for household technologies clearly targeted members of European society alone, sometimes evoking a distinctive kind of consumption logic focused on parties, dances, visits to friends, and even romance.[37] Figure 7.1, an ad for the Bombay Telephone Company, with a female figure clearly drawn to represent an expatriate woman with a servant serving tea in the background, stresses two themes common in ads geared to expatriates: (1) the need of the memsahib to retain ultimate authority over the household and its servants, especially in marketplace activities ("there are some things which she cannot leave to her servants to buy"), and (2) the importance of sustaining the expatriate's social circles ("A dinner party tonight, but she has tired herself out already and will not be able to enjoy herself or be entertaining to her guests").

Other ads stressed the comforts and leisure possibilities that the use of electrical appliances might create for the European household, as in Figure 7.2, also featuring a European woman. It stressed "Electric cooking is so easy," and emphasized how a wife could easily impress her husband by using an electric stove.

The importance of the market of Europeans residing in India was so great to companies involved in the provision of electricity and electrical goods in Bombay that

She's tired herself out

because she wasn't on the TELEPHONE

A dinner party tonight, but she has tired herself out already and will not be able to enjoy herself or be entertaining to her guests. The morning round of the shops in the dust and heat is enough to exhaust anyone, yet there are some things which she cannot leave to her servants to buy, because they must be discussed with the shopkeepers.

How easy it would have been to sit down with the telephone at her elbow and get into direct communication with the suppliers, ask any questions which arose and arrange for her shopping to be sent straight home. How pleasant to be rested and feeling really bright at the prospect of entertaining a few friends to dinner.

Not only is the telephone the most convenient means of communication—it is also the quickest and the cheapest.

TELEPHONE RATES		Payable yearly	Payable quarterly	Payable monthly
Business Lines	.. ..	Rs. 280	Rs. 72-8	—
Residential Lines	.. ..	Rs. 180	Rs. 45-0	Rs. 16
Party Lines (Residences only,		Rs. 135	Rs. 34-0	Rs. 12

BOMBAY TELEPHONE Co., LIMITED,

Home Street, Fort,   •   •   BOMBAY.

Figure 7.1 "She's tired herself out because she wasn't on the TELEPHONE," Bombay Telephone Co., *BC*, April 20, 1936, 12.

their effort to tailor appeals meant for middle-class efforts sometimes seemed halfhearted, resulting in some peculiar advertisements. A series of Gujarati ads featured European actors, often in situations that Indians were unlikely to face. For instance, one pictured a European woman vacuuming her home; a middle-class housewife would have either relied on servant labor to carry out such cleaning tasks or would have at least aspired to do so (and would be unlikely to be motivated by an image of a European doing the job herself).[38] Another pictured a (seemingly European) man standing with his luggage on a quay, having missed his boat for "home" (i.e., to Europe) because he

Figure 7.2 "Electric cooking is so easy," Electric Cookers, BEST, *TI*, October 24, 1938, 13.

had not been reachable by telephone.[39] Figure 7.3 features a European woman (wrapped only in a towel) stepping out of her bath, an image that might have upset middle-class sensibilities if it had pictured an Indian housewife.

Clearly a significant disconnect existed between the visual content of these ads and the objective involved in placing them in a vernacular newspaper. Most likely they simply retained an image that had been used in an English-language version after translating the text into Gujarati or Marathi, thus saving the costs of any investment in new artwork; whereas advertisers in western India often had come to develop differentiated ads for

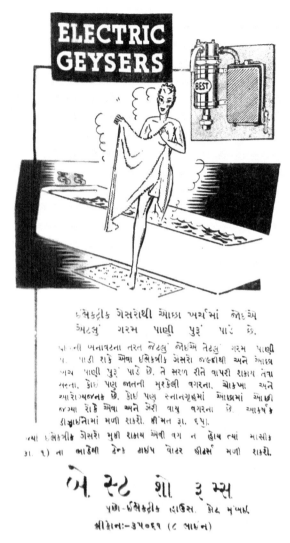

Figure 7.3 "Electric Geysers Provide You as Much Hot Water as you need at Minimum Cost," BEST, *MS*, February 13, 1941, 10.

soaps, medicines, and hot drinks for expatriates and Indians. Electric goods companies at times did not seem to recognize they might be sending mixed messages.

The special commercial motivations of electricity suppliers, especially BEST, also motivated them to advertise a wide variety of electric household technologies even when the prospect for the development of large markets was limited. BEST was a firm initially formed in London in 1905 with British capital; it was incorporated in India around the end of World War I.[40] Before 1920 its primary role had been the extension of the tramways and their electrification (Bombay earlier had a horse-drawn tramway system), but it also was authorized to provide electricity to Bombay shops and homes. At first, BEST tried to generate much of its requirements on its own. In 1910, however, the Tata Hydro-Electric Power Supply Company Limited completed a major power-generating project by constructing large dams at high elevations in the nearby Ghats mountain range. There was a brief period of serious competition between the Tata company and BEST over customers. Ultimately a settlement was reached; BEST would abstain from selling electricity to large industrial concerns, while the Tatas conceded BEST the right to directly supply smaller consumers: small-scale industrial users, shops, and especially urban households.

Within a short time, BEST began to purchase electricity generated by the hydro-project at one anna per unit. At first it tried to produce some of its power requirements, even constructing a major coal-burning station in Bombay during the second decade of the century for this purpose. But when coal prices went up sharply after the war, electricity generated by such means became significantly more expensive than hydropower, and it turned extensively to the Tatas for its supply. For the Tatas, the demand of BEST's consumer-clients, which peaked when business usages ebbed, created a more optimal distribution of the load on the system over the day.[41] For BEST the arrangement meant that it could obtain ample supplies of electricity from the Tatas at lower prices than it could produce itself. At the same time, the infrastructural costs of extending electric transmissions to residential neighborhoods were limited, since the company already had established electric connections in many areas in the city for the tramways.

Local politics in Bombay, however, constrained some of BEST's profit possibilities. The Municipality, for instance, prohibited the company from raising its fares for tramway passengers during the 1920s; Bombay consequently possessed one of the cheapest public transportation networks in the world. Running a loss in its tramway operations, BEST increasingly relied upon earnings from supplying electricity to small-scale users.[42] But the company was also compelled by the municipality to reduce the base rates that it charged household consumers from 8 annas per unit in 1905 to 4 1/2 annas in 1908, 4 annas in 1934, and (after a reduction in rates charged BEST by the Tatas) to 3 annas in 1938.[43] The overall character of this situation—exclusion from the industrial market, an inability to raise prices on the trams or rates charged to consumers, and the relatively small additional costs of establishing new connections—meant that the company's most attractive prospects for increasing profits was to promote the volume of electricity used by individual households, even if the increases would not be dramatic. It was BEST, not the manufacturers of the commodities themselves, that took the lead in advertising most advertising electrical products. Its efforts seemed at times to be concerned with educating consumers about the value of electricity use over the long term rather than urging them to make immediate purchases. In other words, there was little expectation of creating mass demand among the middle class, only marginal increases.

One way BEST sought to promote electricity use was by opening a showroom in 1926 at Electric House on the Colaba causeway where Bombay residents could observe various electrical goods and overcome hesitations about bringing electric appliances into their homes (pictured in Figure 7.4). This location, modeled after similar showrooms in England, possessed a special educational function. Potential customers who entered the premises acquired information about available appliances, received

Figure 7.4 Picture of BEST showroom. Courtesy of BEST.

advice about using these devices, and were offered instruction about the virtues of electric power. The showroom's Lighting Bureau furnished guidance about lighting offices, small factories, and homes; its personnel sometimes visited users in their homes and in shops to design specialized lighting arrangements. A letter published in 1935 in the *Times of India*, written under the pseudonym "Electric," congratulated BEST for the showroom and urged the company to devote itself to converting city-dwellers to the mission of electricity.

> The report that the company is shortly opening a 'show room' at their Head Office in Colaba for the demonstration of domestic appliances for Indian conditions will be received with great joy by all who, though poor, yet possess sufficient 'sanitary conscience' to wish to do away with the foul odour of coal and charcoal gas. . . . The millennium does not appear to be far away when one reads that even at 'Hackney, one of the most unattractive and depressing parts of London, the local authorities, by assiduous service, have so developed the use of electricity for cooking and heating in these small homes that it is becoming the universal agent. . .' But how far the citizens of Bombay will avail themselves of the facilities offered greatly depends upon the efforts the organisers make to spread the 'electrical idea' into the home of every family as well as upon the economic efficiency of the 'new order of things.'[44]

The showroom's purpose was in effect to transform the consciousness of Bombay citizens by exposing them to a fantastic wonder world of electric lights and appliances.

BEST used advertising to carry the same message into the homes, offices, and libraries where middle-class city-dwellers read their newspapers and journals. Advertisements in effect translated the showroom's message into print spaces, creating an imagined sense of what it was like to have a range of electrical devices at one's disposal. BEST committed considerable expenditure to its appeals. In attempting to reach untapped or weakly tapped sets of buyers, advertisers often adopted a pedagogical style aimed at persuading the middle-class family that its modernity was at stake in its decisions about household technologies rather than at adapting to the central concerns of middle-class discourses. To put it differently, they often advanced a kind of civilizing discourse aimed at addressing hesitant consumers ignorant of these products' advantages and intractable in their buying practices; implicitly the reluctant consumer is present as an Other who has to date been too unaware and too tightfisted to appreciate the commodities mentioned in these ads.

In sum, BEST and the manufacturers of household technologies seemingly sensed little immediate potential to cultivate a mass market of middle-class consumers ready to make large numbers of small purchases. They continued to rely heavily for their buyers on persuading European expatriates to buy their goods and on nudging small numbers of Indians to make purchases and thus to use more electricity. Seemingly, they felt little of the pressure, or friction, that prompted advertisers of tonics, medicines, and soaps to adjust existing methods of advertising and develop new appeals that would resonate widely among educated city-dwellers. Capitalists associated with the new technologies advertised extensively, but they did not engage so strongly in the same forms of experimentation nor draw upon "prior meanings" resonant to members of the middle class, and their appeals were not so clearly differentiated in audience between expatriates and members of the middle class. Some campaigns relied heavily on universal principles of modernity that were often found in campaigns outside India at the time. In other cases, they evoked principles of an Indian middle-class conjugality, though there was little overall trend in this direction. An examination of different kinds of ad campaigns reveals these contradictory patterns.

The pedagogies of electricity

Ads promoting the general use of electricity

The most ambitious advertisements designed by BEST championed the general use of electricity. Often addressing European and Indian customers simultaneously, these ads insisted that wide adoption of household technologies—not just electric lighting—was critical to a more complete modernity. Some ads stressed the antiquated, wasteful, and inconvenient methods associated with other sources of energy (whether human, charcoal, or gas) currently being used by Indians in everyday life. Touting what the ads claimed were the many advantages of electricity, they cast non-users and those who used electricity only for lighting as relics of a past age. The instructional tone in these messages was explicit (Figure 7.5):

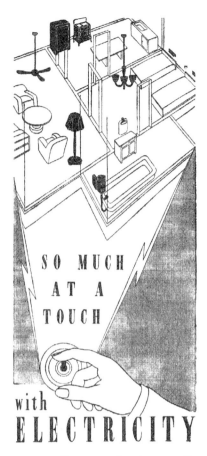

SO MUCH AT A TOUCH

with ELECTRICITY

There comes a time when you realise that the house is getting almost too much for you. Supervising this, that, and the other. Electricity is fool-proof. Household tasks are made lighter —cleaner, briefer and brighter—with the help of electricity. It isn't the people who run their own houses who say the old-fashioned way is the best!

In the past few years the average cost of current has been reduced by half.

In many places all over the country electricity is the cheapest source of power, heat and light. Everywhere it is by far the cleanest, healthiest and most convenient. Are you using electricity?—or only electric light.

THE BOMBAY ELECTRIC SUPPLY & TRAMWAYS CO., LTD.,
Electric House, Fort, BOMBAY.   Tel : 26024 (7 lines).
                                                              BEKS.

Figure 7.5 "So much at a touch with electricity," BEST, *TI,* July 28, 1939, 13.

There comes a time when you realise that the house is getting almost too much for you. Supervising this, that, and the other. Electricity is fool-proof. Household tasks are made lighter—cleaner, briefer and brighter—with the help of electricity. It isn't the people who run their own houses who say the old-fashioned way is best.

...Everywhere it [electricity] is the cleanest, healthiest and most convenient. *Are you using electricity?—or only electric light* (italics mine).[45]

The logic of a universal modernity and of a civilizing mission associated with electricty was particularly overt in a second ad (Figure 7.6), addressed "to every baby in the land." It featured a European-appearing baby (again, a symbol of good health in advertisements generally).

You have arrived in a wonderful age—in the most wonderful age the world has ever known. You will be a healthier, merrier child than it was possible for any baby ever to be, because you are born in Electricity days.... Yes, indeed you are to be congratulated. And later on you will think of former methods of cooking and water heating just as we now think of the stage coach as a pre-historic institution. Then as you get older, you will find more and more uses for this great gift to mankind, rapid new ways of doing your great work in the world.[46]

In effect, the ad inferred that those who hesitated to use electric power represented values that the march of progress would leave behind. The ad's goal clearly was the *conversion* of the householder to a whole range of attitudes and practices rather than of persuading middle-class families to recognize that their existing priorities required use of electric gadgets and appliances.

One of the more interesting themes in some of these advertisements was the relief from drudgery that electricity offered the modern housewife. This theme, one used commonly in North American and European advertisments during this period, was emphasized even more strongly in another ad (Figure 7.7) which pictured a sari-clad woman performing various tasks around the home—cooking, ironing, storing food, and cleaning—with the help of electrical devices. The ad's wording criticized families that allowed women to continue working without broad access to electricity:

"WILL SOMEBODY PLEASE TELL US WHY some women slave away like drudges at household tasks which can be done quicker, cheaper, better by electricity? If they haven't heard of electric cooking, electric water heating, electric cleaning and electric ironing—surely their husbands have?"[47]

The ad critiqued both the ignorant wife who remained stuck in traditional behaviors and the recalcitrant husband who shielded his wife from modern possibilities. Interestingly, servants, who actually performed many of the tasks featured, were missing from the visual frame. Yet in other ads there was a stress on the value of the product as a "servant" in the household. "Electricity," one advertisement in the *Times of India* proclaimed, is "the ideal and cheapest Servant."[48]

TO EVERY BABY IN THE LAND...

You have arrived in a wonderful age—in the most wonderful age the world has ever known. You will be a healthier, merrier child than it was possible for any baby ever to be, because you are born in Electricity days. Of course, you do not know now what that means to you, but your mother does. She knows that by using electric cooking, all your food, your milk and later on your more solid diet, will be heated and boiled and cooked without dirt getting near it, without fumes harming it, with all the nourishment retained. Your mother, enjoying the ease of an electric home will have far more time to give to you, sharing, with you, health and happiness. And when you grow into your teens she will still be young, thanks to the freedom from household drudgery. And you will be bathed soothingly in water easily heated by the same wonderful force of electricity. Your clothes will be washed at any time they need washing, because in these amazing days hot water is always ready in the home equipped to heat water by electricity. Yes, indeed you are to be congratulated. And later on you will think of former methods of cooking and water heating just as we now think of the stage coach as a pre-historic institution. Then as you get older, you will find more and more uses for this great gift to mankind, rapid new ways of doing your great work in the world.

Born in
ELECTRICITY DAYS
— congratulations

Bombay Electric Supply & Tramways Co., Ltd.
Electric House, ... Fort, BOMBAY.
Tel: 26024 (7 lines)

BEK.3.

Figure 7.6 "To every baby in the land," BEST, *TI*, November 18, 1939, 11.

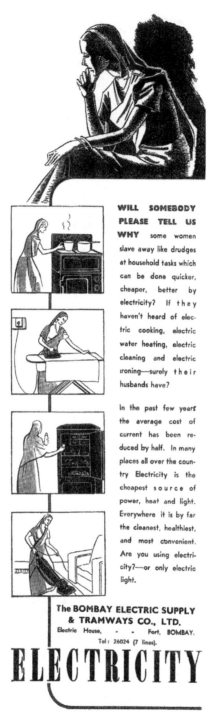

Figure 7.7 "Will Somebody Please Tell Us Why," BEST, *TI*, October 23, 1939, 11.

Here the ad drew upon perceptions of actual servants as unreliable, prone to careless errors, and characterized by a poor sense of judgment, and upon norms that insisted housewives take firmer control over the household, themes discussed in Chapter 2 as being largely confined to appeals to expatriates. In a few cases the use of the products advertised may have involved the housewife displacing the *dhobi* who washed clothes, the *hamal* who took care of lamps in the home, or the *punkahwala* who kept family members cool (in wealthy households) by operating a manual fan. The ads emphasized the housewife's supposedly superior ability to perform these tasks once she was armed with the proper machines. In none of these cases were servants given any agency in making decisions about the products to be used. Servants themselves were disregarded as persons with little relevance to household decisions about consumption. To a great extent the ad reflected a logic that had largely been transferred from a European and North American context or from appeals to expatriates. As I have argued, such an appeal was unlikely to develop much traction among the middle class, where the concern for alleviating the burden of labor performed by servants and housewives was limited. The image of a housewife doing the vacuuming in particular seems improbable during this period.

In short, these general advertisements suggested the incomplete modernity of householders whose use of electrical goods was partial. They adopted a chiding tone, one prompted by the need to overcome the fact that the majority of the ads' readers did not utilize electricity for a wide range of household tasks. They adopted a global logic of progress whose purpose was to embarrass the non-user of the backward state of the practices employed in his/her household; the logic of conjugality is not present. Given the realities of middle-class spending patterns, their impact was less likely to have been to promote a sudden jump in popular consumption of these items than it was to have persuaded Europeans and *small* numbers of Indian consumers to expand their use of electric commodities and electricity incrementally.

Ads for individual products

Most of the advertisements for electrical household technologies, however, sought to convince consumers to purchase specific products. The sales pitch used in these appeals depended greatly on the item. In general, the more radical the alteration of the home environment the product required, the more likely advertisers were to adopt a pedagogical approach steeped in notions of a universal modernity. Advertisers seemingly felt little need to resort to this mode in promoting electric bulbs and electric fans, ads whose purpose was to prompt immediate decisions to make purchases. Often the promoters of these goods sought not to persuade their audience to buy the kind of product in question but to induce them to purchase a specific brand. An ad for Bijlee bulbs (an Indian product), for instance, asks purchasers: "Has your bulb this chemically protected filament? It is new! … Sensational! … Revolutionary! The Chemically Protected Filament in Bijlee makes for the highest light-giving properties"[49] (see Figure 7.8 for a similar Bijlee ad).

An early ad for fans featured a sari-clad female in seeking to convince consumers to buy the G.E. brand: "You can always tell a G.E. FAN GIRL, she is the personification of good health and vivacity, her complexion has that delicate bloom which instantly

Figure 7.8 "It's the Filament that matters in a Bulb," Bijlee, *TI*, November 3, 1937, 19.

reminds one of a delightful Hill Station even though she has never moved out of the city. She takes full advantage of a refreshing breeze from a G.E. fan."[50]

In some cases, BEST deployed advertising to persuade middle-class flat residents using one or two low-intensity bulbs to *expand* their use of lighting. These ads chastised families underusing light, suggesting that they were likely to perform their task poorly or cause their eyesight to deteriorate if they continued to insist on the minimum lighting possible. The presence of a doctor in one ad, scolding a patient for the inadequacy of lighting arrangements in his home, evoked the scientific principles supposedly being neglected by the householder who economized by using lights with low candle power.[51]

With electric appliances that simply replaced non-electric technologies that performed the same task, advertisements often just introduced readers to the practical advantages of the new product. An ad for a BEST electric water heater in the kitchen (an item that would have replaced a coal stove) featured a housewife at work over a sink filled with hot water and emphasized the reliability of water-heaters, informing readers that they could make water warm at any time.[52] A BEST ad in Gujarati for an electric *saghadi* (sigree in English-language ads) for drying clothes—a product that would replace charcoal saghadis that performed the same function—informed the reader there was no need to be concerned about monsoon dampness if the consumer used such an item.[53] Other saghadi ads offered explicit comparisons to existing methods, stressing how the item saved the home from the "foul smell and smoke" produced by charcoal-burning stoves.[54] All of these ads resorted to a logic of straightforward rationality, one that lacked the emotive appeal of home, family, or nation.

When the product advertised involved the introduction of a technology requiring a transformation of prevailing bodily practices, however, advertisers sometimes grounded their rhetoric in terms of values widely present in other appeals to the middle class. In these instances, the advertisement combined the use of a pedagogical voice with the evocation, not of a global ideal of modernity, but of the specific anxieties held by middle class householders of western India, ones grounded in the ideology of modern conjugality. Typically they drew upon prevailing ideas about how the middle-class family might ensure its self-reproduction, as well as upon established modes of representing the family visually, from the larger discourse of commercial advertisment prevalent during the period. They argued in effect that householders who wished to uphold expectations as male providers or as effective female housekeepers needed to purchase the product in question. These ads typically made little reference to relieving women from the "drudgery of labor" or otherwise enhancing family leisure time, insisting instead that the housewife could better execute her existing responsibilities by renting or buying the appliance.

The most prevalent theme of this sort was that of family health. This theme was especially common in ads for refrigerators, whose chief advantage, according to a wide range of advertisements, was ensuring the healthy character of the family's food (rather than keeping drinks cool as in some ads pitched to expatriates). Often these ads featured a sari-clad housewife, the person most responsible for upholding family wellness (see, for instance, Figure 7.9, where the housewife wears her sari in Parsi style). According to one of these ads: "You can not afford to take risks with the health of your family. Hot, humid weather has a bad effect on many foodstuffs which is often undetected until it is too late. . . . An electric refrigerator will keep your food safe and fresh, and will avoid the great dangers of food poisoning."[55] The ad implored: "Is the health of your family worth 8 As [eight annas, the daily cost of renting a refrigerator]? . . . How many people risk their own health and the health of their families by not making sure that all food at home is perfectly fresh?"[56]

By mentioning the immediate cost to the family, it seems clear, the ads clearly were intended to prompt buyers to make the decision to purchase or (more commonly) rent a refrigerator, not just to entertain an imagined future in which refrigerator use might

Figure 7.9 "SAFEGUARD your family's food supply," BEST Refrigerator, *TI,* May 6, 1936, 13.

be possible. Such ads took an instructional tone, but they linked themselves to conceptions of the family as a medicalized unit oriented toward maintaining the well-being of children and ensuring familial self-reproduction; these were conceptions we have seen repeatedly in advertisements examined earlier in the book.[57] They particularly evoked worries among parents about whether they were taking the steps necessary to confront the invisible dangers posed by germs, which modern medical science had determined as the source of dangerous illnesses. And they explicity referred to the difficulties of doing so under Indian sanitary conditions. The comforts associated with the refrigerator were typically mentioned only in ads geared to expatriates.

There also was a similar effort to connect the imperatives of family health to the commodity in some telephone ads. Again, these ads seem intended to persuade consumers to decide to get a telephone in the present. In contrast to appeals explicitly directed to expatriates—which often pictured Europeans on the phone and emphasized the telephone's value for keeping in touch with friends and learning about parties—advertisements for telephones addressed to Indians or to both audiences generally emphasized risks to family well-being associated with the lack of access to a phone. Some ads, for instance, mentioned the need to get in touch with the doctor if a child were suddenly to become ill. In most cases, these ads pictured Indians in a state of anxiety or even panic about some situation that could easily arise in everyday life.[58]

The ad in Figure 7.10 suggests a common theme in ads geared to middle-class families, that of a parent worrying about the health of a child; the ad in effect asked the

Figure 7.10 "UNCERTAINTY can make life a NIGHTMARE," Bombay Telephone Co., *TI*, May 5, 1939, 5.

reader to imagine the dangers to which he or she would be exposing the family through failure to install a phone. The home appears to be an upper-middle class home with modern windows, an elevated bed and a clock. The copy of another ad simply reads "save life, save time, save money";[59] the fact that health concerns came first in this list is noteworthy. Other ads emphasized the value of being able to contact a range of people from doctors to storekeepers and the police, allowing the family to maintain a sense of safety and security.[60] The telephone, such ads insisted, was an indispensable tool needed to insure family survival.

In short, advertisements for household technologies displayed a range of persuasive strategies. They could stress the general value of adopting electrical goods to the process of becoming modern, they could mention the practical advantages of particular products, or they could attempt to evoke central preoccupations of Indian middle-class families. In this sense, they did not follow the common pattern that we have seen in other chapters of convergence around the theme of modern conjugality. What they held in common was a pedagogical style. Advertisers saw themselves as prodding customers whose allegiance to electricity was insufficient, and who were in need of instruction about the value of specific products and electricity in general.

Conclusion

The historian first confronting the widespread presence of discourses about ideal homes and the extensive advertisements for new household techonologies placed in Bombay newspapers during the 1920s and 1930s—both in English and in vernacular languages—might assume that the era of mass consumption had begun. Such a conclusion, however, would be at odds with what we know about actual material practices. Demand for electrical appliances in Bombay was limited, confined to a fairly small group of Europeans, upper-class Indians, and Anglo-Indians with significant enthusiasm about using these commodities on the one hand, and, to a lesser extent, to an Indian middle class whose attitude toward electricity was ambivalent and piecemeal. Middle-class families in Bombay almost certainly regarded the new technologies of the home as prohibitive in cost, as involving the adoption of unsettling new bodily practices, and as bringing about disturbing changes in the performance of household tasks that were currently met through the deployment of servants or unpaid family labor. Yet because BEST was responsible for selling electricity, because its opportunities for profit in its other areas of operation were so constrained, and because the costs of extending electricity to new users were relatively modest, the company still had significant motivation to encourage even marginal increases in consumption. A close reading of local advertisements suggests that the designers of these appeals viewed the middle class as relcalcitrant customers who had to be goaded into using electricity rather than as enthusiastic participants who might embrace a new consumer culture wholeheartedly.

As a whole, advertising for electrical consumer items clearly did not reflect the same efforts at adjustment to the middle-class consumer as the advertising for tonics and soap, medicines, hot drinks, and vanaspati. In earlier chapters of this book, I have suggested that advertisers were continuously engaged in processes of experimentation as they increasingly sought to prompt large numbers of Indian consumers to make habitual purchases of low-cost items. They were involved in collecting knowledge from local actors about middle-class values, priorities, and preoccupations. They adjusted their appeals, their artwork, and their core advertising themes as they reached beyond an audience of expatriates and emulators of the expatriates. But in the case of household technologies such adaptations were limited and uneven, perhaps because the goal of creating a mass consumer culture in urban India was so self-evidently illusory. Many of BEST's ads were developed primarily for an expatriate audience, and in many cases the investment in reworking these ads for middle-class customers was limited. Often BEST invoked universal appeals that were derived from a European or American context: the idea of joining a universal march of progress, the backwardness of non-electric methods of carrying out household tasks, and the need to relieve the drudgery of women's labor. In other cases, they merely mentioned the practical advantages of the products. In a few instances, no doubt, they did stress that use of the new household technologies would make it possible for housewives to manage homes that would otherwise be unruly, unsanitary and dangerous, and that refusal involved exposing a household to unacceptable risks. In these instances, advertisements drew upon a "heightened emotional context of the home" that necessitated that parents, especially housewives, play extensive roles in guarding against a host of potential medical and social threats to their family's well-being.[61] But this was not a dominant approach; there was little tendency to converge around the theme of conjugality or other themes that resonated more deeply in urban society. The view of the home generated by advertising for electrical goods thus proved to be a highly contradictory and fractured one.

Conclusion: Interwar Advertising and India's Contemporary Globalization

A history of advertising in western India before the 1940s is more than an exploration of an entertaining subject that an historian may encounter in newspapers of the time. It provides a valuable historical foundation for appreciating India's "globalization." First, it questions understandings that treat the emergence of the global consumer economy in India and the development of the modern advertising methods as purely a product of the post-liberalization, post-television age. What I have called here "brand-name capitalism" and two central, distinctive structures that accompanied it—the advertising agency and the field of professional advertising—took firm shape in India during the interwar period as international corporations began to seek worldwide markets much more aggressively than before. By the 1930s the advertising business in India was involved in attempting to generate knowledge about Indian society and economy, to deploy "scientific" techniques of copywriting and commercial art that its practitioners saw as an advance over earlier forms of commercial appeal, and to persuade consumers not only to buy certain brands but to transform their bodily practices to incorporate the use of mass-produced commodities. While the dimensions of brand-name capitalism remained relatively small during the interwar years (compared to what they would become), and while the character of advertising has undergone a series of significant changes since that time, the field's early twentieth-century antecedents are critical to understanding how contemporary forms of consumer capitalism acquired their shape.

This book similarly calls into question the radical disjuncture that often exists in South Asian conceptualizations of the history of the Indian "middle class." Historical studies have typically understood the early-twentieth-century middle class by examining non-material concerns such as the quest to acquire English education, nationalism, religious reform, the reformulation of new gender roles, and the emergence of new conceptions of the family. These studies stand in contrast to works on the contemporary middle class in India, which stress its materialism, its drive to distinguish its lifestyle from the urban and rural poor, and its pursuit of consumer commodities. The "old" and the "new" middle classes are imagined as two starkly different phenomena, separated not only by time and social values but also by totally different analytical lenses, indeed by the very criteria one uses to define a middle class. The disciplinary chasm that exists between pre-1940 works by historians and post-1990 studies by anthropologists, sociologists and political scientists accentuates this sense of sharp discontinuity. This book by contrast suggests that material concerns were central in the making of the late colonial middle class by highlighting the efforts of businesses that began to identify this social category as their primary market in India.

One of course cannot deduce middle-class perspectives directly from advertising, but one can appreciate how businesses were starting to understand middle-class consumers as well as the limitations of these efforts. Brand-name capitalism during the interwar period ceased to confine its ambitions to expatriates and a tiny anglicized Indian elite and came to focus its efforts on inducing a larger set of clerks, teachers, and urban professionals, most of them people of modest means, to make collectively tens of thousands of small purchases of low-priced items. For the most part, its exponents still did not yet perceive the rural population or the urban poor as significant customers due to their low levels of literacy and their perceived inability to make purchases beyond their subsistence needs. Nor, if the visual evidence of this book is representative, did it see Muslims and people outside the ranks of high-caste Hindus as part of the middle classes it was trying to reach.

The multinationals' project of making a middle class and making this middle class into buyers of brand-name commodities occurred at the very time when nationalist efforts urging Indians to confine themselves to swadeshi goods and to persuade Indians to simplify their material wants were at their height. The principle of swadeshi could at times be overwhelmed by the barrage of print messages run by multinational firms and by middle-class anxieties about their families' possibilities for self-reproduction. Examining the material priorities of the middle class in effect challenges the pre-eminence of nationalism in the early twentieth-century historiography by suggesting that other critical preoccupations also motivated its members. A study of this subject makes it possible for us to begin tracing historical connections (and discontinuities) in the material attitudes and practices of India's middle classes over time.[1]

Though a form of "globalization" was clearly taking place among the middle class and consumer practices during the interwar period, this development hardly reflected a triumphant, unilinear, or wholesale transplantation into India of economic and cultural forms inaugurated in North America and Europe. Anna Tsing's conception of globalization as a process characterized by *friction*, one in which universalizing projects encounter difference—producing unpredictable, unstable, and messy outcomes— seems particularly apt in understanding the history of consumer-oriented businesses in India and elsewhere in Asia, Latin America, Africa, and eastern Europe.

This study began by discussing the formation of the advertising profession in North America and Europe but it quickly shifted toward examining the ways in which professional advertisers made a myriad of adaptations to circumstances elsewhere in the world and in western India particularly. No doubt, some of the advertising field's leaders viewed their profession as a civilizing mission, as a project of transmitting universal consumer values of modernity and material comfort that they believed all the world's peoples should embrace. But as they entered into awkward encounters with local cultural and social realities, and as they sought to persuade hundreds of thousands of middle-class families to make small purchases of branded commodities, advertisers on the ground were compelled to engage in a series of accommodations, sometimes emphasizing aspects of their appeals that they originally viewed as secondary, sometimes rejecting other elements altogether, sometimes incorporating new articulations they believed might be more emotive to their prospective audiences, and sometimes simply pirating sales pitches indigenous competitors were making at the same time. The results were uneven, disordered, and sometimes unsettling.

While they were convinced they were addressing material desires possessed by all people, professional advertisers operating outside Europe and North America assumed that the world was constituted by difference, and that they would have to adjust their efforts to social and cultural realities in the places where they operated. Built into their own conception of their profession as a "scientific" enterprise was the notion that good advertising required knowledge about consumers in different locales. When it came to building markets in regions such as western India, this involved making efforts to understand local "culture" and engage in forms of market research that I have called commercial ethnology. Because middle-mass markets in India were relatively small, multinational businesses rarely carried out the sophisticated statistical studies they conducted in North America and Europe; they usually relied on less rigorous methods—perusing census records, traveling around the countryside, and interviewing shopkeepers. Sales pitches used by vernacular firms sometimes inspired new approaches by international businesses, as we saw in the example from Wilfred David's novel, which depicted a British businessman who poached language from local ads to devise advertising for his own tonics. Advertisers also relied heavily on input from their own subordinates who translated messages from English into vernacular languages, drew the images pictured in many ads, and provided observations as ads were being constructed in their offices (as the accounts of Prakash Tandon and S. D. Khadilkar examined in Chapters 1, 4 and 5 suggest).

Tandon's narrative of Levers' brief B.O. campaign, and merchant complaints about the marketing methods used by their suppliers, suggest that commercial information may have been conveyed to top corporate managers as much through contestations of existing methods as by the smooth transmission of knowledge from less powerful to more powerful people in business hierarchies. This process is often invisible in the records, and it has to be deduced through an examination of the ads, their differences from ads used in appeals to expatriates or outside India, and especially their transformation over time.

The arrival at the cultural strategies that informed advertisements during the late 1930s involved constant processes of experimentation. With every brand or type of commodity examined in this study, I have sought to explore how advertising specialists adjusted the nature of their campaigns over time. Advertisers, after all, were rewarded by their clients—the multinational manufacturers—largely based upon how successfully their campaigns appeared to be in winning new business.[2] When they faced resistance and hesitations, they were often compelled to devise new strategies or risk irrelevance. Before the late 1920s, global consumer product companies typically placed ads originally designed in their own countries into Indian newspapers. As they came to rely on professional specialists, they increasingly sought to adjust their sales messages to what they viewed as their customers' cultural priorities, often modifying their campaigns' central theme multiple times over the course of the 1930s. Professional advertisers of men's tonics increasingly incorporated the powerful, polysemic cultural theme of male weakness into their printed advertisements and linked their campaigns to notions of conjugal fulfillment. Between 1930 and 1940, J. Walter Thompson shifted its sales pitches for Horlicks from expatriate concerns with the heat and the dangers posed by an inhospitable Indian environment, to the health of Indian children and the value of the product in convalescence, and then again to male anxieties about unemployment and job success and the possibility they might be unable to provide for their families. Ads for beauty soaps increasingly moved away from evoking Western or Westernized "modern girls" to center around the figure of housewives who were modern but who did not challenge the core domestic ideals of the middle class. Such constant adjustments of advertising campaigns were conditioned by the commercial interaction of capitalist actors with Indian society, for instance by the regular flow of information and complaints from shopkeepers who sold these goods and by the perceived successes and failures of specific campaigns in expanding sales.

The fate of international slogans in an Indian environment provides a particularly telling form of evidence about the workings of "friction." The slogan "night starvation" was first used in Horlicks advertisements in the global North when the product was being touted as inducing better nighttime sleep in the early 1930s. The slogan was not introduced into the firm's Indian advertisements for several years, and when it was taken up, it was in the context of a campaign touting the product's ability to enhance men's capacity to work productively in their offices and thus fulfill their responsibilities to provide for their families. The original slogan apparently came to be seen as so distant from the mental universe of male purchasers that copywriters at JWT felt compelled to include a vernacular translation in the English-language text of these ads. These translations literally meant not night starvation at all but "morning weakness," phrasing with a deep multivalent resonance in local society and in local advertising discourse; the term suggested physical incapacity, cowardice in the face of British colonialism, and even sexual dysfunction, all meanings absent in the concept of night starvation.

Similarly, Levers' catch-phrase "B.O." floundered in its Indian advertising for Lifebuoy soap. From the beginning, the company refrained from introducing any reference to romantic and husband-wife contexts, which had been the main foci of its British and North American appeals. The B.O. campaign soon almost completely ran aground when attempts were made to translate it (along with its initials) into regional languages. Eventually the company abandoned the slogan altogether and embraced a sales pitch focused on promoting family health. Levers' advertisers recognized during the later 1930s that touting Lux as the Soap of Stars while using American actresses had lost its selling power in India at a time when nationalism was growing and when the Indian cinema was replacing Hollywood as a key form of public entertainment. By the early 1940s, the company had developed an alternative campaign featuring actresses from the Bombay cinema. But it arrived at this point in a fitful process, finding itself unable for some time to convince Bombay film stars to risk their reputations by appearing in ads and then discovering that some of its competitors had beaten it to the punch in signing Indian actresses to advertising contracts. Levers' ads for many products began to include the phrasing "Made in India from vegetable oils only" in a clear effort to counteract the campaigns of Godrej, which had stressed the nonswadeshi character of its foreign competitors as well as their tendency to use animal fats in the manufacturing process.

The visual character of advertisements also was tranformed through friction. Certainly advertising agencies brought to the subcontinent established practices of commercial art, which had proven to be a valuable mode of conveying images on the printed page. But they ultimately shaped numerous new conventions in the Indian environment. Global firms largely relied on images of Europeans during the 1920s. Their advertisers at the time typically reasoned that not only were many of their customers expatriates but that Indian buyers saw products used by Europeans as more prestigious and would be motivated by images featuring European figures. But by the 1930s, awareness of middle-class nationalism prompted commercial artists to develop depictions that conveyed Indianness. At the same time, advertisers learned to steer away from shading the page to indicate darker skin color as a way of indicating Indian characters in an environment where fair skin was prized by their middle-class customers; the high-caste man and woman came to be depicted using the uncolored newspaper page and Indianness was instead conveyed through clothing and through black hair color. Other conventions emerged: the use of a bindi on the forehead and mangal sutra round the neck to indicate a married woman, a man slumped in his pajamas with his wife standing over him to suggest sexual and physical weakness, cinematic images to convey an aura of romance (within marriage) and light-skinned children in shorts engaged in play to suggest energy and health. Commercial art also came to draw extensively from imagery of vernacular advertisements and other art forms in a self-referencing fashion. Such inter-ocularity, to use Sumathi Ramaswamy's term, proved crucial in the production of a visual culture whose meanings consumer-viewers would recognize.

Processes of friction, I have argued, led to the convergence of many different campaigns during the late 1930s around the principles of modern conjugality, and specifically a medicalized conception of the family that faced a variety of threats to its self-reproduction. This conception was seriously influenced by a eugenic discourse suggesting that, without the appropriate countermeasures, Indian families would be subject to weakness, physical deterioration, lethargy and ineffectiveness. Horlicks advertisements came to crystallize around potential male incapacity to fulfill responsibilities for the household's economic well-being; ads for Ovaltine and for Sunlight soap focused on female obligations for raising hardy, energetic children; appeals for Lifebuoy and Dalda centered around parental preoccupations with the health of the family, again particularly the health of children; even refrigerator and telephone ads sometimes stressed the value of the appliance in safeguarding the family's food supply or in contacting doctors and police in household emergences. As I discussed in Chapter 2, ads targeting expatriates evoked a very different set of themes.

In stressing convergence around the concept of modern conjugality through experimentation, I do not mean to suggest that the cultural preoccupations of middle-class householders were so narrow that only one potential strand of emotive appeal was present. But conjugality was a theme that had great advantages to multinational firms in the 1930s. First, it was a possibility open to them at a time when nationalism, another poweful potential motif, could not easily be adopted because of their self-evidently foreign origins and associations.

Second, it reflected a constellation of powerful discourses circulating widely in middle-class society that were challenging the social and material status quo; it could be deployed to motivate *change* in existing consumption behaviors and conventional body practices. Its invocation was often intended to suggest that modernity itself and the reproduction of the middle-class family and its social position into the next generation were at stake in the decision to purchase and use brand-name commodities. Through the rhetoric of their ads, advertising professionals implicitly asserted over and over again that modern consumption practices were crucial to the making and perpetuation of modern families. Mention of joint families was virtually absent in advertisements I saw between 1925 and 1940. When the mother-in-law began to appear in some ads during the early 1940s, it was often as a figure who represented a rather troublesome challenge to conjugal happiness and the housewife's ability to manage the home by herself.

Third, in a related point, the theme of conjugality particularly jibed with new conceptions of housewives as people who exercised authority as decision-makers about family budgets and as guardians of family health. Marketing experts were beginning to discover that women were not merely reliant on their husbands but played a powerfully determining role in household consumption choices.

Fourth, the emphasis on familial self-reproduction imparted to certain purchases a special urgency in the context of severe budgetary constraints. At a time when appeals to pleasure and luxury generally were of limited motivational value, and households seemingly could not be moved by the desire to keep up with the Mehtas and Patwardhans, evocation of anxieties about the family appeared to have strong motivating power. Appeals to conjugality thus often became a powerful culminating focus when other kinds of sales pitch had been exhausted.

Material realities, not just cultural differences, were also important sources of friction. The middle class that came to be targeted by multinational companies was composed mostly of households with limited disposable income; it was not a category of people with significant newfound buying power, as the term is usually understood in appreciating U.S. history or in analyzing contemporary India. Members of this class were no doubt trying to distinguish their lifestyles from those of the working class, but they often had limited means to do so. Advertisers adjusted their appeals away from approaches they might have used with a more prosperous, less abstemious set of actors (such as the expatriates), often stressing the absolute necessity of consuming the advertised item to familial self-reproduction. At the same time, most firms largely refrained from attempting to appeal to the urban poor and the rural population, which were characterized by more extensive poverty and illiteracy. Yet another constraint was the presence of a huge market of cheap, unbranded goods that typically undersold advertised commodities and commodities marketed by vernacular firms. In encountering the competiton of these commodities, consumer goods firms often found it critical to adjust their sales approaches, for instance by implicitly or explicitly raising the dangers cheaper substitutes represented to family well-being, rather than by suggesting the pleasures that could be obtained from consumption.

Friction also created major obstacles to the sales of some items. Preferences for real ghee (even though it was available mainly in adulterated form) and perceptions that industrially produced cooking mediums possessed unhealthy qualities, continued to plague Levers' effort to make Dalda a ubiquitous household item. Packaged foods made only limited inroads into middle-class consumption patterns. Efforts to advertise electrical household technologies were generally unsuccessful, both because the costs of most of these commodities were high and because saving household labor was hardly a priority in a context where unpaid family labor and cheap servant labor were readily available. Electrical goods manufacturers and electricity products used a variety of sales pitches in their advertising but did not find one that could elicit mass consumer demand. Branded clothing similarly did not acquire a mass market. In this environment, consumerism, defined as the drive to purchase and use an endless new array of goods, did not flourish in the interwar period. Middle-class engagements with brand-name capitalism remained selective and constrained.

In short, the pattern of globalization engendered by multinational consumer goods companies was a limited and messy one even if it set the terrain for more ambitious developments later in the century. Nonetheless, brand-name capitalism gained a foothold in urban India during the interwar period, largely by linking itself to new notions of the family that emerged at this time. If we fail to recognize that a new kind of global project was making serious inroads into the economy during the early twentieth century and that middle-class consumption patterns were being reconfigured as a result of their engagement with these developments, we will continue to be vulnerable to ahistorical understandings of how current social patterns have come to constitute themselves. Advertising became an important feature of Indian society during the interwar period, both in economic and social terms. By tracing the fate of the advertising industry over time we can come to understand critical continuities and transformations in the structures of Indian and global capitalism.

It would be tempting to assume that the processes examined here came to a sudden end with the advent of World War II, and that India's contemporary globalization is part of an autonomous development that began abruptly about 1991; indeed, I myself held this assumption until relatively late stages in my research. No doubt, the war and the formation of a restrictive trade regime after independence greatly reduced the flow of foreign manufactured consumer goods to India. After 1947, moreover, the Congress government took steps to build a socialist economy, taking over control of some industries, and instituting extensive regulation of others as it sought to implement a series of five-year plans. The new regime viewed middle-class consumption with suspicion, as something that distracted the country from addressing its pressing problems of poverty and of building national defense and heavy industry. Advertising itself was criticized heavily, cast as arousing desires that could not be fulfilled because of the limited resources of India's population and thus producing social dissatisfaction in the process. Limited economic growth and the persistence of poverty—for decades, roughly half the population continued to live under conditions of absolute poverty—seemed to offer very unpropitious circumstances for the expansion of consumer industries.

Yet despite all these developments, brand-name capitalism and the field of professional advertising not only persisted but expanded exponentially in the post-1940 environment. Over the next four decades, established firms like J. Walter

Thompson (which became Hindustan Thompson) and Lintas grew many times over, creating new branches, hiring larger staffs, and expanding their turnover dramatically. Many new advertising agencies, most reliant on Indian capital and management alone, were established and flourished. Post-war advertising came to draw upon more rigorous and systematic forms of market research; the efforts to acquire cultural knowledge about consumers during the colonial period would later seem thin and superficial from the perspective of these wide-ranging investigations. New technologies—the use of radio, new forms of print publication, film (and ads at cinema houses) and eventually televison—carried advertisements for large consumer products much more widely over the countryside.

Armed with new sources of knowledge, new technologies for conducting publicity, and a newfound confidence in the receptivity of ordinary people to advertising, Indian manufacturers increasingly turned to professional advertisers in hopes that they could win over consumers who had previously abstained from the purchase and use of brand-name commodities. In many cases, these new efforts involved attempts at ousting unbranded products from Indian markets and transforming the bodily practices that use of the new commodities entailed. Each generation of advertising specialists believed that it was important to develop evermore complex techniques for understanding values and attitudes toward material goods. Each generation also recreated anew the myth that it was the first to make a serious effort to understand the Indian consumer. The expansion of consumer business was not just an inevitable outcome of improved income levels and literacy, it was a product of a myriad of increasingly aggressive campaigns conducted by Indian corporations.

Since the advertising profession was a crucial institution of what I have called brand-name capitalism, its condition, growth, and transformation are a useful gauge of the changing shape of critical features of the Indian economy. Clearly the 1940 to 1990 period was not an interregnum in which the advance of consumer incorporation in new consumer structures was halted. It was instead a time of considerable dynamism and of continued "globalization" in the sense that the profession of advertising, international in its origins and in many of its standard conventions, gained a stronger base in Indian society. By the early 1990s, the firms that were making consumer goods and that conducted publicity for them had thoroughly "Indianized," with Indians assuming all the top positions in their corporate hierarchies, though this process took place within formal business alliances with companies and advertising agencies from outside India. Actually, one might also say they had also "vernacularized" their efforts much more rigorously than their predecssors in that they self-consciously sought to fine-tune their appeals to regional languages and emotive themes specific to particular locales (the reliance on regional cinema stars comes to mind as a most obvious example). These agencies broke away from a simple reliance on the middle class as customers, appealing to the expanded ranks of urban people with disposable income and to the increasingly literate, more prosperous strata of the rural population. Professional advertisers found more and more sophisticated ways of reaching and persuading consumers to buy branded products. Clearly, India's capitalist economy and India's middle class have taken very different forms in the post-1991 environment than they assumed before 1945. Yet they belong to a much longer past of expansion in brand-name capitalism that stretches well into the late colonial period, and continuing to overlook this history creates a flawed understanding of how the structures of the present came to be. This book in particular stresses that the whole history of the advertising profession in South Asia, even when it was dominated by European actors, has involved continuous struggles to understand Indian consumers and to formulate campaigns based upon powerful "prior meanings" that would motivate them to embrace branded products and the larger project of brand-name capitalism.

Notes

Introduction

1   F. R. Eldridge, *Advertising and Selling Abroad* (New York and London: Harper and Brothers, 1930), 1.

2   JWTA, "Memo to Mr. Hutchins, 27 April 1936," 2 in "International Advertising," microfilm reel 257.

3   The limited penetration of advertising culture in India has been discussed in ways that overlap with this study in Markus Daechsel, *The Politics of Self-Expression: The Urdu Middle-Class Milleu in Mid-twentieth Century India and Pakistan* (London and New York: Routledge, 2009).

4   See *Towards a History of Consumption in South Asia*, eds. Douglas E. Haynes, Abigail McGowan, Tirthankar Roy and Haruka Yanigasawa (New Delhi: Oxford University Press, 2010); Daechsel, *The Politics of Self-Expression.*

5   Key works on the middle class during the colonial period are Sanjay Joshi, *Fractured Modernity: Making of a Middle Class in Colonial North India* (New Delhi: Oxford University Press, 2001) and *The Middle Class in Colonial India*, ed. Sanjay Joshi (New Delhi: Oxford University Press, 2019). More extensive references are discussed in Chapter 2.

6   For a few key works, Tanika Sarkar, *The Hindu Wife, Hindu Nation: Community, Religion and Cultural Nationalism* (Bloomington: Indiana University Press, 2001); Mytheli Sreenivas, *Wives, Widows and Concubines: The Conjugal Family Ideal in Colonial India* (Bloomington: Indiana University Press, 2008); Charu Gupta, *Sexuality, Obscenity, Community: Women, Muslims and the Hindu Public in Colonial India* (New York: Palgrave, 2002). A broader discussion of conjugality in South Asia is "Conjugality and Sexual Economies in India," *Feminist Studies*, vol. 38, no. 3 (2011): 1–235. Some other works are mentioned in Chapter 2. The term "family imaginary" has been formulated and developed richly by Sreenivas in her work on colonial South India.

7   For instance, Christopher Pinney, *"Photos of the Gods": The Printed Image and Political Struggle in India* (London: Reaktion, 2004); Sandria B. Freitag, "South Asian Ways of Seeing, Muslim Ways of Knowing: The Indian Muslim Niche Market in Posters," *The Indian Economic and Social History Review*, vol. 44, no. 3 (2007): 297–331; Sumathi Ramaswamy, *The Goddess and the Nation: Mapping Mother India* (Durham, NC: Duke University Press, 2010); *Beyond Appearances? Visual Practices and Ideologies in Modern India*, ed. Sumathi Ramaswamy (New Delhi and Thousand Oaks, CA: Sage, 2003); *Empires of Vision: A Reader*, eds. Martin Jay and Sumathi Ramaswamy (Durham, NC: Duke University Press, 2014), xiv.

8   Ramaswamy, "Introduction" in *Beyond Appearances*, xv.

9   Ibid., xiv.

10 For example, William Mazzarella's seminal study on advertising, while setting forth arguments that have been influential in South Asian Studies, devotes only a few paragraphs to discussion of advertising before 1990. William Mazzarella, *Shoveling*

Smoke: Advertising and Globalization in Contemporary India (New Delhi: Oxford University Press, 2004). Leela Fernandes engages in some discussion of the middle class in colonial India, but leaves out any consideration of its consumption practices, despite the fact she treats consumption as central in her examination of the contemporary middle class. Leela Fernandes, *India's New Middle Class: Democratic Politics in an Era of Economic Reform* (Minneapolis: University of Minnesota Press, 2006).

11 Several substantial non-academic histories, mostly by journalists or insiders to the advertising industry, have been published on advertising in India. But these works rarely address broader questions of socio-cultural or business history to a more limited extent. See Ranabir Ray Choudhury, *Early Calcutta Advertisements, 1875–1925* (Bombay: Nachiketa Publications, 1992); Dasarathi Mishra, *Advertising in Indian Newspapers, 1780–1947* (Berhampur: Ishani Publications, 1987); Arun Chaudhuri, *Indian Advertising: 1780 to 1950 A.D.* (New Delhi and New York: Tata McGraw Hill, 2007); Anand Bhaskar Halve and Anita Sarkar, *Adkathā: The Story of Indian Advertising* (Goa, India: Centurm Charitable Trust, 2011); Ambi Parameswaran, *Nawabs, Nudes, Noodles: India through 50 Years of Advertising* (London: Macmillan, 2016). Another valuable non-academic essay is Vikram Doctor and Anvar Alikhan, "Kyon Na Aazmaye? Part I," *The India Magazine of Her People and Culture* (December 1996): 46–55. A book by Ramya Ramamurthy, *Branded in History* (Gurgaon: Hachette India, 2021) came out just as I was making final preparations of this manuscript for publication, and I regret that I did not have more time to incorporate its perspectives and empirical material.

12 For some key works, see Amiya Kumar Bagchi, *Private Investment in India, 1900–1939* (Cambridge: Cambridge University Press, 1972); Rajnarayan Chandavarkar, *The Origins of Industrial Capitalism in India: Business Strategies and the Working Classes in Bombay, 1900–1940* (Cambridge: Cambridge University Press, 1994); Dwijendra Tripathi, *The Oxford History of Indian Business* (New Delhi and New York: Oxford University Press, 2004); David Rudner, *Caste and Capitalism in Colonial India: the Nattukotai Chettiars* (Berkeley: University of California Press, 1994); Tirthankar Roy, *A Business History of India: Enterprise and the Emergence of Capitalism from 1700* (Cambridge: Cambridge University Press, 2018); Douglas E. Haynes, *Small-Town Capitalism in Western India: Artisans, Merchants and the Making of the Informal Economy, 1870–1960* (Cambridge: Cambridge University Press, 2012).

13 See my essay, "Advertising and the History of South Asia, 1880–1950," *History Compass*, vol. 13, no. 8 (2015): 361–374.

14 For instance, see Rachel Berger, *Ayurveda Made Modern: Political Histories of Indigenous Medicine in North India, 1900–1955* (Houndsmills, Basingstoke, Hampshire: Palgrave Macmillan, 2013); Projit Bihari Mukharji, "Chandshir Chikitsa: A Nomadology of Subaltern Medicine," in *Medical Marginality in South Asia: Situating Subaltern Therapeutics*, eds. David Hardiman and Projit Bihari Mukharji (London: Routledge, 2012), 85–108; Jeremy Schneider, "Reimaging Traditional Medicine: Tracing the Emergence of Commodified Ayurveda in the Interwar Period." MSc. Thesis in Economic and Social History, Oxford University, 2008; Madhuri Sharma, "Creating a Consumer: Exploring Medical Advertisements in Colonial India," in *The Social History of Health and Medicine in Colonial India*, eds. Bisamoy Patti and Mark Harrison (London and New York: Routledge, 2009), 213–228; Madhuri Sharma, *Indigenous and Western Medicine in Colonial India* (New Delhi: Foundation Books, 2012).

15 Kajri Jain, *Gods in the Bazaar: The Economies of Indian Calendar Art* (Durham, NC:
    Duke University Press, 2007); Arvind Rajagopal, "The Commodity Image in the (Post)
    Colony," *Tasveer Ghar: A Digital Archive of South Asian Popular Visual Culture*,
    accessed June 29, 2017, http://www.tasveerghar.net/cmsdesk/essay/100/index_3.html;
    Philip Lutgendorf, "Chai Why?," *Tasveer Ghar*, accessed June 29, 2017, http://
    tasveerghar.net/cmsdesk/essay/89/index.html; Abigail McGowan, "Domestic Modern:
    Redecorating Homes in Bombay in the 1930s," Paper presented in the conference, "The
    Long Indian Century: Historical Transitions and Social Transformations," Yale
    University, April 2014; Sabeena Gadihoke, "Selling Soap and Stardom: The Story of
    Lux," *Tasveer Ghar* accessed July 3, 2017, http://www.tasveergharindia.net/cmsdesk/
    essay/104/index.html. A significant exception to this generalization comes from
    another study of tea advertisements, Gautam Bhadra, *From an Imperial Product to a
    National Drink: The Culture of Tea Consumption in Modern India* (Kolkata: Tea Board
    India, 2005). A more recent and wide-ranging effort is *The Story of Early Indian
    Advertising*, ed. Jyotindra Jain, special issue of *Marg*, vol. 68, no. 3 (March 2017).
16 Daechsel, *The Politics of Self-Expression*; Bhadra, *From an Imperial Product to a
    National Drink*; see also Douglas E. Haynes, "Creating the Consumer? Advertising,
    Capitalism and the Middle Class in Urban Western India, 1914–40," in *Towards a
    History of Consumption*, 108–135. Bhadra's work demonstrates how tea advertisement
    (and other aspects of visual culture) disseminated the practice of tea drinking, first
    among an imperial elite, then within an Indian middle class, and finally among the
    larger population.
17 Rather than defining the two domains largely by language, I define domains also by
    firm type and advertising idiom/style. Vernacular advertising was executed by small
    indigenous firms typically organized on a family basis. Some of these firms advertised
    in English-language papers as well as vernacular ones. Corporate advertising was
    carried out by large, often multinational, corporations, who advertised in English but
    increasingly also in regional languages by the later 1930s.
18 Arvind Rajagopal, "Advertising in India: Genealogies of the Colonial Subject," in
    Oxford Handbook of Modernity in South Asia: Modern Makeovers, ed. Saurabh Dube
    (New Delhi: Oxford University Press, 2011), see especially 218–221. The quotes are
    from p.220. Rajagopal discusses advertising in many different articles, so any summary
    may oversimplify his current position.
19 In using this term, I suggest both the actual act of translation into vernacular
    languages but also the adjustment of advertising pitches to the perceived cultural
    priorities of consumers, even in English-language papers.
20 Mona Domosh, *American Commodities in an Age of Empire* (New York: Routledge,
    2006); Ann MacClintock, *Imperial Leather: Race, Gender and Sexuality in Colonial
    Context* (New York: Routledge, 1995), 31–36; David Ciarlo, *Advertising Empire: Race
    and Visual Culture in Imperial Germany* (Cambridge, MA: Harvard University Press,
    2011); James P. Woodard, "Marketing Modernity: The J. Walter Thompson Company
    and North American Advertising in Brazil, 1929–1939," *Hispanic American Historical
    Review*, vol. 82, no. 2 (May 2002): 257–290.
21 Denise Sutton, *Globalizing Ideal Beauty: How Female Copywriters of the J. Walter
    Thompson Advertising Agency Redefined Beauty for the Twentieth Century*
    (Basingstoke: Palgrave: Macmillan, 2009); Geoffrey Jones, *Beauty Imagined: A History
    of the Global Beauty Industry* (New York: Oxford University Press, 2010); Kristin
    Hoganson, *Consumers' Imperium: The Global Production of American Domesticity,
    1865–1920* (Chapel Hill: University of North Carolina Press, 2007); *The Modern Girl*

Around the World: Consumption, Modernity and Globalization, eds. Modern Girl Around the World Research Group (Durham, NC and London: Duke University Press, 2008).

22 Relli Schecter, "Reading Advertisements in a Colonial/Development Context," 484.

23 Sherman Cochran, *Chinese Medicine Men: Consumer Culture in China and Southeast Asia* (Cambridge, MA: Harvard University Press, 2006). See also Chie Ikeya, *Refiguring Women, Colonialism and Modernity in Burma* (Honolulu: University of Hawaii Press, 2011).

24 Julio Moreno, *Yankee Don't Go Home!: Mexican Nationalism, American Business Culture, and the Shaping of Modern Mexico, 1920-1950* (Chapel Hill: University of North Carolina Press, 2003).

25 Timothy Burke, *Lifebuoy Men, Lux Women: Commodification, Consumption and Cleanliness in Modern Zimbabwe* (Durham, NC: Duke University Press, 1996).

26 As Williamson herself puts the point (and as Burke quotes her): "Advertisers produce knowledge . . . but this knowledge is always produced from something already known, that acts as a guarantee, in its anteriority, for the 'truth' in the ad itself." Judith Williamson, *Decoding Advertisements: Ideology and Meaning in Advertising* (London: Marion Boyars, 1978), 99.

27 Anna Lowenhaupt Tsing, *Friction: An Ethnography of Global Connection* (Princeton: Princeton University Press, 2005), 4.

28 Mazarrella, *Shoveling Smoke*.

29 I also examined some magazines. Many magazines from this period, however, did not include as much advertising as newspapers, especially from larger businesses.

30 Douglas E. Haynes, *Rhetoric and Ritual in Colonial India: The Shaping of a Public Culture in Surat City, 1852-1928* (Berkeley: University of California Press, 1991).

31 For instance, see Ramaswamy, "Introduction" in *Beyond Appearances*, xvi.

32 Ibid.

33 Agents of Unilever noted in an internal report that in some cases "a part of the Indian community" was influenced by advertisements designed to appeal to Europeans, particularly in the most prestigious range of goods. UA, UN/RM/OC/2/2/46/30, "United Traders Ltd., India. Messrs Budget-Meakin's and Knox's Report, 16 January 1936," 19. Such emulation clearly declined over the course of the 1930s.

Chapter 1

1   I have drawn in parts of this chapter, particularly "the globalization of professional advertising" on research from a valuable unpublished honors thesis done under my direction by Jeremy Schneider, "Discourses in Capitalism: Ovaltine Advertisements and Visions of Domesticity in the British Empire during the Interwar Period," Undergraduate Honors Thesis, Dartmouth College, Department of History, 2007. He is in effect a second author of those sections.

2   The discussion of these multinational corporations in India before 1940 has been limited. The best coverage may be Omkar Goswami, "From Bazaar to Industry," in *The Oxford India Anthology of Business History*, ed. Medha Kudaisya (Delhi: Oxford University Press, 2011), 235-257.

3   Darbara Singh Sodhi, "India, a $600,000,000 Market," *AA*, vol. 1, no. 5 (May 1929): 5.

4   See, for instance, Arvind Rajagopal, "Early Publicity in India," *Marg: A Magazine of the Arts*, vol. 68, no. 3 (March 2017): 88-99.

5   Arvind Rajagopal, "Commodity and Commodity Image in the Indian Bazaar: Notes from Trademark Case Law," unpublished essay presented at a workshop, "Transactional Sociality: Market Moralities and Embedded Capital in India," held at the University of Goettingen, December 2016. For a discussion of trademark law and legislation in India, see, for instance, S. Venkateshwaran, *The Law of Trade and Merchandize Marks in India* (Madras: The Madras Law Office, 1937).

6   *Times of India* (hereafter *TI*), April 18, 1939, 6.

7   See Rajagopal, "Advertising as Political Ventriloquism" and "Commodity and Commodity Image in the Indian Bazaar." See also Douglas E. Haynes, "Selling Masculinity: Advertisements for Sex Tonics and the Making of Modern Conjugality in Western India, 1900–1945," *South Asia: Journal of South Asian Studies*, vol. 35, no. 4 (December 2012): 787–831; Douglas E. Haynes, "Brand-Name Capitalism, Soap Advertising and the Making of the Middle Class Family in Western India, 1918–1940," Paper given in a Conference on Material Culture in South Asia, University of Pennsylvania, April 2012.

8   For instance, *TI*, August 3, 1934, 4.

9   For instance, see Frank Perlin, "Proto-Industrialization and Pre-Colonial South Asia," *Past and Present*, vol. 98, no. 1 (1983): 30–95; Prasannan Parthasarathi, *The Transition to a Colonial Economy: Weavers, Merchants and Kings in South India, 1720–1800* (Cambridge: Cambridge University Press, 2001); C. A Bayly, *Rulers, Townsmen, and Bazaars: North Indian Society in the Age of British Expansion, 1770–1870* (Cambridge and New York: Cambridge University Press, 1983).

10   H. V. Bowen, "The Consumption of British Manufactured Goods in India: A Prologue, 1765–1813," *Towards a History of Consumption in South Asia*, ed. by Douglas E. Haynes et. al. (New Delhi: Oxford University Press), 26–50.

11   Anand A. Yang, *Bazaar India: Markets, Society, and the Colonial State in Gangetic Bihar* (Berkeley: University of California Press, 1998).

12   Yang draws this term from the early nineteenth-century British official, Francis Buchanan. Ibid., 227.

13   Douglas E Haynes, "Market Formation in Khandesh, c. 1820–1930," *The Indian Economic & Social History Review*, vol. 36, no. 3 (2016): 275–302.

14   Ibid.

15   Dulali Nag, *The Social Construction of Handwoven Tangail Saris in the Market of Calcutta*, PhD. Dissertation, Michigan State University, University Microfilms International, 1990, 136.

16   Jain, "The Visual Culture of the Indo-British Cotton Trade," in Jain, ed., *The Story of Indian Advertising*, 34–43.

17   For an account of early forms of advertising, including non-newspaper advertising, in South India, see A. R. Venkatachalapathy, "A Magic System?: Print Advertising in Colonial Tamil Nadu," in *Globalizing Everyday Consumption in India: History and Ethnography*, eds. Bhaswati Bhattacharya and Henrike Donner (Delhi: Routledge, 2020).

18   This analysis is based upon analogies to Benedict Anderson's work on nationalism, *Imagined Communities: Reflections on the Origin and Spread of Nationalism* (London: Verso, 1983); Ohmann, *Selling Culture*, 83–117, offers a similar interpretation in discussing advertisement in American magazines.

19   Prithwiraj Biswas, "Advertising and Enterprise in Colonial Bengal: Reflections on Hemendramohan Bose through a study of his advertisements." Paper presented at the North American Conference of British Studies, Washington, D.C., November 2016.

20 These forms of business are discussed more extensively in Douglas E. Haynes, "Vernacular Capitalism, Advertising and the Bazaar in Early Twentieth-Century Western India," in *Rethinking Markets in Modern India: Enbedded Exchange and Contested Jurisdiction*, eds. Ajay Gandhi, Barbara Harriss-White, Douglas E. Haynes, and Sebastian Schwecke (Cambridge: Cambridge University Press, 2020), 116–146.

21 Jeremy Schneider, "Reimaging Traditional Medicine: Tracing the Emergence of Commodified Ayurveda in the Interwar Period," Master of Science in Economic and Social History Thesis, Oxford University, 2008, 15.

22 Similar points have been made in Gupta, *Sexuality, Obscenity, Community*, 66–83; Daechsel, *The Politics of Self-Expression*, 174–175.

23 I suspect the figures of the Europeans in this ad were drawn by someone working at the newspaper office.

24 *Report of the Bombay Economic and Industrial Survey Committee, 1938–1940*, vol. II, Kolaba (Bombay: Government Central Press, 1941).

25 Anvar Alikhan, "Pre-50s: From Raj to Swaraj," in *Adkathā: The story of Indian Advertising*, eds. Anita Sarkar and Anand Halve, 36. See Venkatachalapathy, "A Magic System?" for similar findings in South India.

26 For South India see Venkatachalapathy, "A Magic System?"

27 Doctor and Alikhan, "Kyon Na Aazmaye," 48. They suggest that Dattaram's initially sold advertising space in newspapers and on trams. Dattaram became well known for its ads for the West End Watch Company.

28 J. Walter Thompson, *The Indian Market* (New York: J. Walter Thompson Company, 1959), 32.

29 *EA*, vol. 3, no. 4 (April 1930): 6; *EA*, vol. 2, no. 8 (August 1930): 9; *EA*, vol. 3, no. 3 (March 1931): 5.

30 *EA*, vol. 2, no. 11 (November 1930).

31 L. A Stronach, undated recollection, text provided by Anita Sarkar.

32 Ohmann, *Selling Culture*, 94.

33 See Ohmann, *Selling Culture*, 81–99; Daniel Pope, *The Making of Modern Advertising* (New York: Basic Books, Inc., 1983).

34 See Ohmann, *Selling Culture*, especially 91.

35 Robert P. Hymers and Leonard Sharpe, *The Technique and Practice of Advertising Art* (London: Sir Isaac Pitman & Sons, Ltd., 1939), 1.

36 See for instance, Daniel Starch, *Advertising: Its Principles, Practice and Technique* (Chicago: Scott, Foresman and Co., 1914); Daniel Starch, *Principles of Advertising* (Chicago and New York: A. W. Shaw Co., 1923); Walter Dill Scott, *The Psychology of Advertising: A Simple Exposition of the Principles of Psychology in Their Relation to Successful Advertising* (Boston: Small, Maynard & Company, 1913); F. R. Eldridge, *Advertising and Selling Abroad* (New York and London: Harper and Brothers, 1930); Howard Bridgewater, *Advertising; Or, The Art of Making Known: A Simple Exposition of the Principles of Advertising* (London: Sir Isaac Pitman & Sons, 1910).

37 Ohmann, *Selling Culture*, 97.

38 The most extensive study on the history of advertising research is Peggy Jean Kreshel, "Towards a Cultural History of Advertising Research: A Case Study of J. Walter Thompson, 1908–25," PhD. Thesis, University of Illinois at Urbana-Champaign, 1989.

39 Scott, *The Psychology of Advertising*, 4–5. See also Harold Ernest Burtt, *Psychology of Advertising* (Boston: Houghton Mifflin Company, 1938). These issues are explored in Merle Curti, "The Changing Concept of 'Human Nature' in the Literature of American Advertising," *The Business History Review*, vol. 41, no. 4 (Winter 1967): 335–357.

40 A. J. Greenly, "Reflections on Advertising," *Commercial Art*, vol. XI, no 66 (December 1931): 226–229.

41 Quoted in Schneider, "Discourses in Capitalism," 52.

42 Bridgewater, *Advertising; Or, the Art of Making Known*.

43 See, for instance, Mona Domosh, *American Commodities in an Age of Empire*, esp. 33–45.

44 Jeff Merron, "Putting Foreign Consumers on the Map: J. Walter Thompson's Struggle with General Motors' International Advertising Account in the 1920s," *The Business History Review*, vol. 73, no. 3 (1999): 466.

45 These developments are discussed in Merron, "Putting Foreign Consumers on the Map," 465–502.

46 Donald Renshaw and C. F. Spofford, Jr., *Advertising in India. Trade Information Bulletin No. 318*, Washington: U.S. Department of Commerce (Supplement to Commerce Reports), February 1925; U.S. Department of Commerce, *Channels of Distribution of American Merchandise in India. Trade Information Bulletin 817*, Washington: Government Printing Office, 1933.

47 Jennifer Scanlon, "Mediators in the International Marketplace: U.S. Advertising in Latin America in the Early Twentieth Century," *Business History Review*, vol. 77, no. 3 (2003): 387–415.

48 Domosh has shown that similar conceptions had been associated with American commodity capitalism since the late nineteenth century. See *American Commodities in an Age of Empire*, 3. In coining the term commercial ethnology, I am drawing an analogy to Bernard Cohn's concept of colonial sociology, which refers to principles of knowledge British authorities developed in understanding Indian society. See, for example, Cohn, "The Census, Social Structure and Objectification in South Asia," in *An Anthropologist among the Historians and Other Essays* (Delhi: Oxford University Press, 1987), pp. 224–254; Nicholas Dirks, *Castes of Mind: Colonialism and the Making of Modern India* (Princeton: Princeton University Press, 2001). For a history of official anthropology and its evolution in British India, one that shows how it changed in form during the period covered in this book, see C. J. Fuller, "Colonial Anthropology and the Decline of the Raj: Caste, Religion and Political Change in India in the Early Twentieth Century," *Journal of the Royal Asiatic Society*, vol. 26, no. 3 (July 2016): 463–486.

49 Clement H. Watson, "Markets Are People—Not Places: A Few Thoughts on Export," JWT *News Bulletin*, July 1928, JWTA, Box MN5.

50 Watson, "Markets Are People," 5–6.

51 Watson, "Markets Are People," 11. As Scanlon has pointed out, JWT's efforts were infused with the idea of progress and the role of consumer culture in disseminating the ideal of a global model citizenry, "Mediators in the International Marketplace," 399.

52 Henry C. Miner, Jr., "The American Manufacturer Meets his Foreign Consumer," JWT *News Bulletin*, October 1929, 10, JWT, Box MN5.

53 HATA, HAT/50/1/160/3/12, "Arthur Hobbs, JWT, to Stanley Knott, Scott and Bowne, 19 June 1931," 4.

54 JWTA, Box MN8, "South Africa as a Market," JWT *Newsletter*, June 15, 1929, 4. Note that the newsletter here was referring primarily to white South Africans in this quote. For the most part, advertising professionals saw black South Africans as too poor to purchase branded products.

55 Roger S. Falk, "Advertising in India Must Tackle a Double Sales Problem," *Advertiser's Weekly*, July 11, 1935, 60.

56 JWTA, Box MN8, Harry C. Miner, Jr., "Now A Complete World Service!," *JWT Newsletter*, December 15, 1929, 1.

57 JWTA, "International Advertising," 1935, microfilm reel 257.

58 See the debate over this issue in Allen Reader, "American Copy, Local Copy and Common-Sense Advertising," *EA*, vol. 2, no. 12 (December 1930): 10–11. This issue was also discussed in Eldridge, *Advertising and Selling Abroad*, 11–12.

59 Andrew J. Billings, "Should Advertising Copy Go Native? No—Keep an American Flavor," *AA*, vol. 1, no. 10 (November 1929): 7.

60 J. Francis Dement, "Keep American Appeal in Copy," *AA*, vol. 1, no. 10 (November 1929): 16.

61 Merron, "Putting Foreign Consumers on the Map," 496.

62 José Fajardo, "Should Advertising Copy Go Native? Yes—Make It Fit the People," *AA*, vol. 1, no. 10 (November 1929): 6.

63 1930 JWTA document cited in Schneider, "Discourses in Capitalism," 67.

64 Jarvis, "Artwork in Foreign Advertising," *AA*, vol. 1, no. 6 (June 1929), 10.

65 Ibid.

66 JWTA, "South Africa as a Market," 4.

67 A single office had been established in London in 1899.

68 Falk, "Advertising in India," 60.

69 U.S. Department of Commerce, *Channels of Distribution of American Merchandise in India*, 7.

70 Falk, "Advertising in India," 60.

71 See Schneider, "Discourses in Capitalism."

72 This firm became incorporated as an Indian company in 1937. See https://thelandy.com/2013/02/17/climbing-mt-everest-drinking-ovaltine-all-the-way-2 for a bit of the firm's history. Consulted date 9/23/2018. See Chapter 4 for a more in-depth discussion.

73 Part of a business alliance called the British American Tobacco Corporation.

74 For instance, UA, UNI/RM/OC/2/2/46/18, "Report of Mr. J. Hansard on India, November 1927 to April 1928."

75 UA, "Report of Mr. J. Hansard on India, 1927–8," 13.

76 UA, UNI/RM/OC/2/2/118/3, "Report on Visit to India, Burma and Ceylon by Viscount Leverhulme and W.P. Scott from 19 October, 1929 to 30 November 1929," 16.

77 UNI/RM/OC/2/2/46/31, "Mr. Sidney Van Den Bergh's Report on Lever Bros. (India) Ltd. Business, March 1936," 16–17.

78 UA, UNI/RM/OC//2/2/46/37, "Report on Mr. Barnish's Visit to India, April 1939," Attachment D.

79 Prakash Tandon, *Punjabi Saga (1857–2000): The Monumental Story of Five Generations of a Remarkable Punjabi Family* (New Delhi: Rupa, 2000), 312.

80 UA, "Report on Mr. Barnish's Visit to India," table.

81 Vikram Doctor and Anvar Alikhan indicate that the Bombay firm, Alliance Advertising, was created by ex-army officers in Bombay. See "Kyon Na Aazmaye," 49. Doctor and Alikhan also mention a firm founded by the Tata family called Tata Publicity.

82 L. A. Stronach, "How Modern Advertising and Commercial Art Started in India," *Third Annual Yearbook, Commercial Art Guild* (1952), 21.

83 Alikhan, "Pre-50s: From Raj to Swaraj," 39.

84 Stronach, "How Modern Advertising and Commercial Art Started in India," 21.

85 Ad for Stronach's published in AW, September 24, 1938, 283.

86 Alikhan, "Pre-50s: From Raj to Swaraj," 45.

87 Merron, "Putting Foreign Consumers on the Map."

88 Vikram Doctor, "Edward Fielden," unpublished article dated October 7, 2004.

89 HATA, "Hobbs, JWT, to Knott, Scott and Bowne, 19 June 1931," 2.

90 JWTA, JWT (Eastern) Limited Operating Budget for the year, July–December 1939, dated July 1939 in Treasurer's Office Records, International Offices, Bombay Office, Box 6, Bombay-General, 1939.

91 Doctor, "Edward Fielden"; HATA, "Hobbs, JWT, to Knott, Scott and Bowne, 19 June 1931," 1.

92 HATA, "Hobbs, JWT, to Knott, Scott and Bowne, 19 June 1931," 2.

93 Doctor, "Edward Fielden."

94 JWTA, "Notice to All Members of the Staff, Bombay and Calcutta," February 6, 1939, Treasurer's Office Records, International Offices, Bombay Office, Box 6, Bombay-General, 1939.

95 JWTA, letter from Fielden to Greg Bathon, September 4, 1966, Greg Bathon Papers, Correspondence 1966–8, General.

96 See especially JWTA, letter from the Commissioner, Treasury Department, to JWT, October 1, 1937, in "Incorporation of New Company, 1937," JWT, Treasurer's Office Records, International Offices, Bombay Office, Box 6, 1937.

97 HATA, "Hobbs, JWT, to Knott, Scott and Bowne, 19 June 1931," 3–4.

98 JWTA, "Memorandum on new Branch Office Policy, 7th Feb. 1939." Treasurer's Office Records, International Offices, Bombay Office, Box 6, Bombay-General, 1939.

99 For instance, Doctor and Alikhan, "Kyon Na Aazmaye," 51; Adarts is discussed briefly in Haksar, *Bite the Bullet*, 35–37.

100 This is discussed in Rashmi Kumari (with Chinmay Tumbe and Shashank Velpurcharla), "The Advertising Business of India," a paper written for the World Economic History Congress, Boston, July 2018.

101 See the copies of *Sakal* for parts of 1945 maintained in the Sakal office, where advertising agencies are identified.

102 Advertisement for Stronach's, *AW*, November 24, 1938, 283. See Scanlon, "Mediators in the International Marketplace." I apply the idea of cultural mediation in a somewhat wider sense than in Scanlon's article.

103 HATA, "Hobbs, JWT, to Knott, Scott and Bowne, 19 June 1931," 1.

104 Anvar Alikhan, "Pre-50s: From Raj to Swaraj," 41.

105 Scanlon, "Mediators in the International Marketplace," 401. Scanlon may not sufficiently analyze the importance of these claims to special understandings of local culture in legitimizing the agency's own roles abroad to its clients.

106 HATA, "Hobbs, JWT, to Knott, Scott and Bowne, 19 June 1931," 2. Prakash Tandon performed this activity in Levers during the later 1930s, Tandon, *Punjabi Saga*, 312.

107 One advertising specialist in India concluded that ads should be run only "in first and possibly second line newspapers," concluding that below this level was "worthless as advertising media no matter how good a bargain they will give the advertiser." *EA*, vol. 3, no. 10, (November 1931), 10.

108 *EA*, vol. 3, no. 10, (November 1931), 28–29.

109 HATA, "Arthur Hobbs, JWT, to Stanley Knott, June 19, 1931."

110 JWTA, "International Advertising," 1935, microfilm reel 257, 78.

111 JWTA, "Campaign for Indian Coffee, 1938–9," microfilm reel 232.

112 JWTA, "Report on India, Burma and Ceylon, compiled on the basis of Messrs. Lehn and Fink's questionnaire, 1931," reel 225 of JWT microfilm collection.

113 Ibid., 58.

114 Ibid., 54.
115 Literacy rates were higher in the cities of course but only a bit more than 10 percent of the population lived in places classified as urban.
116 JWTA, "Notes on Indian Advertising—1938," Reel 232 of JWT microfilm collections. Radio was not an option since colonial radio in India did not allow commercial publicity and because too few people owned radios.
117 UA, "Messrs. Budget-Meakin's and Knox's Report," 18.
118 In 1936, one company executive would write: "a good deal of information which might in more sophisticated markets be obtained by questionnaires can be obtained through selling work in the bazaars. The dealers are more closely in touch with the consuming public and are usually also more prepared to talk about our lines and give general information as to their uses." UA, "Messrs. Budget-Meakin's and Knox's Report," 18.
119 See Chapter 4; Tandon, *Punjabi Saga*, 244–245, 252–253.
120 I will suggest in Chapter 4 that the survey had a profound influence on the company's advertising strategies, particularly in leading Levers to focus on female consumers.
121 For a summary of this literature, see my essay "Afterword: Bhagwanlal Indraji, Archaeology and the Intellectual History of Western India," in Virchand Dharamsey, *Bhagwanlal Indraji: The First Indian Archaeologist; Multidisciplinary Approaches to the Study of the Past* (Vadodara: Darshak Itihas Nidhi, 2012). For the role of Indian informants in the British imperial structure in India more generally see C. A. Bayly, *Empire and Information: Intelligence Gathering and Social Communication in India, 1780-1870* (Cambridge: Cambridge University Press, 2009).
122 For Stronach's, see JWTA, "Edward Fielden, Bombay to S.W. Meek, New York, 28 February 1949," Treasurer's Office Records, International Offices, Bombay Office, Box 6, Bombay-General, January–June 1949.
123 The records of JWT discuss at some length the hiring policies for new executives.
124 Tandon, *Punjabi Saga*, 234.
125 For a discussion of Haksar's experience, see several letters in JWTA, Treasurer's Office Records, International Offices, Bombay Office, Box 6, Bombay-General, 1946 and Ajit N. Haksar, *Bite the Bullet: Thirty-Four Years with ITC* (New Delhi: Viking, Penguin Books, 1993). Haksar ultimately decided not to pursue a career in JWT.
126 JWTA, "S.P.S Talyarkhan to Managing Director, JWT (Eastern) Ltd. Bombay16 Feb. 1948," Treasurer's Office Records, International Offices, Bombay Office, Box 6, Bombay-General, January to June 1948.
127 HATA, "Hobbs to Stanley Knott, Scott and Bowne Company, 19 June 1931," 3.
128 JWTA, "Memorandum to Mr. Foote, April 16, 1942," in Treasurer's Office Records, International Offices, Bombay Office, Box 6, Bombay-General, 1942.
129 *Story of the Sir J.J. School of Art, 1857–1957* [Centenary publication], Bombay: Government Central Press, 1957, 174, 5.
130 *Story of the Sir J.J. School of Art, 1857–1957*, esp. 170–172.
131 JWTA, Khadilkar, "Original Artpulls of World War II Advertisements of JWT and Co., Bombay India, 21 October 1996," Pro-American War Posters, Bombay, 1942 with note, Box AP 4.
132 Anvar Alikhan, "Pre-50s: From Raj to Swaraj," 45.
133 V. S. Chakrapani and V. Ramnarayan, *R. K. Swamy: His Life and Times: From Humble Village Origins to the Top Rungs of a Contemporary Profession* (Chennai: Srinivasan K. Swamy, 2007).
134 UA, "Messrs. Budget-Meakin's and Knox's Report, 16 January 1936," 21.

135 See Chapter 5.
136 E. F. Pinner, "Some Aspects of the India Market," *AA*, vol. 1, no. 1 (December 1928), 5.
137 Daniel Starch, *Principles of Advertising*, 927.
138 "These Hints Will Help in Writing Copy in India," *AW*, April 20, 1939. Stronach's book does not seem to have survived, only a brief article describing its contents.
139 Ibid.
140 JWTA, "Memo to Mr. Hutchins, April 27, 1936," 75.
141 Mobeen Hussain, "Race, Gender and Beauty in Late Colonial India c.1900–1950." PhD. Thesis, Newnham College, University of Cambridge, 2021, 245.
142 See *EA,*, vol. 3, no. 10 (November 1931), 11.
143 Ibid., 11.
144 UA, UNI/RM/OC/2/2/46/24, "India: Mr. Mark Vardy's Report, 1935," 68.
145 Peter Johnson, "Thousands of Indians Owe Their Lives to Patent Medicines," *Advertiser's Weekly*, November 24, 1938, 379.
146 *EA*, vol. 3, no. 3 (March 1931), 5.
147 The first use of film in India for such purposes was an effort in Bengal around 1903 for medicines and hair oils by Hiralal Sen. See Projit Bihari Mukharji, *Doctoring Traditions: Ayurveda, Small Technologies and Braided Sciences* (Chicago: University of Chicago Press, 2016), 67. Thanks to the author for this reference.
148 HATA, "Arthur Hobbs to Stanley Knott, Scott and Bowne Company, 19 June 1931," 4.
149 JWTA, "Notes on Indian Advertising—1938," 12.
150 *EA*, November 1931, vol. 3, no. 10, 28.
151 JWTA, "Edward Fielden, Bombay, to Donald C. Foote, New York, 12 August 1949," in JWT Archives, Treasurer's Office Records, International Offices, Bombay Office, Box 6, Bombay-General, July–December 1949, 1.
152 HATA, HAT 50/1/17/3/1, Brand's Essence of Chicken, India/Ceylon. The date on the film script is January 16, 1941.
153 UA, "Report of Mr. J. Hansard on India, November 1927 to April, 1928," 19
154 UA, UNI/RM/OC/2/2/96/4, "Mr. A.D. Gourley's Report on Ceylon, 20.2.1941," 13. The document provides considerable detail on the plan for introducing film into Lever's advertising in Ceylon and mentions that such vans were already in use in India. A film for Dalda is discussed in Chapter 6.
155 See especially the work of Arvind Rajagopal, such as "The Commodity Image" and Kajri Jain, *Gods in the Bazaar*.
156 For these observations, my thanks to Jyotindra Jain, private communication.
157 UA, UNI/RM/OC/2/2/46/14, "Report by Mr. Greenhalgh and Mr. Scott on Their Visit to India, May–June 1926," 12, 13.

Chapter 2

1 E. F. Pinner, "Some Aspects of the India Market," 5.
2 "'Indian Advertisement needs a Thorough Market Research'—Says Madras Mail Manager," *AW*, July 21, 1938, 93.
3 Harold N. Elterich, "Export Advertiser's Media Supplement," *EA,* vol. 3, no. 11 (November 1931), 27, cited in Schneider, "Discourses in Capitalism," 56.
4 Falk, "Advertising in India," 60.
5 UA, "Budget-Meakin's and Knox's Report," 19.

6   *Census of India*, 1931, vol. VIII, part 2, *Bombay Presidency*, 448.
7   *Census of India*, 1921, vol. IX, part 1, *Cities of the Bombay Presidency*, 24. It seems possible that some Anglo-Indians who identified as "Europeans" in 1921 registered as Anglo-Indians in 1931, given the rise in this community's population.
8   The Europeans of Bombay are treated at greater length in my essay, "Bombay's European Community during the Interwar Period," in *Bombay before Mumbai: Essays in Honor of Jim Masselos,* eds. Rachel Dwyer, Manjiri Kamat, and Prashant Kidambi (London: Hurst, 2019), 77–98.
9   *Census of India*, 1921, vol IX, part 1, *Cities of the Bombay Presidency*, 23.
10 The presence of a European underclass consisting of the unemployed, the poor, vagrants and prostitutes, and worries of British officials about dangers this underclass posed to European prestige have been examined in David Arnold, "European Orphans and Vagrants in India in the Nineteenth Century," *The Journal of Imperial and Commonwealth History*, vol. 7, no. 2 (2008): 104–127; Aravind Ganachari, "'White Man's Embarrassment', European Vagrancy in 19th Century Bombay," *EPW*, vol. 37, no. 25 (2002): 2477–2486; Harald Fischer-Tiné, *Low and Licentious Europeans: Race, Class, and "White Subalternity" in Colonial India* (New Delhi: Orient BlackSwan, 2009); Sarmistha De, *Marginal Europeans in Colonial India, 1860–1920* (Kolkata: Thema, 2008); Satoshi Mizutani, *The Meaning of White. Race, Class, and the "Domiciled Community" in British India 1858–1930* (Oxford: Oxford University Press, 2011). Most of this literature focuses heavily on the nineteenth century.
11 *Census of India,*1931, vol. VIII, part 2, *Bombay Presidency*, 448.
12 *Census of India*, 1921, vol. IX, part 1, *Cities of the Bombay Presidency*, 17.
13 Sir Stanley Reed, *The India I Knew, 1897–1947* (London: Odhams Press, Limited, 1952), 23–24.
14 BL, Eur. T. 128/1, Oral Archives Interview with Mr. Albert Norman Walker, born 1892. Walker was an engineer in the Bombay Improvement Trust, beginning 1919 or 1920.
15 Reed, *The India I Knew,* 24.
16 *Census of India*, 1921. vol. IX, part 1, *Cities of the Bombay Presidency*, 15.
17 *Census of India*, 1921, *Cities of the Bombay Presidency*, vol. IX, part 1.
18 For instance, see Anthony King, *Colonial Urban Development: Culture, Social Power and Environment* (London, Henley, and Boston: Routledge and Keegan Paul, 1976).
19 See, for instance, Swati Chattopadhyay, *Representing Calcutta: Modernity, Nationalism and the Colonial Uncanny* (London: Routledge, 2005); William J. Glover, *Making Lahore Modern: Constructing and Imagining a Colonial City* (Minneapolis: University of Minnesota Press, 2008).
20 Reed, *The India I Knew,* 25.
21 Reed, *The India I Knew*, 25. See also Sandip Hazareesingh, *The Colonial City and the Challenge of Modernity: Urban Hegemonies and Civic Contestations in Bombay City, 1905–1925* (Hyderabad: Orient Longman, 2007), 33. *Census of India*, 1921, vol. IX, part 1, B, *Cities of the Bombay Presidency* [Housing Statistics], v.
22 *TI* (Pro-quest), January 30, 1939, 16.
23 British Library, MSS Eur. T. 127, Interview with Prakash Tandon, 5.
24 For a recent account of the Tata family of enterprises, see Mircea Raianu, *Tata: The Global Corporation that Built Indian Capitalism* (Cambridge, MA: Harvard University Press, 2021).
25 British Library, MSS Eur. T. 121, oral transcript of interview with A. T. Robinson, 13.
26 British Library, Diary of W. W. Russell, January 22, 1936, MSS Eur. D. 621/2.

27 Article by D. Karaka, unknown original source, clipping 36, in British Library, Mss Eur. D. 621/27, 1941.

28 For instance, BL, Eur. T. 128/1, Oral Archives Interview with Mr. Albert Norman Walker, JBT.

29 BL, Tandon, Interview, 14–15.

30 See the work of Abigail McGowan, for instance, "Domestic Modern, Redecorating Homes," 424–446. McGowan indicates these ads were also intended to appeal to wealthier Indians.

31 JWTA, "Report on India, Burma and Ceylon," 19.

32 Ibid., 25.

33 Ibid., 27.

34 Ibid.

35 The effect of lighter color was achieved by drawing of lines in the hair with blanks spaces in between.

36 *IWI*, May 25, 1930, 28.

37 "I know you'll like these!" *TI*, February 15, 1937, 9.

38 The importance of club life and parties was explicitly stressed in JWTA, "Report on India, Burma and Ceylon," 19.

39 *TI* (Pro-quest), April 28, 1930, 16.

40 "She wasn't invited because she wasn't on the telephone," *BC*, February 10, 1936, 8.

41 *TI* (Pro-quest), December 11, 1935, 6.

42 *TI* (Pro-quest), December 14, 1933, 13.

43 The use of the term "memsahib" explicitly refers to a European woman.

44 *IWI*, July 20, 1930, 22.

45 Mark Liechty, *Suitably Modern: Making Middle-Class Culture in a New Consumer Society* (Princeton, NJ and Oxford: Princeton University Press, 2003), 64.

46 Quote from B. B. Misra, *The Indian Middle Classes,* cited in *The Middle Class in Colonial India*, ed. Sanjay Joshi, xxxi.

47 Nikhil Rao, *House, but No Garden: Apartment Living in Bombay's Suburbs, 1898–1964* (Minneapolis: University of Minnesota Press, 2013), esp. chapter 2. Rao in turn relies upon documents that used this concept in the interwar period.

48 C. J. Fuller and Haripriya Narasimhan, *Tamil Brahmins: The Making of a Middle-Class Caste* (Chicago: University of Chicago Press, 2014); Fuller and Narasimham sidestep debates among South Asianists, referring instead to theoretical literature associated with Anthony Giddens and other social scientists.

49 Sanjay Joshi, *Fractured Modernity: Making of a Middle Class in Colonial North India* (New Delhi: Oxford University Press, 2001).

50 For instance, L. G. Khare, "The Depressed Middle Classes (part II)," *The Social Service Quarterly*, vol. 3, no. 1, July 1917, 14–19; *Report on the Survey into the Economic Conditions of Middle-Class Families in Bombay City* (Bombay: Indian Statistical Institute, 1952); *Report on an Enquiry into Middle Class Family Budgets in Bombay City* (Bombay: Labour Office, 1928); R. N. Bhonsle, "Clerks in the City of Bombay," MA. Thesis, University of Bombay, 1938, 4. The usage in these sources is discussed in Nikhil Rao's study, *House, but No Garden*, chapter 2.

51 Bhonsle, "Clerks in the City of Bombay," 2–3.

52 Sumit Sarkar, "Kaliyuga, Chakri and Bhakti: Ramakrishna and History Times," in Sarkar, *Writing Social History* (Delhi: Oxford University Press, 1999), 282–357.

53 Here again I depart from Joshi, who seems to treat only the leading professionals of
    Lucknow as members of the middle class, and thus sees them as actors who occupied
    the very top strata of urban society.

54 *TI*, September 10, 1910: 7; August 26, 1916: 11; May 22, 1929: 11; July 19, 1927: 8;
    February 11, 1926: 9; May 16, 1933: 10; May 23, 1934: 13; June 19, 1936: 7; September
    22, 1936: 11.

55 *Times of India*, June 27, 1927: 7; February 27, 1933: 14; April 1, 1912: 8.

56 For instance, a letter signed by a "middle-class Hindu" pointed out that middle-class
    Hindus and Christians "of good education and respectability drawing incomes varying
    from Rs. 40 to 200 per month, are naturally averse to resorting to the existing public
    Hospitals where the poor and the laboring classes are well cared for during sickness."
    TI (Pro-quest), April 1, 1912: 8.

57 Prashant Kidambi, "Consumption, Domestic Economy and the Idea of the 'Middle
    Class in Late Colonial Bombay,' in Late-Colonial Bombay," in *Towards a History of
    Consumption in South Asia*, ed. Haynes et al., 115, 116; N. Raghunathan Iyer, "Middle
    Class Habits of Mind," *Kanara Saraswat*, XXXVI, no. 7 (July 1950), 18.

58 This is primarily derived from Jal Feerose Bulsara, *Bombay: A City in the Making*
    (Bombay: The National Information and Publications Ltd., 1948).

59 Christine Dobbin, *Urban Leadership in Western India: Politics and Communities in
    Bombay City, 1840–1885* (Oxford: Oxford University Press, 1972).

60 Bhonsle, "Clerks in the City of Bombay," 2–3.

61 *Census of India*, 1931, vol. IX, part 1, *Cities of the Bombay Presidency*, 50, 51. These
    numbers had gone up from the 1921 figures of 8,141 males and 2,232 females in
    public administration, 14,163 males and 2,199 females in the professions and liberal
    arts and 43,271 males and 1,695 females in the cashier-clerk category. The shift in the
    former category certainly reflects some change in the counting procedure, but the
    figures from the latter two categories suggest an increase of about 20 percent between
    1921 and 1941.

62 *Census of India*, 1931, vol. VIII, part 1, *Bombay Presidency*, 248, 249.

63 JWTA, "Report on India, Burma and Ceylon," 15. The middle-class category in this
    case included manual workers, which the same report earlier had effectively excluded
    from the ranks of people who would buy Western goods.

64 Bhonsle, "Clerks in the City of Bombay."

65 Bhonsle, "Clerks in the City of Bombay," 60. See Rao, *House, but no Garden*, 74.

66 Bhonsle, "Clerks in the City of Bombay," 18–34.

67 Rao, *House, but No Garden*; Frank Conlon, *Caste in a Changing World: The Chitrapur
    Saraswat Brahmans, 1700–1935* (Berkeley: University of California Press, 1977).

68 J. F. Bulsara: *Bombay: A City in the Making* (Bombay: The National Information and
    Publications Ltd., 1948), 61–62.

69 Richard I. Cashman, *The Myth of the Lokamanya: Tilak and Mass Politics in
    Maharashtra* (Berkeley: University of California Press, 1975), 121.

70 Kidambi, "Consumption, Domestic Economy and the Idea of the 'Middle Class,'"
    111–117; Rao, *House, but No Garden*, 72.

71 This view is predicated upon regarding conjugality as a principle that emerged, and
    achieved dominance, in a complex field of family and household forms that have
    existed in South Asian history, a perspective that has been informed by my
    understanding of the essays (especially the editor's introduction) in Indrani Chatterjee,
    ed., *Unfamiliar Relations: Family and History in South Asia* (New Brunswick, NJ:
    Rutgers University Press, 2004).

72 Bhonsle, "Clerks in the City of Bombay," 79.

73 Ibid., 84, 87.

74 Neeraj Hatekar, Abodh Kumar, and Rajani Mathur, "The Making of the Middle Class in Western India: Age at Marriage for Brahmin Women (1900–50)," *EPW*, vol. 44, no. 21 (May 2009): 40–47.

75 Bhonsle, "Clerks in the City of Bombay," 70.

76 Ibid., 121.

77 Conlon, *Caste in a Changing World*, 114–127.

78 "Poverty and Employment," *KS*, vol. XXII, no. 2 (December 1938): 14. Kidambi, "Consumption, Domestic Economy and the Idea of the 'Middle Class.'"

79 "In Quest of a Son-in-Law," *KS*, vol. XX, no. 4 (April 1936): 7.

80 Ibid., the quote is from "Marriage Made Easy—I" *KS*, vol. XXI, no. 7 (July 1937): 3.

81 Ibid., 3–5.

82 The critical importance of education to familial self-reproduction has been richly discussed by Nita Kumar in "The Middle-Class Child: Ruminations on Failure," in *Elite and Everyman: The Cultural Politics of the Indian Middle Classes*, eds. Amita Baviskar and Raka Ray (New Delhi: Routledge, 2011), 220–245. For the concept of cultural capital, see Pierre Bourdieu, "The Forms of Capital," in *Handbook of Theory and Research for the Sociology of Education*, ed. J. Richardson (Westwood, CT: Greenwood Press, 1986). For an especially valuable application of this theory, see Ajantha Subramanian, *Caste of Merit: Engineering Education in India* (Cambridge, MA: Harvard University Press, 2019), esp. 15–16.

83 N. Raghunathan Iyer, "Middle Class Habits of Mind," *KS*, vol. XXXVI, no. 7 (July 1950): 185.

84 Ibid.

85 L. G. Khare, "The Depressed Middle Classes (Part II)," *The Social Science Quarterly*, vol. 3, no. 1 (July 1917), 14–19.

86 Dipesh Chakrabarty, "The Difference—Deferral of a Colonial Modernity: Public Debates on Domesticity in Colonial Bengal," in *Subaltern Studies VIII: Essays in Honour of Ranajit Guha*, eds. David Arnold and David Hardiman (Delhi: Oxford University Press, 1994), 50–88.

87 Pradip Kumar Bose, "Sons of the Nation: Childrearing in the New Family," in *Texts of Power: Emerging Disciplines in Colonial Bengal*, ed. Partha Chatterjee (Minnesota: University of Minnesota Press, 1996), 118–144; Bose, "Reconstituting Private Life: The Making of the Modern Family in Bengal," in Ghanshyam Shah, ed., *Social Transformation in India: Essays in Honour of Professor I.P. Desai* (Jaipur: Rawat Publications, 1997), 501–531.

88 Charu Gupta, *Sexuality, Obscenity, Community: Women, Muslims, and the Hindu Public in Colonial India* (New York: Palgrave, 2002), 125.

89 Judith Walsh, *Domesticity in Colonial India, What Women Learned When Men Gave Them Advice* (New Delhi: Oxford University Press, 2004), 27.

90 Bose, "Reconstituting Private Life."

91 Ibid., 518.

92 See also Srirupa Prasad, *Cultural Politics of Hygiene in India, 1890–1940: Contagions of Feeling* (Houndmills, Basingstoke, Hampshire: Palgrave MacMillan, 2015); Walsh, *Domesticity in Colonial India*; Hancock, "Home Science and the Nationalization of Domesticity in Colonial India"; and McGowan, "An All-Consuming Subject?"

93 Katherine Mayo, *Mother India* (New York: Greenwood Press, 1955 [1937]), 16.

94 For literature espousing eugenic theories and often suggesting practical steps married
    couples could take to ensure the reproduction of desirable children see Narayan
    Sitaram Phadke, *Sex Problems in India, a Scientific Exposition of Sex Life and Some
    Curious Marriage Customs Prevailing in India from Time Immemorial to the Present
    Day* (Bombay: D. B. Taraporevala Sons & Co., 1929); Sapur Faredun Desai, *Parsis and
    Eugenics* (Bombay: The Author, 1940); Bahman S. J. Banaji, *Ek Mahan Shodh, Marji
    Pramaneno Balak* (Bombay: J. B. Karani Sons, December 1923 [in Gujarati]); Swami
    Shivananda, *Manowanchit Santati: Gruhasthashramache Anubhavsiddha Niyam*
    (Amravati: Rashtroddhar Karyalaya, 2nd ed., 1928).
95 Phadke, *Sex Problems in India*, 68.
96 Mayo, *Mother India*.
97 Ishita Pande, "Curing Calcutta: Race, Liberalism and Colonial Medicine in British
    Bengal, 1830–1900," PhD. Thesis, Princeton University, 2005. Many of these concerns
    were reflected in the articles in *KS* though without an explicitly eugenic focus.
98 For instance, see "Bharaps and Their Physiques," *KS*, vol. XII, no. 4 (April 1929), 8–9.
99 Sreenivas, *Wives, Widows and Concubines*, 120.
100 Chatterjee, "Introduction," in *Unfamiliar Relations*, 13.
101 See Chandra's discussion of the writings of Govardhanram Madhavram Tripathi in
    Sudhir Chandra, *The Oppressive Present: Literature and Social Consciousness in
    Colonial India* (Delhi: Oxford University Press, 1992), 74–82. For a complex
    historical picture of the family in India, see Indrani Chatterjee, ed., *Unfamiliar
    Relations*. Rochana Majumdar examines the competition of joint family values with
    conjugal ideals in the marriage market of Bengal in *Marriage and Modernity: Family
    Values in Colonial Bengal* (Durham, NC and London: Duke University Press, 2009).
102 Rao, *House, but No Garden*.
103 Kaushik Bhaumik, "At Home in the World: Cinema and Cultures of the Young in
    Bombay in the 1920s," in *Towards a History of Consumption*, ed. Haynes et al.,
    136–154.
104 This paragraph has been informed by my reading of Sreenivas, *Wives, Widows,
    Concubines*, especially the conclusion.
105 For a few key works, see Liechty, *Suitably Modern*; Leela Fernandes, *India's New
    Middle Class: Democratic Politics in an Era of Economic Reform* (Minneapolis:
    University of Minnesota Press, 2006), esp. chapter 2; Christiane Brosius, *India's
    Middle Class: New Forms of Urban Leisure, Consumption and Prosperity* (London:
    Routledge, 2010); Kumar, "The Middle-Class Child."
106 Kidambi, "Consumption, Domestic Economy and the Idea of the 'Middle Class." A
    complex picture of dispositions toward consumption in middle-class north India—
    one that sometimes supports the analysis that follows and sometimes runs contrary
    to it—can be found in Markus Daechsel, *The Politics of Self-Expression: The Urdu
    Middle-Class Mileu in Mid-Twentieth Century India and Pakistan* (London and New
    York: Routledge, 2006), 162–204.
107 S. S. Talmaki, "Welcome Address, Kanara Saraswat Conference," *KS*, vol. X, no. 3,
    Supplement to January 1927 issue, 13.
108 Cited in Kidambi, "Consumption, Domestic Economy and the Idea of the 'Middle
    Class," 116.
109 Cited in Rao, *House, but No Garden*, 72–73.
110 "Milestones and Movements, 1886–1936," *KS*, vol. XX, no. 11 (November 1936),
    36.
111 Bhaumik, "At Home in the World."

112 "Bharaps and Their Physiques," 8–9.

113 H. Shankar Rau, "Family Budgets," in *A Chitrapur Saraswat Miscellany* (Bombay: H. Shankar Rau, 1938), 26.

114 Compare the *Report on an Enquiry into Middle Class Family Budgets in Bombay City* with *Report on an Enquiry into Working Class Budgets in Bombay* (Bombay: Labour Office, 1923), 5.

115 *Report on an Enquiry into Middle Class Family Budgets in Bombay City*, 5.

116 Ibid., 8; "Editorial Notes," *KS*, vol. XVII, no. 1 (September 1933), 1.

117 Bhonsle, "Clerks in the City of Bombay," 115. A more anecdotal account providing examples from particular families is provided in L. G. Khare, "The Depressed Middle Classes (Part I)," *The Social Science Quarterly*, vol 2, no. 3 (January 1917): 135–142. My thanks to Abigail McGowan for pointing out this reference.

118 See Haynes, *Rhetoric and Ritual in Colonial India,* esp. 56–58; James Laidlaw, *Riches and Renunciation: Religion, Economy, and Society among the Jains* (Oxford: Clarendon Press, 1995).

119 Abigail McGowan, "Consuming Families: Negotiating Women's Shopping in Early Twentieth Century Western India," in *Towards a History of Consumption in South Asia*, ed. Haynes, et al., 155–184. Gambhirdas Karsandas Bhagat, *Chaha Devinu Charitra ane fashion no faras* (Mumnavad: Published By the author, 1920); Pitambar Gampatram Vyas, *Chalu Jamano Fashion* (Thana: Published By the author, 1920); Hiralal Gagji Brahmabhatt, *Deshdaz (Patriotism)* (Bombay: Royal, 1921); Jivraj Harjivan Thakkar, *Kalyugni Fashionbai* (Ahmedabad: By the Author, 1921); Gordhanlal Shah, *Mumbai Shetan* (Ahmedabad: By the author, 1922); Chimanlal Nagindas Manchharam, *Naval Narangi athva Fahsionyari [Naval Navrangi or the vanity of fashion]* (Bombay: Sanj Vartaman, 1920); Dahyabhai Patel, *Fashionni Fisiyari [Vanity of Fashions]* (Nadiad: Published By the Author, 1921); Dahyabhai Patel, *Fashionni Fisiyari ke Kaliyuga Koonch* (Nadiad, By the Author, 1916). For North India, see Daechsel, *The Politics of Self-Expression,* 195–196.

120 Kidambi, "Domestic Economic and the Idea of the Middle Class" and "Stray Thoughts on Thrift," in *KS,* vol. XI, no. 4 (April 1928): 7-11; "Bharaps and Their Physiques;" "The Saraswat Home," *KS,* vol. XVII, no. 1 (February 1933), 3.

121 Rau, "Family Budgets," 15–31.

122 "Milestones and Movements," 36.

123 Mahatma Gandhi, *Young India*, April 14, 1931, in *Collected Works of Mahatma Gandhi*, vol XLI (Delhi: Government of India, 1971).

124 For this line of argument, see Emma Tarlo, *Clothing Matters: Dress and Identity in India* (New Delhi: Viking Books, 1996), chapter 3.

125 Partha Chattergee, "The Nationalist Resolution of the Women's Question," in *Recasting Women: Essays in Colonial History*, eds. Kumkum Sangari and Sudesh Vaid (New Delhi: Kali for Women, 1989), 240–243.

126 McGowan, "An All-Consuming Subject?"

127 For instance, see McGowan, "An All-Consuming Subject?" Though McGowan looks at literature primarily from an earlier period, these kinds of exhortations certainly persisted later in the twentieth century. See also Gupta, *Sexuality, Obscenity, Commmunity,* 140–151.

128 See, for instance, Emma Tarlo, *Clothing Matters*; Lisa Trivedi, *Clothing Gandhi's Nation: Homespun and Modern India* (Bloomington and Indianapolis: Indiana University Press, 2007). Trivedi discusses clothing advertisement in her study but with a very different purpose than that of this book.

129 Douglas E. Haynes, *Small-Town Capitalism in Western India: Artisans, Merchants and the Making of the Informal Economy, 1870–1960* (Cambridge: Cambridge University Press, 2012), chapter 2.

130 Of course, there were multiple reasons for the limited use of advertising by mills, including the nature of their distributional networks. Producers increasingly resorted to advertising of cloth on an increased scale when some of the cultural constraints I have described eased during World War II.

131 This point has been made earlier but in somewhat different terms by Daechsel in *The Politics of Self-Expression*, 183–185.

132 JWTA, "Report on India, Burma and Ceylon," 4.

133 UA, UNI/RM/OC/2/2/46/23, "Mr. Sidney Van Den Bergh's Report on the Soap Business, December 1934," 2–3.

134 Falk, "Advertising in India," 60.

135 Johnson, "Thousands of Indians Owe their Lives," 379.

136 UA, "Mr. Sidney Van den Bergh's Report on the Soap Business, December 1934," 2.

137 JWTA, "Notes on Indian Advertising," Reel 232 of JWT microfilm collections, 12.

138 UA, "Report of Mr. J. Hansard on India, November 1927 to April 1928," 15.

139 JWTA, "Memo to Mr. Hutchins, April 27, 1936," 1–2.

140 David Arnold, *Everyday Technology: Machines and the Making of India's Modernity* (Chicago and London: University of Chicago Press, 2013), 71–76.

141 The early history of tea advertising is discussed in Bhadra, *From an Imperial Product to a National Drink* and in Erika Rappaport, *A Thirst for Empire: How Tea Shaped the Modern World* (Princeton: Princeton University Press, 2017), esp. 252–262, but there is little discussion of methods used in reaching the countryside during the pre-World War II period.

142 UA, UNI/RM/OC/2/2/46/16, "Mr. W.P. Scott's Report on Visit to India, Feb/ March 1927," 8, 9.

143 UA, "Mr. Vardy's Report, January 1935," 70 and UA, "Mr. Sidney Van den Bergh's Report on Soap Business, December 1934, 16, for descriptions of this system.

144 UA, "Budget-Meakin and Knox's Report, 1936," 20.

145 See UA, "Mr. Vardy's Report, January 1935," 70, and UA, "Mr. Sidney Van den Bergh's Report on Soap Business, December 1934," 16, for descriptions of this system.

146 UA, UNI/RM/OC/2/2/46/38, Letter of unlisted author to W. G. J Shaw, June 17, 1941, report on visit to India by A. D. Gourley, 1941. Correspondence Bundle 1 discusses the conclusions of Gourley on Indian markets.

Chapter 3

1   Wilfrid David, *Monsoon: A Novel* (London: Hamish Hamilton, 1933), 270.

2   *Webster's Third New International Dictionary of the English Language, Unabridged* (Springfield, MA: Merriam-Webster, 2002).

3   *India: Report of the Drugs Enquiry Committee* (Government of India, c. 1931), 65–66.

4   Ibid., 1.

5   Ibid.

6   Schneider, "Reimaging Traditional Medicine," 39.

7   Ibid., 46–47. My thanks also to Kaushik Bhaumik for this information about local practice.

8   See also Markus Daechsel, *The Politics of Self-Expression,* 179. Daechsel also stresses
     that the possibility of self-medication allowed businesses to draw attention about their
     products among consumers located at some distance, allowing them the possibility of
     ordering by mail.

9   Quoted in *India: Report of the Drugs Enquiry Committee,* 369.

10   Mrinalini Sinha, *Colonial Masculinity: The 'Manly Englishman' and the 'Effeminate
     Bengali' in the Late Nineteenth Century* (Manchester and New York: Manchester
     University Press, 1995); Susanne Hoeber Rudolph and Lloyd I. Rudolph, *The
     Modernity of Tradition: Political Development in India* (Chicago: University of Chicago
     Press, 1967), 160–182; Joseph S. Alter, *Gandhi's Body: Sex, Diet, and the Politics of
     Nationalism* (Philadelphia: University of Pennsylvania Press, 2000), 125–126; Richard
     I. Cashman, *The Myth of the Lokamanya: Tilak and Mass Politics in Maharashtra*
     (Berkeley: University of California Press, 1975), 26; Ashis Nandy, *The Intimate Enemy:
     Loss and Recovery of Self under Colonialism* (Delhi and New York: Oxford University
     Press, 1983), 1–63.

11   Indira Chowdhury, quoting the Indian journal, *National Paper,* in *The Frail Hero and
     Virile History: Gender and the Politics of Culture in Colonial Bengal,* SOAS Studies on
     South Asia (Delhi and New York: Oxford University Press, 1998), 21.

12   Ishita Pande, *Medicine, Race and Liberalism in British Bengal: Symptoms of Empire*
     (Abingdon and New York: Routledge, 2010), 151–178.

13   Guy N. A. Attewell, *Refiguring Unani Tibb: Plural Healing in Late Colonial India*
     (Hyderabad: Orient Longman, 2007), 244–247; Ishita Pande, "Curing Calcutta: Race,
     Liberalism and Colonial Medicine in British Bengal, 1830–1900," PhD. Thesis,
     Princeton University 2005.

14   John Rosselli, "The Self-Image of Effeteness: Physical Education and Nationalism in
     Nineteenth-Century Bengal," *Past & Present,* no. 86 (1980): 121–148; Chowdhury, *The
     Frail Hero and Virile History*; Cashman, *Myth of the Lokamanya,* chapters 4 and 5,
     passim; Nandy, *The Intimate Enemy.*

15   Luzia Savary, "Vernacular Eugenics?," *South Asia,* vol. 37, no. 3 (2014), 381–397.

16   M. K Gandhi, quoted in Alter, *Gandhi's Body,* 16. See Rudolph and Rudolph, *The
     Modernity of Tradition,* esp. 183–216.

17   For discussion of historical understandings of the nerves and neurasthenia, see
     Cultures of Neurasthenia from Beard to the First World War, eds. Marijke Giswijit-
     Hofstra and Roy Porter (Amsterdam and New York:Rodopi, 2001); Nancy Rose Hunt,
     A Nervous State: Violence, Remedies and Reverie in Colonial Congo (Durham, and NC
     London: Duke University Press, 2016).

18   Attewell, *Refiguring Unani Tibb,* esp. 244–262.

19   Mark Singleton, *Yoga Body: The Origins of Modern Posture Practice* (Oxford and New
     York: Oxford University Press, 2010), 95–112.

20   Projit Bihari Mukharji, *Nationalizing the Body: The Medical Market, Print and Daktari
     Medicine,* Anthem South Asian Studies (London and New York: Anthem Press, 2009).

21   See, for example, Joseph S. Alter, "Ayurveda and Sexuality: Sex Therapy and the
     'Paradox of Virility,'" in *Modern and Global Ayurveda: Pluralism and Paradigms,* eds.
     Dagmar Wujastyk and Frederick M. Smith (Albany: State University of New York
     Press, 2008), 177–200; James Edwards, "Semen Anxiety in South Asian Cultures:
     Cultural and Transcultural Significance," *Medical Anthropology,* vol. 7, no. 3 (1983):
     51–67. For discussion of early twentieth-century notions relating semen wastage to
     male weakness, see Daechsel, *The Politics of Self-Expression,* 106–113; Guy Attewell,
     Refiguring Unani Tibb, 244–262.

22 For parallel western theories about the importance of "spermatic economy," see, for instance, Michael Edward Melody and Linda Mary Peterson, *Teaching America about Sex: Marriage Guides and Sex Manuals from the Late Victorians to Dr. Ruth* (New York: New York University Press, 1999), chapter 1; Lesley A. Hall and Roy Porter, *The Facts of Life: The Creation of Sexual Knowledge in Britain, 1650–1950* (New Haven: Yale University Press, 1995), 115–121; G. J. Barker-Benfield, *The Horrors of the Half-Known Life: Male Attitudes toward Women and Sexuality in Nineteenth-Century America*, 1st ed. (New York: Harper & Row, 1976), 175–188. For European concepts stressing the harmful effects of masturbation, see Thomas Walter Laqueur, *Solitary Sex: A Cultural History of Masturbation* (New York: Zone Books, 2003).

23 See Arjun Appadurai, "Understanding Gandhi" in *Childhood and Selfhood: Essays on Tradition, Religion, and Modernity in the Psychology of Erik H. Erikson,* ed. Peter Homans (Lewisburg, PA: Bucknell University Press, 1978), 113–144, esp. 120–121, 132; Bhikhu C. Parekh, *Colonialism, Tradition, and Reform: An Examination of Gandhi's Political Discourse* (Newbury Park, CA: Sage Publications, 1989), 177–206; Susanne Hoeber Rudolph and Lloyd I. Rudolph, *Gandhi: The Traditional Roots of Charisma* (Bombay: Orient Longman, 1987), 192–216; Joseph Alter, *Gandhi's Body*, preface and chapter 1. While most of these authors stress the indigenous (usually Hindu) origins of such perspectives, Parekh points out that Gandhi drew as well upon British writers for his concepts of how sexual acts depleted bodily energy. Similar ideas advocated by the religious reformer Dayananda Saraswati have been explored by Anshu Malhotra in "The Body as a Metaphor for the Nation: Caste, Masculinity and Femininity in the *Satyarth Prakash* of Dayananda Saraswati," in *Rhetoric and Reality: Gender and the Colonial Experience in South Asia,* eds. Avril A Powell, and Siobhan Lombert Hurley (New Delhi and New York: Oxford University Press, 2006), 121–153.

24 Parekh, *Colonialism, Tradition and Reform*, 177–178.

25 For a selection of this literature, see Alter, *Gandhi's Body*; 47; Bhikhu Parekh, *Colonialism, Tradition and Reform*, 177; for Dayananda Saraswati, see Malhotra, "The Body as a Metaphor for the Nation"; Charu Gupta, *Sexuality, Obscenity, Community*, 66–84; Shrikant Botre and Douglas E. Haynes, "Understanding R. D. Karve: *Brahmacharya*, Modernity, and the Appropriation of Global Sexual Science in Western India, 1927–1953," in *Global History of Sexual Science, 1880–1960*, eds. Veronika Fuechtner, Douglas E. Haynes, and Ryan Jones (Berkeley: University of California Press, 2018), 163–185; Ishita Pande, "Curing Calcutta: Race, Liberalism, and Colonial Medicine," chapter IV.

26 Douglas E Haynes, "Masculinity, Advertising and the Reproduction of the Middle-Class Family in Western India, 1918–1940," in *Being Middle-Class in India A Way of Life*, ed. Henrike Donner (New York, NY: Routledge, 2011), 23–44.

27 See T. M. Luhrmann, *The Good Parsi: The Fate of a Colonial Elite in a Postcolonial Society* (Cambridge, MA: Harvard University Press, 1996), 130–137. Parsis contributed disproportionately to the makeup of the middle class in Bombay.

28 Pande, "Curing Calcutta: Race, Liberalism and Colonial Medicine."

29 See, for instance, Gandhi, *Hind Swaraj,* rev. ed., 11th reprint (Ahmedabad: Navjivan Publishing, 1996), 53. The ads themselves suggested these kinds of themes.

30 Saratchandra Chattopadhyay's *Devdas*, trans. by Sreejata Guha (New Delhi: Penguin Books, 2002 [1917]); Govardhanram Madhavram Tripathi's *Saraswatichandra*, trans. Tridip Suhrud (Hyderabad: Orient Blackswan, 2015 [1887–1901].)

31 Prashant Kidambi, "Consumption, Domestic Economy and the Idea of the 'Middle Class.'"

32 Gupta, *Sexuality, Obscenity, Community,* 81–82.

33 Ibid., 80–81.

34 Mukharji, "Sex, Medicine and Morality," unpublished, 2009.

35 In what follows, I have given disproportionate representation to ads with visual content because of their especially interesting character.

36 *BC*, December 30, 192, 5.

37 This discussion has been influenced by Projit Bihari Mukharji, *Nationalizing the Body.*

38 My thanks to an anonymous reader of an article I have written on sex tonic advertisement. This literature has been discussed in some recent writings on medical history. See Mukharji, "Sex, Medicine and Morality"; Luzia Savary, "Vernacular Eugenics? Santati-Śāstra in Popular Hindi Advisory Literature (1900–1940)," *South Asia*, vol. 37, no. 3 (2014): 381–397.

39 The linking of these discourses in colonial and postcolonial India, for instance, has been examined by Joseph S. Alter, "Ayurveda and Sexuality," 179.

40 Alter, "Ayurveda and Sexuality."

41 My thanks to Bed Giri for discussing this concept with me; see also Mukharji, "Sex, Medicine and Morality" for discussion of this kind of linking in a wide range of cultural discourses.

42 See *MS*, January 6, 1928, 4; see also *MS*, January 3, 1929, 4; *MS*, January 11, 1927, 13.

43 My thanks to Ramya Sreenivasan for this observation.

44 Mukharji, "Sex, Medicine and Morality"; Savary, "Vernacular Eugenics?"

45 *MS*, January 17, 1934, 5.

46 *BC*, September 15, 1928, 11.

47 The stress on targeting expatriates during this period is discussed in Margrit Pernau, "Modern Masculinity, Bought at Your Local Pharmacist: The Tonic Sanatogen in 20th-Century Indian Advertisements," *Tasveerghar: A Digital Archive of South Asian Popular Culture,*" http://www.tasveergharindia.net/essay/sanatogen-masculine-advert.html, last accessed August 1, 2021.

48 *BC*, May 13, 1926, 10.

49 *BC*, August 19, 1934, 13.

50 *BC*, October 27, 1936, 3.

51 *BC*, September 2, 1935, 2.

52 *BC*, July 23, 1938, 12.

53 *BC*, February 4, 1938, 10.

54 Of course, such ads were not uniquely found in Indian publications; they played on anxieties of young men in a variety of cultures. My point here, however, is that they tied into a much larger discourse about weakness that was particularly pervasive in India.

55 *BC*, October 2, 1929, 8.

56 *BC*, January 19, 1938, 13.

57 *BC*, February 6, 1935, 12.

58 My own review suggests that the *major* British newspapers during this period usually did not raise the issue of sexual dysfunction themes, focusing instead on the value of tonics in overcoming specific ailments or in speeding convalescence. According to colleagues in European history, however, more localized publications in Britain were running ads that promised enhanced male sexual performance.

59 An analysis of some other Okasa ads from North India can be found in Daechsel, *The Politics of Self-Expression,* 179–180.

60 This observation comes from Projit Mukhari, who has explored this development in *Doctoring Traditions,* chapter V.

61 For a rich discussion of Sanatogen ads that echoes many of the themes explored here see Pernau, "Modern Masculinity: Bought at your Local Pharmacist."
62 *MS*, January 24, 1931, 12.
63 *BC*, August 20, 1934, 11.
64 *BC*, October 20, 1934, 17.
65 Images discussed in Pernau's "Modern Masculinity: Bought at your Local Pharamacist" demonstrate that Sanatogen ads also borrowed on the same motif.
66 *MS*, March 28, 1934, 10.
67 A particularly explicit ad depicts a despairing man sitting in a chair holding his head in his hands while his disappointed wife lies sprawled face down on the bed, *MS*, February 13, 1941, 4.
68 *MS*, December 13, 1937, 11.
69 For a wide range of such ads see, for instance, the ads from *MS,* January 24, 1941, 3; February 27, 1941, 3; September 15, 1943, 6; January 12, 1942, 3; February 2, 1942, 3; February 16, 1942, 3; June 1, 1942, 7; July 27, 1942, 3; September 21, 1936, 1.
70 *MS*, June 3, 1942, 2.
71 *MS*, April 29, 1940, 3.
72 *MS*, February 10, 1941, 4.
73 For discussion of the travels and lectures of European and American sexologists in India, see Veronika Fuechtner, "Indians, Jews and Sex: Magnus Hirschfeld and Indian Sexology," in *Imagining Germany, Imagining, Asia: Essays in German-Asian Studies* eds. Fuechtner and Mary Rhiel (Rochester, New York: Camden House, 2013). See Ellen Chesler, *Woman of Valor: Margaret Sanger and the Birth Control Movement in America* (New York: Simon & Schuster, 1992), 355–364.
74 Marie Carmichael Stopes, *Married Love: A New Contribution to the Solution of Sex Difficulties* (NewYork and London: G. P. Putnam's Sons, 1931). Stopes' work was translated into several Indian languages. See Peter Eaton and Marilyn Warnick, *Marie Stopes: A Checklist of Her Writings* (London: Croom Helm, 1977).
75 "Archive: Gandhi and Mrs. Sanger Debate Birth Control," in *Reproductive Health in India: History, Politics, Controversies,* ed. Sarah Hodges (New Delhi: Orient Longman, 2006), 235–247.
76 Karve, *Adhunik Kamashastra* [hereafter AK], 5th ed. (Bombay: Right Agency, 1949 [1932]). See also Karve's journal *Samaj Swasthya, 1927–1953*.
77 *MS*, June 1, 1942, 7.
78 *MS*, January 5, 1942, 2.
79 https://www.healthy-drinks.net/horlicks-ingrediants-health-benefits-and-side-effects/#:~:text=Horlicks%20was%20first%20introduces%20in%20India%20after%20the,Horlicks%20%3A%20Ingrediants%2C%20Health%20Benefits%20And%20Side&20Effects.
80 JWTA, J. Walter Thompson Company (Eastern) Limited, Income Budget for the Year July–December 1939 in Treasurer's Office Records, International Office, Bombay Office, Box 6, Bombay-General, 1939.
81 See *BC*, July 12, 1920, 15: *BC*, July 26, 1920, 12; August 4, 1920, 13; August 23, 1920, 13.
82 JWTA, "Notes on Indian Advertising," 4–5.
83 The effort to link male weakness and middle-class performance in work in tonic advertisement was not unique to Horlicks during this period. See, for instance, ads for Eno's Fruit Salt, *BC*, April 15, 1939, 9.
84 *BC*, October 2, 1939, 9.
85 *BC*, May 14, 1938, 16.

86 *BC*, September 23, 1939, 13.
87 Some of the ads featuring Indian figures were also published in the *Times of India* but the ads featuring European characters were exclusively published in the *Times*.
88 *TI*, April 15, 1939, 17.
89 As we saw with an earlier tonic ad, Europeans could be concerned about being sent home due to underperformance, an act that reflects not only personal failure but failure to maintain the reputation (the "izzat") of the expatriate community.

Chapter 4

1 Amita Kulkarni and Jeremy Schneider worked as research assistants on this book project, then went on to do unpublished research papers or theses under my direction. The discussion of Feluna and Ovaltine advertisements in part reflects not only their research but their interpretative insights in papers they wrote in this context. I fully acknowledge their contributions to this work and thank them for permitting me to draw upon these contributions.
2 Prakash Tandon, *Punjabi Saga*, 245–246.
3 Tani Barlow, "Event, Abyss, Excess: The Event of Women in Chinese Commercial Advertisement, 1910s–1950s," *Differences: Journal of Feminist Cultural Studies*, vol. 24, no. 2 (2013), 52, 53. Similar arguments to Barlow's have been made by Chie Ikeya in *Refiguring Women, Colonialism and Modernity in Burma* (Honolulu: University of Hawaii Press, 2011).
4 See also Barlow, "Buying in: Advertising and the Sexy Modern Girl Icon in Shanghai in the 1920s and 1930s," in Modern Girl Research Group, eds., *The Modern Girl Around the World*, 288–316.
5 For sweeping surveys of this development, see Geraldine Forbes, *Women in Modern India* (Cambridge: Cambridge University Press, 1996); Radha Kumar, *The History of Doing: An Illustrated Account of Movements for Women's Rights and Feminism in India, 1800–1990* (New Delhi: Kali for Women, 1993), 7–72.
6 Meera Kosambi, *Crossing Thresholds: Feminist Essays in Social History* (Raniket: Permanent Black, 2007).
7 See Forbes, *Women in Modern India*; Kumar, *The History of Doing*.
8 Hatekar, Kumar, and Mathur, "The Making of the Middle Class in Western India," *EPW*, vol. 44, no. 21 (2009).
9 For India as a whole, see Tanika Sarkar, "The Hindu Wife and the Hindu Nation: Domesticity and Nationalism in Nineteenth Century Bengal," *Studies in History*, vol. 8, no. 2 (1992): 213–235; Mary Hancock, "Home Science and the Nationalization of Domesticity in Colonial India," *Modern Asian Studies*, vol. 35, no. 4 (2001): 871–903, doi:10.2307/313194; Partha Chatterjee "The Nationalist Resolution of the Women's Question," in *Recasting Women: Essays in Colonial History*, eds. Kumkum Sangari and Sudesh Vaid (New Delhi: Kali for Women, 1989); Swapna Banerjee, *Men, Women, and Domestics: Articulating Middle-Class Identity in Colonial Bengal* (New Delhi and New York: Oxford University Press, 2004); Abigail McGowan "An All-Consuming Subject?" and "Modernity at Home: Leisure, Autonomy and the New Woman in India" (2009), *Tasveer Ghar: A Digital Archive of South Asian Popular Visual Culture* (http://tasveergharindia.net/cmsdesk/essay/95/index_4.html). For domestic tracts in western India see Chapter 2, note 119.

10 "The Education of Girls," *KS*, vol. XXV, no. 4 (April 1941), 85.

11 Ibid.

12 "Women and Employment," *KS*, vol. XXI, no. 9 (October 1937), 10.

13 "Home Sweet Home," *KS*, vol. XX, no. 10 (October 1936), 3.

14 "Some Aspects of the Higher Education of Women," *KS*, vol. XX, no. 10 (November 1936), 18.

15 "Home Sweet Home," 6.

16 Anant Arandol, "Khari Gruhini (true housewife)," *Stri Masik*, June 1933, 613.

17 "Gharcha Jamakharch," *Stri Masik*, December 1943, 326.

18 McGowan, "An All-Consuming Subject?," 51–54.

19 JWT, for instance, had taken gender seriously into its analysis as early as 1931, see its "Report on India, Burma and Ceylon," for instance, 26. This study actually concluded that most middle-class women "did their own shopping as a rule," a sharp contrast to the conclusions reached by Levers.

20 According to one account, the presence of flowers in the hair is a sign of the presence of the goddess Lakshmi in the home and the hope for continued prosperity and consequently symbolizes a desire for the happiness of the husband and family. http://www.boldsky.com/yoga-spirituality/faith-mysticism/2014/significance-of-wearing-flowers-on-hair-039823.html. Consulted October 7, 2018.

21 Modern Girl around the World Research Group, eds., *The Modern Girl Around the World*, back cover. See also Ikeya, *Refiguring Women*; chapter 4 examines the tension between the idea of the modern girl and the model of the modern housewife in commodity culture in Burma during the period covered by this book.

22 Preeti Ramamurthy, "All-Consuming Nationalism: the Indian Modern Girl in the 1920s and 1930s." In The Modern Girl Around the World Research Group, eds., *The Modern Girl Around the World*, 157.

23 Gandhi, "A Student's Shame" from *Harijan*, December 12, 1939, printed in *Self-Restraint vs Self-Renunciation* (Ahmedabad: Navajivan Publishing House, 1947), 168–169.

24 See Chapter 2 for discussion of this issue. See Uma Mullapudi, "Subordinating the Rights of Women: Arguments supporting the 1929 Sarda Act." Dartmouth Independent Study Paper, 2008.

25 "Bharap and Their Physiques," *KS*, vol. XII, no. 4 (April 1929), 8–9.

26 *MS*, January 17, 1934, 11. Ads for this product were also found in Ahmedabad newspapers.

27 *MS*, August 22, 1932, 5.

28 *Prajabandhu*, March 6, 1938, 8.

29 *MS*, January 17, 1934, 11.

30 *Prajabandhu*, January 15, 1930, 16.

31 The concept of imperial or colonial domesticity has been discussed, for instance, in E. M. Collingham, *Imperial Bodies: The Physical Experience of the Raj, c. 1800–1947* (Cambridge: Polity Press, 2001); Schneider, "Discourses in Capitalism."

32 Mary A. Proceda, *Married to the Empire: Gender, Politics and Imperialism in India, 1883–1947* (Manchester: Manchester University Press, 2002), 57.

33 *Cape Times*, May 13, 1935, 14.

34 *Cape Times*, January 24, 1940, 8.

35 *Bantu World*, June 4, 1932, 3.

36 *Bantu World*, October 12, 1933, 11.

37 My thanks to Peter Quella of Boston University who looked over some of the ads in my collection and provided translation and interpretations.

38 *The South African Indian Who's Who and Commercial Directory* (Pietermaritzburg: Natal Witness, 1937), 12. My thanks to Yoshina Hurgobin for this reference.
39 *MS*, July 16, 1927, 6.
40 For instance, see the ad entitled. "Are You Always Ready for the Dance?," *TI*, January 6, 1928.
41 *TI*, March 25, 1936, 20.
42 Translations of vernacular ads were almost undoubtedly carried out in India since few speakers of some of the languages involved, like Marathi, would have been available in South Africa.
43 Amita Kulkarni, "The Societal Conception of the Indian Female Body during the early 19th century through a study of Feluna advertisements," Undergraduate Independent Study Paper, Dartmouth College, 2009. Some of the anslysis here comes directly from Kulkarni's work.
44 *TI*, September 3, 1930, 15.
45 *TI*, March 3, 1931, 14; *TI*, November 18, 1933, 10.
46 *MS*, October 6, 1936, 13.
47 *MS*, February 23, 1931, 11.
48 *MS*, December 1, 1933, 14.
49 http://www.ovaltine.co.uk/about/timeline/. Consulted October 7, 2018. See also Alice Spain's *A Taste of Ovaltine: The Official Story* (Hathfordshire: Alpine Press, 2002).
50 Source P. 302a (January 14, 1937), The Dacorum Heritage Trust, Guard Book J cited in Schneider, "Discourses in Capitalism," 41.
51 The following draws directly from Schneider's work.
52 Adrian Bingham, *Gender, Modernity and the Popular Press in Inter-War Britain* (Oxford: Clarendon Press, 2004), 75.
53 Schneider, "Discourses in Capitalism."
54 *BC*, June 16, 1937, 4.
55 *BC*, May 1, 1936, 5.
56 Schneider, "Discourses in Capitalism," 119, citing *The Forward* (Calcutta), January 9, 1929, 11.
57 Schneider, "Discourses in Capitalism," 119, citing *The Hindu* (Madras), August 10, 1933, 12.
58 Schneider, "Discourses in Capitalism," 134.
59 *Prajabandhu*, January 15, 1939, 18d.
60 Geoffrey Jones, *Beauty Imagined: A History of the Global Beauty Industry* (New York: Oxford University Press, 2010), 15–70.
61 Sutton, *Globalizing Ideal Beauty.*
62 Jones, *Beauty Imagined*, 97–150. Both Sutton and Jones suggest that the diffusion of global commodities involved the dissemination of Western values. This chapter suggests a somewhat more complex model, involving the need to modify sales pitches significantly in the Indian context.
63 The analysis in this section has been helped extensively through discussions with Virchand Dharamsey.
64 Holly Grout, *The Force of Beauty: Transforming French Ideas of Femininity in the Third Republic* (Baton Rouge: Louisiana State University Press, 2015), 8.
65 Grout, *The Force of Beauty.*
66 Sutton, *Globalizing Ideal Beauty.*
67 *MS*, September 23, 1937, 19.
68 *BC*, February 11, 1931, 10.

69 Mobeen Hussain, "Race, Gender and Beauty in Late Colonial India c. 1900–1950," PhD. Thesis, Newnham College, University of Cambridge, 138, esp. 15–17. Hussain particularly discusses the emphasis on skin color. She draws upon other scholars who have tackled this subject, including Margaret L. Hunter, *Race, Gender and the Politics of Skin Tone* (New York: Routledge, 2005), 38.

70 *BC*, November 14, 1936, 2.

71 An exception is Mobeen Hussain's recent Cambridge thesis, "Race, Gender and Beauty," which devotes a full chapter to advertisements of beauty.

72 Sharada Dwivedi and Shalini Devi Holkar, *Almond Eyes, Lotus Feet: Indian Traditions in Beauty and Health* (Mumbai: Eminence Designs Pvt. Ltd., 2006).

73 Ibid., 13–14.

74 Ibid., 46.

75 *BC*, June 11, 1923, 11.

76 Sabeena Gadihoke, "Selling Soap and Stardom: The Story of Lux," *Tasveer Ghar: A Digital Archive of South Asian Popular Visual Culture*, accessed July 3, 2017. http://www.tasveergharindia.net/cmsdesk/essay/104/index.html, 2.

77 *BC*, March 2, 1936, 9. My thanks to Virchand Dharamsey for helping me appreciate the religious imagery involved in this image. In other media the lower half of such a figure was sometimes a map of India, indicating the figure Bharat Mata (Mother India).

78 For examples, see an ad for Colgate talcum powder, *TI*, May 2, 1938, 13.

79 *Kesari*, March 29, 1938, 11.

80 Sutton, *Globalizing Ideal Beauty*, 92–95.

81 JWTA, "Report on India, Burma and Ceylon," 39–42.

82 Eldridge, *Advertising and Selling Abroad*, 25.

83 *IWI*, October 2, 1938, 30.

84 Radhika Parameswaran and Kavitha Cardoza, "Melanin on the Margins: Advertising and the Cultural Politics of Fair/Light/White Beauty in India," *Journalism & Communication Monographs*, vol. 11, no. 3 (September 2009): 213–274.

85 For instance, see Hussain, "Race, Gender and Beauty in Late Colonial India c. 1900–1950."

86 Parameswaran and Cardoza, "Melanin on the Margins."

87 *BC*, July 12, 1935, 3.

88 *BC*, August 9, 1939, 8 for Cleopatra; *MS*, December 7, 1935, 17.

89 Another Unilever product called Lux was used as a laundry soap but this seems to have disappeared by the late 1930s.

90 See Julian Sivulka, *Stronger than Dirt: A Cultural History of Advertising Personal Hygiene in America, 1875–1940* (Amherst, NY: Humanity Books, 2001), 195–196.

91 See also Gadihoke, "Selling Soap and Stardom."

92 UA, UNI/RM/OC/2/2/46/34, "Mr. Sidney Van den Bergh's Report on Lever Brothers (India) Limited and United Traders Limited November 1937," 6. The reason why the actresses refrained from allowing their images to be used was not mentioned. The most obvious explanation would have to do with cultural hesitations and concerns about commercializing their image.

93 *BC*, March 16, 1938, 3.

94 *IWI*, October 23, 1938, 3.

95 *TI*, October 17, 1939, 3, for Padma Devi, *MS*, April 18, 1941, 4, for Khursheed.

96 Sivulka, *Stronger than Dirt*, has shown that film star photographs began to be introduced during the late 1920s in North America, 194–195.

97   *MS*, January 18, 1941, 13.

98   Preeti Ramamurthy, "All-Consuming Nationalism," 147.

99   Ibid.

100 *TI*, August 1, 1939, 13.

101 Ramamurthy, "All-Consuming Nationalism," 163.

102 Gadihoke, "Selling Soap and Stardom."

103 *MS*, May 15, 1942, 5.

104 Tapti Guha-Thakurta, *The Making of a New "Indian" Art: Artists, Aesthetics and Nationalism in Bengal, c. 1850–1920* (Cambridge: Cambridge University Press, 1992).

105 *Indian Artists of Yesteryear*, Nuga Arthouse, 2012. My thanks to Virchand Dharamsey for these interpretive suggestions.

Chapter 5

1   Tandon, *Punjabi Saga*, 233–322. Oral History Interview, Prakash Tandon [written transcript], British Library, European Manuscripts, MSS European T. 127.

2   Harminder Kaur, "Of Soaps and Scents: Corporeal Cleanliness in Urban Colonial India," *Toward a History of Consumption in South Asia*, ed. Haynes et al. (New Delhi: Oxford University Press, 2010), 246–267.

3   Projit Bihari Mukharji, "Soaps, Hair-Oils and Hair-Removers: Towards an Appraisal of Vernacular Capitalism in Colonial Bengal," unpublished paper presented at the Meetings of the American Historical Association, 2011.

4   Timothy Burke, *Lifebuoy Men, Lux Women*, 30–34; Anne McClintock, *Imperial Leather: Race, Gender and Sexuality in the Colonial Context* (New York and London: Routledge, 1995), 207–215, the quote is from page 208.

5   Edmund Hull cited by Kaur, "Of Soaps and Scents," 249.

6   Interview with Shantabai Krishnaji Kamble, Mumbai, April 2006.

7   Soap use is mentioned in a Dalit narrative by Kumud Pawade. See Sharmila Rege, *Writing Caste/Writing Gender: Reading. Dalit Women's Testimonies* (New Delhi: Zubaan, 2006), 243.

8   UA, "India: Mr. Sidney Van den Bergh's Report on Soap Business, December 1934," 6.

9   David K. Fieldhouse, *Unilever Overseas: The Anatomy of a Multinational, 1895–1965* (Stanford: Hoover Institution Press, 1978), 159.

10   *BC*, June 11, 1918, 12.

11   *MS*, May 7, 1930, 3.

12   B. K. Karanjia, *Godrej: A Hundred Years 1897–1997*, Vol. I (New Delhi: Penguin Viking, 1997), 24.

13   GA, Centenary Collection, 1914–1950, "Vancho ane Sikho," "File: Advertisements and Publicity."

14   Fieldhouse, *Unilever Overseas*. See also UA, "India: Report on Visit by Leverhulme and Scott to India, Burma and Ceylon, 1929," 11–12 for evidence of Levers' success.

15   UA, "India: Report on Visit by Leverhulme and Scott to India, Burma and Ceylon, 1929," 11.

16   Fieldhouse, *Unilever Overseas*, 154–162.

17   UA, "Report on Visit by Leverhulme and Scott to India, Burma and Ceylon, 1929," 11–13.

18   *Prajabandhu*, June 12, 1928, 5.

19 UA, "Report on Visit by Leverhulme and Scott to India, Burma and Ceylon,1929," 12.

20 UA, "India: Mr. Sidney Van den Bergh's Report on Soap Business, December 1934," 8.

21 UA, UNI/RM/2/2/118/10, "Mr. Hansard's Report on India, Burma and Ceylon, 1934," 4–5.

22 TCA, Records of Tata Oil Mills Company Ltd., Annual Report, 1933–4, 4.

23 TCA, Records of Tata Oil Mills Company Ltd., Annual Report, 1932–3, 5.

24 UA, "Report on Mr. Barnish's Visit to India, April 1939," 1.

25 This observation was made in GA, Correspondence from Sorabji Khanna, Chief Agent for the Punjab and the Northwest Frontier Provinces for Godrej Toilet Soap, May 13, 1939, "File: Godrej Soaps Ltd. (Sales and Marketing), 1936–1972," Centenary Collection, Reference no. MS06-01-94-90/200801296, Document 32.

26 Trademark infringement was not just a problem for foreign manufacturers; many ads about this issue ran in the papers. See, for instance, an ad by Godrej Soaps mentioning the company's involvement in many legal suits over trademarks, *TI*, November 16, 1934, 24.

27 UA, "Report on Visit by Leverhulme and Scott to India, Burma and Ceylon, 1929," 13.

28 GA, Correspondence from Sorabji Khanna, May 13, 1939.

29 *BC*, August 29, 1934, 3.

30 *BC*, April 6, 1935, 3.

31 *BC*, May 20, 1935 (page unclear).

32 Ibid., 68–69.

33 Kaur has stressed the importance of relying on familiar scents to the process of "indigenization" in "Of Soaps and Scents."

34 Lisa Trivedi, *Clothing Gandhi's Nation: Homespun and Modern India* (Bloomington and Indianapolis: Indiana University Press, 2007).

35 TCA, Records of Tata Oil Mills Company Ltd., Annual Report, 1920, 6.

36 UA, "Mr. Sidney Van den Bergh's Report on Lever Brothers (India) Limited, November 1937," 2, 3.

37 JWTA, "J. Walter Thompson Company (Eastern) Limited, Income Budget for the Year July–December 1939" and Letter from Peter Fielden, J. Walter Thompson (Eastern), to Donald Foote, New York Office, April 22, 1939, 3, in Treasurer's Office Records, International Office, Bombay Office, Box 6, Bombay-General, 1939. The final decision on these discussions is not revealed in the records, but the Tatas had a long-term relationship with JWT.

38 For instance, *MS*, March 21, 1931, 11.

39 *BC*, June 6, 1931, 3.

40 *MS*, February 19, 1934, 11. The price for Hamam was higher than for low-end soaps but apparently lower than Levers' soaps.

41 *BC*, October 15, 1938, 12.

42 *TCA*, Advertisement file from TISCO Review, March 1946.

43 Palmolive's competition is discussed in UA, "Mr. Hansard's Report on India, Burma and Ceylon, 1934," 4; UA, "Mr. Sidney Van den Bergh's Report on Lever Brothers (India) Limited, November 1937," 2.

44 Fieldhouse, *Unilever Overseas*, 160.

45 Ibid., 163–169.

46 UA, "India: Mr. Sidney Van den Bergh's Report on Soap Business, December 1934," 15.

47 Ibid., 2.

48 TCA, Records of Tata Oil Mills Company Ltd., Director's Report, 1934–5, 4–5. These records refer to a "sudden and unduly heavy reduction of soap prices by a large foreign corporation which started its own soap manufacturing in Bombay." That passage almost certainly refers to Lever Brothers.

49 Ibid., 8.

50 UNI/RM/OC/2/2/46/33, "Mr. Hansard's Reports on Lever Brothers (India) Limited, Hindustan Holland Vanaspati Trading Co. Ltd, Ceylon, January/February 1937," 4.

51 UA, "India: Mr. Sidney Van den Bergh's Report on Soap Business, December 1934," 6.

52 UA, "Report on Mr. Barnish's Visit to India, April 1939." Preliminary table.

53 Ibid.

54 Ibid., Attachment D.

55 UA, "Mr. Hansard's Reports on Lever Brothers (India) Limited, Hindustan Holland Vanaspati Trading Co. Ltd, Ceylon, January/February 1937," 4. See also UA UNI/RM/OC/2/2/46/34, "Mr. Sidney Van den Bergh's Report on Lever Brothers (India) Limited, November 1937."

56 UA, "Mr. Sidney Van den Bergh's Report on Lever Brothers (India) Limited, November 1937," 10.

57 UA, "Report on Visit by Leverhulme and Scott to India, Burma and Ceylon, 1929," 53.

58 Sivulka, *Stronger than Dirt*, 186.

59 Ibid. Though Unilever is often accorded credit for coining this term, it had actually been in use for about a decade before it was deployed in publicity for Lifebuoy.

60 *BC*, March 18, 1936, 9.

61 UA, "India: Mr. Sidney Van den Bergh's Report on Soap Business, December 1934," 10.

62 UA, "Mr. Sidney Van den Bergh's Report on Lever Brothers (India) Limited, November 1937," 4–5.

63 *Jam-e-Jamshed*, March 18, 1936, 21.

64 Tandon, *Punjabi Saga*, 237.

65 UA, "Lever Brothers (India), Limited [Discussion of sales], 31 January 1941," 10, 15–16, in 1941 Correspondence Bundle.

66 *TI*, October 6, 1939, 10.

67 For instance, *TI*, October 15, 1939, 17; August 18, 1938, 15.

68 *BC*, October 5, 1938, 3.

69 Prakash Tandon, *Punjabi Saga*, 237.

70 *BC*, August 1, 1940, 6.

71 *BC*, July 21, 1942, 3.

72 http://www.triplepundit.com/special/disrupting-short-termism/unilevers-handwashing-campaign-goes-beyond-csr-and-saves-lives/, accessed June 10, 2015.

73 UA, "Report on Mr. Barnish's Visit to India, April 1939," preliminary table.

74 Ibid., 1.

75 *BC*, April 20, 1938, 8.

76 Similar instructions were provided on boxes of Sunlight soap.

77 The word *kutchha* here is idiomatic phrasing, referring here to low-quality unbranded or cheap soaps.

78 *BC*, September 7, 1940, 13.

79 *MS*, May 28, 1942, 9.

80 *MS*, February 4, 1942, 11.

81 Literally sister, but here meaning a respected female or female friend.

Chapter 6

1 My thanks to Rachel Berger, who generously provided a significant number of references for this chapter and has been a valuable source of intellectual inspiration. Shrikant Botre and Projit Mukharji have also provided useful insights.

2 *Report on an Enquiry into Middle Class Family Budgets in Bombay City*, (Bombay: Labour Office 1928), 1–5.

3 See especially Tracey Deutsch, *Building a Housewife's Paradise: Gender, Politics and American Grocery Stores in the Twentieth Century* (Chapel Hill: The University of North Carolina Press, 2010).

4 Katherine J. Parkin, *Food is Love: Advertising and Gender Roles in Modern America* (Philadelphia: University of Pennsylvania Press, 2006).

5 Alysa Levene, "The Meanings of Margarine in England: Class, Consumption and Material Culture from 1918 to 1953," *Contemporary British History*, vol. 28, no. 2 (2014): 145–165.

6 K. T. Achaya, *The Food Industries of British India* (Delhi: Oxford University Press, 1994).

7 The actual manufacturing of vanaspati was in the hands of an associated company, Hindustan Vanaspati Manufacturing Co. Ltd. (HVM).

8 Arjun Appadurai, "How to Make a National Cuisine: Cookbooks in Contemporary India," *Comparative Studies in Society and History: An International Quarterly,* vol. 30 (1988): 3–24.

9 For a valuable survey of this literature, see Rachel Berger, "Alimentary Affairs: Historicizing Food in Modern India," *History Compass*, vol. 16, no. 2 (2018): 1–10. The history of food and hunger is less relevant in the current context, but see Benjamin Siegel, *Hungry Nation: Food, Famine and the Making of Modern India* (Cambridge: Cambridge University Press, 2018).

10 Bhadra, *From an Imperial Product to a National Drink*; Lutgendorf, "Chai Why?"

11 *Report of the Tarriff Board on the Canned and Bottled Vegetables* (Bombay: Ministry of Commerce and Industry, 1951).

12 For the danger of treating Indian conceptions of food as timeless, see Projit Mukharji, "Historicizing 'Indian Systems of Knowledge': Ayurveda, Exotic Foods and Contemporary Antihistorical Holisms," *History of Science,* vol. 35 (2020): 228–248.

13 For instance, Frank John Ninivaggi, *Ayurveda: Comprehensive Guide to Traditional Indian Medicine for the West* (Westport, CT: Praeger, 2001), 91–104, 153–184; https://www.yogajournal.com/food-diet/digest-this, accessed October 27, 2018.

14 Mukharji, *Nationalizing the Body*, 123.

15 These quotes come from H. Shankar Rau, "Family Budgets," in Rau, ed., *A Chitrapur Saraswat Miscellany,* 72. Rau in turn cited the Gita as the source of these quotations.

16 Ibid.

17 Shrikant Botre, "Nutrition and the Making of Marathi Sexology, 1920–1950," Paper presented at workshop on "Caste-ing Nutrition: The Politics of Health and Food in Modern India," University of Warwick, June 2018.

18 Ibid., 3–4.

19 See Mukharji, *Nationalizing the Body,* esp. 129–130.

20 Mckim Mariott, "Caste Ranking and Food Transactions: A Matrix Analysis," in Milton Singer and Bernard S. Cohn, eds., *Structure and Change in Indian Society* (Chicago: Aldine Publishing Company, 1968), 133–172.

21 Abigail McGowan, "An All-Consuming Subject," 31–54; Judith Walsh, *Domesticity in Colonial India*; Mary Hancock, "Home Science and the Nationalization of Domesticity in Colonial India."

22 Y. G. Pandit, *Report on the Oil-Pressing Industry of the Bombay Presidency* (Bombay: Government Central Press, 1914), 20. See also An Industrialist (anonymous author), *The Vegetable Oil Industry: A treatise for manufacturing oils from the Indian oil seeds with detailed processes of filtering, refining, bleaching, deodorizing and hydrogenating the oil* (Calcutta: Industry Publishers, 1941, 3rd ed.); Gopal Hattiangdi, *The Vanaspati Industry* (Hyderabad: Indian Central Oilseeds Committee, 1958), 2.

23 Pandit, *Report on the Oil-Pressing Industry*, 13.

24 Note by C. N. Surya Prakas, Vice-President, Bangalore Municipal Commission. BL India Office Records, Dept of Education, Health and Lands, October 1930, Health-A Proceedings.

25 For a more thorough discussion of the use and perception of ghee in South Asian society, see Rachel Berger, "Clarified Commodities: Managing Ghee in Interwar India," *Technology and Culture,* vol. 60, no. 4 (2019): 1004–1026.

26 K. T. Achaya, *Indian Food: A Historical Companion,* paperback edition (Delhi: Oxford University Press, 1998), 65.

27 B. Dass, *A Note on the Scarcity of Ghee and Milk* (Lahore: Punjab Hindu Sabha, 1913), 1.

28 Vaidya Jatashankar Liladhar Trivedi, *Khanpan: Khorak (Food): Bhag Pehelo* (Ahmedabad: Published by Author, 1920 [edition of 2,500]), 118.

29 Hattiangdi, *The Vanaspati Industry,* 4.

30 Trivedi, *Khanpan: Khorak,* 118–119. Newspaper accounts from the period regularly discussed the practice of adulteration and prosecutions of traders for adulteration after the adoption of the Bombay Prevention of Adulteration Act. See for instance, *TI,* July 2, 1941, 10; July 25, 1934, 5; September 4, 1934, 5; October 9, 1937, 17.

31 N. N. Godbole and Sadgopal, *Butter-Fat (Ghee): Its Composition , Nutritive Value, Digestibility, Rancidity, Adulteration, Its Detection and Estimation* (Varanasi: Benares Hindu University, 1939), especially Chapter V; Trivedi, *Khanpan: Khorak,* 118–20.

32 UA, UNI/RM/OC/2/2/46/22, "India: Mr. Sidney Van den Bergh's Report on Edible Business, December 1934," 13.

33 *TI,* August 11, 1937, 16.

34 *BL,* Letter from the Secretary to Chief Commissioner of Coorg, Bangalore, to the Secretary to the Government of India, Dept. of Commerce, no. 1281/64-12, Dated the 16 of May 1929, India Office, Records, Dept. of Education, Health and Lands, October 1930, Health-A Proceedings.

35 Utsa Ray, *Culinary Culture in Colonial India: A Cosmopolitan Platter and the Middle-Class* (Delhi: Cambridge University Press, 2015), 158–159.

36 David Arnold, *Toxic Histories: Poison and Pollution in Modern India* (Cambridge: Cambridge University Press, 2016), 216–217.

37 Ibid., 163.

38 This date comes from *BL*, Comments by Rai Bahadur Ram Saran Das, State Council Debates found in India Office Records. Dept. of Education, Health and Lands, June 1931, Health-A Proceedings.

39 Hattiangdi, *The Vanaspati Industry,* 4.

40 Fieldhouse, *Unilever Overseas*, esp. 169–170. Rachel Berger has particularly highlighted to me the importance of Van den Berghs during this early period of vanaspati.

41 G. Balachandran, *Globalizing Labour?: Indian Seafarers and World Shipping, c. 1870–1945* (New Delhi: Oxford University Press, 2012).

42 TA, *Tata Oil Mill Company Ltd: Annual Report: 1925–26,* 3.

43 Godbole and Sadgopal, *Butter-Fat (Ghee),* 5.

44 National Archives of India, Note by G. L. Corbett, "Indian Trade," in Government of India, Department of Education, Health and Lands, Health-B Proceedings, November 1930, Pros. 175–177. My thanks to Rachel Berger for this reference.

45 UA, UNI/RM/OC/2/2/46/40, "India: Report of Mr. A. D. Gourley on His Visit, 1944," esp. 46.

46 For these companies, see UA, "India: Mr. Sidney Van den Bergh's Report on Edible Business, December 1934," 2; UNI/RM/OC/2/2/46/31, "Mr. Sidney Van den Bergh's Report on H.H.V.T. Business," March 1936, 6–7.

47 Hattiangdi, *The Vanaspati Industry.*

48 UA, "India: Mr. Sidney Van den Bergh's Report on Edible Business, December 1934," 1–2.

49 UA, "Mr. Sidney Van den Bergh's Report on H.H.V.T. Business, March 1936," 6–7.

50 UA, "Mr. Sidney Van den Bergh's Report on H.H.V.T. Business, March 1936," 8.

51 The Chemical Analyzer was a scientist working for the Government of Bombay responsible for examining medico-legal issues. The role of this office in various provinces (usually called the Chemical Examiner) has been discussed, more in the context of poisons than food adulteration, in Arnold, *Toxic Histories,* esp. 111–117.

52 *MS,* January 12, 1929, 17.

53 TCA, TOMCO, *Annual Report,* 1920, 6.

54 TCA, TOMCO, *Annual Report,* 1922–23, 5; see also *Annual Report,* 1923–24.

55 TCA, TOMCO, *Annual Report,* 1923–24, 3.

56 Ibid., 4–5.

57 TCA, TOMCO/T43/AGN Minutes of Sixth Ordinary General Meeting of TOMCO, October 8, 1924, 57 of file.

58 TCA, TOMCO, *Annual Report,* 1926–27, 3.

59 *MS,* August 11, 1927, 5.

60 My thanks to Projit Mukharji for this observation.

61 *BC,* May 21, 1927, 14.

62 *TI,* July 5, 1933, 4.

63 *TI,* May 31, 1933, 14.

64 *TI,* February 18, 1931, 18.

65 *TI,* September 3, 1930, 13.

66 *TI,* February 5, 1933, 15.

67 UA, "India: Mr. Sidney Van den Bergh's Report on Edible Business, December 1934," 2, 20.

68 Ibid., 2. Tata itself was making three times as much vanaspati as Cocogem by this time.

69 TCA, TOMCO, *Annual Report,* 1923–24, 4.

70 https://www.hul.co.in/about/who-we-are/our-history/, consulted October 28, 2018. For this history, see also Fieldhouse, *Unilever Overseas,* 164–175.

71 UA, "Mr. Sidney Van den Bergh's Report on H.H.V.T. Business," March 1936, 2.

72 Ibid., 9.

73 Discussions of these issues repeatedly occurred during the 1930s, see both the A Proceedings in the British Library and the B Proceedings in the National Archives of India for this discussion. My thanks to Rachel Berger for pointing these materials out to me.

74 For one example, see Council of State Debates, Legislative Assembly Debates, February 13, 1931 in BL, Indian Office Library, Dept. of Education, Health, and Lands, A Proceedings, June 1931.

75 For a discussion of this issue, see Berger, "Clarified Commodities," which focuses primarily on the Punjab.

76 UA, "Mr. Sidney van den Bergh's Report on Edible Business, December 1934," 12.

77 UA, "Report on Visit to India by A. D. Gourley—1944," 55.

78 Ibid.

79 For a bit more detailed history of Dalda, see UA, "Report on Visit to India by A. D. Gourley—1944," 55–60. Achaya, *The Food Industries,* 212, dates Dalda to the early 1930s rather than 1938.

80 UA, UNI/RM/OC/2/2/46/35, "Mr. Sidney Van den Bergh's Report on HHVT Co Ltd., Bombay, November 1937," 19. This source indicates that the company should stop viewing the product as a simple substitute for ghee and, "sell Vanaspati on its own merits as a healthy body-building food containing vitamins, which can be used for cooking and baking and with all foods."

81 UA, "Report on Visit to India by A. D. Gourley—1944," 56.

82 Bose, "Sons of the Nation"; Bose, "Reconstituting Private Life."

83 My thanks to Virchand Dharamsey for discussing the meaning of these ads with me.

84 The first Dalda cookbook was published in 1942. I was able to find the third edition, which published more than 50,000 copies. *The Dalda Cookbook*, 3rd ed., compiled by Mrs. Z. P. Kukde (Bombay: The Dalda Advisory Service, 1951?). My thanks to Maya Malhotra for making a copy available.

85 Appadurai, "How to Make a National Cuisine." Appadurai explores cookbooks in a later period, when more intensive sociality across community lines would have heightened pressures for middle-class housewives to demonstrates their cosmopolitan capabilities.

86 My thanks to Shrikant Botre, now specializing in the history of nutrition, for discussing the translation of this ad quite closely.

87 Prakash Tandon, *Beyond Punjab, 1937–1960* (London: Chatto and Windus, 1971), 114, 123.

88 Hattiangdi, *The Vanaspati Industry.*

89 UA, Report on Visit to India by A. D. Gourley—1944, 53.

90 Ibid.

91 Ibid., 58.

92 Gandhi, "Vanaspati and Ghee", April 8, 1946 in https://www.mkgandhi.org/health/diet_reform/40vanaspati_and_ghee.html, accessed June 26, 2019.

93 UA, UNI/RM/OC/2/2/46/44, "Chairman's Visit to India, November/December 1947," 18.

94 Ibid., 19.

95 Interviews by author with ex-Levers' and ex-Lintas officers, such as Gerson da Cunha, 2006 and 2017; Aspi Modi, 2006, Alyque Padamsee, 2006; and Rajni Chaddha, 2018. See also Tandon, *Beyond Punjab,* 169–180.

96 Tandon, *Beyond Punjab,* 169–180.

97 Interview with Rajni Chaddha.

98 Alyque Padamsee and Arun Prabhu, *A Double Life: My Exciting Years in Theatre and Advertising* (New Delhi: Penguin Books, 1999), 49.

99 See Hattiangdi, *The Vanaspati Industry* and Alyque Padamsee and Arun Prabhu, *A Double Life*, on Hindustan Levers' efforts to counteract the reputation of Dalda for harming eyesight.

100 https://www.business-standard.com/article/management/40-years-ago-and-now-how-dalda-built-and-lost-its-monopoly-115030501153_1.html, consulted January 21, 2019.
101 Padamsee and Prabhu, *A Double Life,* 49, 50.
102 Interviews by author with Gerson da Cunha, 2006, and Aspi Modi, 2006.

Chapter 7

1   Caroline Davidson, *A Woman's Work Is Never Done: A History of Housework in the British Isles 1650–1950* (London: Chatto and Windus, 1982).
2   The larger history of BEST is discussed in Prestonji D. Mahaluxmivala, *History of the Bombay Electric Supply & Tramways Company, Limited: 1905–1935* (Bombay: BEST, 1936).
3   Arvind Rajagopal, "Advertising, Politics and the Sentimental Education of the Indian Consumer," *Visual Anthropology Review*, vol. 14, no. 2 (1998): 14–31.
4   Bhonsle, "Clerks in the City of Bombay," 131.
5   Ibid., Chapter IX.
6   "Bharaps and Their Physiques," *KS*, vol. XII, no. 4 (April 1929): 8–9.
7   Bhonsle, "Clerks in the City of Bombay," 130; Nikhil Rao, *House, but No Garden*, 97–136.
8   Abigail McGowan, "Ahmedabad's Home Remedies: Housing in the Re-Making of an Industrial City, 1920–1960," *South Asia: journal of South Asia Studies*, vol. 36, no. 3 (2013): 397–414; McGowan, "Consuming Domesticity: Creating Consumers for the Middle-Class House in India, 1920–1960," in Bhaswati Bhattacharya and Henrike Donner, eds., *Globalizing Everyday Consumption in India: History and Ethnography* (New York: Routledge, 2020).
9   Rao, *House, but No Garden*, 97–136.
10   In a personal communication, Frank Conlon has mentioned that housing in the co-operative housing complex of the Saraswat Brahmans of Bombay, built in Gamdevi around 1915, possessed electric service.
11   The relatively quick adoption of electric lighting as a replacement for gas lights in Europe has been discussed by Wolfgang Schivelbusch, *Disenchanted Night: The Industrialization of Light in the Nineteenth Century,* trans. Angela Davies (Berkeley: University of California Press, 1988). My thanks to Shekhar Krishnan for this reference.
12   Communication from Shekhar Krishnan.
13   For instance, see Raghunath Shripad Deshpande, *Modern Ideal Homes for India* (Poona: United Book Corporation, rev. ed., 1948 [1st edition 1939]); Deshpande, *Cheap and Healthy Homes for the Middle Classes of India* (Poona: United Book Corporation, 7th edn, 1969 [1st edition 1935]). For recent analyses of these studies, see McGowan, "Ahmedabad's Home Remedies" and "Consuming the Home."
14   *TI* (Pro-quest) May 28, 1934; 5. My thanks to Abigail McGowan for this and the following reference. Other *Times of India* references were located in original copies of the newspaper.
15   *TI,* December 15, 1936, 7.
16   The Dhanraj Mahal complex still survives today, though it would no longer be recognized as a structure once touted as being ahead of its time.
17   *TI*, May 27, 1936, 17–20.

18 The exhibition has been discussed by Nikhil Rao in *House but No Garden,* 137–170; Gyan Prakash, *Mumbai Fables* (Princeton: Princeton University Press, 2010), 97–98; and Abigail McGowan, "Domestic Modern: Redecorating Homes in Bombay in the 1930s," *Journal of the Society of Architectural Historians,* vol. 75, no. 4 (December 2016): 424–446. This article elaborates significantly on the concept of the ideal home and also discusses advertisements (including a couple of ads I discuss here) but in a different analytical frame than offered here. I read the published version of this highly relevant article only during the final days of completing this manuscript though I had attended an earlier conference presentation of this paper, also cited in the bibliography.

19 The role of the architectural association in this event is discussed in McGowan, "Domestic Modern."

20 *BC,* November 3, 1937, 14.

21 *BC,* November 4, 1937, 8.

22 *TI,* November 3, 1937, 15.

23 Ibid., 2.

24 Ibid., 19.

25 Ibid., punkah refers to a fan (here, an electric fan). "Boy" obviously refers to a male house-servant (in a demeaning term).

26 *TI,* November 3, 1937, 19.

27 For the washing machine in the U.S., see Joann Vanek, "Household Technology and Social Status: Rising Living Standards and Status and Residence Differences in Housework," *Technology and Culture,* vol. 19, no. 3 (1978): 361–375.

28 American and European use of household appliances before 1940 should not be exaggerated. Electricity use was still largely urban in character, and the adoption of electric household goods was gradual. In the United States, one-third of American homes possessed electricity in 1920; the figure was two-thirds by 1930. In Britain only 6 percent of British homes were wired for electricity in 1918. By 1935, 35 percent of American families owned a washing machine and 44 percent owned a vaccuum cleaner, two of the most popular household technologies. Only 13 percent owned a refrigerator. Less than 10 percent of households owned washing machines in England and Finland at the end of World War II. See, for instance, Vanek, "Household Technology and Social Status," 361–375; Davidson, *A Woman's Work is Never Done,* chapter 2; Tanis Day, "Capital-Labor Substitution in the Home," *Technology and Culture,* vol. 33, no. 2 (1992): 302–327; Ruth Schwartz Cowan, "The 'Industrial Revolution' in the Home: Household Technology and Social Change in the 20th Century," *Technology and Culture,* vol. 17, no. 1 (1976): 1–23; Cowan, *More Work for Mother: The Ironies of Household Technology from the Open Hearth to the Microwave* (New York: Basic Books, 1983); Sue Bowden and Avner Offer, "Household Appliances and the Use of Time: The United States and Britain since the 1920s," *The Economic History Review* vol. 47, no. 4 (November 1, 1994): 725–748; Ronald R. Kline, "Resisting Development, Reinventing Modernity: Rural Electrification in the United States before World War II," *Environmental Values,* vol. 11, no. 3 (2002): 327–344; Mika Pantzar, "Tools or Toys—Inventing the Need for Domestic Appliances in Postwar and Postmodern Finland," *Journal of Advertising,* vol. 32, no. 1 (2003): 83–93.

29 *Report on an Enquiry into Middle Class Family Budgets in Bombay City,* 1–5.

30 *A Chitrapur Saraswat Miscellany,* ed. H. Shankar Rau (Bombay: Published by Author, 1938), 22; my thanks to Frank Conlon for this reference.

31 These figures were included in some of the ads cited later.

32 Cowan, *More Work for Mother;* Day, "Capital-Labor Substitution in the Home."

33 Measuring this growth is unfortunately not possible because of the changing nature of census categories. See *Census of India*, 1911 and *Census of India*, 1931 (the former used workers and dependents, the latter only workers).

34 Partha Chatterjee, "The Nationalist Resolution of the Women's Question."

35 Walsh, *Domesticity in Colonial India*; McGowan, "An All-Consuming Subject."

36 European business firms in Bombay were often expected to provide salaries that would facilitate the sustenance of lifestyles comparable to those possible at "home"; this included the adoption of electrical appliances used in Europe.

37 See Chapter 2.

38 *Mumbai Samachar,* January 19, 1942, 10.

39 *Jame Jamshed,* March 12, 1936, 11.

40 The dating of BEST's establishment varies in different accounts because the firm went through several different stages.

41 The account of BEST's history in the above two paragraphs comes from *Electricity in India being a History of the Tata Hydro-Electric Project with Notes on the Mill Industry in Bombay and the Progress of Electric Drive in Indian Factories* ed. S. M Rutnagur (Bombay: Indian Textile Journal, 1912); Mahaluxmivala, *History of the Bombay Electric Supply*; H. K. Gandgadhariah, *Electric Law and Practice in India* (Bombay: Examiner Press, 1935); Shripad Narayan Pendse, *The B.E.S.T. Story,* trans. M. V. Rajadhyaksha (Bombay: Bombay Electric Supply & Transport Undertaking, 1972).

42 The history of Bombay's tramway system has been explored in Frank Conlon, "Tramways and the Urban Development of Colonial Bombay," in *Mumbai Past and Present: Historical Perspectives and Contemporary Challenges*, ed. Manjiri Kamat (Bombay: Nehru Centre, Indus Source, 2013), 80–112.

43 Pendse, *The B.E.S.T. Story,* 28–34; Mahaluxmivala, *The History of BEST,* 326–345.

44 Quoted in Pendse, *The B.E.S.T Story,* 28–29.

45 *TI*, December 16, 1939, 13.

46 *TI*, November 18, 1939, 11.

47 *TI*, October 23, 1939, 11.

48 *TI*, April 3, 1935, 5.

49 *BC,* December 18, 1937, 16.

50 *BC,* May 19, 1924, 11.

51 *MS,* January 8, 1938; see also *BC,* December 7, 1937, 3.

52 *MS,* August 27, 1932, 4.

53 *MS,* August 13, 1932, 14.

54 *BC,* July 11, 1936, 16.

55 *TI,* May 20, 1936, 11.

56 *TI,* May 6, 1936, 13.

57 Pradeep Kumar Bose, "Sons of the Nation."

58 See also *TI,* May 5, 1939, 5.

59 *TI,* May 20, 1936, 17.

60 *TI,* July 16, 1938, 8.

61 I borrow this notion from Ruth Cowan's work, *More Work for Mother*, on American housewives and household techniques during the same time. Cowan's concept coincides nicely with publications on India by such scholars as Judith Walsh, *Domesticity in Colonial India*; Abigail McGowan, "An All-Consuming Subject?"; and Mary Hancock, "Home Sciences and the Nationalization of Domesticity in Colonial India." See also Susan Strasser, *Never Done: A History of American Housework* (New York: Pantheon Books, 1982).

Conclusion

1   It also suggests that we define the contemporary middle class broadly, to include the hundreds of millions of people buying small quantities of consumer goods rather than to use "western" material standards as our basis. Using the latter standards would exclude most people defining themselves as middle class early in the century and move us away from how South Asians are defining themselves in the present.

2   There is usually no direct empirical evidence proving whether these perceptions were actually correct.

Bibliography

Official archives

British Library

European Manuscripts
India Office. Records, Department of Education, Health and Lands. Health-A Proceedings.
India Office. Records, Department of Education, Health and Lands. Health-B Proceedings.

Maharashtra State Archives

Bombay Provincial Banking Enquiry Files

Business archives

Godrej Archives, Centenary Collection, 1914–1950 [GA], Mumbai, India
History of Advertising Trust Archives [HATA], Raveningham, Norfolk, UK
J. Walter Thompson Archives [JWTA], Hartman Center for Sales, Marketing and
    Advertising History, Duke University, Durham, NC.
Tata Central Archives [TCA], Pune, India
Unilever Archives [UA], Port Sunlight, England, UK

Interviews conducted by author

Interview with Alyque Padamsee, 2006
Interview with Aspi Modi, 2006
Interviews with Gerson da Cunha, 2006 and 2017
Interview with Maya Malhotra, 2017
Interview with Rajni Chaddha, 2018
Interview with Ratan Sohoni, May 2006
Interview with Shantabai Krishnaji Kamble, Mumbai, April 2006
Interview with Virchand Dharamsey, April 2006

Advertising profession periodicals

Advertiser's Weekly [UK]
Advertising Abroad (subsequently *The Export Advertiser*) (US)
Commercial Art
Printer's Ink
Yearbook, Commercial Art Guild (India)

Pre-1950 journals

Kanara Saraswat
Stri Bodh
Stri Masik

Newspapers

Bantu World (various languages, South Africa)
The Bombay Chronicle (Bombay, English)
Cape Times (English, Capetown, South Africa)
Gujarat Mitra (Surat, Gujarati)
Illustrated Weekly of India (Bombay, English)
Jam-e-Jamshed (Bombay, Gujarati)
Kesari (Poona, Marathi)
Kirloskar (Poona, Marathi)
Mumbai Samachar (Bombay, Gujarat)
Prajabandhu (Ahmedabad, Gujarati)
Rhodesian Herald (Rhodesia, English)
Times of India (English, Bombay)
Times of India (Pro-quest)

Miscellaneous Paper

L. A. Stronach, undated recollection, text provided by Anita Sarkar

Official reports

Bureau of Foreign and Domestic Commerce, United States "Channels of Distribution of American Merchandise in India." Washington: United States Government Printing Office, 1933.
India: Report of the Drugs Enquiry Committee. Government of India, c. 1931.
Pandit, Y. G. *Report on the Oil-Pressing Industry of the Bombay Presidency.* Bombay: Government Central Press, 1914.
Renshaw, Donald, C. B. Spofford, and U.S. Bureau of Foreign and Domestic Commerce. *Advertising in India.* Trade Information Bulletin, No. 318. Washington: Government Printing Office, 1925.
Report on an Enquiry into Middle Class Family Budgets in Bombay City. Bombay: Labour Office, 1928.
Report on an Enquiry into Working Class Budgets in Bombay. Bombay: Labour Office, 1923.
Report on the Survey into the Economic Conditions of Middle Class Families in Bombay City. Bombay: Indian Statistical Institute, 1952.
Report of the Tarriff Board on the Canned and Bottled Vegetables. Bombay: Ministry of Commerce and Industry, 1951.

Census reports

Census of India, 1911

Census of India, 1921, vol VIII, part 1, *Bombay Presidency*
Census of India, 1921, vol VIII, part 2, *Bombay Presidency*
Census of India, 1921, vol. IX, part 1, *Cities of the Bombay Presidency*
Census of India, 1931, vol. VIII, *Bombay Presidency*
Census of India, 1931, vol. IX, part 1, *Cities of the Bombay Presidency*

Pre-1950 non-official published sources (not including popular journal articles and essays written for trade journals, which are fully cited in the notes)

Banaji, Bahman S. J. *Ek Mahan Shodh, Marji Pramaneno Balak*. Bombay: J. B. Karani Sons, December 1923.
Bhagat, Gambhirdas Karsandas. *Chaha Devinu Charitra ane fashion no faras*. Mumnavad: Published by the Author, 1920.
Brahmabhatt, Hiralal Gagji. *Deshdaz (Patriotism)*. Bombay: Royal, 1921.
Bridgewater, Howard. *Advertising; Or, The Art of Making Known; A Simple Exposition of the Principles of Advertising*. London: Sir Isaac Pitman & Sons, 1910.
Burtt, Harold Ernest. *Psychology of Advertising*. Boston: Houghton Mifflin Company, 1938.
Chattopadhyay, S. *Devdas*. Translated by Sreejata Guha. New Delhi: Penguin Books, 2002 [1917].
Dass, B. *A Note on the Scarcity of Ghee and Milk*. Lahore: Punjab Hindu Sabha, 1913.
The Dalda Cookbook, 3rd Edition. Compiled by Mrs. Z. P. Kukde. Bombay: Dalda Advisory Service, 1951? [1st ed. 1942].
David, Wilfrid. *Monsoon: A Novel*. London: Hamish Hamilton, 1933.
Desai, Sapur Faredun. *Parsis and Eugenics*. Bombay: Published by author, 1940.
Deshpande, Raghunath. *Modern Ideal Homes for India*. Poona: United Book Corporation, revised edition 1948 [first edition 1939].
Eldridge, F. R. *Advertising and Selling Abroad*. New York and London: Harper and Brothers, 1930.
Gandhi, Mahatma. "Change of Heart", May 14, 1931 (from *Young India*). In *Collected Works of Mahatma Gandhi*, vol XLVI. Delhi: Government of India, 1971.
Gandhi, Mahatma. *Hind Swaraj*, revised ed., 11th reprint (Ahmedabad: Navajivan Publishing, 1996).
Gandhi, Mahatma. "A Student's Shame" from *Harijan*, December, 12 1939, printed in *Self-Restraint vs Self-Renunciation*. Ahmedabad: Navajivan Publishing House, 1947.
Gandhi, Mahatma. "Vanaspati and Ghee", April 8, 1946 in https://www.mkgandhi.org/health/diet_reform/40vanaspati_and_ghee.html. Accessed June 26, 2019.
Godbole, N. N. and Sadgopal. *Butter-Fat (Ghee): Its Composition, Nutritive Value, Digestibility, Rancidity, Adulteration, Its Detection and Estimation*. Varanasi: Benares Hindu University, 1939.
Gandgadhariah, H. K. *Electric Law and Practice in India*. Bombay: Examiner Press, 1935.
Hymers, Robert P. and Leonard Sharpe. *The Technique and Practice of Advertising Art*. London: Sir Isaac Pitman & Sons, Ltd., 1939.
Karve, R. D. *Adhunik Kamashastra*, 5th ed. Bombay: Right Agency, 1949 [1932] (in Marathi).
Khare, L. G. "The Depressed Middle Classes." Part I, *The Social Science Quarterly* 2, no. 3 (January 1917): 135–142; Part II, *Social Science Quarterly* 3, no. 1 (July 1917): 14–19.
Mahaluxmivala, Prestonji D. *History of the Bombay Electric Supply & Tramways Company, Limited: 1905–1935*. Bombay: BEST Co., 1936.

Manchharam, Chimanlal Nagindas. *Naval Narangi athva Fashionyari [Naval Navrangi or the vanity of fashion]*. Bombay: Sanj Vartaman, 1920.

Mayo, Katherine. *Mother India*. New York: Greenwood Press, 1955 [1937].

Patel, Dahyabhai. *Fashionni Fisiyari [Vanity of Fashions]*. Nadiad: Published by the Author, 1921.

Phadke, Narayan Sitaram. *Sex Problems in India, a Scientific Exposition of Sex Life and Some Curious Marriage Customs Prevailing in India from Time Immemorial to the Present Day*. Bombay: D. B. Taraporevala Sons & Co., 1929.

Pillay, A. P. *The Art of Love and Same Sex Living, Based on Ancient Precepts and Modern Teachings*. Bombay: Taraporevala, 15th ed., c. 1947.

Rau, H. Shankar, ed. *A Chitrapur Saraswat Miscellany*. Bombay: Published by author, 1938.

Rutnagur, S. M., ed. *Electricity in India being a History of the Tata Hydro-Electric Project with Notes on the Mill Industry in Bombay and the Progress of Electric Drive in Indian Factories*. Bombay: Indian Textile Journal, 1912.

Scott, Walter Dill. *The Psychology of Advertising: A Simple Exposition of the Principles of Psychology in Their Relation to Successful Advertising*. Boston: Small, Maynard & Company, 1913.

Shah, Gordhanlal. *Mumbai Shetan*. Ahmedabad: Published by the Auuthor, 1922.

Shivananda, Swami. *Manowanchit Santati: Gruhasthashramache Anubhavsiddha Niyam*. Amravati: Rashtroddhar Karyalaya, 2nd edition, 1928.

Starch, Daniel. *Advertising: Its Principles, Practice, and Technique*. Chicago: Scott, Foresman and Co., 1914.

Starch, Daniel. *Principles of Advertising*. Chicago and New York: A. W. Shaw Co., 1923.

Stopes, Marie Carmichael. *Married Love: A New Contribution to the Solution of Sex Difficulties*. Authorized ed. New York and London: G.P. Putnam's Sons, 1931.

Thakkar, Jivraj Harjivan. *Kalyugni Fashionbai*. Ahmedabad: Published by the Author, 1921.

The South African Indian Who's Who and Commercial Directory. Pietermaritzburg: Natal Witness, 1937.

Tripathi, Govardhanram Madhavram. *Saraswatichandra*. Translated by Tridip Suhrud. Hyderabad: Orient Blackswan 2015– (1887–1901).

Trivedi, Vaidya Jatashankar Liladhar. *Khanpan: Khorak (Food): Bhag Pehelo*. Ahmedabad: published by author, 1920.

Vyas, Pitambar Gampatram. *Chalu Jamano Fashion*. Thana: Published by the Author, 1920.

Unpublished theses and course papers

Ahmed, Shaheen. "Decoding the Fetish: A Dialectical Understanding of the Notion of the Fetish in Advertisements in India from 1970 to 1993." M. Phil. Dissertation, JNU University, 2016.

Bhonsle, R. N. "Clerks in the City of Bombay." M.A. Thesis, University of Bombay, 1938.

Hussain, Mobeen. "Race, Gender and Beauty in Late Colonial India c. 1900–1950." PhD. Thesis, Newnham College, University of Cambridge, 2021.

Kreshel, Peggy Jean. "Towards a Cultural History of Advertising Research: A Case Study of J. Walter Thompson, 1908–25." PhD. Thesis, University of Illinois at Urbana-Champaign, 1989.

Kulkarni, Amita. "The Societal Conception of the Indian Female Body during the early 19th century through a study of Feluna advertisements." Undergraduate Independent Study Paper, Dartmouth College, 2009.

Mullapudi, Uma. "Subordinating the Rights of Women: Arguments supporting the 1929 Sarda Act." Dartmouth Independent Study Paper, 2008.

Nag, Dulali. "The Social Construction of Handwoven Tangail Saris in the Market of Calcutta." PhD. Dissertation, Michigan State University. University Microfilms International, 1990.

Pande, Ishita. "Curing Calcutta: Race, Liberalism, and Colonial Medicine in British Bengal, 1830–1900." PhD. Thesis, Princeton University, 2005.

Schneider, Jeremy. "Discourses in Capitalism: Ovaltine Advertisements and Visions of Domesticity in the British Empire during the Interwar Period." Undergraduate Honors Thesis, Dartmouth College, Department of History, 2007.

Schneider, Jeremy. "Reimaging Traditional Medicine: Tracing the Emergence of Commodified Ayurveda in the Interwar Period." Master of Science in Economic and Social History Thesis, Oxford University, 2008.

Unpublished conference papers

Biswas, Prithwiraj. "Advertising and Enterprise in Colonial Bengal: Reflections on Hemendramohan Bose through a study of his advertisements." Paper presented at the North American Conference of British Studies, Washington, D.C., November 2016.

Botre, Shrikant. "Nutrition and the Making of Marathi Sexology, 1920–1950." Paper presented at workshop on "Caste-ing Nutrition: The Politics of Health and Food in Modern India," University of Warwick, June 2018.

Doctor, Vikram. "Edward Fielden." Unpublished article, dated October 7, 2004.

Haynes, Douglas. "Brand-Name Capitalism, Soap Advertising and the Making of the Middle Class Family in Western India, 1918–1940." Paper presented at the Conference on Material Culture in South Asia, University of Pennsylvania, April 2012.

Kumari, Rashmi, with Chinmay Tumbe and Shashank Velpurcharla. "The Advertising Business of India." Paper written for the World Economic History Congress, July 2018.

McGowan, Abigail. "Domestic Modern: Redecorating Homes in Bombay in the 1930s." Paper presented at the conference, "The Long Indian Century: Historical Transitions and Social Transformations," Yale University, April 2014.

Mukharji, Projit Bihari. "Sex, Medicine and Morality: The Modernization of Sexed Bodies." Unpublished chapter draft, 2009.

Mukharji, Projit Bihari. "Soaps, Hair-Oils and Hair-Removers: Towards an Appraisal of Vernacular Capitalism in Colonial Bengal." Unpublished Paper presented at the Meetings of the American Historical Association, 2011.

Rajagopal, Arvind. "Advertising as Political Ventriloquism: Agency, Corporation and State in the Shaping of India's Branded Market." Unpublished essay, 2014.

Rajagopal, Arvind. "Commodity and Commodity Image in the Indian Bazaar: Notes from Trademark Case Law." Unpublished essay presented at a workshop, "Transactional Sociality: Market Moralities and Embedded Capital in India," held at the University of Goettingen, December 2016.

Post-1950 publications

Achaya, K. T. *The Food Industries of British India.* Delhi: Oxford University Press, 1994.

Achaya, K. T. *Indian Food: A Historical Companion,* paperback edition. Delhi: Oxford University Press, 1998.

Bayly, C. A. *Empire and Information: Intelligence Gathering and Social Communication in India, 1780–1870.* Cambridge: Cambridge University Press, 2009.

Bayly, C. A. *Rulers, Townsmen, and Bazaars: North Indian Society in the Age of British Expansion, 1770–1870.* Cambridge and New York: Cambridge University Press, 1983.

Berger, Rachel. *Ayurveda Made Modern: Political Histories of Indigenous Medicine in North India, 1900–1955.* Houndsmills, Basingstoke, Hampshire: Palgrave Macmillan, 2013.

Berger, Rachel. "Alimentary Affairs: Historicizing Food in Modern India." *History Compass* 16, no. 2 (2018): 1–10.

Berger, Rachel. "Clarified Commodities: Managing Ghee in Interwar India." *Technology and Culture* 60, no. 4 (2019): 1004–1026.

Bhadra, Gautam. *From an Imperial Product to a National Drink: The Culture of Tea Consumption in Modern India.* Kolkata: Teaboard India, 2005.

Bhaumik, Kaushik. "At Home in the World: Cinema and Cultures of the Young in Bombay in the 1920s." In *Towards a History of Consumption in South Asia.* Edited by Douglas E. Haynes et al. New Delhi: Oxford University Press, 2010.

Bingham, Adrian. *Gender, Modernity and the Popular Press in Inter-War Britain.* Oxford: Clarendon Press, 2004.

Bose, Pradip Kumar. "Reconstituting Private Life: The Making of the Modern Family in Bengal." In *Social Transformation in India: Essays in Honour of Professor I.P. Desai.* Edited by Ghanshyam Shah. Jaipur: Rawat Publications, 1997, 501–531.

Bose, Pradip Kumar. "Sons of the Nation: Childrearing in the New Family." In *Texts of Power: Emerging Disciplines in Colonial Bengal.* Edited by Partha Chatterjee. Minnesota: University of Minnesota Press, 1996, 118–144.

Botre, Shrikant, and Douglas E. Haynes. "Understanding R. D. Karve: *Brahmacharya*, Modernity, and the Appropriation of Global Sexual Science in Western India, 1927–1953." In Veronika Fuechtner, Douglas E. Haynes, and Ryan Jones, eds., *Global History of Sexual Science, 1880–1960.* Berkeley: University of California Press, 2018.

Bourdieu, Pierre "The Forms of Capital." In J. Richardson (ed.), *Handbook of Theory and Research for the Sociology of Education.* Westwood, CT: Greenwood Press, 1986.

Bowden, Sue, and Avner Offer. "Household Appliances and the Use of Time: The United States and Britain since the 1920s." *The Economic History Review* 47, no. 4 (November 1994): 725–748.

Bowen, H. V. "The Consumption of British Manufactured Goods in India: A Prologue, 1765–1813." In *Towards a History of Consumption in South Asia.* Edited by Douglas E. Haynes et al. New Delhi: Oxford University Press, 2010.

Brosius, Christiane. *India's Middle Class: New Forms of Urban Leisure, Consumption and Prosperity.* London: Routledge, 2010.

Bulsara, Jal Feerose. *Bombay: A City in the Making.* Bombay: The National Information and Publications Ltd., 1948.

Burke, Timothy. *Lifebuoy Men, Lux Women: Commodification, Consumption, and Cleanliness in Modern Zimbabwe.* Durham, NC: Duke University Press, 1996.

Cashman, Richard I. *The Myth of the Lokamanya: Tilak and Mass Politics in Maharashtra.* Berkeley: University of California Press, 1975.

Chakrabarty, Dipesh. "The Difference—Deferral of a Colonial Modernity: Public Debates on Domesticity in Colonial Bengal." In *Subaltern Studies VIII: Essays in Honour of Ranajit Guha.* Edited by David Arnold and David Hardiman. Dehli: Oxford University Press, 1994, 50–88.

Chakrapani, V. S. and V. Ramnarayan. *R. K. Swamy: His Life and Times: From Humble Village Origins to the Top Rungs of a Contemporary Profession.* Chennai: Srinivasan K. Swamy, 2007.

Chandra, Sudhir. *The Oppressive Present: Literature and Social Consciousness in Colonial India*. Delhi: Oxford University Press, 1992.

Chandavarkar, Rajnarayan. *The Origins of Industrial Capitalism in India: Business Strategies and the Working Classes in Bombay, 1900–1940*. Cambridge: Cambridge University Press, 1994.

Chatterjee, Indrani, ed. *Unfamiliar Relations: Family and History in South Asia*. New Brunswick, NJ: Rutgers University Press, 2004.

Chatterjee, Partha. "The Nationalist Resolution of the Women's Question." In *Recasting Women: Essays in Colonial History*. Edited by Kumkum Sangari and Sudesh Vaid. New Delhi: Kali for Women, 1989.

Chattopadhyay, Swati. *Representing Calcutta: Modernity, Nationalism and the Colonial Uncanny*. London: Routledge, 2005.

Chattopadhyay, S. *Devdas*. Translated by Sreejata Guha. New Delhi: Penguin Books, 2002 [1917].

Chaudhuri, Arun. *Indian Advertising: 1780 to 1950 A.D.* New Delhi and New York: Tata Mc-Graw Hill, 2007.

Chesler, Ellen. *Woman of Valor: Margaret Sanger and the Birth Control Movement in America*. New York: Simon & Schuster, 1992.

Choudhury, Ranabir Ray. *Early Calcutta Advertisements, 1875–1925*. Bombay: Nachiketa Publications, 1992.

Chowdhury, Indira. *The Frail Hero and Virile History: Gender and the Politics of Culture in Colonial Bengal*. SOAS Studies on South Asia. Delhi and New York: Oxford University Press, 1998.

Ciarlo, David. *Advertising Empire: Race and Visual Culture in Imperial Germany*. Cambridge, MA: Harvard University Press, 2011.

Cochran, Sherman. *Chinese Medicine Men: Consumer Culture in China and Southeast Asia*. Cambridge, MA: Harvard University Press, 2006.

Cohn, Bernard. "The Census, Social Structure and Objectification in South Asia." In *An Anthropologist among the Historians and Other Essays*. Delhi: Odord University Press, 1987, 224–254.

Collingham, E. M. *Imperial Bodies: The Physical Experience of the Raj, c. 1800–1947*. Cambridge: Polity Press, 2001.

"Conjugality and Sexual Economies in India," *Feminist Studies [Special Issue]* 38, no. 3 (2011), 1–235.

Conlon, Frank. *Caste in a Changing World: The Chitrapur Saraswat Brahmans, 1700–1935*. Berkley: University of California Press, 1977.

Conlon, Frank. "Tramways and the Urban Development of Colonial Bombay." In *Mumbai Past and Present: Historical Perspectives and Contemporary Challenges*. Edited by Manjiri Kamat. Bombay: Nehru Centre, Indus Source, 2013, 80–112.

Cowan, Ruth Schwartz. *More Work for Mother: The Ironies of Household Technology from the Open Hearth to the Microwave*. New York: Basic Books, 1983.

Cowan, Ruth Schwartz. "The 'Industrial Revolution' in the Home: Household Technology and Social Change in the 20th Century." *Technology and Culture* 17, no. 1 (1976): 1–23.

Curti, Merle. "The Changing Concept of 'Human Nature' in the Literature of American Advertising." *The Business History Review* 41, no. 4 (Winter 1967): 335–357.

Daechsel, Markus. *The Politics of Self-Expression: The Urdu Middle-Class Milleu in Mid-Twentieth Century India and Pakistan*. London and New York: Routledge, 2006.

Davidson, Caroline. *A Woman's Work Is Never Done: A History of Housework in the British Isles 1650–1950*. London: Chatto and Windus, 1982.

Day, Tanis. "Capital-Labor Substitution in the Home." *Technology and Culture* 33, no. 2 (1992): 302–327.

De, Sarmistha. *Marginal Europeans in Colonial India, 1860–1920.* Kolkata: Thema, 2008.

Deshpande, Raghunath Shripad. *Cheap and Healthy Homes for the Middle Classes of India,.* Poona: United Book Corp., 1969.

Dirks, Nicholas. *Castes of Mind: Colonialim and the Making of Modern India.* Princeton: Princeton University Press, 2001.

Deutsch, Tracey. *Building a Housewife's Paradise: Gender, Politics and American Grocery Stores in the Twentieth Century.* Chapel Hill: The University of North Carolina Press, 2010.

Dobbin, Christine. *Urban Leadership in Western India: Politics and Communities in Bombay City, 1840–1885.* Oxford: Oxford University Press, 1972.

Doctor, Vikram, and Anvar Alikhan. "Kyon Na Aazmaye? Part I." *The India Magazine of Her People and Culture* (December 1996): 46–55.

Domosh, Mona. *American Commodities in an Age of Empire.* New York: Routledge, 2006.

Dwivedi, Sharada, and Shalini Devi Holkar. *Almond Eyes, Lotus Feet: Indian Traditions in Beauty and Health.* Mumbai: Eminence Designs Pvt. Ltd., 2006.

Eaton, Peter, and Marilyn Warnick. *Marie Stopes: A Checklist of Her Writings.* London: Croom Helm, 1977.

Edwards, James. "Semen Anxiety in South Asian Cultures: Cultural and Transcultural Significance." *Medical Anthropology* 7, no. 3 (1983): 51–67.

Ewen, Stuart. *Captains of Consciousness: Advertising and the Social Roots of the Consumer Culture.* New York: McGraw Hill, 1976.

Fernandes, Leela. *India's New Middle Class: Democratic Politics in an Era of Economic Reform.* Minneapolis: University of Minnesota Press, 2006.

Fernandes, Naresh. *Taj Mahal Foxtrot: The Story of Bombay's Jazz Age.* New Delhi: Lustre Press, 2012.

Fieldhouse, David K. *Unilever Overseas: The Anatomy of a Multinational, 1895–1965.* Stanford: Hoover Institution Press, 1978.

Fischer-Tiné, Harald. *Low and Licentious Europeans: Race, Class, and "White Subalternity" in Colonial India.* New Delhi: Orient BlackSwan, 2009.

Forbes, Geraldine. *Women in Modern India.* Cambridge: Cambridge University Press, 1996.

Fox, Stephen R. *The Mirror Makers: A History of American Advertising and its Creators.* New York: Morrow, 1984.

Freitag, Sandria B. "South Asian Ways of Seeing, Muslim Ways of Knowing: The Indian Muslim Niche Market in Posters." *The Indian Economic and Social History Review* 44, no. 3 (2007): 297–331.

Fuechtner, Veronika. "Indians, Jews and Sex: Magnus Hirschfeld and Indian Sexology." In *Imagining Germany Imagining Asia: Essays in Asian-German Studies.* Eds. Veronika Fuechtner and Mary Rhiel. Studies in German Literature, Linguistics, and Culture. Rochester, New York: Camden House, 2013.

Fuller, C. J. "Colonial Anthropology and the Decline of the Raj: Caste, Religion and Political Change in India in the Early Twentieth Century." *Journal of the Royal Asiatic Society* 26, no. 3 (July 2016): 463–486.

Fuller, C. J., and Haripriya Narasimhan. *Tamil Brahmins: The Making of a Middle-Class Caste.* Chicago: University of Chicago Press, 2014.

Gadihoke, Sabeena. "Selling Soap and Stardom: The Story of Lux." *Tasveer Ghar: A Digital Archive of South Asian Popular Visual Culture,* accessed July 3, 2017. http://www.tasveergharindia.net/cmsdesk/essay/104/index.html.

Ganachari, Aravind. "'White Man's Embarrassment', European Vagrancy in 19th Century Bombay." *EPW* 37, no. 25 (2002): 2477–2486.

Ghosal, Subhas. "Advertising in Marketing: A Look Ahead (1971)." In *Advertising: Gleanings From Subhas Ghosal*. Delhi: MacMillan India, 2002.

Giswijit-Hofstra, Marijke, and Roy Porter, eds. *Cultures of Neurasthenia from Beard to the First World War*. Amsterdam and New York: Rodopi, 2001.

Glover, William J. *Making Lahore Modern: Constructing and Imagining a Colonial City*. Minneapolis: University of Minnesota Press, 2008.

Goswami, Omkar. "From Bazaar to Industry." *The Oxford India Anthology of Business History*. Ed. Medha Kudaisya. Delhi: Oxford University Press, 2011.

Gove, Philip Babcock, and Inc. Merriam-Webster. *Webster's Third New International Dictionary of the English Language, Unabridged*. Springfield, MA: Merriam-Webster, 2002.

Grout, Holly. *The Force of Beauty: Transforming French Ideas of Femininity in the Third Republic*. Baton Rouge: Louisiana State University Press, 2015.

Guha, Ramachandra. *A Corner of a Foreign Field: The Indian History of a British Sport*. London: Picador, 2003.

Guha-Thakurta, Tapti. *The Making of a New "Indian" Art: Artists, Aesthetics and Nationalism in Bengal, c. 1850–1920*. Cambridge: Cambridge University Press, 1992.

Gupta, Charu. *Sexuality, Obscenity, Community: Women, Muslims, and the Hindu Public in Colonial India*. New York: Palgrave, 2002.

Hall, Lesley A., and Roy Porter. *The Facts of Life: The Creation of Sexual Knowledge in Britain, 1650–1950*. New Haven: Yale University Press, 1995.

Halve, Anand Bhaskar, and Anita Sarkar. *Adkathā: The Story of Indian Advertising*. Goa: Centurm Charitable Trust, 2011.

Hancock, Mary. "Home Science and the Nationalization of Domesticity in Colonial India." *Modern Asian Studies* 35, no. 4 (2001): 871–903.

Haksar, Ajit. *Bite the Bullet: Thirty-Four Years with ITC*. New Delhi: Viking, Penguin Books, 1993.

Hatekar, Neeraj, Abodh Kumar, and Rajani Mathur. "The Making of the Middle Class in Western India: Age at Marriage for Brahmin Women (1900–50)." *EPW* 44, no. 21 (2009); 40–47, 49.

Hattiangdi, Gopal. *The Vanaspati Industry*. Hyderabad: Indian Central Oilseeds Committee, 1958.

Haynes, Douglas E. "Advertising and the History of South Asia, 1880–1950." *History Compass* 13, no. 8 (2015): 361–374.

Haynes, Douglas E. "Afterword: Bhagwanlal Indraji, Archaeology and the Intellectual History of Western India." In Virchand Dharamsey, *Bhagwanlal Indraji: The First Indian Archaeologist; Multidisciplinary Approaches to the Study of the Past*. Vadodara: Darshak Itihas Nidhi, 2012.

Haynes, Douglas E. "Creating the Consumer? Advertising, Capitalism and the Middle Class in Urban Western India, 1914–40." In *Towards a History of Consumption in South Asia*. Edited by Douglas E. Haynes, Abigail McGowan, Tirthankar Roy, and Haruka Yanagisawa. New Delhi: Oxford University Press, 2010, 108–135.

Haynes, Douglas E. "Bombay's European Community during the Interwar Period." In *Bombay before Mumbai: Essays in Honor of Jim Masselos*. Edited by Rachel Dwyer, Manjiri Kamat, and Prashant Kidambi. London: Hurst, 2019, 77–98.

Haynes, Douglas E. "Market Formation in Khandesh, 1820–1930." *The Indian Economic & Social History Review* 36, no. 3 (2016): 275–302.

Haynes, Douglas E. "Masculinity, Advertising and the Reproduction of the Middle-Class Family in Western India, 1918–1940." In *Being Middle-Class in India: A Way of Life*, ed. Henrike Donner. Routledge Contemporary South Asia Series 53. New York: Routledge, 2011, 23–44.

Haynes, Douglas E. *Rhetoric and Ritual in Colonial India: The Shaping of a Public Culture in Surat City, 1852–1928*. Berkeley: University of California Press, 1991.

Haynes, Douglas E. "Selling Masculinity: Advertisements for Sex Tonics and the Making of Modern Conjugality in Western India, 1900–1945." *South Asia: Journal of South Asian Studies* 35, no. 4 (December 2012): 787–831.

Haynes, Douglas E. *Small-Town Capitalism in Western India: Artisans, Merchants and the Making of the Informal Economy, 1870–1960*. Cambridge: Cambridge University Press, 2012.

Haynes, Douglas E. "Vernacular Capitalism, Advertising and the Bazaar in Early Twentieth-Century Western India." In Ajay Gandhi, Barbara Harriss-White, Douglas E. Haynes, and Sebastian Schwecke, eds., *Rethinking Markets in Modern India: Enbedded Exchange and Contested Jurisdiction*. Cambridge: Cambridge University Press, 2020.

Hazareesingh, Sandip. *The Colonial City and the Challenge of Modernity: Urban Hegemonies and Civic Contestations in Bombay City, 1905–1925*. Hyderabad: Orient Longman, 2007.

Hoganson, Kristin L. *Consumers' Imperium: The Global Production of American Domesticity, 1865–1920*. Chapel Hill: University of North Carolina Press, 2007.

Hunt, Nancy Rose. *A Nervous State: Violence, Remedies and Reverie in Colonial Congo*. Durham, NC and London: Duke University Press, 2016.

Hunter, Margaret L. *Race, Gender and the Politics of Skin Tone*. New York: Routledge, 2005.

Ikeya, Chie. *Refiguring Women, Colonialism and Modernity in Burma*. Honolulu: University of Hawaii Press, 2011.

Indian Artists of Yesteryear, Nuga Arthouse, 2012.

J. Walter Thompson Company. *The Indian Market, 1959*. New York: J. Walter Thompson Co., 1959.

Jain, Jyotindra, ed. *The Story of Early Indian Advertising*. Special issue of *Marg: A Magazine of the Arts* 68, no. 3 (March 2017).

Jain, Jyotindra. "The Visual Culture of the Indo-British Cotton Trade." In *The Story of Indian Advertising*, 34–43.

Jain, Kajri. *Gods in the Bazaar: The Economies of Indian Calendar Art*. Durham, NC: Duke University Press, 2007.

Jay, Martin, and Sumathi Ramaswamy, eds. *Empires of Vision: A Reader*. Durham, NC: Duke University Press, 2014.

Jones, Geoffrey. *Beauty Imagined: A History of the Global Beauty Industry*. New York: Oxford University Press, 2010.

Joshi, Sanjay. *Fractured Modernity: Making of a Middle Class in Colonial North India*. New Delhi: Oxford University Press, 2001.

Joshi, Sanjay, ed. *The Middle Class in Colonial India*. New Delhi: Oxford University Press, 2019.

Karanjia, B. K. *Godrej: A Hundred Years 1897–1997*, Vol. I. New Delhi: Penguin Viking, 1997.

Kaur, Harminder. "Of Soaps and Scents: Corporeal Cleanliness in Urban Colonial India." In *Toward a History of Consumption in South Asia*. Edited by Douglas Haynes et al. New Delhi: Oxford University Press, 2010, 246–267.

Kidambi, Prashant, "Consumption, Domestic Economy and the Idea of the 'Middle Class' in Late Colonial Bombay." In *Towards a History of Consumption in South Asia*. Edited by Douglas E. Haynes et al. New Delhi: Oxford University Press, 2010, 108–135.

King, Anthony Douglas. *Colonial Urban Development: Culture, Social Power and Environment*. London, Henley, and Boston: Routledge and Keegan Paul, 1976.

Kline, Ronald R. "Resisting Development, Reinventing Modernity: Rural Electrification in the United States before World War II." *Environmental Values* 11, no. 3 (2002): 327–344.

Kosambi, Meera. *Crossing Thresholds: Feminist Essays in Social History*. Raniket. Permanent Black, 2007.

Kumar, Nita. "The Middle-Class Child: Ruminations on Failure." In Amita Baviskar and Raka Ray, eds., *Elite and Everyman: The Cultural Politics of the Indian Middle Classes*. New Delhi: Routledge, 2011, 220–245.

Kumar, Radha. *The History of Doing: An Illustrated Account of Movements for Women's Rights and Feminism in India, 1800–1990*. New Delhi: Kali for Women, 1993.

Laidlaw, James. *Riches and Renunciation Religion, Economy, and Society among the Jains*. Oxford: Clarendon Press, 1995.

Laird, Pamela Walker. *Advertising Progress: American Business and the Rise of Consumer Marketing*. Baltimore, MD: The Johns Hopkins University Press, 1998.

Laqueur, Thomas Walter. *Solitary Sex: A Cultural History of Masturbation*. New York: Zone Books, 2003.

Lears, T. J. Jackson. *Fables of Abundance: A Cultural History of Advertising in America*. New York: Basic Books, 1994.

Levene, Alysa. "The Meanings of Margarine in England: Class, Consumption and Material Culture from 1918 to 1953." *Contemporary British History* 28, no. 2 (2014): 145–165.

Liechty, Mark. *Suitably Modern: Making Middle-Class Culture in a New Consumer Society*. Princeton, NJ and Oxford: Princeton University Press, 2003.

Luhrmann, T. M. *The Good Parsi: The Fate of a Colonial Elite in a Postcolonial Society*. Cambridge, MA: Harvard University Press, 1996.

Lutgendorf, Philip. "Chai Why?" *Tasveer Ghar: A Digital Archive of South Asian Popular Visual Culture*, http://tasveerghar.net/cmsdesk/essay/89/index.html. Accessed June 29, 2017.

Majumdar, Rochana. *Marriage and Modernity: Family Values in Colonial Bengal*. Durham, NC and London: Duke University Press, 2009.

Malhotra, Anshu. "The Body as a Metaphor for the Nation: Caste, Masculinity and Femininity in the Satyarth Prakash of Dayananda Saraswati." In *Rhetoric and Reality: Gender and the Colonial Experience in South Asia*. Edited by Avril A. Powell and Siobhan Lambert-Hurley. SOAS Studies on South Asia. New Delhi and New York: Oxford University Press, 2006.

Marchand, Roland. *Advertising the American Dream: Making Way for Modernity, 1920–1940*. Berkeley: University of California Press, 1985.

Mariott, Mckim. "Caste Ranking and Food Transactions: A Matrix Analysis." In Milton Singer and Bernard S. Cohn, eds., *Structure and Change in Indian Society*. Chicago: Aldine Publishing Company, 1968.

Mazzarella, William. *Shoveling Smoke: Advertising and Globalization in Contemporary India*. New Delhi: Oxford University Press, 2004.

McClintock, Anne. *Imperial Leather: Race, Gender and Sexuality in the Colonial Context*. New York and London: Routledge, 1995.

McGowan, Abigail. "Ahmedabad's Home Remedies: Housing in the Re-Making of an Industrial City, 1920–1960." *South Asia: Journal of South Asia Studies* 36, no 3 (2013): 397–414.

McGowan, Abigail. "An All-Consuming Subject? Women and Consumption in Late-Nineteenth and Early-Twentieth-Century Western India." *Journal of Women's History* 18, no. 4 (2006): 31–54.

McGowan, Abigail. "Consuming Domesticity: Creating Consumers for the Middle-Class House in India, 1920–1960." In Bhaswati Bhattacharya and Henrike Donner, eds., *Globalizing Everyday Consumption in India: History and Ethnography*. New York: Routledge, 2020.

McGowan, Abigail. "Domestic Modern: Redecorating Homes in Bombay in the 1930s." *Journal of the Society of Architectural Historians* 75, no. 4 (2016): 424–446.

McGowan, Abigail. "Selling Home: Marketing Home Furnishings in Late Colonial Bombay." In *Bombay before Mumbai: Essays in Honor of Jim Masselos*. Edited by Prashant Kidambi, Manjiri Kamat, and Rachel Dwyer. London: Hurst, 2019.

Melody, Michael Edward, and Linda Mary Peterson. *Teaching America about Sex: Marriage Guides and Sex Manuals from the Late Victorians to Dr. Ruth*. New York: New York University Press, 1999.

Merron, Jeff. "Putting Foreign Consumers on the Map: J. Walter Thompson's Struggle with General Motors' International Advertising Account in the 1920s." *The Business History Review* 73, no. 3 (1999): 465–503.

Mishra, Dasarathi. *Advertising in Indian Newspapers, 1780–1947*. Berhampur: Ishani Publications, 1987.

Mizutani, Satoshi. *The Meaning of White. Race, Class, and the "Domiciled Community" in British India 1858–1930*. Oxford: Oxford University Press, 2011.

Modern Girl Around the World Research Group (eds.,) *The Modern Girl Around the World: Consumption, Modernity and Globalization*. Durham, NC and London: Duke University Press, 2008.

Moreno, Julio. *Yankee Don't Go Home!: Mexican Nationalism, American Business Culture, and the Shaping of Modern Mexico, 1920–1950*. Chapel Hill: University of North Carolina Press, 2003.

Mukharji, Projit Bihari. "Chandshir Chikitsa: A Nomadology of Subaltern Medicine." In *Medical Marginality in South Asia: Situating Subaltern Therapeutics*. Edited by David Hardiman and Projit Bihari Mukharji, 2012, 85–108.

Mukharji, Projit Bihari. "Historicizing 'Indian Systems of Knowledge': Ayurveda, Exotic Foods and Contemporary Antihistorical Holisms." *History of Science* 35 (2020): 228–248.

Mukharji, Projit Bihari. *Nationalizing the Body: The Medical Market, Print and Daktari Medicine*. Anthem South Asian Studies. London and New York: Anthem Press, 2009.

Mukharji, Projit Bihari. *Doctoring Traditions: Ayurveda, Small Technologies and Braided Sciences*. Chicago: University of Chicago Press, 2016.

Nandy, Ashis. *The Intimate Enemy: Loss and Recovery of Self under Colonialism*. Delhi and New York: Oxford University Press, 1983.

Ninivaggi, Frank John. *Ayurveda: Comprehensive Guide to Traditional Indian Medicine for the West*. Westport, CT: Praeger, 2001. https://www.yogajournal.com/food-diet/digest-this, consulted October 27, 2018.

Ohmann, Richard M. *Selling Culture: Magazines, Markets, and Class at the Turn of the Century*. London and New York: Verso, 1996.

Padamsee, Alyque, and Arun Prabhu. *A Double Life: My Exciting Years in Theatre and Advertising*. New Delhi: Penguin Books, 1999.

Pande, Ishita. *Medicine, Race and Liberalism in British Bengal: Symptoms of Empire*. Routledge Studies in South Asian History 5. Abingdon and New York: Routledge, 2010.

Pantzar, Mika. "Tools or Toys—Inventing the Need for Domestic Appliances in Postwar and Postmodern Finland." *Journal of Advertising* 32, no. 1 (2003): 83–93.

Parameswaran, Ambi. *Nawabs, Nudes, Noodles: India through 50 Years of Advertising.* London: Macmillan, 2016.

Parameswaran, Radhika, and Kavitha Cardoza. "Melanin on the Margins: Advertising and the Cultural Politics of Fair/Light/White Beauty in India." *Journalism & Communication Monographs* 11, no. 3 (September 2009): 213–274.

Parekh, Bhikhu C. *Colonialism, Tradition, and Reform: An Examination of Gandhi's Political Discourse.* Newbury Park, CA: Sage Publications, 1989.

Parkin, Katherine J. *Food Is Love: Advertising and Gender Roles in Modern America.* Philadelphia: University of Pennsylvania Press, 2006.

Parthasarathi, Prasannan. *The Transition to a Colonial Economy: Weavers, Merchants, and Kings in South India, 1720–1800.* Cambridge: Cambridge University Press, 2001.

Punathambekar, Ashwin. "Ameen Sayani and Radio Ceylon: Notes Toward a History of Broadcasting and Bombay Cinema." *Bioscope: South Asian Screen Studies* 1, no. 2 (2010): 189–197.

Pendse, Shripad Narayan. *The B.E.S.T. Story.* Translated by M. V. Rajadhyaksha. Bombay: Bombay Electric Supply & Transport Undertaking, 1972.

Perlin, Frank. "Proto-Industrialization and Pre-Colonial South Asia." *Past and Present* 98, no. 1 (1983): 30–95.

Pernau, Margrit. "Modern Masculinity, Bought at Your Local Pharmacist: The Tonic Sanatogen in 20th-Century Indian Advertisements." *Tasveerghar: A Digital Archival of South Asian Popular Culture,* http://www.tasveergharindia.net/essay/sanatogen-masculine-advert.html. Last accessed August 1, 2021.

Pinney, Christopher. *"Photos of the Gods": The Printed Image and Political Struggle in India.* London: Reaktion, 2004.

Pope, Daniel. *The Making of Modern Advertising.* New York: Basic Books, Inc., 1983.

Prakash, Gyan. *Mumbai Fables.* Princeton, NJ: Princeton University Press, 2010.

Prasad, Srirupa. *Cultural Politics of Hygiene in India, 1890–1940: Contagions of Feeling.* Houndmills, Basingstoke, Hampshire: Palgrave Macmillan, 2015.

Proceda, Mary A. *Married to the Empire: Gender, Politics and Imperialism in India, 1883–1947.* Manchester: Manchester University Press, 2002.

Raianu, Mircea. *Tata: The Global Corporation that Built Indian Capitalism.* Cambridge, MA: Harvard University Press, 2021.

Rajagopal, Arvind. "Advertising in India: Genealogies of the Colonial Subject." In *Oxford Handbook of Modernity in South Asia: Modern Makeovers.* Edited by Saurabh Dube. New Delhi: Oxford University Press, 2011.

Rajagopal, Arvind. "Advertising, Politics and the Sentimental Education of the Indian Consumer." *Visual Anthropology Review* 14, no. 2 (1998): 14–31.

Rajagopal, Arvind. "The Commodity Image in the (Post) Colony." *Tasveer Ghar: A Digital Archive of South Asian Popular Visual Culture.* http://www.tasveerghar.net/cmsdesk/essay/100/index_3.html. Accessed June 29, 2017.

Rajagopal, Arvind. "Early Publicity in India." *Marg: A Magazine of the Arts* 68, no. 3 (March 2017): 88–99.

Ramamurthy, Preeti. "All-Consuming Nationalism: the Indian Modern Girl in the 1920s and 1930s." In *The Modern Girl Around the World.* Durham, NC: Duke University Press, 2008.

Ramamurthy, Ramya. *Branded in History.* Gurgaon: Hachette India, 2021.

Ramaswamy, Sumathi, ed. *Beyond Appearances? Visual Practices and Ideologies in Modern India*. New Delhi and Thousand Oaks, CA: Sage, 2003.

Ramaswamy, Sumathi. *The Goddess and the Nation: Mapping Mother India*. Duhram, NC: Duke University Press, 2010.

Rao, Nikhil. *House, but No Garden: Apartment Living in Bombay's Suburbs, 1898–1964*. Minneapolis: University of Minnesota Press, 2013.

Rappaport, Erika. *A Thirst for Empire: How Tea Shaped the Modern World*. Princeton: Princeton University Press, 2017.

Ray, Utsa. *Culinary Culture in Colonial India: A Cosmopolitan Platter and the Middle-Class*. Delhi: Cambridge University Press, 2015.

Reed, Stanley. *The India I Knew, 1897–1947*. London: Odhams Press, 1952.

Rege, Sharmila. *Writing Caste/Writing Gender: Reading. Dalit Women's Testimonies*. New Delhi: Zubaan, 2006.

Rosselli, John. "The Self-Image of Effeteness: Physical Education and Nationalism in Nineteenth-Century Bengal." *Past & Present*, no. 86 (1980): 121–148.

Roy, Tirthankar. *A Business History of India: Enterprise and the Emergence of Capitalism from 1700*. Cambridge: Cambridge University Press, 2018.

Rudner, David. *Caste and Capitalism in Colonial India: the Nattukotai Chettiars*. Berkeley: University of California Press, 1994.

Rudolph, Susanne Hoeber, and Lloyd I. Rudolph. *The Modernity of Tradition: Political Development in India*. Chicago: University of Chicago Press, 1967.

Rudolph, Susanne Hoeber, and Lloyd I. Rudolph. *Postmodern Gandhi and Other Essays: Gandhi in the World and at Home*. Chicago: University of Chicago Press, 2006.

Sarkar, Sumit. "Kaliyuga, Chakri and Bhakti: Ramakrishna and History Times." In Sarkar, ed., *Writing Social History*. Delhi: University Press, 1999.

Sarkar, Tanika. "The Hindu Wife and the Hindu Nation: Domesticity and Nationalism in Nineteenth Century Bengal." *Studies in History* 8, no. 2 (1992): 213–235.

Sarkar, Tanika. *The Hindu Wife, Hindu Nation: Community, Religion and Cultural Nationalism*. Bloomington: Indiana University Press, 2001.

Savary, Luzia. "Vernacular Eugenics? Santati-Śāstra in Popular Hindi Advisory Literature (1900–1940)." *South Asia* 37, no. 3 (2014): 381–397.

Scanlon, Jennifer. "Mediators in the International Marketplace: U.S. Advertising in Latin America in the Early Twentieth Century." *Business History Review* 77, no. 3 (2003): 387–415.

Schivelbusch, Wolfgang. *Disenchanted Night: The Industrialization of Light in the Nineteenth Century*. Translated by Angela Davies. Berkeley: University of California Press, 1988.

Sharma, Madhuri. "Creating a Consumer: Exploring Medical Advertisements in Colonial India." *Social History of Health and Medicine in Colonial India*, eds. Bisamoy Patti and Mark Harrison. London and New York: Routledge, 2009, 213–228.

Sharma, Madhuri. *Indigenous and Western Medicine in Colonial India*. New Delhi: Foundation Books, 2012.

Shechter, Relli. "Reading Advertisements in a Colonial/Development Context: Cigarette Advertising and Identity Politics in Egypt, c.1919–1939." *Journal of Social History* 39, no. 2 (2005): 483–503.

Siegel, Benjamin. *Hungry Nation: Food, Famine and the Making of Modern India*. Cambridge: Cambridge University Press, 2018.

Singleton, Mark. *Yoga Body: The Origins of Modern Posture Practice*. Oxford and New York: Oxford University Press, 2010.

Sinha, Mrinalini. *Colonial Masculinity: The 'Manly Englishman' and 'The Effeminate Bengali' in the Late Nineteenth Century*. Studies in Imperialism. Manchester and New York: Manchester University Press, 1995.

Sinha, Mrinalini. *Specters of Mother India: The Global Restructuring of an Empire*. Durham, NC: Duke University Press, 2006.

Sivulka, Juliann. *Stronger than Dirt: A Cultural History of Advertising Personal Hygiene in America, 1875-1940*. Amherst, NY: Humanity Books, 2001.

Spain, Alice. *A Taste of Ovaltine: The Official Story*. Hathfordshire: Alpine Press, 2002.

Story of the Sir J.J. School of Art, 1857-1957. Centenary publication. Bombay: Government Central Press, 1957.

Sreenivas, Mytheli. *Wives, Widows and Concubines: The Conjugal Family Ideal in Colonial India*. Bloomington: Indiana University Press, 2008.

Strasser, Susan. *Never Done: A History of American Housework*. New York: Pantheon Books, 1982.

Strasser, Susan. *Satisfaction Guaranteed: The Making of the American Mass Market*. New York: Pantheon Books, 1989.

Stronach, L. A. "How Modern Advertising and Commercial Art Started in India." *Third Annual Yearbook, Commercial Art Guild*, p. 21, 1952.

Subramanian, Ajantha. *Caste of Merit: Engineering Education in India*. Cambridge, MA: Harvard University Press, 2019.

Sutton, Denise. Globalizing *Ideal Beauty: How Female Copywriters of the J. Walter Thompson Agency Redefined Beauty for the Twentieth Century*. Basingstoke: Palgrave Macmillan, 2009.

Sutton, Denise. *Globalizing Ideal Beauty: Women, Advertising, and Power of Marketing*. Basingstoke: Palgrave Macmillan, 2012.

Tandon, Prakash. *Beyond Punjab, 1937-1960*. London: Chatto and Windus, 1971.

Tandon, Prakash. *Punjabi Saga (1857-2000): The Monumental Story of Five Generations of a Remarkable Punjabi Family*. New Delhi: Rupa, 2000.

Tarlo, Emma. *Clothing Matters: Dress and Identity in India*. New Delhi: Viking Books, 1996.

Tripathi, Dwijendra. *The Oxford History of Indian Business*. New Delhi and New York: Oxford University Press, 2004.

Trivedi, Lisa. *Clothing Gandhi's Nation: Homespun and Modern India*. Bloomington and Indianapolis: Indiana University Press, 2007.

Tsing, Anna Lowenhaupt. *Friction: An Ethnography of Global Connection*. Princeton, NJ: Princeton University Press, 2005.

Vanek, Joann. "Household Technology and Social Status: Rising Living Standards and Status and Residence Differences in Housework." *Technology and Culture* 19, no. 3 (1978): 361–375.

Venkatachalapathy, A. R. *In Those Days There Was No Coffee: Writings in Cultural History*. New Delhi: Yoda Press, 2006.

Venkatachalapathy, A. R. "A Magic System?: Print Advertising in Colonial Tamil Nadu." In *Globalizing Everyday Consumption in India: History and Ethnography*. Edited by Bhaswati Bhattacharya and Henrike Donner. Delhi: Routledge, 2020.

Venkateshwaran, S. *The Law of Trade and Merchandize Marks in India*. Madras: The Madras Law Office, 1937.

Walsh, Judith E. *Domesticity in Colonial India, What Women Learned When Men Gave Them Advice*. New Delhi: Oxford University Press, 2004.

Williamson, Judith. *Decoding Advertisements: Ideology and Meaning in Advertising*. London: Marion Boyars, 1978.

Woodard, James P. "Marketing Modernity: The J. Walter Thompson Company and North American Advertising in Brazil, 1929–1939." *Hispanic American Historical Review* 82 (2002): 257–290.

Yang, Anand A. *Bazaar India: Markets, Society, and the Colonial State in Gangetic Bihar.* Berkeley: University of California Press, 1998.

Non-academic web sources

https://www.business-standard.com/article/management/40-years-ago-and-now-how-dalda-built-and-lost-its-monopoly-115030501153_1.html. Accessed January 21, 2019.

https://www.healthy-drinks.net/horlicks-ingredients-health-benefits-and-side-effects/#:~:text=Horlicks%20was%20first%20introduces%20in%20India%20after%20the,Horlicks%20%3A%20Ingrediants%2C%20Health%20Benefits%20And%20Side%20Effects. Last accessed August 29, 2021.

https://www.hul.co.in/about/who-we-are/our-history. Accessed October 18, 2018.

http://www.ovaltine.co.uk/about/timeline/. Accessed October 7, 2018.

https://thelandy.com/2013/02/17/climbing-mt-everest-drinking-ovaltine-all-the-way-2. Accessed September 23, 2018.

http://www.triplepundit.com/special/disrupting-short-termism/unilevers-handwashing-campaign-goes-beyond-csr-and-saves-lives/. Accessed June 10, 2015.

https://www.yogajournal.com/food-diet/digest-this. Accessed October 27, 2018.

Index

The letter *f* following an entry indicates a page with a figure.
The letter *t* following an entry indicates a page with a table.